CUNNING FOLK AND
FAMILIAR SPIRITS

To Hamish and Dylan

CUNNING FOLK AND FAMILIAR SPIRITS

*Shamanistic Visionary Traditions in Early
Modern British Witchcraft and Magic*

~

EMMA WILBY

sussex
ACADEMIC
PRESS

BRIGHTON • PORTLAND

Copyright © Emma Wilby, 2005

The right of Emma Wilby to be identified as Author of this work has been asserted in accordance with the Copyright, Designs and Patents Act 1988.

2 4 6 8 10 9 7 5 3 1

First published 2005 in Great Britain by
SUSSEX ACADEMIC PRESS
PO Box 2950
Brighton BN2 5SP

and in the United States of America by
SUSSEX ACADEMIC PRESS
920 NE 58th Ave   Suite 300
Portland, Oregon 97213–3786

All rights reserved. Except for the quotation of short passages for the purposes of criticism and review, no part of this publication may be reproduced, stored in a retrieval system, or transmitted, in any form or by any means, electronic, mechanical, photocopying, recording or otherwise, without the prior permission of the publisher.

British Library Cataloguing in Publication Data
A CIP catalogue record for this book is available from the British Library.

Library of Congress Cataloging-in-Publication Data
Wilby, Emma.
    Cunning-folk and familiar spirits : shamanistic visionary
    traditions in early modern British witchcraft and magic /
    by Emma Wilby.
    p. cm.
    Includes bibliographical references and index.
    ISBN 1-84519-078-5 (hardcover : alk. paper) —
    ISBN 1-84519-079-3 (pbk. : alk. paper)
        1. Witchcraft—Great Britain—History—16th century.
        2. Witchcraft—Great Britain—History—17th century.
        3. Magic—Great Britain—History—16th century.
        4. Magic—Great Britain—History—17th century. I. Title.
    BF1581.W54 2005
    133.4'3'094109031—dc22

                                            2005005582

Typeset and designed by G&G Editorial, Brighton & Eastbourne
Printed by TJ International, Padstow, Cornwall
This book is printed on acid-free paper.

CONTENTS

ILLUSTRATIONS

The author and publisher gratefully acknowledge the permission granted to reproduce the copyright material in this book. Every effort has been made to trace copyright holders and to obtain their permission for the use of copyright material. The publisher apologizes for any errors or omissions in this list and would be grateful if notified of any corrections that should be incorporated in future reprints or editions of this book.

PAGE 140 Alualuk's spirits from *Intellectual Culture of the Iglulik Eskimos* by Knud Rasmussen (1976). Original drawings, the National Museum of Denmark; *Healing the Sick*. Smithsonian Institution National Anthropological Archives (NAA-30981-c).

PAGE 172 Helping spirit from *Intellectual Culture of the Iglulik Eskimos* by Knud Rasmussen (1976). Original drawings, the National Museum of Denmark; Demon familiar from *The examination and Confession of certayn Wytches at Chensforde* . . . (1566) Lambeth Palace Library (ZZ 1587. 12. 03); *Flight of the Shaman* by Jessie Oonark (1970) Stonecut and stencil on paper. 52.0 × 66.8 cm (sheet) cm (imp.) Art Gallery of Ontario, Toronto: Gift of the Klamer Family, 1978. Copyright: Public Trustee for Nunavut, estate of Jessie Oonark.

PAGE 173 *The Witches' Sabbath* by Hans Baldung Grien (1485–1545). Chiaroscuro woodcut printed from two blocks in grey and black. Block/image: 37.8 × 26.0 cm (14 7/8 × 10 in.) Museum of Fine Arts, Boston: Bequest of W. G. Russell Allen (69.1064).

PAGE 182 A cunning man in a trance from *Historia de Gentibus Septentrionalibus* by Olaus Magnus (1567), Book 3, Chapter 17. University of Pennsylvania; Untitled Ledger Drawing, Galloping, Littleman, Kiowa or Sweetwater, Cheyenne, December 1894–January 1895. Pencil, ink and crayon on paper. Buffalo Bill Historical Centre, Cody, Wyoming: Gift of Mr and Mrs Joseph M. Katz (48.59.8).

PAGE 227 *Saint Anthony Tormented by Demons* by Martin Schongauer (1470–75) Engraving. Philadelphia Museum of Art: Purchased with the W. P. Wilstach Fund, 1950.

PAGE 235 *The Annunciation* from Albrecht Dürer's Small Passion series (1510); Joan Prentice and her familiars, from *The Apprehension and confession of three notorious Witches* . . . (1589) Lambeth Palace Library (ZZ 1597.15.03).

PAGE 248 *Death and the Child* from the Dance of Death series by Hans Holbein the Younger (1523–26); Frontispiece from *The history of Tom Thumb* . . . by Richard Johnson. Imprinted at London: [by A. Mathewes?] for Tho: Langley, 1621. The Pierpont Morgan Library, New York (PML 45444).

PREFACE

Walking with Spirits
A Cunning Woman's Tale

At the Edinburgh assizes, November the eighth, 1576, a Scotswoman named Bessie Dunlop was tried for sorcery and witchcraft. * *A wife and mother, Bessie had been arrested several months previously at or near her home in the parish of Dalry, Ayrshire, and taken before the Bishop of Glasgow. The Bishop had considered her case either grave or problematic enough to send her to a higher court. By the time she reached the Edinburgh assizes Bessie had been imprisoned for many weeks and had undergone several interrogations.*[1] *At this final hearing she stood in a crowded courtroom while her previous confessions were read out before the judge, the jury, and a press of onlookers, and recorded in meticulous detail by the assize clerks.*[2] *Their records state that:*

---

* The confession reproduced here is a copy of the transcription of the original trial records made by the Scottish historian, Robert Pitcairn, in the early nineteenth century. I have made some minor modifications to Pitcairn's text in order to make it more accessible to the modern reader. The punctuation and spelling has been modernized wherever possible. Obsolete words for which an exact translation can be found have been changed to their modern equivalent, such as 'thow: you' or 'quhen: when'. Antiquated words and phrases for which I have not found a precise enough translation have been retained, alongside a conjectural interpretation in parentheses, and are glossed on their first appearance only. Occasionally words have been parenthesized to clarify the grammatical sense of a phrase or passage.

[ ]   Square brackets enclose words or phrases added by me to clarify the sense of passage.
[*]   Square brackets containing a word or phrase preceded by an asterisk enclose a conjectural translation of an obscure word or phrase.
[?]   Square brackets containing a word or phrase preceded by a question mark indicates that the meaning is very obscure and that the translation amounts to an educated guess.

ELIZABETH or BESSIE DUNLOP, spouse to Andrew Jack in Lyne,[3] [is] accused of the using of Sorcery, Witchcraft and Incantation, with Invocation of spirits of the devil, continuing in familiarity with them at all such times as she thought expedient [and] dealing with charms and abusing the people with [the] devilish craft of sorcery forsaid by the means after specified. [She] used these [magical practices for] diverse years bypast, specially at the times and in [the] manner following:

1. IN the first, That forasmuch as the said Elizabeth being asked[4] by what art and knowledge she could tell diverse persons of things they tynt [?lost] or were stolen away, or help sick persons she answered and declared that she herself had no kind of art nor science for to do, but diverse times, when any such persons came ather [?] to her she would ask one Tom Reid, who died at Pinkie,[5] as he himself affirmed, who would tell her whenever she asked.

2. ITEM, She being asked what kind of man this Tom Reid was, declared he was an honest well [*quite/very] elderly man, grey bearded, and had a grey coat with Lombard sleeves of the old fashion, a pair of grey breeches and white stockings gartered above the knee, a black bonnet on his head, cloise [?close] behind and plain before, with silken laces drawn through the lippis [*edges] thereof and a white wand in his hand.

3. ITEM, Being asked how and in what manner of place the said Tom Reid came to her [she] answered that it was as she was going between her own house and the yard of Monkcastle, driving her cattle to the pasture and making heavy fair dule [*sorrow] with herself, gretand [*weeping] very fast [*earnestly, strongly] for her cow that was dead, her husband and child that were lying sick in the land ill [*famine or epidemic] and she newly risen out of child-bed. The forsaid Tom met her by the way, hailed her and said 'Good day, Bessie.' And she said 'God speed you, goodman'. 'Sancta Marie' said he 'Bessie, why make you such great dule and fair greting [*weeping] for any worldly thing?'. She answered 'Alas! Have I not great cause to make great dule [*feel so sad], for our gear is trakit

[?] Square brackets containing a question mark only indicates that no translation could be found.
( ) Round brackets are original to Pitcairn's transcription.

Despite my modernizations, the text is still complex and difficult to read. As with so many trial records from the period, interrogator's questions, first person narratives, third person narratives, direct and reported speech, along with various tenses jostle together with little to differentiate them. To make the major modifications necessary to iron out all these complexities of grammar and sense, however, would be to lose the original voice of the text.

[*dwindled away] and my husband is on the point of death and a babe of my own will not live and myself at a weak point. Have I not good cause then to have a fair [?faint] hart?'. But Tom said 'Bessie, you have angered God and asked something you should not have done, and therefore I counsel you to mend to him, for I tell you your baby shall die, and the sick cow, before you come home; your two sheep shall die too, but your husband shall mend and be as hail and fair as ever he was.' And then I was something happier for he told me that my goodman would mend. Then Tom Reid went away from me in through the yard of Monkcastle, and I thought he went in at a narrow hole of the dyke nor ony [?that no] earthly man could have gone through and fwa [?so/then] I was something afraid'. This was the first time that Tom and Bessie met.

4. ITEM, The third time[6] he appeared to her as she was going between her own house and the Thorn [tree] of Damstarnock, where he tarried a good while with her and asked her 'If she would not trust in him?' [To which] she said 'She would trust in anybody [who] did her good.' And Tom promised her both gear, horses, and cow, and other graith [*possessions] if she would deny her Christianity and the faith she took at the font. Whereunto she answered 'That if she should be revin at horif-taillis [*dragged at a horse's tail] she should never do that.' But she promised to be loyal and true to him in anything she could do. And further, he was something angry with her that (she) would not grant to that which he spoke.

5. ITEM, The third[7] time he appeared in her own house to her, about the twelfth hour of the day, where there were sitting three tailors and her own goodman. And he took her apron and led her to the door with him, and she followed, and went up with him to the hill-end where he forbade her to speak or fear for any thing she heard or saw. And when they had gone a little way forward she saw twelve persons, eight women and four men. The men were clad in gentlemens' clothing and the women had all plaids round about them and were very seemly like to see. And Tom was with them. And [the interrogators] demanded if she knew any of them. [She] answered – none, except Tom. [Being] asked what they said to her [she] answered [that] they bade her sit down and said 'Welcome Bessie, will you go with us?' But [she said] she answered not, because Tom had forbidden her. And she further declared that she knew not what purpose they had among them, only she saw their lips move, and within a short space they parted all away and a hideous ugly fowche [*squall] of wind followed them; and she lay sick until Tom came again back from them.

6. ITEM, She being asked whether she asked Tom what persons they were. [She] answered that they were the gude wychtis [*good neighbours/fairies] that dwelt in the Court of Elfame [*Elf-home/fairyland]

who came there to desire her to go with them. And further, Tom desired her to do the same, to which she answered [that] 'She saw no profit to go thai kynd of gaittis [*along that route], unless she knew what for!' [To which] Tom said 'Do you not see me, both meit-worth, claith-worth [*well supplied with food and clothing] and good enough like in person and [that] (he?) should make her far better than ever she was?' She answered 'That she dwelt with her own husband and children and could not leave them.' And fwa Tom began to be very angry with her and said 'If fwa she thought, she would get little good of him.'

7. [Being] asked if she had sought anything from Tom to help her self or any other with [she] answered that when sundry persons came to her to seek help for their animal, their cow or ewe, or for a child that was taken away with an evil blast of wind, or elf-gripped, she went and asked Tom what might help them. And Tom would pull a herb and give [it to] her out of his own hand and bade her strain the same with any other kind of herbs and open the beast's mouth and put them in and the beast would mend.

8. ITEM, Tom gave her, out of his own hand, a thing like the root of a beet, and bade her either seethe and make an ointment of it, or else dry it and make powder of it, and give it to sick persons and they should mend. [She was] asked how she knew the person would heal. [She] declared that as soon as she rubbed the salve upon the patient, man or woman or child, and it soaked in, the child would mend; but if it sweated out, the person would die.

9. ITEM, [Being] asked to whom she applied that kind of medicine [she] answered that she cured John Jacks's child, and Wilson's of the town, and her goodman's sister's cow. [And she said that] three times Tom gave her such a herb out of his own hand. And [she was] asked [by the interrogators] to whom she applied the powder in drink. [She] declared that the Lady Johnston, elder, sent to her a servant of the said ladies, called Catherine Dunlop, to help a young gentlewoman, her daughter, now married to the young laird of Stanley. And [she said that] she thereupon asked ounfall[?] at Tom. And he said to her that her sickness was a cold blood that went about her heart that caused her to dwam and vigous [*swoon or faint] away. And Tom bade her take one part of ginger, cloves, anniseeds, liquorice, and some strong ale, and seeth them together, and strain it and put it in a vessel. And [Tom told her to tell her client to] take a little quantity of it in a mutchekin cane [*measuring vessel], and some white refined sugar among it [and to] take and drink thereof each day in the morning [and to] walk a while after, before meat, and she would be well. [Being] asked where she gave the gentle woman the drink [she] answered – in her own sister's house, the young Lady Blackhallis. [Being]

asked what she got for her doing [she] declared – a peck of meal and some cheese.

10. ITEM, [Being] asked if any other persons had been to her for the like cause, [she] declared that the Lady Kilbowie, elder, sent for her, and desired to see if she could make her any help for her leg that was crooked, to whom [Bessie had] promised answer as soon as she had spoken with Tom. But Tom [had] said 'she would never mend because the marrow of the bone was consumit [*wasted away, destroyed] and the blood dofinit [*dull, heavy], and if she sought any further help it would be worse with her!'

11. ITEM, She being asked if she could do any good to any women that were in travel of thair chyld bed-lare [*having a difficult labour] [she] answered that she could do nothing until she had first spoken with Tom; who laid down to her [?gave her] a green silken lace, out of his own hand, and bade her attach it to their under-dress and knit [it] about their left arm and without delay the sick woman would be deliver [?give birth]. But the said lace being laid once down by Tom, she could never apprehend it, and made great seeking therefore. Item, [She] declared that when she herself was lying in child-bed with her last son, Tom came to her, in her own house, and bade her 'take a good heart to her for nothing should ail her'.

12. [Being] asked if she could tell of anything that was away [?not in sight] or anything that was to come [*in the future] [she] answered that she could do nothing her self but [only] as Tom told her. And [she] further declared that many folks in the country (came to her?) to get knowledge of gear stolen from them. [Being] asked what persons they were [she] answered [that] the Lady Thridpairt, in the Barony of Renfrew, sent for her and asked her who was it that had stolen from her two horns of gold and a crown of the sun, out of her purse. And, after she [she] had spoken with Tom, within twenty days, she sent her word who had them and she got them again. Item, James Cunningham, chalmerlane [?chamberlain] of Kilwinning, came to her about some beir [?beer] that was stolen forth of the barn of Cragance and she told him where it was and he got it again. Item, The Lady Blair sundry times had spoken with her about some clothes that were stolen from her; a pair of woollen hose, a pair of sheets, a pillowcase, linen cloths, shirts and serviettes, for the which she dang and wrackit [*beat and tormented] her own servants. But Tom [had] told her 'That Margaret Simple, her own friend [*relative] and servant had stolen them.' Item, Being asked by William Kyle, burgess of Irvine, as he was coming out of Dumbarton, who was the stealer of Hugh Scott's cloak, a burgess of the same town. [She asked Tom and] Tom answered 'That the cloak would not be gotten because it wane [?was] taken away by Mally

Boyd, dweller in the same town, and was put out of the fashion of a cloak [and re-made] in[to] a kirtle. And although the said William had promised that she should not be troubled for the declaration of the same, yet, as soon as she came to the market of Irvine she was put in the tolbooth and struck, but was relieved by James Blair, brother to William Blair of the Strand.

13. ITEM, [Being] asked (If she had been applied to?) by Henry Jameson and James Baird of the Manse of Watterston, to get them knowledge of who had stolen their plough-irons, fittick [?] and musell [*bridle of a plough] [she] declared [that] she should give them answer as soon as she had spoken with Tom, who showed her that John Black and George Black, smiths, had stolen the same and that the cowtir [*coulter of a plough] and fok [?] were lying in his own house between the mekle ark [*large meal or grain chest] and a great kist [*big wooden box]. And [she] further said that when they came there to the ryping [?reaping] they should not find them because that Jamie Dougall, sherriffs officer, who then presently was with them, should ressais [?receive] three pounds for the concealing of them; for the which cause also, she was apprehended by the said smiths, and brought to my Lord of Glasgow.[8]

14. [Being] asked how she knew that this man was Tom Reid that died at Pinkie, [she] answered [that] she never knew him when he was in life, but that she should not doubt that it was he bade her go to Tom Reid, his son, now official in his place to the laird of Blair, and to certain others [of] his kinsmen and friends there, whom he named, and bade them restore certain goods and mend other offences that they had done. And that it was he that sent them word thereof 'Remember . . . [9] that when he and he went together to the black Saturday; and that the said . . . would have been another gait [*way/distance]. He drew him by the church of Dalry and there bought a pound of figs and gave [them to] him, and put them in his napkin. And so they went together, until they came to the field.'[10]

15. ITEM, [Being] asked if Tom, at his own hand, had sent to any person to show them things to come, [she] declared that he sent her to no creature in Middle-earth, but to William Blair of the Strand, and his eldest daughter, who was contracted and shortly to be married with . . . Crawford, young laird of Baidland, and [was told to] declare unto them that if she married that man, she should either die a shameful death, slay her self, cast herself down over a crag, or go mad. Whereby the said marriage was stayed and the laird forsaid married her youngest sister. Tryit to be of veritie [*Proven by Law]

16. [Being] asked what she thought of the new law [the Reformed Religion], [she] answered that she had spoken with Tom about that matter

but Tom [had] answered that this new law was not good and that the old faith should come home again but not such as it was before. [Being] asked if ever she had been in [a] suspect place with Tom, or had carnal dealings with him, [she] declared – not upon her salvation and condemnation, but [that] once he took her by the apron and would have had her go with him to Elfame.

17. ITEM, [Being] asked what time of the day or night he [Tom] most came to her, [she] answered that at the twelfth hour of the day was his common appearing.

18. [Being] asked if she had seen him going up and down the world [she] declared that once she saw him going in the churchyard of Dalry, among the people.

19. [Being] asked if she said anything to him [she] answered – no, because he had forbidden her. [He had told her] that wherever she saw him or met with him she should never speak to him unless he spoke to her first. Item, She saw him going up and down on the street of Edinburgh upon a market day, where he leuch [?laughed] upon her, and went up and down among the people and put his hands to the lavis [?loaves of bread] as other folk did.

20. [Being] asked if she never asked him wherefore he came to her more [than] to any other body [she] answered, remembering her, when she was lying in child-bed-lair with one of her sons, that a stout woman came in to her, and sat down on the form beside her and asked a drink from her, and she gave [one to] her. The woman also told her that that babe would die, and that her husband should mend of his sickness.[11] The said Bessie answered that she remembered well thairof and Tom said that [she] was the Queen of Elfame [Queen of the Fairies] his mistress, who had commanded him to wait upon her and to do her good.

21. [Being] asked if ever she had spoken with him at a loch and water side, [she] answered – never, save once, when she had gone afield with her husband to Leith[12] for home-bringing of meal. Going afield to tether her nag at Restalrig Loch there came a company of riders by that made such a din as [if] heaven and earth had gone together, and suddenly they rode into the loch, with many [a] hideous rumble.[13] But Tom told [her] it was the gude wichtis that were riding in Middle-earth.

22. [Being] asked when she spoke last with Tom [she] declared – on the morning after Candlemas-day last was,[14] where she spoke with him and he told her of the evil weather that was to come.

23. [Being] asked if she never asked [Tom] what trouble should come to her for [being in] his company [she] declared that [Tom had told her] she would be troubled therefore, but bade her seek an affayis[15] of her neighbours and no thing should ail her. [She] further declared that [Tom

told her?] she should be brought to Glasgow and [if?] she come in the Bishop's hands she would be well treated and sent home again.

24. ITEM, the said Bessie declared that the laird of Auchinskeith is riding with the ffair-folk [*the fairies], albeit he died nine years since.

APUD *Dalkeith*, xx *September, anno* 1576.[16]

25. BESSIE DUNLOP being re-examined, in [the] presence of the laird of Whittingham and George Auchinlek of Balmanno, and being asked how often Tom Reid came to her before she[17] confessed that he came thrice, and that she had no power at na [?any] time to try or tell any other, in the meantime, of his coming. He required her sundry times to pass with him and because she refused he shook his head and said that he should cause her forthink it [*to think again]. [She] confessed further that she has spoken with him at diverse times by [*over] the space of four years.

26. BEING asked about the plough-irons stolen from Henry Jameson and James Baird [she] confessed that she asked Tom Reid who declared to her that Gabriel Black and Geordie Black in Lokarsyde stole them and brought them to their father's house, named John Black, upon a grey gelding on a Saturday in the night – which she told again to the said Henry Jameson and James Baird.

27. ITEM, [She] confessed that four years since, or thereabouts, she saw the laird of Auchinskeith at a [fairy] thorn beyond Monkcastle – the which laird died more than five years since. Thereafter she, at the desire of Lady Auchinskeith, asked Tom Reid if such a man was among them [the fairies]? Who answered that he was among them.[18]

[We, the members of the jury, find] the said Elizabeth Dunlop, to be guilty and charged of the haill [?whole/entire] points above written, and of using of Witchcraft, Sorcery, and Incantation, with Invocation of spirits of the devil, continuing in familiarity with them at all times, as she thought expedient, and thereby dealing with charms, and abusing the people with her devilish craft of sorcery forsaid, by the means above specified.

On the margin of the document recording Bessie's trial are written the words 'Convict, and burnt'. It is likely that Bessie, along with other convicted felons, would have been taken by open cart to Castle Hill in Edinburgh, either immediately after the trial or during the subsequent few days. Once there, she would have been encouraged to publicly repent of her sorcery and witchcraft.[19] After her repentance she would have been strangled, and her body burnt to ashes before the expectant crowd.

ACKNOWLEDGMENTS

I owe a great debt of gratitude to the late Gareth Roberts, without whose encouragement and generosity this book would never have been written. I am also indebted to Ronald Hutton, who kindly read an early draft of the manuscript and gave me much valuable comment. Special thanks must also go to my publisher, Anthony Grahame, for his vision and patience.

Parts of chapters 4–7 have appeared in the journal *Folklore* (2000, vol. 111, pp. 283–305). My grateful thanks to the editors and to Taylor & Francis (www.tandf.co.uk) for permission to re-use this material. I am also grateful for advice and encouragement from Gillian Bennett, Marion Gibson, Andy Gurr, Christine Johns, Mog Morgan, Kate Pink and Joanna Redstone. The efforts of Rob Ford, of Exeter University Library, have also been much appreciated.

Last but not least I wish to thank my family – particularly my sons, Hamish and Dylan, for their forbearance, and therapeutic nonchalance regarding all things literary; Annie and Sue, for their unwavering support in all weathers; and most of all, Jamie, who has been right beside me every step of the way.

Part I

Demon and Fairy Familiars
The Historical Context

INTRODUCTION TO PART I

'In the name of God, what art thou?'
Elizabeth Bennett, 1582

In her role as a 'cunning woman', or popular magical practitioner, Bessie Dunlop worked at the rock face of sixteenth-century Scottish life: she delivered babies, healed the sick, consoled the bereaved, identified criminals and recovered lost and stolen goods. But the keystone of Bessie's magical practice – the source of all her knowledge and power – was her relationship with a ghost, a familiar spirit who she called Tom Reid. And Bessie was not alone in this. Of the hundreds of trials for witchcraft which took place across the length and breadth of Britain in the sixteenth and seventeenth centuries, from the Orkney Isles to Cornwall, a significant number produced confessions detailing descriptions of pivotal encounters between popular magical practitioners and some kind of spirit. That belief in familiar spirits was widespread among the common people in this period is also corroborated by references found in the writings of contemporary intellectuals and theologians and in plays, ballads and pamphlets. In these sources the magical practitioner might be defined in any number of ways – as a 'witch', 'sorcerer', 'wizard', 'wise man', 'cunning woman' and so on – and their spirit-familiar might be variously described as an 'imp', 'demon', 'fairy', 'angel' or, most commonly, 'the Devil'. Whatever the definitions employed, however, in all these descriptions of encounters with familiar spirits, the working relationship between the human and the spirit followed the same basic format as that enjoyed by Bessie Dunlop and the man who 'died at Pinkie'.

Trial confessions which contain descriptions of familiar-encounters all share a contradictory mix of the everyday and the fantastic. Bessie's narrative, for example, resonates with vivid details about daily life: a grey-bearded man in a coat with old-fashioned 'Lambart' sleeves, cloves and strong ale seething in a medicine vessel, a pound of eggs received and carefully wrapped up in a napkin and, more poignantly, a countrywoman driving her cattle to pasture, heavy with sadness at the thought of her husband and newborn baby lying at home close to death. And yet, at the same time, there are elements in the narrative that are so uncanny and numinous that they evoke the fascination of the fairy tale: the well-dressed gentleman disappearing through a narrow hole in a dyke that 'no earthly man could have gone through', the noisy company of 'gude wychtis' (fairies) riding into Restalrig Loch with 'many a hideous rumble' and the ghost of a dead man tugging at a woman's apron and begging her to go with him into fairyland.

So how are we to approach this complex material? What are we to make of these contradictions? Were these descriptions of encountering spirits elaborate fictions? Or did women like Bessie Dunlop believe that they genuinely encountered supernatural beings? And if so, what was actually going on when these encounters were believed to be taking place?

Magical practices surrounding the use of familiar spirits are alive and well in Britain today. In many modern pagan traditions beliefs surrounding encounters with 'spirit-like' beings, either defined as supernatural entities, or in psychological terms, 'personal' or 'transpersonal' aspects of the psyche, play a significant role. Instructions for the development of relationships with spirit-familiars feature in magical belief systems as diverse as Hermetic and Thelemic magic, Wicca, Heathenism, angel lore, spiritualism and the many forms of neo-shamanism. Relationships with autonomous envisioned entities also play a key role in a number of modern psychological therapies – such as analytic and archetypal psychology. Books, articles and experiential workshops consistently claim to show interested individuals the way to encounter familiar spirits, defined variously as spirit-guides, ancestors, elemental spirits, fairies, guardian angels, archetypes, power animals and so on.

Writers from these traditions are primarily interested in the familiar's usefulness. They focus on the experiential: How can such familiars be invoked? What can you do with them when they appear? What can you learn about yourself from your familiar? While these writers often claim a link between modern familiar beliefs and popular familiar beliefs found in sixteenth- and seventeenth-century Britain, justification for these claims tends to be slender, usually amounting to the paraphrasing of a couple of notorious witch trials in which familiars played a prominent role. The reason for this brevity is not one of inaccuracy, for the intuitions of these writers are undoubtedly correct, but because the historical perspectives available with which to back up their claims are few and far between.

Over the past century, witchcraft in early modern Europe has been of intense interest to academic historians and a rich and varied body of research has accumulated on the subject. Despite this long-standing interest, however, most scholars in the British field have been concerned with the political, social and religious ramifications of witch trials, and as a consequence beliefs and practices surrounding familiar spirits remain largely overlooked. Until relatively recently, descriptions of familiar-encounters found in trial records of the period were usually dismissed as derivative of one or more of the following: mental illness (the accused was 'senile' or 'delusional'), prosecutorial coercion (the accused was pressurised by interrogators into fabricating stereotypical stories about encounters with the Devil) or misapprehension (the accused had mistakenly assumed that previous meetings with 'real' men or animals had been encounters with spirits). Over the past few decades, however, a growing body of research has rendered such a reductionistic range of explanations untenable. Historians such as Carlo Ginzburg, Gábor Klaniczay and Éva Pócs have argued that descriptions of sabbath experiences and familiar-encounters found in early modern European witch trials were expressions of popular experiential traditions rooted in pre-Christian shamanistic beliefs and practices. As a result of this work, most scholars now acknowledge that there was a genuinely folkloric component to European witch beliefs in this period, although opinions still differ as to its extent. Despite these changes in perspective, however, the majority of historians concerned with British witchcraft and magic continue to discuss the familiar-encounter, its folkloric significance, and the mystery of its genesis, in passing. Most notably, none have followed Ginzburg's lead and explored familiar beliefs in the context of their possible shamanistic origins.

Over the years this lack of attention to familiar lore has had inadvertent, and far more serious implications than the mere overlooking of a specialized set of historical beliefs. By not giving adequate weight to descriptions of encountering spirits, the academic portrayal of popular magical belief and practice in early modern Britain often comes across as reductionistic: an exposition of a fundamentally pragmatic system of self-help primarily designed to alleviate material suffering. A system in which popular magical practitioners accessed practical magical solutions to remedy day-to-day problems – ranging from the more superficial, such as a sour batch of beer, a lost purse, or a refused demand for alms, to the more serious, such as a difficult labour, or sickness in humans or animals. Although historians have produced a number of perceptive studies which bear testament to the sophistication and efficacy of popular magical traditions in this period, and which extol, in particular, the value of 'cunning' or 'wise' folk as policemen, detectives and doctors – something remains missing from the picture. An experiential or 'spiritual' dimension.

Historians have long recognized that there was an experiential dimension to learned or 'high' magical traditions in early modern Britain, and that this dimension possessed a spiritual significance for practitioners. They readily acknowledge the fact that learned magicians performed rituals in order to facilitate mystical experience or revelation, and that their attempts to visually encounter spirits could play an integral role in this context. The magical beliefs and practices of common folk in this period, however, are seldom elevated by historians in this way. Such an oversight is deeply illogical. Visional spirituality has never been the preserve of the learned. The influential sixteenth-century German magician, Cornelius Agrippa, claimed that encounters with certain types of spirit were *more* likely to occur to 'children, women, and poor and mean men' than the educated magician because the former naturally possessed the 'singleness of the wit, innocency of the mind . . . firm credulity, and constant silence' necessary for the task. Insights into the ontological nature of the spirit-encountering experiences of Britain's 'poor and mean men', however, and into the mystical significance which these encounters may have possessed for them, remain largely absent from the history books.

This work, therefore, is a preliminary attempt to explore this overlooked dimension of Britain's native spiritual heritage. Taking a multidisciplinary approach, it will draw on historical, anthropological, psychological and comparative religious perspectives to examine popular familiar beliefs in early modern Britain, paying particular attention to their experiential dimension and spiritual significance. The book has been written and structured in such a way as to make it useful to both the general reader and the historian.

Part I is purely historical in tone, and begins with an overview of popular magical belief in Britain in the period and an appraisal of the social function of popular magical practitioners – the latter being subdivided into 'cunning folk', who were associated with good magic, and 'witches', who were associated with harmful magic. It then goes on to examine in some detail the familiar beliefs held by both types of magical practitioner through referencing and cross-referencing between a wide range of 'encounter-narratives' – that is, descriptions of encounters with spirits – taken from trial records for witchcraft and sorcery from throughout Britain in the period, and backed up with relevant contributions from contemporary élite writings. By this analytic process Part I aims to achieve two things: first, to illustrate in some detail, the event-pattern, emotional dynamics and social function of the alleged familiar-encounter, and secondly to illustrate how encounter-narratives were not merely élite fictions, that is, the result of learned prosecutors superimposing their demonological preconceptions onto cunning folk and witches, but were rooted in folk belief and came, in significant part, from the magical practitioners themselves.

In Parts II and III the book moves away from the early modern period and away from purely historical methodologies. Part II draws systematic comparisons between the encounter-narratives given by early modern cunning folk and witches, and descriptions of encounters with familiar spirits given by shamans from Siberia and the Americas in the late nineteenth and early twentieth centuries. These anthropological comparisons serve two purposes. First, they corroborate the argument for the folkloric origins of the encounter-narrative put forward in Part I. Secondly, they facilitate the exploration, undertaken in Part III, into the ontological nature of these alleged spirit-encounters.

Part III begins by arguing that the encounter-narratives given by cunning folk and witches were not just accumulations of folk beliefs and stories, but that they were, like comparable narratives given by shamans, descriptions of visionary experiences – actual psychic events which occurred in historical time and geographical space. It is suggested that, taken together, these widespread and yet mutually coherent narratives could be interpreted as evidence that popular shamanistic visionary traditions, of pre-Christian origin, survived in many parts of Britain during the early modern period.

Part III then goes on to explore the possible spiritual significance of these traditions. Through an analysis of the way recent developments in the fields of comparative religion and psychology have enabled scholars to acknowledge the mystical status of the shaman's spirit-encountering experiences, it asserts the mystical status of the British familiar-encounter. This assertion is then supported by an examination of some of the cultural assumptions that have historically made it difficult for academic historians to recognize the experiential dimension, and the spiritual significance, of popular magical belief and practice in this period. In the penultimate chapter, the role of the familiar as 'envisioned spiritual guide' is examined through an exploration of visional mysticism in the Christian contemplative traditions of medieval Europe. The book concludes by looking at the significance these perspectives have for our understanding of spirituality in Britain, both in the early modern period and in the twenty-first century.

CHAPTER ONE

A Harsh and Enchanted World

Bot Thom said, 'Bessie, thow hes crabit [angered] God, and askit sum thing you suld nocht haif done; and, thairfoir, I counsell thee to mend to him:[1]

In order to understand popular beliefs surrounding familiar spirits in early modern Britain, we need to put these beliefs in context by taking a general look at the mental climate of the time. Bessie Dunlop and her contemporaries lived in a world very different from the one we inhabit today. During the sixteenth and seventeenth centuries Britain underwent a great many epoch-making religious and political changes: the break with Rome, the rise of Protestantism, the execution of a king and the establishment of the Commonwealth. The State saw the fledgling emergence of those two great pillars of the modern age: rationalism and industrialism. For the majority of people during these two hundred years, however, everyday life changed little. Only a small minority of the population enjoyed any amount of wealth or education. The remainder, whom we can loosely term 'the common people/folk' or 'the poor',[2] led a rural hand-to-mouth existence immersed in and wholly dependent upon nature and dominated by the need to produce food. Daily life was an unremitting round of hard physical labour, constantly overshadowed by the threat of poverty and disease.

While it is difficult for most westerners today to imagine the rigours of the early modern physical environment, it is just as difficult for us to imagine the mental worlds of those who struggled within it. To the common people in this period, the harsh and unyielding physical world was also an enchanted one.[3] Powerful occult forces permeated life at every level. The air teemed with invisible supernatural entities which constantly influenced the natural world and the lives of men. A prayer could be answered. A spell could cure. A look could kill. A spirit or deity could be at your ear at any time of the night or day – guiding your spinning-hand

Cour de ferme by Jan Siberechts (1662). Flemish artist Siberechts evokes the business of daily life as it was for many people throughout Europe in the early modern period.

or your plough-arm, charming the crops in the fields or the animals in the barns, bringing good luck and gold, or raining down famine and disease. Everyday life was sympathetically linked to the heavens, and even the smallest event could possess a cosmic significance. From the moment of birth, the early modern poor were immersed in this magical universe and as they grew, if they were lucky, to maturity, they accumulated the skills needed to negotiate a way through it. While their practical abilities enabled them to deal as best they could with the visible physical world, it was their beliefs and rituals which enabled them to deal with the invisible web of supernatural forces which lay behind it.

The matrix of belief and ritual inherited by the common people of early modern Britain can be provisionally subdivided into those beliefs and rituals which were 'religious' and those which were 'magical'. Although this categorization is simplistic, it is useful insofar as it highlights the basic difference between the 'supplicatory' and the 'coercive' methods of dealing with supernatural powers. Keith Thomas sums up this difference as follows:

> the essential difference between the prayers of a churchman and the spells of a magician was that only the latter claimed to work automatically; a prayer had no certainty of success and would not be granted if God chose not to concede it. A spell, on the other hand, need never go wrong, unless some detail of ritual observance had been omitted or a rival magician had been practising stronger counter-magic. A prayer, in other words, was a form of supplication: a spell was a mechanical means of manipulation. Magic postulated occult forces of nature which the magician learned to control, whereas religion assumed the direction of the world by a conscious agent who could only be deflected from his purpose by prayer and supplication.[4]

Religious Beliefs

Religious beliefs in early modern Britain are well documented and extensively researched. Historians have closely examined the ideological, political and social implications of the break with Rome, the establishment of the Church of England and the rise of Protestant sects throughout England and Scotland and as a consequence there is plenty of evidence to hand that Protestant belief and ritual had a strong popular impact in this period. The new perspectives offered by Protestantism provoked intense spiritual excitement, not only among scholars and clerics, but also among the common folk. The translation of the Bible into English, the diminishing of the institutional role of the Church and clergy and the doctrinal emphasis on man's individual relationship with God, freed many people to explore religious belief and practice in a more intense and direct way than ever before. Such fervent religiosity, however, was not the prerogative of the Protestant. Work by historians such as Eamon Duffy have emphasized the fact that the 'auld ffayth', that is, Roman Catholicism, still claimed the hearts of many common folk in this period.[5] Although ordinary people could not generally read religious writings, or understand the Latin of the Mass, the passage of their days and seasons were chequered with vivid and emotive ritual: the performance of the sacraments (baptism, confirmation, matrimony, the Eucharist, holy orders, penance and extreme unction); the observation of the liturgical calendar (special days or weeks in the year where particular rituals were performed); pilgrimages to holy places; and the ubiquitous and fervent worship of the saints. In addition, the Catholic faith, though underpinned by a preoccupation with sin and death, was in practice often celebratory, providing many ritual opportunities for communal festivity which could include dancing, singing, processions, pageant plays and feasting. Although England officially ceased to be Catholic in the early 1530s (Scotland following in 1560) and the subsequent decades saw the desecration of churches, the abolition or dilution of the sacraments, the abandonment of the Latin Mass and the denial of the intercessionary abilities of the saints, many ordinary people, including a good proportion of the clergy, maintained their close bond with Catholic belief and ritual. A Puritan document in 1584 claimed that 'Three parts at least of the people' were 'wedded to their old superstition still' and nearly fifty years later an English vicar could still lament that he found 'the whole body of the common people popishly addicted'.[6] Beliefs and rituals pertaining to the Virgin Mary and the cult of the dead were recorded in Britain right up to the end of the seventeenth century and beyond, as were seasonal rituals associated with fertility, good fortune and the banishment of evil. Devotion to the saints also persisted and many Protestant clergy lamented the persistence of pilgrimages to sacred wells, springs and other holy places and the high-spirited celebrations which often took place in churches and churchyards on the eve of saints' days. The use of rosaries, primers, vestments, altars and images also continued among the common folk long after they were officially outlawed, while the use of Catholic prayers and phraseology was even more persistent. A continuing belief in the power of the saints can be seen in the healing charm used by Morayshire cunning man William Kerrow, in 1623:

The quaquand fever and the trembling fever
And the sea fever and the land fever,

Bot and the head fever and the hart fever,
And all the fevers that God creatit.
In Sanct Johnes name, Sanct Peteris name,
And all the sancts of heavin's name
Our Lord Jesus Chrystis name.[7]

Even Latin prayers, so despised by the Protestants, survived the rigors of the Reformation and frequently re-emerged in folk charms. One late seventeenth-century cunning woman from Orkney, for example, performed a spell by rubbing a herb between her middle finger and thumb and saying *'In nomine patris filii et spiritus sancti'*.[8] This continuing adherence to the outward forms of Catholicism could be accompanied by strong spiritual conviction. When Tom Reid tried to persuade Catholic sympathizer Bessie Dunlop to deny her Christian faith she replied, with great affront, that 'gif sche suld be revin at horis-taillis [dragged at a horse's tail], sche suld neuir do that'.[9] Similarly, Bessie's claims that Tom Reid attributed her misfortunes to her having 'crabit [angered] God' and that he urged her to 'mend to him' also indicate a lively religious conscience at work.[10] Many ordinary people like Bessie, who had the pressing business of physical survival on their hands, outwardly endured the Reformation but in their hearts they hoped that 'the auld ffayth suld cum hame agane'.[11]

Magical Beliefs

During the early modern period popular Christian beliefs, however strongly held, were often intermingled with beliefs and practices of a more magical nature. The first scholar to comprehensively examine this traditionally-overlooked dimension of British history was Oxford historian Sir Keith Thomas. In his seminal work *Religion and the Decline of Magic* (1971), Thomas argued that in sixteenth- and seventeenth-century England, magical beliefs permeated both learned and popular thought with a subtlety and extent hitherto unrecognized by historians. The book became an instant classic, and remains unsurpassed, although some of its arguments and emphases have since been challenged.[12] The brief sketch of religious and magical belief in the period presented in the first two chapters of this book owes much to Thomas's scholarship.

One of the sources of magical belief and practice in early modern Britain was, ironically, the enduring popular attachment to Catholicism. The 'old faith' was riddled with magic and superstition, much of it promoted and supported by the Church itself. Although its central concerns were theoretically otherworldly or 'spiritual' (that is, concerned with the fate of the soul and the afterlife as opposed to physical existence on earth) and ecclesiastics were anxious to emphasize the intercessionary nature of church ritual, in practice, and particularly at a grass-roots level, the Catholic Church encouraged people to use prayers and rites magically. When priests asked penitents to repeat a stated number of Paternosters, Aves and Creeds in Latin – a language which they could not understand – they were encouraging the idea that repeating prayers would have a mechanical efficacy. In this sense, the prayer was no different from the magical charm. The sacraments of the Church were used and administered in a similar way. Attendance at Mass, for example, conferred instant benefits such as protection during travel, ease in childbirth, recovery of lost goods and so on, regardless of the extent to which one understood the ceremony, the state of mind in which one attended it or even the moral nature of one's deeds committed before or after attendance there. One medieval theologian claimed that during mass 'anyone who saw a priest bearing the Host would not lack meat or drink for the rest of that day, nor be in any danger of sudden death or blindness'.[13] Ritual objects were also seen as possessing magical power. Holy water, for example, could be drunk by humans and animals to cure them of sickness, scattered on fields to promote a good harvest or sprinkled onto houses to drive away demons and protect from fire. Among common folk it was believed that the individual who did not eat the communion bread during Mass, but slipped it under his tongue and took it home with him, was then in possession of a powerful magical object which could be used to cure sickness, fertilize fields, protect crops against pests or act as a good-luck charm. The worship of saints and their relics, pilgrimages to holy places, seasonal rituals such as the perambulation of the parish in Rogation Week and so on, could all possess a magical efficacy.[14]

In essence, almost any element of the Catholic religion, whether physical or liturgical, could be used magically and for many ordinary people, as Keith Thomas claims, the old faith may have been little more than 'an organized system of magic designed to bring supernatural remedies to bear upon earthly problems'.[15] This magical dimension of Catholicism was roundly condemned by English Protestant reformers, who were anxious to emphasize the distinction between magic and religion. William Tyndale, for example, denounced the Catholics for 'a false kind of praying, wherein the tongue and lips labour . . . but the heart talketh not . . . nor hath any confidence in the promises of God; but trusteth in the multitude of words, and in the pain and tediousness of the length of the prayer; as a conjurer doth in his circles, characters, and superstitious words of his conjuration.'[16] An enduring attachment to Catholicism, however, was not the only origin of magical belief and practice in the early modern period, for the common folk's thirst for magic also drew on roots which reached down into pre-Christian subsoils.

Pre-Christian Influences

Historians have long recognized that magical beliefs and practices of pre-Christian origin survived into the early modern period, however in recent decades there has been a growing acknowledgement that these beliefs were more pervasive and influential than previously thought. One scholar has gone so far as to claim, for example, that 'pre-Reformation European peasants were virtually pagan, that they held animist beliefs in a spirit world which had to be appeased in order to maintain their crops and live-stock, that these beliefs were overlaid in varying degrees by Christian notions which were to a large extent adapted to animism.'[17] There is no doubt that allegiance to nature spirits and pagan deities masqueraded behind the worship of the saints; that ancient traditions of ancestor worship lay at the core of the cult of the dead and that the most sacred events in the Christian calendar, such as Christmas and Easter, were superimposed over already-existing pre-Christian religious festivals. The same was true of many annual agricultural rituals, such as those performed on Plough Monday or during Rogation Week, and the seasonal fire rituals performed on holy days such as St John or St Peter's Eve. More light-hearted pursuits such as Church Ales, May games, Hocktide sports, morris dancing, mumming, dancing with hobby horses and celebrations involving the Lords of Misrule or the Summer Lords and Ladies and so on, possessed an even thinner veneer of Christianity. Folk charms from the period also clearly reveal this assimilation of the new faith by the old. The core of this Shetland version of a widely-used healing charm is believed to be pre-Christian, while the appeal to the Christian God found in the first and last lines is a later addition:

> The Lord rade
> And the foal slade
> He lighted
> And he righted
> Set joint to joint
> Bone to bone
> and sinew to sinew
> Heal in the Holy Ghost's name.[18]

Despite the fact that Catholicism was incredibly successful at assimilating pre-Christian magical belief and practice, this process of absorption was in no way complete. The guiding principles in the lives of many ordinary people in early modern Britain were essentially 'animist' rather than Christian, and some of the most cherished beliefs and rituals paid little lip service to Christianity at all. In our own century, novelists and film-makers unconsciously perpetuate the notion of the idyllic Christian community of Britain past: every member of the parish, from the poorest cottar in his homespun jerkin to the lord of the manor in his velvets and ruff, all coming together to worship in a candle-lit church – the gulf in rank and earthly fortunes which normally separated them being momentarily bridged by the metaphysical certainties and emotional comforts of established belief. But the reality was rather different. In many parts of England and Scotland churches were without a resident priest. Those parishes with incumbent priests all too frequently found their man of God guilty of immorality, greed or negligence and saw the disproportionate wealth of the Church failing to see its way to where it was needed. Some people responded to the failings of the Church by focusing on reform, meeting their worldly and spiritual needs through Protestantism. For others, however, the response was less vivacious.

A significant proportion of common folk seldom attended church at all. Contemporaries complained that it was quite common for only half of the parish to be present at Sunday worship and in 1635 one pamphleteer lamented that it 'really was a case of two or three persons gathered together in God's name'.[19] The Scottish witch, Janet Man, who was tried in 1659, would not have been alone when she claimed that 'she was guiltie of manie other sinnes such as neglect of the ordinances for the spaice of Tuentie yeires she had not receaved anie beniffeitt of the kirk'.[20] Of those who attended church, many just went through the motions with little real understanding. A large proportion of the laity could not recite the Lord's Prayer or Ten Commandments and knew little of Christian scripture or doctrine, one observer complaining in 1606 that people 'knew more about Robin Hood than they did about the stories in the Bible'.[21] Another described the words of a dying man of sixty who had attended church several times a week throughout his lifetime:

> Being demanded [on his death bed] what he thought of God, he answers that he was a good old man; and what of Christ, that he was a towardly young youth; and of his soul, that it was a great bone in his body; and what should become of his soul after he was dead, that if he had done well he should be put into a pleasant green meadow ... But, my brethren, be assured this man is not alone; there be many a hundred in his case who come to

15

church and hear much, haply a hundred and fifty sermons in a year; yet at the year's end are as much the better for all, as the pillars of the church against which they lean, or the pews wherein they sit.[22]

Some individuals were not only ignorant concerning Christian belief and ritual, they were openly irreverent. People chatted, told jokes, spat and fell asleep during church services. When, for example, a sermon given by the Elizabethan curate of Stogursey, Somerset, went on too long, a parishioner shouted out that it was 'time for him to come down so that the maids might go milking'.[23] In 1547, bishop and statesman Stephen Gardiner described a parish in Cambridge where 'when the vicar goeth into the pulpit to read that [he] himself hath written, then the multitude of the parish goeth straight out of the church, home to drink', and in the same county forty-one years later a man was charged with indecent behaviour in church after his 'most loathsome farting, striking, and scoffing speeches' had caused 'the great offence of the good and the great rejoicing of the bad'.[24]

Others lived their lives virtually untouched by Christian belief, not knowing or feeling strongly enough about Christianity to bother to satirize it. Puritan John Penry claimed that in Elizabethan Wales, thousands of people knew little of Christ – 'yea almost that never heard of him' – and in 1607, Fulham cartographer John Norden claimed that the people living in scattered hamlets in the depths of the New Forest lived 'far from any church or chapel, and are as ignorant of God or of any civil course of life as the very savages among the infidels'.[25] Such extreme ignorance, however, was not only to be found in the remote areas, it was also present in the more central counties of Essex, Wiltshire, Hampshire and even London. Keith Thomas concludes that theologian Richard Hooker 'may have been right when he observed that there were very few persons by whom God was "altogether unapprehended" . . . But a concept of God as vague as this was compatible with all sorts of beliefs of which the Church strongly disapproved.'[26]

Although some common folk seldom attended church and possessed limited knowledge of, or respect for, Christian teachings, this does not mean that they believed their world to be devoid of supernatural influences, or that they did not consider belief and ritual to be of the utmost importance. The lives of even the most isolated and theologically-unaware individuals would have been hedged about with a complex body of magical beliefs and rituals inherited from their pre-Christian ancestors, many of which remained largely untouched by the long fingers of the Church. One of the most coherent matrices of non-Christian belief extant on a popular level in this period was the body of accumulated knowledge and custom relating to fairies.[27] The early modern 'fairy faith', if we can call it that, was an amalgamation of many of the animistic beliefs and rituals surrounding nature spirits, deities, ghosts and so on which had not been completely homogenized into Catholic hagiolatry and the cult of the dead. And it is here, in this surviving bedrock of pre-Christian animism, that we can trace the origins of the early modern familiar.

The Fairy Folk

> Remembring hir, quhen sche was lyand in chyld-bed-lair, with ane of hir laiddis, that ane stout woman com in to hir, and sat doun on the forme besyde hir, and askit ane drink at hir, and sche gaif hir . . . and Thom said, That was the Quene of Elfame his maistres, quha had commandit him to wait upoun hir, and to do hir gude.[28]

In early modern Britain, disbelief in the existence of spirits was tantamount to atheism. The overwhelming majority of people, whether rich or poor, educated or uneducated, believed in the existence of a countless number and variety of invisible supernatural beings. Different types of people were concerned with different types of spirits: for the devout Christian, angels and demons stood centre stage; for the élite magician, spirits originating from classical cosmologies could be equally significant while the uneducated country people placed a greater emphasis on the 'fairy folk'. Trying to make any hard and fast distinction between categories of spirits in early modern Britain is impossible because supernatural beings were labelled differently, depending on geography, education and religious perspective and definitions overlapped considerably. The term 'fairy', for example, is a misleadingly broad generic term which, in the period, covered a wide range of supernatural entities.[29] On a popular level there was often little difference between a fairy and an angel, saint, ghost, or devil. We find the popular link between fairies and angels, for example, expressed in the confession of a cunning man on trial for witchcraft in Aberdeen, in 1598. The magical practitioner, who was identified in the trial records as 'Andro Man', claimed that his familiar (described by the interrogators as the Devil) was an angel who, like Tom Reid, served the queen of the fairies. The records state 'Thow confessis that the Devill, thy maister, quhom thow termes Christsonday, and supponis to be ane engell, and Goddis godsone, albeit he hes a thraw by God, and swyis to the Quene of Elphen, is rasit be the speking of the word *Benedicte*.'[30]

The grass-roots association between fairies and the Devil was also, from a Christian perspective, rather ambiguous. In orthodox theological terms the name 'devil' denoted a purely malevolent spirit who was either the Devil himself or a demon in his service. On a popular level, however, the term was less morally specific. In 1677 a Scottish clergyman refers to a type of fairy familiar whom 'the vulgar call white deviles, which possibly have neither so much power nor malice as the black ones have, which served our great grandfathers under the names of Brouny, and Robin Goodfellow, and, to this day, make dayly service to severals in quality of familiars'.[31]

The most consistent association to be found, however, is the link between fairies and the dead. In the mid seventeenth century, political philosopher Thomas Hobbes claimed that 'The Fairies are Spirits and Ghosts. Fairies and Ghosts inhabit Darknesse, Solitudes, and Graves' while a few decades later Scottish theologian James Garden, in a letter to the English antiquarian, John Aubrey, asserted that Scottish magical practitioners, or 'seers', were people who converse with 'ghosts & spirits, or as they commonly call them, the fairies or fairie-folk'.[32] Similarly, Garden's contemporary, Robert Kirk, a clergyman from Aberfoyle, Stirling, who wrote the famous treatise on seventeenth-century Scottish fairy belief, *The Secret Commonwealth of Elves, Fauns and Fairies*, recorded how one local seer, or magical practitioner, claimed that the fairies were 'departed souls attending a whil in this inferior state'.[33] That these learned commentators accurately reflected popular belief is illustrated by the fact that many people claimed to have seen dead friends and relatives in fairyland. Bessie Dunlop maintained that Tom Reid was the spirit of a man who had died at the Battle of Pinkye thirty years earlier, and yet Tom lived in fairyland and served Bessie by command of the queen of the fairies. The relationship between fairies and the dead was even closer for Orkney cunning woman Elspeth Reoch, whose trial dittays of 1616 state that she was visited by a man who 'callit him selff ane farie man quha wes sumtyme her kinsman callit Johne Stewart quha wes slane be Mc Ky at the doun going of the soone'.[34]

The heterogenous group of spirits which came under the umbrella term of 'fairy', did, nevertheless, share many characteristics. They were often portrayed as possessing a human-like appearance and living an uncanny simulacrum of human life. They wore clothes (adopting local fashions, often quaintly out-of-date); they rode horses and hunted game; they grew crops and held markets; they worked at domestic tasks such as spinning and washing clothes; and they spent their leisure time playing games, dancing and making music. On a more personal level, they could marry, set up house, enjoy sexual relations and in some cases give birth to children. Fairies were also capable of all-too-human emotions: they could feel anger, hatred, jealousy, sympathy or joy – and they could fall in love. Fairy society, like that of early modern Britain, was presided over by a monarchy, and the fairy king and queen, sometimes accompanied by an entourage of aristocratic henchmen, reigned over a mannered and lavish court. Although fairies were often associated with the natural landscape, particularly hills and subterranean caverns, in principle the fairies could be found almost anywhere. One early modern writer claimed that 'They occupy various places of this world; as Woods, Mountains, Waters, Air, fiery Flames, Clouds, Starrs, Mines, and hid Treasures: as also antient Buildings, and places of the slain. Some again are familiar in Houses, and do frequently converse with, and appear unto mortals.'[35] The folklorist Katharine Briggs divides traditional British fairies into two groups: 'solitary' and 'trooping'.[36] Solitary fairies live alone or in small groups and themselves can be subdivided into 'domestic' and 'non-domestic'; that is, fairies who live alongside people in their houses or outhouses (such as the brownie) and those who live in the countryside, away from human society. Trooping fairies, alternatively, live in big groups away from human habitation. In reality, the two categories overlap considerably, solitary fairies spending time with trooping fairies and members of the trooping fairies often appearing individually.

Although fairies were believed to resemble humans in appearance and behaviour, ontologically they were considered to be vastly different. The finer details concerning the exact origin and nature of different kinds of spirits was the subject of vigorous ongoing debate in theological and academic circles, however it was commonly thought that the fairy possessed some kind of semi-material or 'astral' form, putting them somewhere on the spectrum between human flesh and bones and pure spirit. Yorkshire biographer Durant Hotham claimed, for example, that fairies were 'lodg'd in Vehicles of a thinner-spun thred than is (otherwise than by condensation) visible to our dim sight'; Robert Kirk that fairies possessed 'light changable bodies (lik those called Astrall) somewhat of the nature of a condens'd cloud' and Somerset surgeon John Beaumont, with chilling empiricism, that the hand of a fairy which he himself encountered 'yielded to my touch, so that I could not find any sensible resistency in it'.[37] The supernatural form of the fairy possessed correspondingly supernatural powers: fairies could, for example, live long beyond the allotted human span; they could become visible or invisible at will; they could shapeshift between animal and human form and they could fly, sometimes travelling vast distances at great speed. They could also divine the future, heal the sick and possess knowledge of objects and events in far off places. Despite their supernatural status, however, early modern

19

fairies possessed an ambiguous moral nature which was often all-too-human in its superficiality and ambivalence. This nature spanned the good–bad spectrum: some fairies were completely malicious, to be avoided by humans at all costs and others (a small minority) were totally benign. The majority of fairies, however, including most of the rather inaccurately named 'good' fairies, were generally considered to have been morally ambivalent, capable of both virtue and malevolence in varying proportions. Whatever their moral nature, however, and wherever they lived, most fairies were reluctant to be seen. Although folk tales, ballads, anecdotes and trial confessions from the period describe chance encounters between ordinary people and fairy folk it is clear that consistent and purposeful visual encounters with fairies were believed to be the preserve of magical practitioners, that is, those individuals who were specialists in the practice of magic. This special relationship between the popular magical practitioner and the fairy will be examined in detail in subsequent chapters.

Although the majority of ordinary people did not encounter the fairies directly, many still considered their relationship with these spirits to be of the greatest importance. Fairies were believed to be able to use their supernatural powers to influence almost any aspect of the natural world, including the lives of humans, and as a consequence people were very anxious to curry fairy favour. At night, housewives across the length and breadth of Britain would leave out bowls of water or milk and plates of bread or cake on the kitchen floor for the fairies. By day, out in the fields and the animal sheds, their husbands would tie cords and bury bones and mutter charms in an effort to please these capricious spirits of the land. In return for this solicitude, the fairies might help the housewife to a fine batch of butter or a strong brewing of ale, or may even leave fairy silver in her boots; while they might treat the farmer to a fine August, a good lambing season, or help him turn up a crock of fairy gold with the plough. While human attempts to please the fairies were motivated by the desire for good fortune, however, they were just as strongly motivated by fear. These same housewives strove to keep their kitchens clean and be generous to their neighbours in the belief that the fairies abhorred slovenliness and meanness, and their husbands avoided ploughing in a spot of land or felling a tree if it was believed to be sacred to the fairies, for fear of upsetting them. Any of the mishaps which occurred around the homestead could be attributed to fairy displeasure. Keith Thomas writes that, if neglected, the fairies were believed to 'avenge themselves by washing their children in the beer, stealing milk from the cows and corn from the fields, knocking over buckets, frustrating the manufacture of butter and cheese, and generally making nuisances of themselves'.[38] From this perspective, rituals performed for the fairies were simultaneously precautionary and supplicatory.

While the fairies were considered to be powerful agents in domestic and farming affairs, they also played a further, far more sinister and yet far more exalted role in the lives of common folk in this period. The same spirits who concerned themselves with the cleanliness of a pan or the provision of a good supper were also beings of terrifying numinosity who possessed powers over time, space, life and death. When a man or woman wished to enlist fairy help in relation to the graver or more difficult aspects of human life they often chose to do so through a magical practitioner who would consult with the fairies on their behalf. In these matters, as in the domestic sphere, fairies could cause as much harm as good, and nowhere was this ambivalence more apparent than in the business of human health. On the one hand, fairy skill in physic was believed to be unparalleled, Oxford scholar Robert Burton accurately echoing popular belief when he claimed that fairies and other spirits 'cause and cure most diseases' and know 'the virtues of herbs, plants, stones, minerals, &c. of all creatures, birds, beasts, the four elements, stars, planets; [and] can aptly apply and make use of them as they see good'.[39] Despite having these skills at their disposal, however, fairies were also able to shoot a man dead with an 'elf-arrow' or relentlessly 'haunt' him until he wasted away. Some cunning folk managed this fairy ambivalence with dexterity. In the early fifteenth century Agnes Hancock, for example, claimed that she 'freely consulted the subterranean people [the fairies] whenever she felt in need of advice or information' and yet her professional specialism was in the diagnosing and curing of sickness caused by fairy malevolence.[40] Similarly, over a hundred years later, Bessie Dunlop claimed that she gained her healing skills from the fairies (by virtue of the fact that Tom Reid, her familiar, served her at the command of the fairy queen) and yet she was able to bring these fairy-derived skills to bear when curing children and animals who had been 'elf-grippit', that is, harmed by the fairies.[41]

Fairy Belief – Mythology or Matter of Fact?

Although it is indisputable that fairy beliefs were found throughout Britain in this period, and that they were taken very seriously by some people, the extent of their scope and influence among the populace as a whole is still a matter of debate among historians. In 1959 folklorist Katharine Briggs, in one of the few books devoted to the study of early modern fairy beliefs, concluded that these beliefs were 'widely held . . . among the common people'.[42] This view was echoed a few years later by Barbara Rosen, who claimed that fairies were 'still powerful agents of superstition among countryfolk and the simpler townsmen' in the period.[43] Against these opinions, however, must be set the more reserved views of other, more prominent, historians of the period. In *Religion and the Decline of Magic*, for example, Keith Thomas's brief discussion of fairy beliefs contains contradictory assertions. On the one hand, he claims that 'For *many* persons fairies thus remained spirits against which they had to guard themselves by some ritual precaution [my italics]' while on the other he concludes that by the Elizabethan age 'fairy lore was primarily a store of mythology rather than a corpus of living beliefs, but it was *sometimes* still accepted literally at a popular level [my italics].'[44] Although in more recent years scholars such as Edward Cowan, Lizanne Henderson, Peter Maxwell-Stuart and Diane Purkiss have produced work which points to the vivacity of fairy belief in this period, ambiguity still remains.[45] Only four years ago James Sharpe maintained that in England there was 'a powerful folklore which saw fairies as active, large, and frequently mischievous and sometimes malevolent beings' and that this folklore was 'widespread' – but tempered this assertion by adding that educated people may have been 'rejecting fairy beliefs, and even among the population at large such beliefs, by the later seventeenth century at least, may have been regarded as something most appropriate for servant girls and children'.[46]

Although some of the educated may have had their reservations, many sources from the period suggest that fairy belief was indeed a 'powerful folklore' among common folk at this time. In 1597, King James VI of Scotland penned a treatise on witchcraft and sorcery, *Daemonologie*, in which he referred condescendingly to the 'simple creatures' who believe in fairies, claiming them to be deluded by the Devil. Such people, he wrote, believe that:

> there was a King and Queene of Phairie, of such a jolly court & train as they had, how they had a teynd, & dutie, as it were, of all goods: how they naturallie rode and went, eate and drank, and did all other actiones like naturall men and women: I thinke it liker VIRGILS Campi Elysij, nor anie thing that ought to be beleeved by Christians . . . the devil illuded the senses of sundry simple creatures, in making them beleeve that they saw and harde such thinges as were nothing so indeed.[47]

A similarly vivid portrait of how seriously the common folk of seventeenth-century Scotland held their fairy beliefs, and one which also includes an insight into how these beliefs related to popular Christianity, is painted by Robert Kirk, who describes how the Scots believed that fairies went abroad to new lodgings at each new quarter of the year and that some local people, in order to avoid any terrifying encounters with these bands of spirits, would:

> keep Church duly everie first Sunday of the quarter, to sene or hallow them-selves, their corns and cattell, from the shots and stealth of these wandring Tribes. And many of these superstitious people will not be seen in Church again till the nixt quarter begin, as if no dutie were to be learned or don by them, but all the use of worship and sermons were to save them from those arrowes that fly in the dark.[48]

Such beliefs were not only the preserve of the Scots. In 1579, the June glosse of *The Shepheardes Calender* claimed that 'The opinion of faeries and elfes is very old, and yet sticketh very religiously in the myndes of some', while clergyman John Penry claimed that in late sixteenth-century Wales the fairies were held in 'astonishing reverence' and that the people there dared not 'name them without honour'.[49] Similarly, in 1584 the Kentish squire, Reginald Scot, saw fit to lament that 'we are so fond, mistrustfull and credulous, that we feare more the fables of Robin good-fellow; astrologers, & witches, & beleeve more the things that are not, than the things that are' while nearly forty years later the Yorkshire poet and translator Edward Fairfax claimed that 'so many are the strange follies, rooted in the opinion of the vulgar, concerning the walking of souls in this or that house, the dancing of Fairies on this rock or that mountain, the changing of infants in their cradles, and the like'.[50] In the latter half of the seventeenth century, Wiltshire antiquary John Aubrey said of the fairies that 'When I was a Boy our Countrey-people would talke much of them' while Somerset Squire Richard Bovet echoed that he had often heard the 'Country People' talk of fairy encounters.[51] Similar comments can also be found in *The Displaying of Supposed Witchcraft* (1677) where the author, Yorkshire schoolmaster John Webster, claims of the fairies that 'there are many that do believe and affirm that there are such people' and provides a particularly graphic account of the temerity with which people from the North of England held onto their fairy beliefs in an increasingly rationalist world:

> for the most part the common people, if they chance to have any sort of the Epilepsie, Palsie, Convulsions or the like, do presently perswade themselves that they are bewitched, forespoken, blasted, fairy-taken, or haunted with some evil spirit, and the like; and if you should by plain reason shew them, that they are deceived, and that there is no such matter, but that it is a natural disease, say what you can they shall not believe you, but account you a Physician of small or no value, and whatsoever you do to them, it shall hardly do them any good at all, because of the fixedness of their depraved and prepossessed imagination.[52]

As late as 1725, Henry Bourne claimed in his *Antiquitates Vulgares* that 'Another Part of this Conversation generally turns upon Fairies. These, they tell you, have frequently been heard and seen, nay that there are some still living who were stollen away by them and confined seven Years.'[53] The strength of fairy belief in early modern Britain can also be discerned from some of the trial records and pamphlets describing the methods by which thieves or 'coseners' were believed to have swindled money out of gullible victims. In the early seventeenth century, Fulham cunning folk Alice and John West, for example, allegedly tricked many people out of their savings by claiming to have a special relationship with the king and queen of the fairies. Only by exploiting a sincerely-held belief in the material generosity of the fairies could Alice West have persuaded a young woman 'to sit naked in a garden a whole frostie winters night, with a pot of earth in her lap, promising that ere morning the queene of fayries should turne it into gold'.[54]

By far the most compelling and persuasive testimony to the strength of popular fairy belief in this period, however, is to be found in the confessions taken down in trials for sorcery and witchcraft. Here we find descriptions of encounters with fairies (both solitary and in groups), journeys undertaken with fairies and visits to fairyland. The ecclesiastics and men of law who interrogated suspected witches were interested in evidence of maleficent magic and association with the Devil and found references to fairy belief irrelevant or inaccurate, either attempting to omit these references altogether, as in the famous trial of Nairnshire witch Isobel Gowdie in 1662, or re-defining them in order to fit them into a stereotypically demonological format.[55] We can safely assume, therefore, that any direct references to fairy belief found in witch confessions are likely have originated from the accused. As the folklorist Katharine Briggs claimed, confessions for witchcraft are 'a valuable if painful testimony, because, however fantastic they may seem, they bear witness to a real belief and cannot be dismissed as poetic embroidery'.[56]

This overview of the magical beliefs held by common folk in early modern Britain, though general, provides us with a context from which we can more confidently begin to examine contemporary beliefs concerning familiars. We have seen that a wide range of religious and magical belief, of both pre-Christian and Christian appearance and origin, existed in Britain in this period, and that the institution of the Church had a varying degree of sway over the hearts and minds of the common people. We have also seen how a coherent and widespread matrix of fairy belief is likely to have underpinned the popular world-view. In order to find out more about how beliefs surrounding familiar spirits fit into this complex picture we must now turn our attention away from the general populace and towards those specialized individuals who acted as a bridge between the ordinary world and the magical world of the spirits. If we are to find the familiar among the obscurity and chimeras of the early modern enchanted universe, then we must now let the cunning folk and witches be our guides.

CHAPTER TWO

Cunning Folk and Witches

The common people of early modern Britain possessed a wide repertoire of spells and rituals with which they could practise magical self-help, but in those instances where more sophisticated magical knowledge was needed, they turned to a magical practitioner. In contemporary sources these practitioners were referred to under a wonderful variety of generic names: wise man or woman, cunning man or woman, witch (white or black), wizard, sorcerer, conjurer, charmer, magician, wight, nigromancer, necromancer, seer, blesser, dreamer, cantel, soothsayer, fortune-teller, girdle-measurer, enchanter, incantantrix and so on. These generic names, like those used to define categories of spirit, overlapped considerably and were often interchangeable. At any given time, the term used to define a magical practitioner would have depended upon the type of magic they practised, where they lived, whether they were liked or disliked and whether the person defining them was illiterate or literate, rural or urban, Puritan or Catholic and so on. The same practitioner, for example, could be referred to as a 'wise man' by one person, a 'witch' by another and a 'conjurer' by yet another. These complexities make it difficult for a historian to settle on a working terminology. Many of these generic names have survived until the present day. 'Sorcerer', 'wizard', 'magician' and 'witch', for example, are energetic and numinous terms, but they have been so distorted and embellished by the twentieth-century imagination that, with the exception of the latter, they are now seldom employed by academic historians. Given such difficulties, we shall follow contemporary scholars in the field and employ the following terms. Any individual who practised magic in a professional capacity, whether for good or ill, will come under the umbrella term of 'magical practitioner'. Those magical practitioners primarily associated with the practice of maleficent magic will, in the absence of any viable alternative, be termed 'witches'. Those primarily associated with the use of beneficent magic will be termed 'cunning folk' – a title which, although popular in the early modern period, has not survived into the present day and therefore is not overlaid with modern connotations. All these terms possess the benefit of being non-gender specific, however when they are employed here in the general singular, they will be used in the feminine. This choice does not reflect any perceived gender bias in the terms per se, but mirrors the fact that in the source material used, the majority of magical practitioners, cunning folk and witches referred to are women.[1]

The term 'cunning folk' will be used here to denote popular as opposed to learned magical practitioners, that is, the kind of individuals that ordinary people would have turned to when they needed help. Such a usage necessitates drawing a hypothetical line through early modern culture, separating it into 'élite' (educated and moneyed) and 'popular' (uneducated and poor) segments. In reality, such a division did not exist. Society in this period was highly stratified, with many individuals inhabiting the middle ground between the élite and popular demographic poles, and these many levels of society were in constant interaction. As a result of this, a significant minority of cunning folk – who were to all intents and purposes 'popular' magical practitioners – would have possessed some degree of literacy and, as historian Owen Davies has recently shown, have prized magical manuals and written charms as magical aids and status symbols.[2] Consequently, while our discussion focuses on popular magical practitioners, most of whom were by definition illiterate, it will inevitably embrace a proportion of literate or semi-literate cunning folk who enhanced their magical practice by drawing from learned magical traditions.

The Cunning Folk

The cunning man or woman, in the guise of sorcerer, wizard or magician, is a prominent and numinous figure in the twenty-first-century imaginal landscape – being frequently represented in film, television, visual art and literature. Until relatively recently, however, the historical reality of these magical practitioners and the popular magical traditions they worked within, have been largely overlooked by modern historians. The cunning folk of early modern England were first brought to the general attention of scholars over thirty years ago with the publication of Alan Macfarlane's *Witchcraft in Tudor and Stuart England* and Keith Thomas's *Religion and the Decline of Magic* in 1970 and 1971 respectively.[3] Although the latter works were influential, to the extent that no subsequent study of English witchcraft neglects to explore, to a greater or lesser degree, the activities of cunning folk in this period, it is only in recent years, with the publication of Owen Davies's *Cunning Folk: Popular Magic in English History* (2003), that a historian has taken the baton from Thomas and Macfarlane and examined the reality of English cunning folk in any detail.[4] The cunning folk of early modern Scotland have received separate and equally infrequent attentions, prominent among these being Peter Maxwell-Stuart's *Satan's Conspiracy: Magic and Witchcraft in Sixteenth-Century Scotland.*[5]

Although historians have attempted to unearth information about cunning folk from contemporary writings and unpublished archival records, they still emphasize that it is difficult to ascertain with any accuracy the number of popular magical practitioners working in early modern Britain. Trial records of sorcery cases, for example, can only illuminate a percentage of the individuals practising in any given area, and to further frustrate matters, these records themselves remain largely unexamined. Thomas laments that:

> the risk of prosecution was great enough to deter the cunning man from courting unnecessary publicity, and this makes it all the more difficult to determine just how common a figure he was. No useful statistics can be derived from the records of the secular courts, where his appearance was only desultory. The church courts, however, unearthed wizards with great regularity. No one can say how many of their names are contained in the voluminous and almost entirely unpublished court books and visitation records which survive, often in their hundreds, for virtually every diocese in England. It would be the work of a lifetime for an individual to produce even an approximate answer to the question.[6]

There is good reason to assume that cunning folk were widespread and numerous throughout Britain in this period. In Essex, where the only fully systematic inquiry into the subject has been made, Alan Macfarlane identified at least 60 cunning men or women appearing in court records between 1560 and 1680, which means, in effect, that nobody was likely to have lived more than ten miles from one.[7] These findings are corroborated by the fact that contemporary writers often remark upon their ubiquity. In 1584, Reginald Scot claimed that he had heard local ministers affirm that 'they have had in their parish at one instant, xvii. Or xviii' practising cunning folk, while nearly forty years later Robert Burton wrote that 'Sorcerers are too common; cunning men, wizards, and white witches, as they call them, in every village'.[8] This general picture is strengthened by the fact that cunning folk were still common in the nineteenth century, one commentator claiming in 1807 that 'a cunning man, or a cunning woman, as they are termed, is to be found near every town'.[9]

Despite the fact that cunning folk were undoubtedly widespread in this period, their activities went largely unrecorded. While learned magical practitioners detailed their magical beliefs and practices in journals and books, the usually illiterate cunning folk consulted no written works and committed nothing to paper. Their magical knowledge and technique would have been acquired through observation and word of mouth and been practised and developed in the 'secret, unchartered areas of peasant exchange'.[10] To obscure matters even further, fear of legal reprisal, beliefs surrounding fairy taboos and the desire for self-mystification would have prevented many cunning folk from talking about their magical practices, even with their closest associates.

Notwithstanding these obstacles, it is still possible to garner a considerable amount of information about the activities of popular magical practitioners from other sources. References can be found in the works of several learned writers from the period and we can also hear the voices of the practitioners themselves in trial records, where the descriptions of the accusations levelled against them and their replies to these accusations can provide us with vivid first-hand information about their magical beliefs and practices. Trial records relating to sorcery cases remain largely unexamined and unpublished; however, records relating to witchcraft cases have received a wholly different fate and consequently provide us with the lion's share of our information about cunning folk in this period.

Throughout early modern Europe theologians, intellectuals and rulers became increasingly concerned with the subject of witchcraft and the persecution of witches became so intense and obsessive that it has been aptly named the period of the 'witch-craze'. In Britain, as in the rest of Europe, Church and State made no distinction, in theory, between 'white' magic, the magic predominantly associated with cunning folk, and 'black' magic, the magic predominantly associated with malevolent witches. Any kind of magical belief or practice which had not been officially sanctioned by the Church was considered heretical. This blanket condemnation is expressed in the query of the Ecclesiastical Commission in 1559, which condemned the employment of 'charms, sorceries, enchantments, invocations, circles, witchcrafts, soothsaying or any like crafts or imaginations, invented by the Devil' and also condemned any application to cunning folk 'for counsel and help'.[11] The language used in witch trials reflects this attitude, charges usually listing accusations of 'witchcraft' alongside those of 'sorcery', 'enchantment', 'invocation' and so on with no material distinction being made between the different terms.[12] Despite the fact that practitioners of both white and black magic were equally culpable in theory, in practice most cunning folk were not zealously persecuted. If they kept their heads down and didn't tread on anyone's toes, they had a good chance of either evading the law altogether, or, at worst, being presented in an ecclesiastical court on a sorcery charge from which they could usually escape with a warning or a light sentence. But a significant minority of cunning folk were not so lucky and found themselves presented before secular courts on charges involving witchcraft. Many of these were treated as harshly as the malevolent witch and received the highest penalty. In the last fifty years or so witch-trial records have been extensively analysed both in Britain and on the Continent and as a consequence of this a large amount of archival material, rich with fascinating detail, has been assiduously transcribed and published. Those witch-trial records which describe the magical activities of cunning folk provide us with much of the information presented in this book.

Any attempt to use early modern witch-trial records as a resource for building up a picture about popular belief in the period confronts the question of the 'accuracy' of the source material, that is, how far trial confessions can be seen as reflections of the actual words, thoughts, feelings and experiences of the accused. Historians have frequently argued that witch-trial confessions were corrupted by a variety of factors, the most obvious being manipulative questioning of the 'how long have you been a witch?' variety, and coercion, which in Scotland sometimes involved torture, and in England, where torture was illegal, verbal intimidation and/or suspiciously 'torture-like' methods such as sleep deprivation and pricking.[13] Confessions were also distorted by trial clerks, and again, more seriously, by pamphleteers, who took trial records and attempted to craft them into 'popular literature'. Historians like Diane Purkiss and Lyndal Roper have also emphasized the distorting effects of 'collusion', a subtle process whereby the suspect responds to the flattering attentions of her educated male interrogator by becoming an actor and storyteller – weaving, in response to his questions, a complex narrative web of memory, fantasy and wish-fulfilment.[14]

We must set against these conclusions the fact that confessions also clearly reflected real beliefs and experiences. The close links between events described by suspects and those described by victims and accusers cannot all be attributed to interrogatorial manipulation. Similarly, the picture of the suspect as an oppressed and/or impressionable victim is challenged by the fact that there are examples of accused witches and cunning folk resisting suggestions which they did not agree with, being non-compliant, and/or flatly denying accusations made against them. Others, conversely, refused to withdraw their self-damning confessions even when sympathetic (and probably sceptical) interrogators were attempting to release them from their charges. In *Reading Witchcraft: Stories of Early English Witches,* in which Marion Gibson employs close textual analysis in an attempt to unpick the elements of accuracy and distortion in a number of English trial records, it is asserted that such examples question:

> both the views that witches are simply victims, or that they are particularly compliant storytellers. They neither accept proffered representations of themselves gratefully, contributing little to their own stories, nor do they necessarily fantasise willingly, jumping at the chance to receive attention, to be treated seriously by their male social superiors, and to talk about their inner lives. They do not seem to be easily exploited, but neither are they to blame for their own downfall.[15]

In conclusion, Gibson occupies a middle-ground. On the one hand, she warns against 'regarding [witch-trial records] as if they were objective and unproblematic' but on the other asserts that the suspect was 'an author/co-author of original material in his or her own right' and that 'The dynamics of surviving witchcraft examinations seem to be about cooperation, co-authorship and negotiation.'[16] Where witch-trial records relate to the interrogation of cunning folk, the latter option is even more likely. In a witch trial, where the judiciary was concerned with establishing whether or not an individual had performed harmful magic with the aid of the Devil, any claims to the use of beneficent magic or fairy aid are highly unlikely to come from anyone but the suspect themselves. While these complexities must be kept in mind, in the present discussion there is no scope for close textual analysis of trial material. In Part I it will be sufficient for our purposes to provisionally use this material as read, on the premise that a proportion of it is likely to have some connection with the beliefs and experiences of popular magical practitioners in this period. The perceptual advantages to be gained from initially assuming this inclusive and 'indulgent' position with regard to the authenticity of trial confessions will become evident in Parts II and III, where we will be analysing elements of these confessions from anthropological and psychological perspectives.

Healing

sundrie persounes cam to hir to seik help for thair beist, thair kow or yow, or for ane barne that was tane away with ane evill blast of wind, or elf-grippit.[17]

The most important magical service provided by cunning folk was that of healing, and their value in this respect cannot be over-emphasized. The many faces of sickness and disease were all too familiar to the early modern poor. The improvements in diet, living conditions and medicine enjoyed by modern Britons were as yet undreamt of. A large proportion of the population were chronically undernourished, even at the best of times, and the balance between food production and need was so fine that just one weak or failed harvest represented real hunger for many people. This dietary inadequacy combined with unsanitary living conditions and frequent epidemics to produce an astonishingly low life expectancy.[18] It was not only the precariousness of human health, however, which troubled common folk in the period. The delicate balance between food production and need was highly dependent upon the health of animals. Most rural, and many urban, people kept animals: cows, sheep, pigs, geese, chickens and so on which provided vital protein in the form of dairy produce, eggs and meat and useful body parts such as wool for spinning, oils for tallow, hides for leather and so on. Alternatively, animals or their products could be sold at market, thereby generating money for essential purchases not produced at home, such as salt, metal tools or kitchen equipment. For a poor family the loss, or even temporary unproductivity of an animal represented genuine hardship. In such a context Bessie's lamentations about the death of her cow, voiced in the same breath as her concerns about the mortal illness of her husband and child, would not have been inappropriate.

The early modern poor struggled against the spectre of disease in many ways. There was a rudimentary organized medical profession in the period, through which physicians and surgeons could be trained and licensed. However, these official medical practitioners were few and far between and their services were often too expensive for the average man. For those living in the towns, a viable alternative to the physician could be found in the apothecary, who was apprentice-trained, and could both sell herbs and medicines and prescribe cures. But although cheaper than physicians, apothecaries were still relatively costly and their numbers could not meet public demand. For many of the poor, the physician and the apothecary were not viable options and throughout the period, as Keith Thomas emphasizes, 'the impact of organized medicine upon the lower reaches of the population was seldom more than superficial'.[19] These 'lower reaches of the population' were forced to find other ways.

Medicinal self-help went some way towards alleviating health problems and most housewives would have possessed a working knowledge of herbs and basic magico-medical techniques handed down through the centuries.[20] If an ailment was beyond self-help, however, the first port of

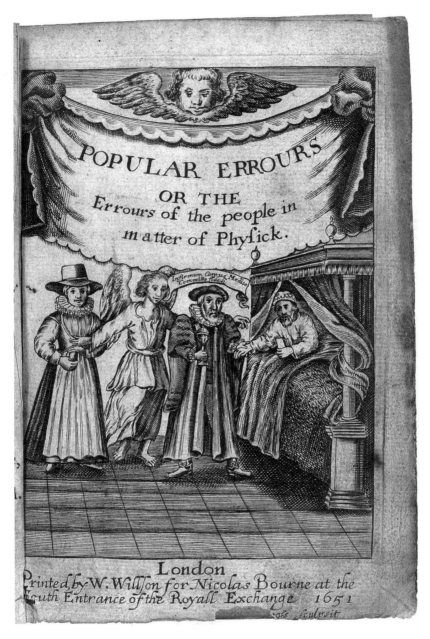

POPULAR ERROURS

OR THE
Errours of the people in
matter of Physick.

Infirmum Corpus Medico
Committe fideli.

London
Printed by W. Willson for Nicolas Bourne at the
South Entrance of the Royall Exchange 1651
ols sculpsit.

In the frontispiece to James Primrose's *Popular Errours or the Errours of the people in matter of Physick* (1651) an angel prevents a cunning woman from treating a sick man and encourages a male physician to minister in her stead. Primrose's efforts, in the text, to challenge the medical expertise of cunning women, only serve to emphasise the latter's status among the common folk in this period.

call would have been the cunning man or woman. Highly regarded for their healing skills, they were also reasonably cheap, often accepting payment in kind and sometimes accepting no payment at all. Cunning folk also had the advantage of being easy to reach, usually living in a village within easy walking distance from their prospective client, although there is some evidence to suggest that people were prepared to travel a long way to visit a prestigious healer. In the early eighteenth century, for example, people travelled up to fifty miles to see the Scottish cunning man, Adam Donald, who was famous for his skills in treating the lingering illnesses thought to be caused by witchcraft.[21] The value put on the healing skills of cunning folk is similarly illustrated in Robert Burton's observation that 'if they be sought unto, [they] will help almost all infirmities of body and mind'.[22] Such glowing recommendations also tempted the wealthy, who, although they could well afford the physician, nevertheless called upon the services of these unofficial doctors. A number of Bessie Dunlop's clients, for example, were from the Scottish nobility.

Cunning folk could work with a sick person in a wide variety of ways, from the simple laying on of hands to the use of elaborate rituals. Traditional plant medicine could be used, and herbal prescriptions could be complex and precise. In order to cure the 'cauld blude' which 'gaid about' her heart, for example, the Lady Blackhaillis was advised by Bessie Dunlop to:

> tak ane pairt of ginger, clowis, annetsedis, licorese, and sum stark aill, and seith thame togidder, and schyre it, and put it in ane veschell, and tak ane lytill quantetie of it in ane mutchekin cane, and sum quhyte sucker caffin amang it; tak and drink thairof ilk day, in the morning; gang ane quhyle eftir, befoir meit; and sche wald be haill.[23]

Charms and prayers were also frequently used. Prayers were often no different from those recited in church, or recommended by the priest for private contemplation. After the Reformation, however, many of the prayers traditionally used by cunning folk became controversial because they retained their Catholic content, often to the extent of being recited in garbled medieval Latin. Charms were more idiosyncratic, many of them seamlessly merging Christian elements with folkloric material of clearly pre-Christian origin. In 1607 Scottish cunning woman Bartie Paterson claimed to have used the following charm to cure sick cattle: 'I CHARME the for arrow-schot, for dor-schot, for wondo-schot, for ey-schot, for tung-schote, for lever-schote, for lung-schote, for hert-schot, all the maist, in the name of the Father, the Sone and the Haly Ghaist. AMEN.'[24] Similar charms were used by English cunning woman 'Goodwife Veazy', a specialist in the cure of 'ringworm, tetter-worm and canker-worm', around the turn of the sixteenth century. Before applying honey and pepper to the affected part she recited three times: 'In the name of God I begin and in the name of God I do end. Thou tetter worm (or thou canker-worm) begone from hence in the name of the Father, of the son, and of the Holy Ghost.'[25] Prayers and charms could also be written onto pieces of parchment or paper which were then either stitched up, sealed with wax and/or incorporated into magical amulets. Clients were advised to keep such charms about their person (around their neck, in a bag or sewn into clothing and so on) or to hide them in the home or farmstead (above a door or window, in a pot, bottle or hole in the ground etc.).

Cunning folk also used religious substances and artefacts for healing purposes: holy water, Eucharist wafers (sneaked out of the church after Communion), candle wax, scrapings from religious statues and water from holy wells were all employed outside the parameters of official church usage. Less elevated objects could also be used as magical aids. Bartie Paterson, for example, recommended that his client carry wheat, salt and pieces of rowan tree about with him 'for his helth'.[26] Bessie Dunlop, on the other hand, helped to ease a woman's labour by attaching a green silken lace to the woman's underdress and then tying the lace about her left arm.[27] Alternatively, a combination of magical tools were used by Agnes Sampson, a cunning woman from Haddington, near Edinburgh. In 1591 Agnes claimed that to ease the first labour of gentlewoman Euphame MacCalzean, she had given her a 'bored stone' (probably a fairy stone, containing a natural hole formed by water) to lay under her bolster and enchanted moulds and powders (made from the ground-up bones and body parts of dead men) wrapped in a piece of paper to roll up in her hair and then advised her that when her labour began she should take her husband's shirt, fold it up and put it under her feet.[28] Live animals were also used as magical aids. In 1604 Northumberland cunning women Katherine Thompson and Anne Nevelson were convicted for putting the bill of a white duck to a patient's mouth and then mumbling charms.[29] Frogs and spiders could also be either ingested or put onto afflicted parts. Many such cures were based on ancient beliefs in the dynamic inter-relationship or 'sympathy' between different elements of nature or creation. Bessie Dunlop prescribed 'hot' spices like ginger and cloves to cure the 'cauld blude' which ran about the Lady Blackhaillis's heart, while the 'bored stone' which Agnes Sampson gave Euphame MacCalzean was designed, by sympathy, to assist the baby through the birth canal. Similarly, many cures were based upon the belief that any object belonging to an individual, whether it be a cup, clothes or body parts such as fingernail parings, locks of hair, urine, excrement and even sweat, were materially connected to that person's existence. In 1654, a cunning woman from the North-East of England, named Anne Green, saw no illogicality in claiming to have cured a headache caused by bewitchment through boiling a lock of the client's hair in urine and then throwing it in the fire – believing that the maleficent spell would have been destroyed along with the hair and urine.[30]

One of the cunning woman's most esoteric healing techniques was that of sickness transferal: the ability to magically take the sickness out of a patient and transfer it onto an animal, or less commonly, themselves. Agnes Sampson's prescription to ease the labour of Euphame MacCalzean cited above, culminated in Euphame's labour pains being 'cast off . . . upon a dog which ran away and was never seen again'.[31] Less than ten years later a cunning man from Aberdeenshire named 'Andro Man' confessed that he cured a client, Alexander Simpson, by putting him 'nyne tymes fordwart throch ane hesp of unvatterit yarne, and than thow tuik a cat, and pat hir nyn tymes bakvart throw the sam hesp, and said thy orationis on him, and put on the seiknes on the cat, quha instantlie deit, and the said Alexander immediatlie recoverit of his disease'.[32] Sickness could also be transferred onto inanimate objects. In Dumfries in 1650 Bessie Graham claimed to do so by chanting 'God teach me to pray to put the ill away, out of the flesh blood and bane into the earth and calld staine and nevir to come again in Gods name.'[33] The literal manner in which this healing technique was understood is illustrated by the fact that the object into which sickness had been transferred could be considered dangerous. Perthshire cunning woman Isobel Haldane claimed in 1623 to have cured a child by washing him in water and then discarding the water, along with the child's shirt, into a stream. Isobel claimed to have been worried, however, because on the way to the stream she spilt some of the water into which she had transferred the sickness, claiming that 'if onye hed gone ower it, thay hed gottyn the ill'.[34]

Other less dramatic forms of physical healing were also commonly used by cunning folk. Massage and manipulation could accompany the use of herbs and charms, as could spiritual healing through touching or stroking. In 1645, Cornish cunning woman Anne Jefferies claimed to have cured her mistress's leg by stroking it, while in Northumberland, eight years later, Margaret Stothard was alleged to have used her breath to literally suck a sickness out, putting her lips to a child's mouth and making such 'chirping' and 'sucking' noises 'that the mother of the said child thought that she had sucked the heart of it out, and was sore affrighted'.[35] Cunning folk could also use physical healing techniques in a more obviously ritualistic sense. In 1650, Dumfrieshire cunning woman Janet Dickson was accused of having attempted to cure a sick child by ritually manouvering both herself and the child. Janet allegedly asked that the child be taken to 'St Jergan's Well' and when there she:

> did cast the [child's] clothes in the welle which sank to the bottom and eftir did wash the child in the well and theraftir the said Jonet cam to ane thorne beside the well and roune thrise about the said thorn withershines and in the morneing the said Janet with her mother . . . cam to sie the child and performe hir uthir charmes – who Laid the child betwixt tuo dorrs and used her charmes and theirafter took the fyre off the hearth and did putt the craddle and the child therin on the hearth and turned their back to the craddle rocking the same.[36]

Not only did cunning folk need to possess a wide variety of healing techniques – they also needed to be skilled at medical diagnosis. As with healing methods, ways of diagnosing sickness were many and varied, ranging from the more empirically-based, such as reading a patient's urine, to the rather more esoteric. The measuring of girdles or shoes, for example, in the belief that the length of the object would reflect the wearer's condition, was a common diagnostic method. In 1566, Cambridgeshire cunning woman Elizabeth Mortlock described how she would first pray, and then 'measureth the girdle or band of any such persons being sick or haunted, from her elbow to her thumb, craving God for Saint Charity's sake that if [they] be haunted with a fairy, yea or no, she may know, and saith that if it be so the band will be shorter and her cubit will reach further than commonly it doth.'[37]

Finding Lost Goods

> And farder declarit, That mony folkis in the countre (came to hir?) to gett witt of geir stollin fra thame [38]

If the most important service provided by cunning folk was that of healing, the second was that of retrieving stolen goods and identifying criminals. Again, the importance of this 'policing' role can only be appreciated in the context of the degree of suffering caused by theft at this time. In twenty-first-century Britain, most people have adequate money (to maintain physical survival), many possessions and ample insurance protection. In sixteenth- and seventeenth-century Britain, conversely, people had very little money, very few possessions and no insurance protection at all. For the majority of the population, who hovered near the breadline, even having to replace objects as mundane as a shirt stolen off a line, a spade filched from an outhouse or a fowl taken from the garden, represented hours or weeks of hard labour, either through having to re-make the object or, if it could not be manufactured at home, providing the money or barter goods to replace it. More serious thefts such as that of a plough, or a purse, could seriously affect a poor man's livelihood. Without recourse to a police force, and with only nominal protection from crime offered by local constables and justices of the peace, the victims of theft would often turn to a cunning man or woman for remedy. In the mid seventeenth century, for example, a labourer from Molesworth, near Huntingdon, described how, after losing a purse containing seven shillings, he was 'swearing, cursing, raging, and wishing to himselfe that some wise body (or Wizzard) would helpe him to his purse and money again'.[39] Even the rich approached cunning folk if they wished to recover lost goods. Bessie Dunlop claimed that she had been approached by Lady Blaire about some stolen clothes, and by Lady Thridpairt about 'twa hornis of gold, and ane croune of the sone' which had disappeared from her purse.[40] Although cunning folk sometimes devised magical formulae to directly injure a criminal (by way of punishment or to prevent him from making away with his stolen goods), they primarily acted as sources of information – disclosing the whereabouts of the lost goods and/or identifying the thief and then leaving the client, armed with this information, to do the rest. Bessie was able to tell Lady Thridpairt 'quha had thame [the contents of her purse]; and sche [Lady Thridpairt] gat thame agane'.[41] Bessie's information, like that of many cunning folk, could be incredibly precise. When Williame Kyle approached Bessie about the whereabouts of a lost cloak she told him that 'the cloak wald nocht be gottin; because it wane tane away be Malye Boyde, duellare in the sam toun, and was put out of the fassoun of a cloik, in [into] ane kirtill'.[42] Cunning folk could even be approached to find missing persons. In 1617 it was reported that John Redman of Sutton, in Cambridgeshire, on discovering that his wife had left him, 'went from wizard to wizard, or, as they term them, "wise men", to have them bring her again'.[43]

Cunning folk recovered lost goods and identified criminals using a variety of magical techniques. Some of these were part of the basic repertoire of magical self-help skills used by ordinary people. Among them was the 'sieve and shears', a simple technique whereby a sieve was hung on the point of some shears and then the names of suspects were recited, the sieve swinging round at the name or the touch of the guilty party. Also common was the 'Bible and key', and its many variants, whereby pieces of paper bearing the names of suspects were consecutively inserted into the hollow end of a key placed between the pages of the Holy Book, the latter moving when the guilty party's name was put inside. Another technique involved writing the names of suspects on individual pieces of paper and then rolling them up into clay balls which were immersed in water, the ball which opened first revealing the criminal's name.[44] Sometimes such magical techniques would be performed before a group of suspects.[45] Other techniques used by cunning folk, such as astrological divination and geomancy, were less available to common folk. Also more specialized was the technique of criminal detection and remote viewing through crystal balls, fingernails, bowls of water, polished mirrors and so on. In 1578 an Essex man went to a cunning man to find out who had stolen some of his linen. The man took his client into his hall and 'browghte with him a looking glasse, and did hange the said glasse up over the benche in his said hawle, upon a nyle, and had the said examinate look in yt, and said as farr as he could gesse, he shulde see the face of him that had the said lynnen'.[46] There is no doubt that the cunning man or woman's skills in this area were highly esteemed. The comments of an almanac-maker in 1609 illustrate how fear of their detecting skills could be enough to prompt thieves to return goods. The author reports how an individual who had lost something might claim that they had been:

'with such a man who is exceeding learned, and he did shew me in a glass the party that had my ring, and he told me where it is, and that if it be not brought me again before tomorrow morning that I shall go to him again, and he will make it come again to the cost of the party that hath it', etc. Now this is spoken where all the household shall hear it (yet seeming to be said in secret). He or she who hath it (through fear) is moved to convey it to some place where it may soon be found; and then flyeth out a report that such a cunning man hath caused it to be brought again.[47]

Although healing, finding lost goods and identifying criminals were central concerns for a large proportion of cunning folk, they also, between them, possessed a range of other skills. Many were believed capable of divining the future and it was not uncommon for them to be asked to make predictions, and give subsequent advice, on a wide variety of matters. Robert Kirk, for example, claims that Scottish seers:

prognosticate many future events, only for a moneth space, from the shoulder-bone of a sheep, on which a knife never came . . . By looking into the bon they will tel if whoredom be committed in the Ouners house; what money the Master of the sheep had, if any will die out of that house for that moneth, and if anie cattell there will take a Trake (as if planet-struck) called earchal[?]. Then will they prescribe a preservative and prevention.[48]

Bessie Dunlop was also forearmed with knowledge of the future when she told William Blair of the Strand that if his eldest daughter went ahead as planned and married the young 'Lard of Baidland' the girl would either 'die ane schamefull deid, slay hir self, cast hirself doun our ane crag, or ga reid-wod [mad]'.[49] Often cunning folk were skilled at predicting the likelihood of a person's death, several claiming to do so by the process of noting carefully the points at which they faltered during the recital of a particular prayer.[50] Others could be even more specific. Kirk claimed that particularly experienced seers could have a vision of a man wearing a shroud and 'conjecture at the neerness or remoteness of his death by the more or less of his body that is covered by it'.[51] James Garden pointed out, on the other hand, that the object of the seer's predictions were 'not only sad & dismall; but also joyfull & prosperous: thus they foretell of happy marriages, good children, what kind of life men shall live, & in what condition they shall die: also riches, honour, preferment, peace, plentie & good weather'.[52]

Cunning folk were also valued for their role as mediators between the living and the dead. Keith Thomas claims that 'To deal with haunted houses, contemporaries often called in the cunning folk' while it was commonly believed that a ghost who wished to complete unfinished business would be able to communicate it to a cunning man or woman.[53] Kirk maintained that ghosts which caused disruption in houses were likely to be 'Souls that have not atteaneed their Rest, thorough a vehement desyre of revealing a murther, or notable injury don or receav'd, or a Treasure that was forgot in their Lyftime on Earth, which when disclos'd to a Conjuror alon the Ghost quite removes.'[54] The magical practitioner's skill in matters of death was often matched by their skill in matters of love. In 1591 Edinburgh gentlewoman Euphame MacCalzean was condemned for asking an acquaintance 'if she knew any witty or skilful women in the country that will either cause your husband love you or else get your will of him'.[55] In the previous year a cunning man was taken before the church authorities in Canterbury, confessing that he had given three men 'magical writings' to 'secure them the love of maids' and had also given a woman a charm 'to make her husband love her, for which he was paid six and eightpence plus two half-kirtles and a gold ring'.[56] Aside from the lofty matters of love and death, cunning folk could be applied to for help in a wide variety of other matters, from farming, fishing, weather, travel, business, sporting pursuits, law suits and hunting to treasure-seeking, gambling and even social climbing.[57] More important still, was their unique ability to identify sickness or other misfortunes which were caused by malevolent witchcraft and to magically counteract these effects. In 1618, Leicestershire mother Joan Gill claimed that she had been so worried about her sick child that she called on the services of cunning woman Anne Baker, asking her to 'look on the child and tell her whether it was forespoken or no'.[58] Such beliefs are reflected in an account given by one of the characters in Essex Puritan George Gifford's semi-fictional *Dialogue Concerning Witches and Witchcrafts:*

> There is also a woman at R.H. five and twentie miles hence, that hath a great name, and great resort there is daily unto her. A neighbour of mine had his child taken lame, a girl of ten yeares old, and such paine in her backe, that she could not sit upright. He went to that woman, and she told him that he had some bad neighbour, the child was forespoken, as she suspected . . . and so told him what he should do, and he had remedie: the girle is well at this day, and a pretie quicke girle.[59]

Methods used to detect witchcraft were many and varied, ranging from the standard diagnostic use of prayer recital to more unusual techniques. When a 'cow keeper's wife' went to see Wapping cunning woman Joan Peterson in the mid seventeenth century, in the suspicion that one of her cows had been bewitched, the latter boiled up some of the cow's urine which then 'rose up in bubbles, in one of which she shewed her the face of the woman which the cow keeper's wife suspected to have bewitched it'.[60] Yorkshire cunning man Cuthbert Williamson, on the other hand, claimed in 1594 that if his eyes ran with tears while he was with a client then their illness was caused by witchcraft, while other cunning folk believed that if they could not see their reflection in their client's eyes, then the latter had been bewitched.[61]

While many cunning folk were multi-talented, possessing a variety of skills with which to tackle the problems brought before them, there was also ample scope for specialization. Many were known for being particularly skilled in a given area of magical expertise, whether the latter was simple charming or the more subtle business of communicating with the dead. Seventeenth-century playwright Thomas Heywood waxes lyrical (and ironical) on the subject:

> You have heard of Mother Nottingham, who for her time was prettily well skilled in casting of waters; and after her, Mother Bomby; and then there is one Hatfield in Pepper Alley, he doth pretty well for a thing that's lost. There's another in Coleharbour, that's skilled in the planets. Mother Sturton in Golden Lane, is for fore-speaking; Mother Phillips, of the Bankside, for the weakness of the back; and then there's a very reverend matron on Clerkenwell Green, good at many things. Mistress Mary on the Bankside is for 'recting a figure; and one (what do you call her?) in Westminster, that practiseth the book and the key, and the sieve and the shears: and all do well, according to their talent.[62]

Witches

In early modern Britain the term 'witch' generally denoted an individual who was seen by others, or perceived by themselves, as being able to employ magical powers to do harm. The type of harmful magic most feared by contemporary villagers was 'maleficium'. Maleficium was witchcraft at its most basic – the manipulation of occult forces at a distance with malevolent intent. Like cunning folk, witches could deploy occult forces in a wide variety of ways, ranging from a simple act of will to the use of complex ritual: trial records reveal them causing harm through a glance of the eyes, a touch, a curse, a charm, spirit-aid, and the use of magical objects and physical actions, some of which involved body parts (such as hair or nails) or other objects belonging to the victim. Common people in this period could attribute just about any kind of misfortune to maleficium: sickness or death in humans and animals; the disruption of domestic activities such as milking, spinning, brewing beer and making butter; and problems associated with farming such as the upset of a plough team or the failure of a crop. Bad weather, shipwrecks and impotence were also traditionally blamed on maleficium. Witch-trial records are full of case after case of recriminations and counter-recriminations involving children or animals which became sick, or died; brewings of beer which went sour, batches of butter which would not curdle and so on. In the majority of these cases the accuser makes a circumstantial link between the misfortune and the alleged witch, often maintaining that the witch performed the maleficium after being angered in some way. The records pertaining to the trial of Dumfries witch Elizabeth Maxwell, in 1650, record that 'Thair befell a contraversie betwixt hir [Elizabeth] and one bessie baitie spous to Robert Rennick anent the change of ane halff crown and parting in wraith the said Bessie becam frantick and continews so to this day having contractit hir frensie within a day or two eftir this debait.'[63] The anger of the accused witch was very frequently attributed to the refusal of a demand for food. At the trial of Alice Manfield (also known as 'Mother Manfield') in 1582, a neighbour claimed that 'Mother Manfield came unto her and asked her a mess of milk, who answered that she had but a little, not so much as would suckle her calf, whereat she departed; and she [the neighbour] saith, that that night her calf died, being very lusty and 20 days old.'[64] Many accusations, like the two quoted above, do not describe the actual method through which the angered witch was believed to have caused the harm, however a significant minority are more specific. The records from the

1579 trial of Berkshire witch Elizabeth Style, for example, state that the witch 'did kill one Saddock [her neighbour] with a clap on the shoulder, for not keeping his promise for an old cloak to make her a safeguard, who presently went home and died'.[65] At other times the alleged act of maleficium was linked to a witch's curse. The records of the trial of Scottish witch Elspeth Thomson, taken down at Dumfries in 1671, state that 'you haveing required James meghie . . . to give you a dayes work and he haveing refuised the same ye threatened him and said that he should not work so much work for a zeires time. And by your sorcerie and witchcraft within fyve dayes yrefter he contracted a cruell seikness and disease. And hes nevir bein in perfect health since'.[66] Other trial records describe the performance of specific maleficent rituals. Some of these were very simple: in 1583, for example, Norfolk witch 'Mother Gabley' was accused of killing no less than thirteen men by 'boiling or rather labouring of certain eggs in a pail full of cold water'.[67] Others were more complex: records from the 1579 trial of Essex witch Mother Staunton state that a woman twice denied Mother Staunton's request for milk and on the second occasion barred the door against her, whereapon the witch 'sat down upon her heels before the door and made a circle upon the ground with a knife. After that, she digged it full of holes within the compass, in the sight of the said wife, her man and her maid, who, demanding why she did so, she made answer that she made a shitting-house for herself after that sort, and so departed. The next day the wife coming out at the said door was taken sick . . . and to this day is not restored to health.'[68] The ritual use of magical objects could also be very complex. Cecil Ewen records how, in Hertfordshire in 1606, a witch's chest was found to contain a set of human bones, a collection of hair of all colours and a parchment which seems to have performed the function of the classic 'wax doll'. The parchment bore a drawing of a man's heart and around the drawing:

> " . . . fitting even to the very brim of the parchment, were coloured in severall colours very curiously divided braunches, on which hung dangling things like ashen keys, and at the ends of them in some places figured, and others proportioned a mouth, in briefe the whole joints and artiers of a man".
>
> Upon examination, the Witch confessed that she had power, in virtue of the bones, hair and parchment, and with the help of her spirits (one for men, and one for cattle), to inflict torture in any joint, sinew, or part of the body, by pricking the corresponding part in the parchment chart.[69]

Neighbourhood Tensions

While it is acknowledged that witch beliefs, and in particular beliefs about maleficium, can be found in the majority of pre-modern societies around the world, historians have struggled to explain why there was such a dramatic increase in the number of prosecutions in many parts of Britain and Continental Europe throughout the early modern period. Attention has traditionally rested on élite involvement, with historians such as Hugh Trevor-Roper and Norman Cohn arguing that the European 'witch-craze' was largely attributable to the political and religious concerns of the ruling classes, with witch prosecution being used as a method of stamping out dissent and promoting political and religious uniformity.[70] Among British scholars, this paradigm was challenged in the 1970s by Alan Macfarlane and Keith Thomas, who emphasized the popular contribution to the rise in witch prosecutions in England in this period.[71] According to Thomas, witch accusations were an expression of tension between villagers living in close-knit communities existing at subsistence level, and the majority of those accused were poverty-stricken women – often old, often widows – who were forced to rely heavily on community support, particularly after the demise of monastery based alms-giving, and elicited fear and resentment in the process. Although historians have since argued that a significant number of those accused of witchcraft did not fit Thomas's stereotype, and that the societal stresses which preceded their arrest were often more complex than those he described, it is now generally acknowledged that although élite forces played a significant role in the pattern of British witchcraft prosecution, on a village level witch accusations were the inevitable consequence of intense and frequent suffering combined with compulsory neighbourly interdependence and an unquestioned belief in the ability of human beings to employ magical powers to maleficent ends – an explosive combination. The mother who watches her third child waste away and die painfully before her eyes, or the struggling labourer, with ten people dependent on his earnings, who loses the use of an arm in a freak accident, would have been sorely tempted to attribute their misfortunes to a disliked or mistrusted neighbour, particularly one who already possessed a 'bad name'. In the following extract from the trial of Essex witch Elizabeth Bennett, in 1582, we see how the most innocent of gestures could be interpeted as malevolent by a distressed mind, and how even friendship was no defence against accusations of witchcraft. William Bonner described how:

the said Elizabeth Bennett and his wife were lovers and familiar friends, and did accompany much together; and saith that since Candlemas last his wife hath complained of a lameness in her knee, and that since also she hath been much troubled. And saith also that not ten days past the said Elizabeth Bennett being with his wife, she being sickly and sore troubled, the said Elizabeth used speeches unto her, saying 'Ah good woman, how thou art loden,' and then clasped her in her arms and kissed her. Whereupon presently after her upper lip swelled and was very big, and her eyes much sunked into her head, and she hath lain since in a very strange case.[72]

Alternatively, when the child of Ely mother Alice Wade became sick and 'fell shrieking out and would not suck' the distraught woman attributed the sickness to the fact that Dorothy Ellis, who was subsequently tried as a witch in 1647, had previously 'laid her hand upon the the cheek of her child and mumbled words to herself'.[73] Those individuals who, for whatever reason, believed themselves to possess magical powers were particularly vulnerable to accusations of witchcraft. At the turn of the fifteenth century, for example, Michael Trevisard, from Hardness in Devon, whose whole family had long been suspected of practising witchcraft, made an ambiguous prediction which was later interpreted by its recipient as an act of maleficium. Bereaved mother Alice Butler (who had previously lost at least two children in infancy) claimed at Michael's trial that she had been standing in the street near to him when she had observed: '"I would my child were able to run as well as any of these children that run here in the street". He [Michael] said, "It shall never run". "No? That's hard!" said Examinate. "No, it shall never run till thou hast another", answered Trevisard. The same week the child sickened, and after languishing for seventeen weeks, died.'[74]

Men and women such as Elizabeth Bennett, Dorothy Ellis and Michael Trevisard became unwittingly, or wittingly, tangled up in their neighbours' darkest emotions. However sophisticated the methods of its learned orchestrators, these emotions were the raw material of the British witch-craze. Whatever a prejudiced and manipulative judge chose to do with a witch once they stood at the bar before him, in the majority of cases they stood there because their friends and neighbours had hounded them in.

CHAPTER THREE

The Magical Use of Spirits

The Witch's Familiar

In early modern Britain both cunning folk and witches claimed to perform magic with the help of familiar spirits, but it is the witch's demon familiar, whether in the form of a man or an animal, which is most recognizable to people today. Although many centuries separate us from the beliefs and practices of the men and women described in this book, there are few who would not recognize the stereotypical image of the black cat perched on the end of the witch's broomstick, or the lascivious horned devil standing at the witch's shoulder, inciting her to evil. This long-standing notoriety of the witch's familiar is largely due to an intense preoccupation with witchcraft on the part of the early modern Church and State: a preoccupation which generated many trials and produced painstakingly detailed records, and spin-off pamphlets, many of which contain 'encounter-narratives', that is, descriptions of encounters with spirits.

Encounter-narratives are found in witch-trial records throughout the period. Complex cases from as early as 1566 suggest that there was a well-established familiar lore before the witch-craze really gained momentum in Britain.[1] Nevertheless, a review of witch-trial material cannot give us an accurate idea of the real extent of familiar use. In his study of witchcraft and sorcery in the Home Counties from 1560 to 1680, Alan Macfarlane discovered that a slender 28 out of 503 indictments for offences under the Witchcraft Statutes in Essex involved demon familiars.[2] The real number of familiars involved, however, was almost certainly more. The indictment, which is the only remaining record of most trials, contains the barest essentials of a case. The former relating to the trial of Ellen Smyth which took place in 1579, describes how she bewitched a child who later died. However when the same case was described in a pamphlet no less than five familiars were allegedly involved.[3]

Despite the consistent appearance of encounter-narratives in witch trials and pamphlets, historians have made little attempt to explore the popular basis of this dimension of witchcraft. As we have already seen, until recently there has been a general disinterest in the popular component to early modern magic in general. More specifically, however, until recently most scholars dismissed descriptions of witches' familiars found in trial records as largely, if not wholly, learned or 'élite' in origin – a phantasm conceived and nurtured in the minds of medieval theologians and bearing little relation to the beliefs of ordinary people. There is some documentary support for this view. Since the Middle Ages ideas surrounding demonic familiar spirits had been written about and discussed by theologians and scholars throughout Europe. The coalition between witches and the Devil and/or demons was, for the theologian, a logical one. Any magical beliefs which did not easily assimilate into Christian doctrine and ritual were associated with the Devil, and beliefs concerning the use of spirits to perform magic were obvious targets. As the study of spirits, both good and bad, increasingly fascinated medieval scholars and ecclesiastics, so the spirit-encountering activities of the witch (and her learned counterpart, the magician) became increasingly tangled up in their complex ideological web. The more lengthy books and treatises that appeared on the subject, the more the plot thickened. Theologians argued that the Devil, always eager to capture human souls, saw witches (with their taste for magic and their corrupt natures) as an easy target. They believed that the Devil, or a demon sent on behalf of the Devil, directly approached witches and tempted them to make a 'pact' with him, a pact in which the witch promised to surrender her immortal soul to the Devil in return for certain favours, most commonly the bestowal of magical powers through which to gain riches or be revenged upon enemies. By agreeing to the pact, the witch played into the Devil's hands. His legion was swelled by the addition of the witch's soul and the world's suffering was increased through the witch's maleficium. On a more subtle level, the witch encouraged others to ally themselves with the Devil, either explicitly, through encouraging them to become witches, or implicitly, by encouraging them to gain some benefit from her magical powers and thereby become party to her sin. Satan was believed to be amassing an 'army' of witches with which to wage war on mankind, and, in this context, the practices of the witch threatened not only the local community, but the whole of Christendom.

Many of the relationships between witches and their familiar spirits described in trial records resemble this theological stereotype and historians have traditionally asserted that these resemblances represent evidence of élite contamination. Trial contents referring to overt commitment to the Devil or his demons, which we can term the 'specifically demonological elements', were assumed to have been introduced during the interrogatorial process (by prosecutors, armed with these demonological preconceptions, manipulating testimony to secure a conviction) or, if they did originate from the witch, to have been the result of élite ideas imposing themselves on the minds of the common people through a process of downward filtration. According to the latter hypothesis, prosecutorial suggestion during witchcraft trials, in witchcraft pamphlets, pulpit teachings and so on served to gradually impress the idea of the witch's familiar 'from above' into the popular imagination, where it then became a vehicle for the sensationalist and paranoid fantasies of the witch and her neighbours. In the last few decades, historians of witchcraft have increasingly questioned this simplistic view, although some have not abandoned it completely. As recently as 2003, a leading historian of English witchcraft maintained that 'One possible explanation for the popular belief in familiars . . . was the downward diffusion and subsequent folklorization of élite ideas.'[4]

The discarding of the 'élite-origin-only' theory of the genesis of British familiar belief reflects a wider paradigm shift in European witchcraft studies as a whole over the last thirty years or so. As we shall explore in more detail in later chapters, pioneering research by Continental scholars into beliefs surrounding the witches' sabbath has clearly illustrated that demonological ideas about witchcraft merged with popular witch lore in a far more complex manner than any dualist and hierarchical élite/popular abstraction allows. Consequently, there has been a growing recognition that there was a genuinely folkloric component to many aspects of witch belief throughout Europe in this period, and Robin Brigg's claim, in the mid-1990s, that '[European witch] narratives combined elements of folklore and official demonology, which were fitted around social and pyschological determinants' can now be seen to represent the majority view.[5] This paradigm shift is increasingly reflected in the British field. Nearly ten years ago James Sharpe claimed, in reference to English witch belief, that 'we should never forget that notions about witchcraft were part of a much wider set of beliefs, incorporating both 'superstition' and popular religion . . . Unravelling these beliefs and tracing the connections between them are tasks which historians have only just begun to undertake.'[6] Recent attempts to 'unravel these beliefs' and 'trace these connections' have been made by several scholars, among them Darren Oldridge, who has examined how folkloric ideas about the Devil played a significant role in English witch beliefs; Frederick Valletta, who has

A Detection
of damnable driftes, practi-
zed by three VVitches arraigned at
Chelmiffo2De in Effer, at the
laſte Aſſiſes there holden, whiche
were executed in Ap2ill.
1 5 7 9.

Set fo2the to difcouer the Ambuſhementes of
Sathan, whereby he would furp2ife vs
lulled in fecuritie, and hardened
with contempte of Gods
vengeance th2eatened
fo2 our offences.

Imprinted at London for Edward White,
at the little North-dore of Paules.

A Detection of damnable driftes . . . (1579). This pamphlet relating to the trial of a group of Essex witches is typical of those believed to have disseminated learned ideas about demon familiars. The familiar depicted here seems to be an amalgam of a hedgehog and an owl.

looked at how popular beliefs about portents, ghosts, and prodigies contributed to the English witch-craze and Joyce Miller, who has examined evidence of folk healing in seventeenth-century Scottish witchcraft.[7]

The aspect of folklore which has the greatest relevance for our understanding of beliefs surrounding the British witch's familiar, however, is that of fairy belief. The close connections between the witch's familiar and the fairy have consistently been pointed out by scholars over the past century. In 1921, in a paper for the journal *Folklore*, J. A. MacCulloch discussed the close links between the Scottish Devil and the fairy men of folklore, and in 1959 Katharine Briggs touched on these links in her comprehensive study of early modern fairy belief, *The Anatomy of Puck*.[8] In the early 1970s, Jeffrey Russell noted that 'The small demons that became the witches' familiars of the later Middle Ages were originally dwarves, trolls, fairies, elves, kobolds, or the fertility spirits called Green men, any of whom could be either frightening or funny' and Keith Thomas claimed that the cunning man's fairy helper belongs 'to the same genre as the witch's familiar or the conjurer's demons'.[9] The connections between witches' familiars and fairies have been more recently touched on by Diane Purkiss in *The Witch in History* (1994) and *Troublesome Things* (2001) and by myself in the paper, *The Witch's Familiar and the Fairy in Early Modern England and Scotland* (2000).[10] The significance of this line of enquiry has since been acknowledged by James Sharpe in the paper, *The Witch's Familiar in Elizabethan England*.[11] The links between beliefs about the Devil and fairy belief in a specifically Scottish context have been recently discussed by Lizanne Henderson and Edward Cowan in *Scottish Fairy Belief* (2001) and by Peter Maxwell-Stuart in *Satan's Conspiracy* (2001).[12] Research into the folkloric component of witch beliefs undertaken by Continental scholars in the last few decades has also uncovered the links between fairy beliefs and beliefs surrounding encounters with the Devil and other spirits, however there still remains much work to be done in this area. As recently as 2003 Darren Oldridge claimed that 'The role of fairy beliefs in European witchcraft is a subject that awaits fuller investigation.'[13]

Despite the widespread references cited above, British familiar lore, its folkloric credentials and in particular its connections with fairy belief, is still primarily discussed in passing, as an adjunct to other matters. Historians of British witchcraft and magic continue to spend the bulk of their time discussing élite ideas and activities surrounding witch-belief, unpicking trials for evidence of élite contamination and analysing the neighbourhood tensions and personal life-stories that contributed to accusation and confession. As a consequence, British beliefs surrounding witches' familiars, arguably among the most vivid and idiosyncratic in

Europe, remain substantially unexplored. In 1971 Keith Thomas lamented that the English animal familiar was 'largely unaccounted for'.[14] So little has changed in the last thirty years that in 2001 James Sharpe could still find cause to lament that 'a detailed investigation into the phenomenon of familiars is currently one of the most urgent items on the agenda for future research into English witchcraft history'.[15]

The Cunning Woman's Familiar

If the familiar spirits used by witches have received little attention from historians, those used by cunning folk have received even less. While scholars have always been ready to acknowledge that learned magicians of the period made frequent use of spirit familiars, the ways in which cunning folk were acquainted with this branch of magical practice has been largely overlooked. In *Religion and the Decline of Magic*, still the most comprehensive examination of English popular magic in this period, Keith Thomas seldom mentions the use of familiar spirits by cunning folk. Comments such as 'usually the precise source of the wizard's skill seems to have been left conveniently undefined . . . *In rare cases* he might purport to employ a familiar spirit [my italics]', reflect Thomas's overall implication that the role of spirits in the magical practice of cunning folk was minimal.[16] No historians have subsequently contradicted Thomas's assertions and the cunning man or woman's familiar is largely absent from academic studies of early modern British magic and witchcraft. Owen Davies's recent work on English cunning folk maintains Thomas's emphasis. Despite acknowledging that 'learned conjurors with their grimoires commanded demons, spirits and angels to come to their aid, [while] the more humble could, instead, call upon the services of the fairies', Davies only touches briefly on popular fairy-conjuring activities.[17]

One of the problems facing historians who wish to explore this area of early modern popular magic is the perceived lack of evidence. While there are many published witch-trial records describing the ways in which witches used familiars, plain sorcery cases remain largely unexamined, and, as Thomas points out, the few which have been unearthed seldom mention familiar spirits. What has been generally overlooked, however, is the value of witch-trial records as sources to be mined on this subject. Many of the significant minority of witch trials which clearly describe the magical activities of cunning folk also describe the use of familiar spirits.[18] The fact that these cases, though small in number, are widely distributed and share an inherent congruity, raises the possibility that familiar use by cunning folk was widespread in early modern Britain. From these sources alone it is difficult to determine how prevalent and how vigorous such a popular conjuring tradition might have been, yet comments found in contemporary élite writings suggest that the tradition may have been strong. John Beaumont devoted a good proportion of his *Historical, Physiological, and Theological Treatise of Spirits* (1705) to familiar spirits, and his study makes many references to anecdotes and beliefs of popular origin.[19] Comments by other writers suggest that the tradition was not only widespread, but was also vigorous. In *The Secret Commonwealth* Robert Kirk frequently talks about the use of familiars by Scottish seers, while in 1677 a fellow countryman wrote that some kinds of fairies 'to this day, make dayly service to severals in quality of familiars'.[20] Such a tradition was not unique to Scotland, however. In 1654 Durant Hotham claimed that the familiar spirit, rather than being a rarity as Thomas implies, was in fact a standard magical aid, stating that 'he [the cunning man] was of that sort we call white Witches, which are such as do cures beyond the ordinary reasons and deductions of our usual practitioners, and are supposed (and most part of them truly) to do the same by the ministration of spirits'.[21] Reginald Scot, similarly, mentions the use of familiars by cunning folk in passing as if it were an accepted fact which would go unchallenged by his readers. Scot (who used the term 'witch' to cover both black witches and healers) claimed that 'where a man shuld seeke comfort and counsell, there shall hee be sent . . . to the coosening witch, who will not sticke to take upon hir, by wordes to heale the lame . . . yea, with hir familiar & charmes she will take upon hir to cure the blind'.[22]

The comments of these writers are also corroborated by more official sources. Whenever the early modern Church spoke out against extant pre-Christian superstitions, the invocation of spirits was usually high up on the list. This concern with spirits was not purely a result of the witch-craze, for similarly worded condemnations concerning the magical use of spirits by ordinary people had been delivered by the Church throughout previously recorded history.[23] In 1548–9 English bishop John Hooper spoke out against those who 'give faith unto the conjuration or sorcery of superstitious persons' and among the conjurer's offences he lists 'seeking the help of damned spirits, or of such souls as be departed out of this world, as Saul did . . . These men . . . in English be called conjurers, who useth arts forbidden by God's laws'.[24] Similarly the conjuration of spirits is high on the list of magical practices criticized by the Bishop of Worcester in 1569. He condemns 'charms to cure men or beast; invocations of wicked spirits; telling where things lost or stolen are become by key, book, tables, shears, sieves; looking into crystals or other casting of figures'.[25]

These concerns were reflected in secular legislation. All of the statutes against witchcraft and sorcery passed in the early modern period (1542, 1563 and 1604) were greatly concerned with the invocation of spirits. The wording of these statutes made it clear that it was not only the witch's familiar with which they were concerned. The Henrician Bill of 1542, for example, stated:

> FOR REFORMATION whereof be it enacted by the King our sovereign lord with the assent of the Lords spiritual and temporal and the Commons in this present Parliament assembled and by authority of the same, that if any person or persons, after the first day of May next coming, use, devise, practise or exercise, or cause to be used, devised, practised or exercised, any invocations or conjurations of spirits, witchcrafts, enchantments, or sorceries, to the intent to get or find money or treasure, or to waste, consume or destroy any person in his body, members or goods, or to provoke any person to unlawful love, or for any other unlawful intent or purpose, or by occasion or colour of such things or any of them, or for despite of Christ, or for lucre of money, dig up or pull down any cross or crosses, or by such invocations or conjurations of spirits, witchcrafts, enchantments or sorcery, or any of them, take upon them to tell or declare where goods stolen or lost shall become, That then all and every such offence and offences, from the said first day of May next coming, shall be deemed accepted and adjudged felony.[26]

Cunning Woman or Witch?

The success or failure of the attempt to identify the presence of a cunning woman's familiar spirit in witch-trial records rests largely upon accurate definition of the magical practitioner involved. In a significant minority of records, the presence of a cunning man or woman can be identified with certainty. Bessie Dunlop's case is a prime example. Bessie was not brought to court because she had performed maleficium, but because a local family had protested that she had falsely accused them of theft. She performed only good magic and her familiar had fairy connections. Most witch-trial records, however, are not so clear cut, and it is difficult to say with any certainty whether the individual who stood before the bench was a cunning woman or a witch. One of the reasons for this difficulty is the fact that there was a great deal of overlap between the two types of magical practitioner in the period. While historians often make a distinction between cunning folk, who performed good magic, and witches, who performed bad magic, in the early modern period this distinction was often blurred. Although some cunning folk had a reputation for being wholly good, a large proportion of them were considered ambivalent, that is, that they could employ their magical powers to both help and harm. Christina Larner describes this dual nature in a Scottish context:

> The healer is a source of hope in the community. But his power is two-edged. If he should fail, demand extortionate and uneconomic returns for his services, or become hostile, then he becomes a source of menace and a focus for anxiety. The refusal of Canon Law to distinguish between black and white magic . . . regardless of whether it is intended to heal or harm, in fact reflects a peasant reality: that the healer can be dangerous.[27]

The trial records of East Lothian cunning woman Beigis Tod, who was accused of witchcraft in 1608, echo this popular perception when they claim that Beigis was known to be skilled in *both* 'on-laying and af-taiking of seiknes'.[28] There is no doubt that some cunning folk were tempted to use their magical skills to do harm, often at the request of a client. Mary Woods from Norfolk, for example, claimed in 1612 that 'she was asked by Mrs Suckling to tell when her husband, Dr Suckling, would die, and that she [Mary] refused a large reward to poison him'.[29] East Lothian cunning woman Agnes Sampson, on the other hand, seems not to have been so restrained, claiming in 1591 that when her client, Barbara Napier, came to her asking to be revenged on a man called 'Archie', she [Agnes] made 'a bonny small picture of yellow wax which she enchanted and conjured under the name of "Archie"' and instructed Barbara to put it by the fire so that 'as it should melt away before the fire, so should that man whose picture it was consume and pine away'.[30] Similarly John Beaumont describes how, in the early sixteenth century, a parishioner went to a cunning man with a grievance against a vicar who would not let him ring the church bell for fear it would disturb the local landowner. The cunning man (described as a 'Cantel') replied: 'Does he [the landowner] not love ringing? He shall have enough of it: And from that time, a Bell began to toll in his House, and continued so to do till [the] *Cantel's* Death.'[31] While Agnes Sampson and the Somersetshire Cantel performed maleficium at the behest of a client, others performed it in response to a perceived injury against themselves. When Wapping cunning woman Joan Peterson (1652) successfully cured a client only to find that he refused to pay her the agreed price for her services, she cried 'you had been better you had given me my money for you shall be ten times worse than ever you were'.[32] Having the reputation of being able to perform maleficium could even be good for business, Barbara Rosen claiming that 'London in the reigns of Elizabeth and James supported swarms of seedy, disreputable conjurors, who played up their black reputations as advertisement for their skills in palm-reading, fortune-telling, finding lost things, providing love-philtres and poisons.'[33] Given the ambivalent nature of early modern cunning folk, therefore, when we are presented with trial records describing them performing both good and bad magic, it is difficult to establish with any certainty whether the cited practitioner was a cunning woman or a witch. Similar difficulties arise when it comes to identifying their familiar spirits.

Guessing the Riddle

It is difficult to distinguish the cunning woman's familiar from the witch's familiar in trial records because, just as Church and State made no distinction, in theory at least, between 'black' and 'white' magic, so they also made no distinction between familiars which were used to harm and familiars which were used to heal: both were considered to be evil, that is, of the Devil. English bishop John Hooper, as we have already seen, was greatly concerned with those who heal through 'seeking the help of damned spirits' while the preface to a pamphlet documenting the trial of four witches in Windsor in 1579, laments that 'the fondness and ignorance of many is such that they succour those devilish imps, have recourse to them for the health of themselves or others, and for things lost, calling them by the honourable name of 'wise women'. Wherein they know not what honour they do to the devil.'[34] The statute passed by James VI & I in 1604 reflected the growing societal concern with the stereotypical witch's familiar, condemning as felons (that is, serious criminals) any persons who 'after the said Feast of St. Michael the Archangel next coming, shall use practice or exercise any invocation or conjuration of any evil and wicked spirit, or shall consult, covenant with, entertain, employ, feed, or reward any evil and wicked spirit to or for any intent or purpose'.[35] As it had done in the earlier statutes of 1542 and 1563, however, the term *'for any intent or purpose'* indiscriminately covered not only the use of familiars (and any other form of 'witchcraft, enchantment, charm, or sorcery') to 'hurt or destroy any person in his or her body', but also their employment for far more benign purposes, such as finding out 'where goods or things lost or stolen should be found or become' or 'what place any treasure of gold or silver should or might be found or had' and so on.[36]

By virtue of this statute, judicial prosecutors were legally bound to define any kind of familiar spirit employed for magical purposes as wholly malevolent, whether the practitioner who used it was a witch or a cunning woman, and whether they employed the spirit to maleficent or beneficent ends. Some trial records show this process of prosecutorial demonization very clearly. Bessie Dunlop's confession, for example, makes it clear that she perceived Tom Reid to be a classic ghost (classic in the sense that he despatched her with messages to his still-living relatives) with fairy connections (in that he served her at the behest of the fairy queen) who also helped her to perform beneficent magic. Despite Bessie's convictions, however, the prosecutors categorized Tom as a 'spretis of the devill'.[37] This demonizing process is even more blatantly revealed in the trial dittays of Orkney cunning woman Elspeth Reoch, dated 1616, which state that a 'blak man cam to her . . . And callit him selff ane farie man quha wes sumtyme her kinsman callit Johne Stewart quha wes slane be Mc Ky'. Elspeth's interrogators obviously did not find her definition of John Stewart (fairy man or ghost) sufficient, for the dittay later reads 'she confest *the devell* quhilk she callis the farie man lay with hir [my italics]'.[38] The way in which the familiar used by Aberdeenshire cunning man 'Andro Man' was similarly distorted by his prosecutors can be clearly seen in his trial records, dated 1598, which refer to 'the Devill, thy maister, quhom thow termes Christsonday, and supponis to be ane engell, and Goddis godsone'.[39]

Given these difficulties, the encounter-narratives found in witch-trial records present us with a series of riddles. We have two types of practitioner, the 'cunning man or woman' and the 'witch'; two types of magic, 'white' and 'black'; and various different types of familiar spirit, all enmeshed together in convoluted ways. The remainder of this book is concerned with teasing out some of the threads which make up this complex tapestry. Chapters FOUR to SEVEN are primarily concerned with definition and genesis. We will investigate, in some detail, the structure and dynamics of the relationship between cunning folk and witches and their respective familiar spirits. Through doing so we will attempt to answer several questions: What was the nature of the alliance between magical practitioner and familiar spirit? How did witches' familiars differ from – and how did they resemble – the familiars used by cunning folk? To what extent did the witch's familiar have roots in popular belief and to what extent was it a theological stereotype? The answers to these questions will then be used as a platform to support subsequent arguments developed in the book (chapters EIGHT to FOURTEEN), arguments which have implications not only for our understanding of the use of spirit familiars in early modern Britain, but also for our understanding of the experiential dimension of popular magic in this period.

In order to clearly distinguish the witch's familiar spirit from that of the cunning woman, the following terminology will be employed. The familiars used by cunning folk shall be termed 'fairy familiars'. As we have already seen, cunning folk frequently described their familiars as either being fairies, or being connected to the fairies through serving the fairy king or queen or having access to/living in fairyland. Although it was not uncommon for cunning folk to define their familiar spirits in a variety of other ways, calling them, for instance, 'angels', 'saints', 'sprites', 'imps', or 'spirits of the dead' and so on, there is enough correlation between popular conceptions of these types of spirit and the heterogenous group of folk spirits defined as fairies to justify the usage of the term 'fairy familiar' here. The familiar spirit used by the witch, on the other hand, will be defined as a 'demon familiar'. Although the term 'demon' was used to describe many different kinds of spirits in the period, including fairies, it shall be used here in the sense that it points to a spirit which, unlike the fairy, was more commonly associated with purely malevolent acts.

The bulk of the evidence used in the chapters FOUR to SEVEN will be derived from encounter-narratives found in witch-trial records, with additional findings from the records of sorcery trials and contemporary élite writings. The intense concern over both maleficium and demonological witchcraft in this period means that trial records featuring the relationship between witches and demon familiars far outnumber those pertaining to cunning folk and fairies. However, although records relating to the trials of cunning folk are fewer, there exists a significant minority which are rich in detail, such as, for example, those relating to Bessie Dunlop, Alison Peirson, Andro Man, Agnes Sampson, Joan Willimot and so on.[40] These detailed records are similar enough structurally, both to each other and to the larger number of extant shorter or fragmented trial records which exist, to be able to make generalizations about their subject matter. The basic criteria used here to distinguish trial records pertaining to cunning folk from those pertaining to witches will be the amount of beneficient magic described. A substantial minority of witch-trial records, such as those of Scottish witches Isobel Gowdie and Jonet Rendall, report that the accused performed a relatively equal number of both maleficent and beneficent acts, and in these cases it is not clear whether the magical practitioner would be more accurately defined as a witch or as a cunning man or woman.[41] In these instances I have made personal decisions as to definition, based on any background information available and on the general tenor of the confession, although some of these decisions could be contested. Owing to the considerable overlap between the activities of witches and cunning folk in the period, such ambiguity cannot be avoided.

In the following chapters we will be referring to, and cross-referencing between, a wide variety of cunning folk and witches from many regions of Britain in the early modern period. In order to sustain clarity and readability, while still providing as much helpful information as possible, details as to county or region of Britain in which the cunning woman or witch practised, and the date of their trial, shall be placed in brackets after their name. Thus Agnes Sampson, a cunning woman who practised in East Lothian and who was tried in 1591, would be referred to as either 'East Lothian cunning woman Agnes Sampson (1591)' or, where more brevity is possible, as 'Agnes Sampson (East Lothian, 1591)'.

And finally, for the purposes of this discussion, the term 'demon familiar' will be used in an unusually broad and inclusive sense. Historians have, quite rightly, made distinctions between the stereotypical 'animal familiar', which primarily appeared in England, and the Devil in the form of a man, who primarily appeared in Scotland. This categorization, however, means that the two types of spirit can be seen as separate phenomena and the relationship between witches and the Scottish Devil, for example, examined without reference to the concept of 'familiar spirits' at all. While the distinction between these two types of spirit is significant and would benefit from further study, here we are focusing on resemblances: the Devil in the form of a man appears frequently in English trial records throughout the period, while animal familiars appear consistently, though less frequently, in records from Scotland. And in the large majority of cases, both types of spirit behave in fundamentally the same way. For the purposes of the discussion hereafter the defining criteria for the term 'demon familiar' will be 'any spirit which enters into a relationship with a witch and gives her magical assistance'. Consequently, the terms 'demon familiar', 'animal familiar' and 'the Devil' will be interchangeable. As the book progresses the advantages to be gained from looking at witches' familiars from this broad perspective will increasingly become clear.

CHAPTER FOUR

Human and Spirit: The Meeting

Smallhead sat down, and was crying bitterly when a short grey cat walked in and spoke to her. 'Why do you cry and lament so?' asked the cat. 'My sisters abuse me and beat me,' answered Smallhead. 'This morning they said they would kill me in the evening unless I had all the needles in the straw outside gathered before them.' 'Sit down here,' said the cat, 'and dry your tears.' The cat soon found the twenty needles and brought them to Smallhead.[1]

Then she cried aloud, and began to weep bitterly for the loss of her golden ball. Presently she heard a voice exclaiming: 'Why do you weep, O king's daughter? Your tears could melt even the stones to pity you!' She looked at the spot from whence the voice came, and saw a frog stretching his thick ugly head out of the water. 'Oh! There you are, old water-paddler,' she said. 'Well, then, I am crying for the loss of my golden ball that has fallen into the fountain.' 'Then weep no more,' answered the frog; 'I can get it for you . . . '[2]

Most people today would consider themselves to have little or no knowledge about early modern familiars. In reality, however, the basic dynamics of the relationship between a cunning woman or witch, and her spirit ally, is easily recognizable to all of us, being encapsulated in narrative themes running through traditional folk tales and myths from throughout the world. Classics such as Rumpelstiltskin, Puss-in-Boots, the Frog Prince and so on, are representative. In these tales the protagonist usually finds themselves alone and in some kind of trouble, when a supernatural being appears suddenly before them and offers to help in some way. These fairy stories and myths originate from the same reservoir of folk belief as the descriptions of familiar-encounters given by cunning folk and witches in early modern Britain.

The Appearance of the Spirit

Those engaged in the task of questioning popular magical practitioners about their dealings with spirits were always keen to establish the circumstances surrounding the first encounter with a familiar. The information they collected in trial records reveals that, in its early stages, the cunning woman's initial familiar-encounter was very similar to that of the witch. In both cases, this meeting was usually 'spontaneous', that is, sudden and unexpected as opposed to being deliberately sought out. Both types of magical practitioner were usually alone in the countryside or at home and engaged in everyday occupations, when the spirit suddenly appeared as if from nowhere, unsolicited.[3] This type of spontaneous encounter with a familiar seems to have made a marked impression upon those who experienced it, for many individuals were able to pinpoint with astonishing accuracy, often many years later, exactly where they were and what they were doing when the event occurred. Among witches, Isobel Smith (Angus, 1661), for example, was 'one the head off the hill of Fineheaven, whill shee wes alone gathering heather' when she first met the Devil; Joan Prentice (Essex, 1589) was 'alone in her chamber, and sitting upon a low stool preparing herself to bedward'; Elizabeth Southerns (Lancashire, 1612) was 'coming homeward from begging . . . near unto a stonepit in Goldshaw in the said Forest of Pendle' and Rebecca Jones (Essex, 1645) was 'going to St Osyth, to sell her said masters butter'.[4] Cunning folk describe similar circumstances: Bessie Dunlop was 'between her own house and the yard of Monkcastle, driving her cattle to pasture'; Elspeth Reoch (Orkney, 1616) was 'at the Loch syd awaiting quhen the boit sould fetch hir in'; Agnes Sampson (East Lothian, 1591) was 'out in the fields from her own house at Keith betwix five and six at even, being her allane'; Anne Jefferies (Cornwall, 1645) was 'knitting in an arbour in our garden'; and Donald McIlmichall (Argyll, 1677) met his fairy associates 'on a night in the moneth of November 1676 he travelling betwixt Ardturr and Glackiriska at ane hill'.[5]

The second most common way for cunning folk and witches to first encounter the familiar was through receiving it as a gift from another magical practitioner, often a family member. Essex witch Rebecca West (1645) claimed that 'about seven yeares since, shee began to have familiaritie with the Devil, by the instigation of her mother Anne Weste; who hath appeared unto the said Rebecca at severall times, in diverse shapes; at one time in the likenesse of a proper young man'.[6] Similarly, Liverpool witch Margaret Ley (1667) claimed before a court that that when her mother died 'she [her mother] had nothing to leave her [and her sister] . . . but her two spirits, and named them, the elder spirit to this widow, and the other spirit to her, the said Margaret Ley'.[7] Leicestershire cunning woman Joan Willimot (1618), on the other hand, received her fairy familiar from someone she intriguingly described as 'her master', claiming that '[her master] willed her to open her mouth and he would blow into her a fairy which should do her good. And that she opened her mouth, and that presently after his blowing, there came out of her mouth a spirit which stood upon the ground in the shape and form of a woman'.[8] It was also not uncommon for both types of magical practitioner to claim that they had received their familiar from another, more powerful spirit. In 1646 Huntingdonshire witch Jane Wallis claimed that:

> as she was making of her bedde in her Chamber, there appeared in the shape of a man in blacke cloaths and blackish cloaths about five weeks past, and bid her good-morrow, and shee asked what his name was, and he said his name was *Blackeman*, and asked her if she were poore, and she said I; and then he told her he would send one *Grissell* and *Greedigut* to her, that shall do anything for her . . . and after *Blackeman* was departed from her, within three or 4 dayes, *Grissell* and *Greedigut* came to her, in the shapes of dogges with great brisles of hogges haire upon their backs, and said to her they were come from *Blackeman* to do what she would command them, and did aske her if shee did want anything, and they would fetch her any thing.[9]

Similarly, Aberdeenshire cunning man Andro Man (1598) claimed to possess an angel familiar who 'swyis to the Quene of Elphen', and Bessie Dunlop that Tom Reid had been sent to her by the fairy queen who had 'commandit him to wait upon hir'.[10]

For both cunning folk and witches, the encounter with the familiar-spirit was primarily a visual one.[11] They *saw* the spirit. The modern imagination is most likely to associate the visual form of a spirit with the smoky, undefined form of the stereotypical ghost; however, descriptions of familiar spirits given by early modern magical practitioners reveal that these men and women experienced spirits manifesting before them in clearly defined, three-dimensional human or animal forms, vivid with colour and animated by movement and sound. Most descriptions are so matter-of-fact and realistic that you could be forgiven for assuming, as some historians have done, that the narrators were describing encounters with real flesh-and-blood beings. Bessie's finely drawn description of Tom Reid is a particularly detailed example:

> Sche being inquirit, quhat kynd of man this Thom Reid was? Declarit, he was ane honest wele elderlie man, grey bairdit, and had ane gray coitt with

Lumbart slevis of the auld fassoun; ane pair of grey brekis and quhyte schankis, gartanit abone the kne; ane blak bonet on his heid, cloise behind and plane befoir, with silken laissis drawin throw the lippis thairof; and ane quhyte wand in his hand.[12]

Not only is Tom Reid's visual form striking in its realism, but it is also striking in its ordinariness. Such ordinariness was the norm, however. Even in less detailed confessions than Bessie's, there is still a pervading sense of naturalism. Although some descriptions of the demon familiar conform to a devilish stereotype (black in body and dress/cloven feet/fearsome aspect etc.) and some descriptions of fairy familiars are fantastic (tiny or giant size/shadowy/glowing with light/hollow-backed etc.), in most instances both types of familiar resemble relatively ordinary humans or animals with only slight, if any, visual anomalies. There is also little to distinguish between the appearance of the demon familiar and the appearance of the fairy familiar. There is scant heterogenesis, for example, between the sober appearance of the fairy man described by Walter Ronaldson of Aberdeenshire in 1601 as 'ane litill bodie, haiffing a scheavin berd, cled in quhyt lening, lyk a sark' and that of the demon familiar described by Aberdeenshire witch Ellen Gray (1597) as 'in the scheap of ane agit man, beirdit, with a quhyt gown and a thrummit hatt'.[13] Similarly, there is little to distinguish the king of the fairies, described by Nairnshire witch Isobel Gowdie (1662) as 'a braw man, weill favoured, and broad faced', from the demon familiar described by Angus witch Isobel Smith (1661) as 'ane braw gentleman' or by Essex witch Rebecca Jones (1645) as 'a very handsome young man'.[14] There is also little difference between the familiars who appeared before Aberdeenshire cunning man Andro Man (1598) 'in liknes of ane fair angell, and clad in quhyt claythis' and before Orkney cunning woman Jonet Rendall (1629) 'claid in quhyt cloathis with ane quhyt head and ane grey beard' and before East Lothian witch John Fian (1591) 'with white raiment'.[15] The Devil in the form of a man, as he appeared in Scotland, was often described as 'mickle' or tall and we correspondingly find an early modern traveller in Scotland remarking that 'A SPIRIT, by the Country People call'd *Browny*, was frequently seen . . . in the shape of a tall Man'.[16] By way of contrast, other familiars seem to have been notably small ('half long', 'littill' etc.), also redolent of small fairy hobmen as they appear in early modern and, with more frequency, later fairy sources.

Both demon and fairy familiars could appear dressed wholly in black, or wholly in white, or in any variety of colours in between. In many accounts the Devil appears in green, a colour which was often associated with the fairies. Jonet Watson (Midlothian, 1661) claimed, for example, that 'THE DEIVILL apeired vnto her, in the liknes of *ane prettie boy, in grein clothes* . . . and went away from her in the liknes of *ane blak doug*'.[17] Like many familiars, Jonet's 'prettie boy' was believed to shapeshift, a magical skill which was also associated with the fairies. Huntingdonshire witch Jane Wallis (1646) claimed that her familiars '*Grizell*, and *Greedigut* did come in severall shapes, yet most commonly like hounds with Brissells on their backes'.[18] Similarly, Dorset cunning man John Walsh (1566) claimed that his spirit appeared 'like a gray-blackish culver [dove], and sometime like a brended dog, and sometimes like a man in all proportions, saving that he had cloven feet'.[19] Both fairy and demon familiars could appear in a variety of animal guises ranging from apes, stags, horses, lambs, ferrets, dogs, cats and mice to birds, bees, spiders, grasshoppers, snails and frogs. As several scholars have illustrated, long before the witch-craze and the furore about demon familiars, on both a popular and élite level the Devil was believed to assume animal forms.[20] Some of the less-intimate early modern English animal familiars resemble the more 'permanent' fairy animals which were less close to mankind than the friendly fairy hobman in animal form. The most common permanent fairy animal to be found in English and Scottish sources up to the nineteenth century, the dog, was also one of the forms most frequently assumed by the animal demon familiar.

To match their down-to-earth appearance both demon familiars and fairy familiars were often given down-to-earth, and frequently affectionate, nicknames. And again, we find a great deal of overlap. As we have already seen, the terms 'familiar' and 'devil' were interchangeable between the two types of spirit. Similarly interchangeable, according to one source, was the term 'imp' (often used to denote the English animal familiar) and the term 'puckrel', with its obvious fairy associations.[21] The same types of personal names (often diminutive) which were given to individual fairies, were also given to familiars, particularly in England, reflecting the affectionate and intimate relationship often found between magical practitioners and their spirits. Several familiars, for example, shared a first name with the ubiquitous hobman Robin Goodfellow. The Devil in the form of a man who reportedly appeared before a group of Somerset witches in 1664, sounds very much like the versatile fairy hobman. An account of the meeting reads that 'on *Thursday* Night before Whitsunday last, about the same place met *Catharine Green* . . . and *Henry Walter*, and being met they called out *Robin*. Upon which instantly appeared a little Man in black Clothes to whom all made obeysance, and the Man put his hand to his Hat, saying, How do ye? Speaking *low* but *big*.'[22] Other name-correspondences from the period are (citing demon familiar name first and fairy equivalent in brackets): Hob (Hobb/Hobgoblin); Great or

Little Browning (Browny/Brouny); Bowman (Bogle); Oberycon (Oberon); Piggin (Pigwiggen); Pluck/Puppet (Puck/Puckle); Ball/Bidd (Billy); Willet/William/Walliman (Will o' the Wisp); Tibb (Tib); Jill (Jill/Jin). There are several examples of the name 'Tom' bridging the divide between the two types of familiar. There are records of demon familiars called Tom Twit, Vinegar Tom and Thomas a Fearie and likewise of fairies called Tom Tumbler, Tom Thumbe and Tom Tit Tot.[23]

The following excerpt from a confession given by Nairnshire witch Isobel Gowdie (1662) clearly indicates the closeness between the fairy familiar and the demon familiar. Although Isobel was condemned as a witch and confessed to having consorted with the devil and performed maleficent magic, her description of the spirits which the Devil gave to her and her companions is pure folklore, and the familiars described are indistinguishable from fairies in both appearance and name. Isobel claimed that:

> ilk on of us has a SPIRIT to wait upon us, quhan we pleas to call upon him. I remember not all the Spritis names; bot thair is on called 'SWEIN,' quhilk waitis upon the said Margret Wilson in Aulderne; he is always clothed in grass-grein; and the said Margret Wilson hes an nicknam called, 'PICKLE NEIREST THE WIND.' The nixt Sprit is called 'RORIE,' who waitis upon Bessie Wilsone, in Aulderne; he is still clothed in yallow; and hir niknam is 'THROUGH THE CORN YAIRD' [. . . .]. The third Spirit is called 'THE RORING LYON' who waitis upon Issobell Nicoll, in Lochlow; and [he is still clothed] in sea-grein; her niknam is 'BESSIE RULE.' The fourth Sprit is called 'MAK HECTOR' quho [waitis upon Jean] Martein, daughter to the said Marget Wilson; he is a young-lyk Devill, clothed still in grass- [green. Jean Martein is] MAIDEN to the Coven that I am of; and her niknam is 'OVER THE DYKE WITH IT' . . . The nam of the fyft Sprit is 'ROBERT THE [RULE' and he is still clothed in] sadd-dun, and seimis to be a Comander of the rest of the Spritis; and he waittis upon Margret Brodie, in Aulderne. [The name of the saxt Spirit] is called 'THEIFF OF HELL WAIT UPON HIR SELFE;' and he waitis also on the said Bessie Wilson. The name of the sevinth [Sprit is called] 'THE READ REIVER;' and he is my owin Spirit, that waittis on my selfe, and is still clothed in blak. The aucht Spirit [is called] 'ROBERT THE JACKIS,' still clothed in dune, and seimes to be aiged. He is ane glaiked gowked Spirit! The woman's [niknam] that he waitis on, is 'ABLE AND STOWT!' The nynth Spirit is called 'LAING;' and the woman's niknam that he waitis on, is 'BESSIE BAULD.' The tenth Spirit is named 'THOMAS A FEARIE,' &c.[24]

Frontispiece to *The Discovery of Witches* by Matthew Hopkins (1647). The notorious Suffolk Witch-finder is here depicted alongside two witches and various animal familiars.

The Offer of Assistance

Encounter-narratives which detail the intial meeting between a magical practitioner and a familiar spirit generally describe the spirit appearing to the cunning person or the witch when they are in some kind of need and offering them help. This narrative theme can be seen in its classic form in the following confession given by a seventeenth-century cunning man from the North of England, as recorded by John Webster, who was present at the trial:

> one night before the day was gone, as he was going home from his labour, being very sad and full of heavy thoughts, not knowing how to get meat and drink for his Wife and Children, he met a fair Woman in fine cloaths, who asked why he was so sad, and he told her that it was by reason of his poverty, to which she said, that if he would follow her counsel she would help him.[25]

This same basic narrative theme can also clearly be seen running through Bessie Dunlop's description of her first encounter with Tom Reid. When Bessie first encountered Tom, one of her cows had just died, her husband and child were mortally ill, and she herself was weak both through lack of food and from the rigours of recent childbirth. Out of dire necessity, Bessie was driving her remaining cattle to pasture, and it was in the depths of this physical and emotional anguish that Tom Reid first appeared and offered her comfort and advice:

> 'Sancta Marie,' said he, 'Bessie, quhy makis thow sa grit dule and fair greting for ony wardlie thing?' Sche ansuerit, 'Allace! Haif I nocht grit caus to mak grit dule? Ffor our geir is trakit; and my husband is on the point of deid, and ane babie of my awin will nocht leve; and myself at ane waik point; haif I nocht gude caus thane to haif ane fair heart?' Bot Thom said, 'Bessie, thow hes crabit God, and askit sum thing you suld nocht haif done; and, thairfoir, I counsell thee to mend to him: for I tell thee thy barne shall die, and the seik kow, or yow cum hame, thy twa scheip sall de to: bot thy husband sall mend, and be als haill and feir as euier he was.' And than I was sumthing blyther, fra he tauld me that my gudeman wald mend.[26]

The type of help which the familiar offered the magical practitioner depended upon the nature of their problems and upon the solution they desired. And it is here, at this juncture, that the encounter-narratives of cunning folk begin to differ significantly from those of their darker counterparts.

The Helpful Fairy

In the majority of encounter-narratives given by cunning folk, it is evident that their problems, prior to encountering the familiar for the first time, were primarily rooted in the struggle for physical survival – the lack of food or money, bereavement, sickness, loss of livelihood and so on. Webster's northcountry cunning man, cited above, first met his fairy familiar when he was desperately trying to find food for his family; Bessie Dunlop, when she was weak and her husband and baby mortally ill; Alison Peirson (Fifeshire, 1588) when she was sick, and lying in bed alone; and Agnes Sampson (East Lothian, 1591) when she was struggling to provide for herself and her children after the untimely death of her husband.[27] In these cases the fairy familiar alleviated the individual's suffering through making its magical powers available to them, an offer which enabled them to increase both their material wealth and their social standing by setting themselves up as a magical practitioner. In some narratives this transaction was clearly verbalized. Susan Swapper (Wales, 1607), for example, claimed that she had been told by a companion that if she knelt to the queen of the fairies the latter would give her 'a living' while Joan Tyrry (Somerset, 1555) claimed that the fairies 'taught her such knowledge that she getteth her living by it'.[28] Other narratives do not spell it out so clearly, but indicate a similar state of affairs. Jonet Rendall (Orkney, 1629) was told by her fairy familiar 'Walliman' that 'He sould learne yow to win almiss be healling of folk', while Anne Jefferies (Cornwall, 1645), by virtue of the healing powers she gained as a result of her liaison with the fairies, had 'monies, at all times, suffcent to supply her wants.'[29] Bessie Dunlop's narrative is equally suggestive. Although Tom offered Bessie goods and livestock, he did not manifest these things directly, but enabled Bessie to set herself up as a magical practitioner and thereby earn the money necessary to purchase them.[30] The meeting between Webster's northcountry cunning man, whom we met earlier, and his fairy familiar, effected the same result. Webster observed that the magical practitioner was 'a very simple and illiterate person to any mans judgement, and had been formerly very poor, but had gotten some pretty little meanes to maintain himself, his Wife and diverse small children, by his cures'.[31]

Although fairy familiars were employed by cunning folk in a variety of ways, they were primarily used in healing. Almost all of the encounter-narratives given by cunning folk record the use of fairy familiars for this purpose. Webster's northcountry cunning man was advised by the fairy woman to get a 'good living' through 'doing of good and curing sick people'; the records of the trial of Andro Man (Aberdeenshire, 1598) state that 'the Quene of Elphen, promesit to the [Andro Man], that thow suld knaw all thingis, and suld help and cuir all sort of seikness'; and Alison Peirson (Fifeshire, 1588) claimed that her healing skills were gained from a spirit called William Sympson (a dead uncle who lived with the fairies) and who 'haillit hir and teichit hir all thingis'.[32] Tales of the fairy-assisted healing powers of Anne Jefferies (Cornwall, 1645), on the other hand, 'made such a noise over all the county of Cornwall, as that people of all distempers came not only so far off as the Land's-end, but also from London, and were cured by her'.[33] The exact nature of the fairy familiar's help in this field could vary, but it commonly involved predicting the patient's fate, diagnosing the causes of illness and prescribing cures. When Agnes Sampson (East Lothian, 1591) was 'sent for to heal the old Lady Edmiston when she lay sick', she immediately went away, invoked her familiar, and 'demanded whether the lady would live or not'.[34] Similarly, Joan Willimot (Leicestershire, 1618) claimed that 'her spirit came weekly to her and would tell her of divers persons that were stricken or fore-spoken' and that 'the use which she had of the spirit was to know how those did which she had undertaken to amend'.[35] In a variation on this theme, John Beaumont describes one cunning woman using a whole 'jury' of fairies in this way:

> being ask'd by the Judge, how she came by her knowledge, as to the Death, or recovery of Persons sick; she told him, she could give no other Account of it, but that when any Person was sick, and she had a Mind to know the Issue, a Jury of Fairies came to her in the Night time, who consider'd of the Matter; and if afterwards they look'd cheerful, the Party would recover.[36]

Bessie Dunlop, on the other hand, gained more concrete help from Tom Reid, claiming that when a sick person came to her she 'sperit at Thom, Quhat mycht help thame? And Thom wald pull ane herb, and gif hir out of his awin hand'.[37] Similarly, Janet Trall (Perthshire, 1623) claimed that a 'bonny white' fairy man told her how to 'do good to poor folks: and he shewed me the means how I might do this, which was by washing, bathing, speaking words, putting sick persons through hesps [hanks] of yarn, and the like'.[38] Webster's northcountry cunning man, meanwhile, performed his cures by virtue of a 'little white box full of . . . white powder' which he obtained from the queen of the fairies, being told to 'give 2 or 3 grains of it to any that were siek, and it would heal them'.[39]

Second to healing, fairy familiars were commonly employed to use their magical powers to help cunning folk in their attempts to discover the whereabouts of lost goods, identify criminals and divine the future. John

Walsh (Dorset, 1566) claimed that he would raise his familiar spirit 'of whom he would then ask for anything stolen – who did it, and where the thing stolen was left'.[40] Similarly, when interrogators asked Bessie Dunlop 'Gif sche culd tell of ony thing that was away, or ony thing that was to cum', she answered that 'sche culd do nathing hir selff, bot as Thom tald hir'.[41] The divinatory skill of a familiar spirit was also responsible for the fame of a seventeenth-century seer from Colonsay in the Scottish Hebrides. When the seer was asked:

> who gave her such sights and warnings, she said, that as soon as she sett three crossess of straw upon the palm of her hand, a great ougly Beast sprang out of the Earth, neer her and flew in the air. If what she enquired had success according to her wish, the Beast would descend calmly, and lick up the crossess: If it would not suceid, the Beast would furiously thurst her and the crossess over on the ground, and so vanish to his place.[42]

Some familiars bestowed the skill of divination, or 'second-sight' directly onto the cunning woman. Isobel Sinclair (Orkney, 1633) claimed that 'shoe hath bein controlled with the Phairie; and that be thame, shoe hath the *second sight*' while Christian Lewinstoun (East Lothian, 1597) confessed that her divinatory skills came from her daughter, who 'was tane away with the Farie-folk . . . and that all the knawledge scho had was be hir dochter, wha met with the Fairie'.[43] Similarly, Elspeth Reoch (Orkney, 1616) claimed that a fairy man told her 'he wald lerne her to ken and sie ony thing she wald desyre . . . And she being desyrous to knaw said how she could ken that. And he said Tak an eg and rost it And tak the sweit of it thre Sondayis And with onwashin handis wash her eyes quhairby she sould sie and knaw ony thing she desyrit.'[44]

Cunning folk also used their fairy familiars to converse with the dead. As we have already seen, in this period fairies were often defined as either departed souls themselves, or as existing in, or having access to, a spirit-realm inhabited by the dead. Tom Reid, who, like a number of fairy familiars, was defined as both a familiar and a departed soul, asked Bessie to act as a mediator between himself and his family, commissioning her to go to his son 'and to certain utheris his kynnismen and friendis thair, quhom he naimit; and bade thame restoir certane guidis, and mend uthir offencis that thai had done'.[45] The access to the fairies which Bessie gained through Tom enabled her to bring news of the dead to the living: her trial dittays stating that she 'saw the Laird of Auchinskeyth, at a thorne, beyond Monkcastell; quhilk Lard deit mair nor fyve zeir syne. Thaireftir, sche, at the desyre of the Ladye Auchinskeyth, inquirit at Thom Reid, Giff sic ane mann was amangis thame? Quha answerit, That he was amangis thame.'[46] In this case, Bessie's client seems to have desired simple reassurance as to her deceased husband's location, however sometimes the cunning woman's role in such delicate matters was more challenging. As we have seen earlier, the latter's ability to communicate with spirits meant that she could be called upon to negotiate with disruptive souls who had not 'atteaneed their rest' because they carried unfinished business over from their 'Lyftime on earth'.[47]

The Helpful Demon

When she first encountered her demon familiar, the witch was usually in similar straits to the cunning woman. She was living on or near the bread-line, and suffering some kind of hardship or tragedy, often involving bereavement.[48] Even learned writers on witchcraft acknowledged that the suffering of the witch was significant in this context. King James VI noted that it was the witches' 'great miserie and povertie' which drove them into the arms of the Devil, who, 'finding them in an utter despair . . . he either by a voyce, or likenesse of a man inquires of them, what troubles them: and promiseth them, a suddaine and certaine waie of remedie'.[49] A substantial proportion of encounter-narratives describe witches entering into a relationship with a demon familiar because it offers to alleviate the sufferings caused by the struggle for survival. This offer was often, as historian Christina Larner noted, articulated as the promise of freedom from 'want'.[50] Bessie Wilson (Scotland, 1661), for example, was told by the Devil that 'thee art a poor puddled (overworked) body. Will thee be my servant and I will give thee abundance and thee sall never want', while Agnes Wobster (Aberdeenshire, 1597) was charged that 'Thow confessis that thairefter Satan apperit to the in the liknes of a calff, and spak to the in the manner forsaid, and baid the be a gude servand to him, and thow suld never want.'[51] This offer could be phrased in other ways. A demon familiar in the form of a man asked Susannah Edwards (Devon, 1682) whether she were a poor woman, and upon her assent told her that 'she need never want again for meat or drink or clothing'; another, in the form of a polecat, told Anne Usher (Suffolk, 1645) that 'he would bring her victuals'; three more, in the the form of grey rats, told Ellen Shepheard (Huntingdonshire, 1646) that if she made a pact with them she should 'have all happinesse' while the 'meickle black man' who appeared before eighteen-year-old Marie Lamont (Renfrewshire, 1662) at the sabbath told her that if she served him 'it sould be weel with her'.[52]

While the desire for freedom from want was clearly a significant moti-vating force behind the witch's relationship with the demon familiar, contemporary sources also suggest that the witch's motives in this context could be more complex. Despite their acknowledgement that the sufferings caused by poverty were significant, learned writers such as King James placed heavy emphasis upon the theological conviction that it was the witch's greed and malevolent intent (often described as the 'desire for revenge') which also motivated her to ally herself with a familiar. James defines this conventional 'alliance theory' thus:

> These Witches . . . being intised ether for the desire of revenge, or of worldly riches, their whole practises are either to hurte men and their gudes, or what they possesse, for satisfying of their cruell mindes in the former, or else by the wracke in quhatsoever sorte, of anie whome God will permitte them to have power off, to satisfie their greedie desire in the last poynt.[53]

Evidence from trial records both confirm and contradict James's claims. Encounter-narratives only occasionally describe the 'greedie desire' for, and reciprocal promise of, 'worldly riches' as being significant in the initial relationship forged between a witch and her demon familiar – one of the few clear examples being found in the narrative of Lancashire witch Anne Whittle (1612), where she claims that her demon familiar promised her 'gold, silver, and worldly wealth at her will'.[54] In the majority of cases the demon familiar's gifts of wealth were rather more modest, to say the least. Jane Wallis (Huntingdonshire, 1646), for example, who was so poor she could not even feed her familiars, claimed that 'divers times [the familiars] cames to her afterwards, and brought her two or three shillings at a time'.[55] Even less generous was the demon familiar used by Joan Williford (Kent, 1645), who brought her 'sometimes one shilling, sometimes eight pence, never more at once'; while the Devil who appeared before John Tailzour (Angus, 1661) when he was ploughing, was even more temperate, offering, rather cannily, to 'len [lend]' him some money because 'he knew he was going to some mercates [markets]'.[56]

The élite notion that greed lay at the heart of the relationship between a witch and her familiar is also thrown into question by the fact that the promise of riches is just as commonly found in the encounter-narratives given by cunning folk. Fairies were traditionally associated with the acquisition of money or treasure: Fulham cunning woman Alice West (1613) claimed that the fairy king and queen 'had in their power the command of inestimable treasure', while Suffolk woman Agnes Clerk (1499) maintained that a holly stick allegedly given to her daughter by the fairies could be used 'in order to find hidden treasure'.[57] Similar beliefs lay behind an Aberdeenshire man's claim in 1601 that a spirit in the form of a little man, almost certainly a fairy, woke him up to tell him 'thou art under wraik, gang to the weachmanis houss in Stanivoid and thair thou sall find baith siluer and gold'.[58] However, despite such associations, monetary gifts from the fairies seldom lived up to their promise. Like gifts from the demon familiar, they often turned out to be fraudulent or insubstantial, turning into a pile of dust, or a handful of leaves.[59]

While the Jamesian theory that the witch's relationship with the demon familiar was motivated by greed for riches is only partially supported by the sources, there is more evidence to support his claim that this relationship was motivated by the witch's malevolent desire for 'revenge' and to 'hurte men and their gudes'.[60] Trial records frequently associate malevolent intent on the part of the witch with the appearance of, and subsequent alliance with, the familiar. Elizabeth Francis (Essex, 1579), for example, had asked a neighbour if she could borrow some yeast, however 'being denied the same . . . she cursed Poole's wife and bade a mischief to light upon her for that she would give her no yeast. Whereapon, suddenly in the way she heard a great noise, and presently there appeared unto her a spirit of a white colour, in seeming like to a little rugged dog, standing near her upon the ground, who asked her whither she went.'[61] A similar pattern can be seen in the narrative of John Fian (East Lothian, 1591), who claimed he was 'lying in his bed in Tranent in Thomas Trumbill's chamber, musing and pensing how he might be revenged of the said Thomas, who had offended him in not spargeing [white-washing] of his chamber as he had promised, his face being toward the wall, the devil appeared to him . . . And also [the Devil promised him] that he should be revenged of his enemies.'[62] The records of the trial of John Palmer (St Albans, 1649), on the other hand, simply state that 'Being of a fretful and revengeful nature, he made a compact with the Devil'.[63]

References to malevolent intent found in encounter-narratives could have been the result of interrogatorial intervention, that is, introduced by prosecutors eager to superimpose their Jamesian stereotype of the demonic pact onto the suspect's confession. They could also have originated in the unjust accusations of a hostile community. However, it is also possible that they came from the accused themselves. There is no doubt that the types of resentments described in encounter-narratives would have been very prevalent in the lives of common folk in this period. Village life was intensely inter-dependent and the privations of one individual would have frequently been connected in some way to the actions of another. That this was the case is supported by the fact that in witch-trial records, reference to malevolent intent on the part of the witch frequently exists side by side with reference to some kind of suffering. When she first encountered her demon familiar Margaret Johnson (Lancashire, 1634) was 'beeing at her house at Marsden in great passion & anger & distracted' – but she was also 'withall oppressed w[i]th some want'.[64]

Similarly, Dorothy Ellis (Cambridgeshire,1647), who used her demon familiar to lame neighbours and kill cattle, claimed that it first came to her when she was 'much troubled in her mind'.[65] The trial records of Jonet Watson (Midlothian, 1661) describe the protagonist's grievances in more detail. At first we have the classic encounter between a witch and the Devil: Jonet 'come home to hir awne house, being verrie grieved and angrie . . . [and] wished to have amendse of *Jean Bughane*. Upon the which THE DEIVILL apeired unto her . . . and asked, "What aild her?"' Further reading of the confession reveals, however, that just prior to this meeting with the Devil Jonet had attended a funeral where she had lost her rightful share, as one of the poorest in the parish, to a portion of the 'rix-dollar' because Jean Bughane had 'run away with the said money, so that she got no part of it'.[66]

It was this type of resentment and anger which set the witch apart from the cunning woman. Whereas the latter alleviated her suffering by using the magical services of the familiar to set herself up as a magical practitioner, a role which generally benefited others, the former alleviated her suffering by using the magical services of the familiar to harm those individuals she deemed responsible for her privation. Witch-trial records contain long lists of the ways in which witches allegedly used demon familiars to perform malevolent acts, or 'maleficium'. Some of these malicious errands were relatively minor. Margaret Grevell (Essex, 1582) was reported to have 'caused her imps to destroy several brewings of beer and batches of bread . . . A brewing at Read's, a brewing at Carter's and a brewing of three or four bushels of malt at Bruce's.'[67] Others were more serious, involving the sickness, or death, of precious livestock. Elizabeth Bennett (Essex, 1582), having fallen out with her neighbour of three years, William Byatt, sent a demon familiar (called 'Lierd') in the shape of a lion 'to go and to plague the said Byatt's beasts unto death; and the spirit returning told this examinate that it had plagued two of his beasts, the one a red cow, the other a black. And saith, that the spirit told her that he plagued the black cow in the back, and the red cow in the head'.[68] Witches were also accused of employing their demon familiars to commit even more serious crimes. Angus witch Isobel Shirie (1661) claimed that, with the help of her demon familiar, she killed a man:

> shoe [Isabel] wronged Balillie Wood by braying to pouder two toads heads, and ane peice of ane dead man's scull, and ane peice of dead man's flesch, quhich the divill perfumed. And having condescended with the divill therwith to be baillie Wood's deith, the divill declaired that within a month or 20 days, as shoe pleased, he sould die; and that shoe went thereafter to Baillie Wood's house and enquyred for a pan, quhich was befor that tyme

poinded fra hir for ces, the baillie called on hir and gave hir a drinke, and befor shoe delyvered the cup to him againe shoe put the pouder in it, and he died within the tyme prescribed.[69]

Francis Moor (Huntingdonshire, 1646), on the other hand, murdered a man with the help of a demon familiar in the form of a white cat called 'Tissy', claiming that 'one *William Foster*, about sixteen years since, would have hanged two of her children for offering to take a piece of bread; and for that cause about six years since she cursed the said *William Foster*; whereupon the white Cat went to him, and he immediately fell sick, and lying in great paine for the space of seven or eight days, and then dyed'.[70] Even more dramatically, the octogenarian witch John Lowes (1645), who was the vicar of Brandeston, in Suffolk, for fifty years, used his familiars to sink ships at sea. On one occasion, while 'walking upon the wall' near Landguard Fort, Harwich, he 'saw a great sail of ships pass by, and bidding his yellow imp go and sink a new vessel stationed about the middle of the fleet . . . By this act he made fourteen widows in a quarter of an hour, for which he did not grieve, but rejoiced in realizing the power of his imps.'[71]

Back-to-Front Familiars

The basic correlation between the demon familiar and bad magic and the fairy familiar and good magic presented here was not always so clear cut. In this period the overlap between cunning woman and witch, fairy and demon, was so great that it was often difficult to draw lines between categories of magical practitioner and familiar spirit. Consequently it is hardly surprising to find instances in encounter-narratives where witches allegedly used their demon familiars to perform good magic and cunning folk used their fairy familiars to perform maleficium. The demon familiar used by Nairnshire witch Isobel Gowdie (1662) helped her to wither crops and kill a man, however it also taught her spells with which to to heal broken limbs, pains in the head and fevers, and how to remove sickness from a child who was forspoken.[72] Lancashire witch Anne Whittle (1612), meanwhile, who performed magic with the help of a familiar called 'Fancy', also used charms to cure those who were bewitched.[73] Demon familiars could also help with the finding of lost goods and divining the future. Angus witch Helen Guthrie (1661) boasted that she 'knowes assuredlie that Elspet Pigotis cloath, which wes in wanting laitlie, was taken away by a gentleman's servand who lodgit in the house at ane certane tyme, and that shee wes assured of this by a spirit which she hes besyde other folkes, yea, besyde all the witches in Angus'.[74] At other times demon familiars did not help others, but they assisted their human ally around the homestead in much the same way as a traditional brownie. The spirit shared by Essex witches Elizabeth Francis and Agnes Waterhouse (1566), for example, helped the latter by killing one of her hogs for her and the former by bringing sheep into her pasture.[75] The familiar who appeared before Devon witch Temperance Lloyd (1682), on the other hand, offered, rather disarmingly, to help her carry a heavy load: 'I was going for brooms,' Temperance claimed, 'and he [the Devil] came to me and said, "This poor woman has a great burthen"; and he would help ease me of my burthen.'[76]

We can set against these cases the fact that many encounter-narratives given by cunning folk contain descriptions of malevolent intent on the part of the magical practitioner and evidence that they employed their fairy familiars to do harm. Agnes Sampson (1591), for example, was a highly-respected and largely benevolent cunning woman from Haddington, near Edinburgh, who cured the sick and "sought her haill responses" from her familiar (described variously as a dog and a man and whom she seems to have invoked by calling 'Elva'). Agnes was originally tempted into an alliance with this spirit, however, not only because he offered her a way out of her suffering, but also because he offered her the 'power to be revenged on her enemies'. Agnes claimed he taught her how to perform maleficent magic and that she helped him raise winds in order to cause shipwrecks.[77] Similarly, the fairy familiars who appeared before renowned Cornish healer Anne Jefferies (1645), made a woman's leg sore because she angered them.[78] Perthshire cunning woman Isobel Haldane (1623), who first met her fairy familiar when he helped her to escape from fairyland, was also not above using him to punish her enemies. When neighbour Stephen Ray accused Isobel of stealing some beer she cursed him with the words 'he that delyveret me frome the ffarye-ffolk sall tak amendis (on) thé!'[79] Orkney cunning woman Jonet Rendall (1629), on the other hand, first met her fairy familiar when she was 'being above the hill of Rendall having soucht charitie and could not have it'. The spirit, whom she called 'Walliman', acknowledged her resentment of those neighbours who would not give her alms and promised that in future 'quhasoever sould refus yow almiss and quhatever ye craved to befall thame sould befall thame'. As a result of this alliance, Jonet could heal the sick by praying to her fairy familiar, but if her neighbours refused her alms the same spirit 'wald be angrie and mak thair beastis die'.[80]

In the context of fairy beliefs of the time, such maleficent acts on behalf of the fairy familiar would not have been surprising. We have already seen in chapter ONE that although fairies were associated with healing skills, good fortune and so on, they were also associated with malevolence. Some contemporary descriptions of fairy familiars make them sound stereotypically demonic. Kirk claimed that 'they are ever readiest to go on hurtfull earands, but seldom will be the Messengers of great good to men' and Robert Burton that 'Terrestrial devils are those *Lares, Genii, Faunes, Satyrs,* Wood-nymphs, Foliots, Fairies, *Robin Goodfellowes, Trolli,* &c. which as they are most conversant with men, so they do them most harm.'[81] This conception of fairy nature was also expressed by Perthshire cunning woman Janet Trall (1623), who described a terrifying encounter with a group of fairies, the chief of whom told her 'to do ill, by casting sickness on people'.[82] This touchy fairy nature, quick to malevolence, is well-illustrated in a later tale concerning the Manx 'Fenoderee' or brownie:

> A man sent by his wife to invoke the Fenoderee to cure their little red cow says the correct incantation but forgets to cross himself for safety. The Fenoderee comes in a mischievous mood, cures the cow but begins to carry off the man, who remembers just in time to cross himself, but not before he had inadvertently devoted the cow to the Fenoderee.[83]

The domestic brownie, despite being one of the fairies most intimate with man, was notorious for being touchy and later sources suggest that, like the demon familiar, he was particularly feared outside his own home and quite capable of helping his human 'master' at the expense of someone else.[84]

CHAPTER FIVE

The Working Relationship

The duration of the working relationship between a cunning man or woman and their familiar could range from a few short weeks to several decades. Bessie Dunlop worked with her fairy familiar for three years, John Walsh for five, Isobel Sinclair for seven, Isobel Haldane for ten, Alison Peirson for sixteen, Jonet Drever for twenty-seven and Andro Man for thirty-two. The situation was similar for witches.[1] Ellen Shepheard worked with her demon familiar for five years, Meribel Bedford for six, Francis Moore for eight, Alexander Sussums for sixteen, Elizabeth Weed for twenty-one and Anne Cate for twenty-two.[2] Given the fact that these figures represent relationships which were mostly brought to a close through imprisonment or execution, it seems reasonable to surmise that long-term relationships between both types of magical practitioner and their familiar spirits were the norm. Witches sometimes claimed that their demon familiars lived in a specific place in or near the house, and in this respect they resembled the domestic fairy, or brownie. Trial records contain references to demon familiars living in glass or leather bottles; crystals; baskets; boxes; earthenware pots lined with wool kept under the stairs or by the hearth; under borders of 'green herbs' in the garden and under the roots or in the hollows of trees.[3]

In most cases, after the initial encounter, the relationship between magical practitioner and familiar spirit seems to have settled into a pattern. Some familiars consistently appeared spontaneously before their human allies, even when unwanted and unbidden. Huntingdonshire witch Elizabeth Chandler (1646), for example, lamented of her two familiars (whom she called Beelzebub and Trullibub) that 'she did never willingly invoke or employ the same, but hath prayed to God to deliver her therfrom'.[4] Equally persistent, but more welcome, was the familiar which served Lancashire witch Elizabeth Southerns (1612). Elizabeth claimed that 'the said spirit or devil appeared at sundry times unto her this examinate about daylight-gate, always bidding her stay, and asking her this examinate what she would have or do'.[5] However, such consistently random appearances on the part of the familiar do not seem to have been the norm. Although most familiars retained their autonomy, and sometimes exercised it by appearing before the magical practitioner unbidden, on a day-to-day level they usually appeared in response to some kind of request.

In a minority of sources we find clear indications that this 'request' could take the form of an overt conjuration. In 1692 Robert Kirk claimed of the Scottish seer that, 'The Tabhaisder or Seer that corresponds with this kind of Familiars, can bring them with a spel to appear to himselfe or others when he pleases, as readily as Endor Witch did those of her own Kind.'[6] Kirk's claim is supported by trial records such as those relating to the East Lothian cunning man, Alexander Hamilton (1630), which state that he was given a 'battoun of fir' by the Devil, and that 'be streking of the said battone thryse upone the ground the devill was in use sumtymes to appeir to the said Alexr in the liknes of ane corbie [raven] at uther tymes in the schape of ane katt and at uther tymes in the schape of ane dog and thereby the said Alexr did ressave responsis frome him'.[7] Other trial records describe a variety of alternative invocatory methods: Essex witch Joan Cunny (1589), for example, claimed that a magical practitioner called 'Mother Humphrey of Maplestead' told her that 'she must kneel down upon her knees and make a circle on the ground, and pray unto Satan the chief of the devils, and that then the spirits would come unto her'; Wiltshire cunning woman Anne Bodenham (1653), who was literate, could 'raise spirits by reading books'; Angus witch Elspet Bruice (1661) 'reased the divell' through 'turning the sive and the sheires'; and Edinburgh cunning woman Jonet Boyman (1572) conjured 'ane grit blast' like a whirlwind in which her familiar appeared.[8] Some conjurations were essentially verbal. When East Lothian cunning woman Agnes Sampson (1591) wished to talk to her familiar she 'charged the devil, calling him 'Eloa', to come and speak to her'.[9] Others combined verbal commands or entreaties with the use of ritual. Essex witch Margaret Moone (1645) allegedly performed her invocatory ritual before her 'searcher', Francis Milles, who claimed that 'she [Margaret] said, if she might have some bread and beere, she would call her said impes: which being given unto her, she put the bread into the beere, and set it against an hole in the wall, and made a circle round about the pot, and then cried, Come Christ, come Christ, come Mounsier, come Mounsier'.[10] The familiar spirit belonging to Aberdeenshire cunning man Andro Man (1598) was slightly more sophisticated, for it was 'rasit be the speking of the word B*enedicte,* and is laid agane be taking of a dog under thy left oxster in thi richt hand, and [by Andro Man] casting the same in his mouth, and speking the word

Maikpeblis'.[11] English tailor and cunning man William Wycherley (1549), on the other hand, who was likely to have been literate and have some leanings towards learned magic, invoked a spirit called 'Ambrose Waterduck' with the use of a great circle, a sword and a ring.[12] The conjuration of spirits could sometimes be accompanied by fasting.[13] William Barckseale, a cunning man from Southampton, used to 'fast and pray three days before engaging in the detection of stolen goods' while Cornish cunning woman Anne Jefferies (1645), who frequently conversed with fairy familiars, was famous for eating barely enough to sustain life. For a number of cunning folk and witches, encounters with familiar spirits were also associated with a particular time and place. The mid seventeenth-century 'Fairy Boy from Leith' met the fairies 'every *Thursday* Night . . . under yonder Hill (pointing to the great Hill between *Edenborough* and *Leith*)', while Dorsetshire cunning man John Walsh (1566) went to meet the fairies 'upon hills, whereas there is great heaps of earth, as namely in Dorsetshire. And between the houres of 12 and one at noon, or at midnight he useth them'.[14] Ayrshire cunning man John Stewart (1618), alternatively, 'met with the fairies every Saturday at seven o'clock. He also saw them every Halloween, sometimes on Lanark Hill and other times on Kilmaurs Hill'.[15] Some Scottish witches also travelled to churchyards, roadside crosses or remote open places in order to meet the Devil.

Despite the instances quoted here, and notwithstanding the fact that 'invocations' and/or 'conjurations' were frequently condemned by witch-craft statutes throughout the period, in a substantial majority of witch-trial records there is no clear evidence of overt ritual conjuration. In many of the latter, the manner in which the spirit was allegedly contacted is not mentioned at all, reference only being made to the fact that the magical practitioner 'sent', 'caused' or 'willed' their spirits to perform magical acts and 'asked', 'commanded' or 'demanded' their familiar to come to them. Bessie Dunlop claimed, for example, that 'diverse tymes, quhen onye sic persounes come ather to hir, sche wald inquire at ane Thome Reid, quha deit at Pinkye, as he himselff affirmit; wha wald tell hir, quhen evir sche askit'.[16] Historians generally assume that descriptions of overt ritual conjuration found in witch-trial records are attributable to the influence of learned magical ideas. In reference to the conjuring activities of Dorset cunning man John Walsh (1566), for example, who claimed that 'he had a book of his said master which had great circles in it, wherein he would set two wax candles across of virgin wax, to raise the familiar spirit, of whom he would then ask for anything stolen', the historian Barbara Rosen noted that 'This is not a witch's familiar, but a conjurer's; it comes only in response to ceremonies, and then in differing shapes.'[17] This type of emphasis on the links between

A. *A Witch.* B *A Spirit raised by the Witch.*
C *A Friar raising his Imps.*   D *A Fairy Ring.*
E *A Witch rideing on the Devill through the Aire.*
F *An Inchanted Castle.*

The frontispiece to Richard Bovet's *Pandaemonium, or the Devil's Cloyster* (1684) brings together popular and élite conjuration, fairies, demon familiars and the witches' sabbath.

overt ritual conjuration and learned magic, which continues to be upheld by more recent historians, has the inadvertent effect of minimizing the role which invocatory techniques may have played in the activities of popular magical practitioners. On the one hand, the scarcity of reference to overt conjuration in witch-trial records may be rooted in the fact that most interrogators were concerned with finding evidence to prove that suspects had used their familiar spirits to perform maleficium (and as we shall see in chapter SIX made a 'pact' with the Devil), and that they had little to gain from detailing the methods by which these spirits had been invoked. On the other hand if, as is more generally assumed, the scarcity of these references accurately reflects the fact that overt ritual conjuration was not routinely employed by popular magical practitioners, this does not necessarily mean that other types of conjuration were not taking place. As we shall explore more fully in later chapters, the methods used to conjure spirits did not need to be overt, or ritualistic, to be deemed effective and the popular magical practitioner's simple process of 'asking' or 'demanding' that their familiar come to them may have masked powerful, but externally minimalist, invocatory techniques.

Strange Intimacies

The tenor of the relationship between magical practitioner and familiar spirit could vary widely. An element of formality, for example, often existed between a Scottish witch and their demon familiar, particularly if their relationship involved attendance at the sabbath, where groups of witches congregated together in the presence of 'the Devil'. Accounts of sabbath and pre-sabbath meetings often describe the Devil making 'demands' and 'commands', acting as master of ceremonies, sitting at the head of the table, giving sermons, bestowing names and so on. The following late sixteenth-century account from one of the famous North Berwick witches is representative.

> The devil start up himself in the pulpit, like a mickle black man and called every man by his name, and every one answered . . . The first thing he demanded was if they kept all promise and been good servants, and what they had done since last time they had convened at his command . . . Then he commanded them to keep his commandments, which were to do all the evil they could. Before they departed they kissed his arse. He had on him a gown and a hat which were both black; and they that were assembled, part stood and part sat. John Fian was ever nearest to the devil at his left elbow; 'Grey Meal' kept the door.[18]

The formality often present in the relationship between Scottish witches and the Devil was also often found in the relationship between cunning folk and the fairy monarchy. Although there are exceptions, the fairy king and queen were generally kindly but formal figures, who bestowed magical gifts on the worthy, on their own terms. When Webster's north-country cunning man was given healing powders from the fairy queen he described how he 'came to a fair hall, wherein was a Queen sitting in great state, and many people about her, and the Gentlewoman that brought him, presented him to the Queen, and she said he was welcom'.[19] Similarly Susan Swapper (Wales, 1607) was told by a group of spirits to kneel down before the queen of the fairies.[20]

Whether the relationship was formal or not, both witches and cunning folk could be scared by their familiars. When Essex witch Elizabeth Bennett (1582) first met one of her familiars she was so afraid she cried out: 'In the name of God, what art thou? Thou wilt not hurt me?' while Cornish cunning woman Anne Jefferies (1645) was 'so frighted' to see 'six persons, of a small stature, all clothed in green' jump over the garden hedge that she 'fell into a kind of convulsion-fit'.[21] Perthshire cunning woman Janet Trall (1623), on the other hand, was so terrified by one visit from the fairies that she nearly lost her mind, claiming that 'they [the fairies] drave me down, and then I was beside myself, and would have eaten the very earth beside me'.[22] Even the kindly Tom Reid could some-times provoke fear, Bessie claiming that on one occasion Tom 'gait in at ane naroware hoill of the dyke nor onye erdlie man culd haif gane throw; and swa I was sumthing fleit'.[23] It was often the sudden, unexpected nature of the familiar's appearance which caused such anxiety. Robert Kirk claimed that the Scottish seer 'is not terrified with their sight when he calls them [his familiars] – but seeing them in a surprise (as often he dos) frights him extreamly'.[24] East Lothian cunning woman Agnes Sampson (1591) was certainly scared when her fairy familiar 'came in over the dyke in likeness of a dog, and came so near to her that she was effrayed and charged him on the law that he lived on to come no nearer'.[25]

Despite such references to formality and fear, a large number of relationships between magical practitioner and familiar spirit were informal and intimate. The relationships between English witches and their animal familiars, in particular, were notoriously close. Essex witch Joan Prentice (1589) and her spirit, which appeared to her in the form of a ferret, had an affectionate relationship which centred around the sucking of blood. When the familiar first appeared to Joan as she was sitting in her chamber at an almshouse in Sible Hedingham, she was very frightened. After it had comforted her by saying, 'fear me not, my coming unto thee is to do thee no hurt', their relationship quickly improved, and before long she was calling her familiar to her in much the same way as you would summon a beloved pet, crying 'Bid, Bid, Bid, come Bid, come Bid, come suck, come suck, come suck'. On some occasions, the two seemed to chat like an old married couple; Joan's trial records stating that Bid came to her 'in the night time as she was sitting upon a little stool, preparing herself to bedward . . . "Joan, wilt thou go to bed" [asked the ferret] to whom she answered, "Yea, that I will by God's grace"; then presently the ferret leapt upon her lap, and from thence up to her bosom, and laying his former feet upon her left shoulder, sucked blood out of her left cheek.'[26] Edmonton witch Elizabeth Sawyer (1621), on the other hand, claimed that her familiar, whom she called 'Tom', came to her 'sometimes as a large black dog, and at other times as a small white dog' and that she 'used to stroke him on the back, whereat he wagged his tail in contentment' while those belonging to Essex witch Elizabeth Clarke (1645), and who appeared in the shape of two dogs, were seen 'skipping into her lap and kissing her'.[27] Even interactions with the more formal Scottish Devil could have their affectionate moments. Angus witch Helen Guthrie (1661) claimed that when she and several other witches 'made them selfes mirrie' in a churchyard in Forfar, the Devil 'made much of them all' and 'kist them all'.[28]

The sheer intensity of the closeness which could develop between demon familiar and witch is vividly evoked by the comments of Alice Nokes (1579), from Lambourne in Essex, who, being reproved at church for disputing with a neighbour, claimed 'in a fume' that 'she cared for none of them all as long as Tom [her familiar] held on her side'.[29] A similar intensity is illustrated in a mid seventeenth-century eye-witness account of an English execution which states that 'A mother and daughter, condemned for witchcraft, being on the point of execution, were urged to repent and forsake the Devil. The Mother declined to renounce the faithful friend of threescore years, and "died in her obstinacy".'[30] As we shall see in chapter SIX, elements of affection could also be expressed through a sexual relationship.

Although the relationship between a cunning woman or witch and their familiar was intimate, it was a very 'human' kind of intimacy, which embraced a wide spectrum of emotion. The dynamics between Tom Reid and Bessie Dunlop were representative. On the one hand, their relationship was a very supportive one – not only did Tom facilitate Bessie's magical practices but he also helped her on a more personal level. When Bessie was undergoing a difficult labour, for example, he told her to 'tak ane gude hart to hir, for nathing suld aill hir'. On the other hand, Bessie and Tom could get angry with each other. Tom became 'verrie crabit' with Bessie when she would not do what he wanted, and 'schuke his heid, and said he suld caus hir forthink it'.[31] Similarly Joan Prentice, despite her bedtime intimacies with her familiar, was not afraid to show her displeasure when she discovered that he had disobeyed her instructions and had harmed a child more seriously than she intended: 'Thou villain! [Joan cried] What hast thou done? I bid thee to nip it but a little and not to hurt it, and thou hast killed the child?'[32] Sometimes such relationships could get physically violent. When Lancashire witch Elizabeth Southerns (1612) refused to perform some maleficent magic, her demon familiar, whom she called 'Tibb', became very angry and 'shove[d] or pushed this examinate [Elizabeth] into the ditch, and so shed the milk which this examinate had in a can or kit, and so thereupon the spirit at that time vanished'.[33] On the other hand, when the familiars belonging to Essex witch Joan Pechey (1582) were too forceful, she talked to them as if they were wayward children, a neighbour claiming that he heard her shouting to them: 'Yea, are you so saucy? are ye so bold? you were not best to be so bold with me. For if you will not be ruled, you shall have a Symond's sauce – yea . . . I perceive if I do give you an inch you will take an ell.'[34] Even the more formal human-spirit relationships could accommodate such bickering. East Lothian cunning woman Agnes Sampson (1591) was not too scared to confront her fairy familiar, despite his sometimes authoritarian manner, claiming that on one occasion, 'she quarrelled her master the devil, and that in respect she had never gotten good of him, and said she would renounce him, but did it not. And he promised to her at that time that nothing should go against her.'[35]

Sabbaths and Elf-Homes

For some magical practitioners the relationship with the familiar involved travelling with them to, or meeting them in, a different place. The witch, notoriously, journeyed to the sabbath (these experiences being predominantly recorded in Scottish witch trials), while the cunning woman journeyed to fairyland or, as it was called in the period, 'elfhame' (literally 'elf-home'). A few magical practitioners claimed that they first met their familiars in fairyland, or at the sabbath; however, a greater number claimed that their journey to these places had been initiated by the familiar's invitation.[36] Nairnshire witch Isobel Gowdie (1662), for example, first met the Devil as she was 'goeing betwix the townes of *Drumdewin* and *the Headis*' where she 'promeisit to meit him, in the night time, in *the Kirk of Aulderne*; quhilk I did'.[37] Bessie Dunlop claimed that on one occasion Tom Reid 'tuke hir be the aproun, and wald haif had hir gangand [go} with him to Elfame', and that on another, she met a group of 'gude wychtis that wynnit in the Court of Elfame; quha come thair to desyre hir to go with thame'.[38] Scattered throughout encounter-narratives from Southern England, where descriptions of sabbath and fairyland experiences are seldom found, we still find references to familiars attempting to lure magical practitioners to 'go with them', although the destination is not specified. Huntingdonshire witch Ellen Shepheard (1646), for example, claimed that 'a Spirit, somewhat like a Rat, but not fully so big, of an iron-grey colour . . . said you must goe with me', whilst nearly seventy years earlier Essex witch Elizabeth Bennett maintained that a familiar spirit in the form of a black dog asked her to 'go with it'.[39] Animal-spirits could sometimes lead Scottish witches to the sabbath, Argyllshire witch John Reid (1697) claiming that "he and the haggs were summoned [to the sabbath] by a black dog with a chain about his neck, the tinkling of which they followed'.[40] Such invitations on the part of the familiar were sometimes refused. Bessie Dunlop, for example, resisted Tom's entreaties by saying 'Sche saw no proffeit to gang thai kynd of gaittis [along that route], unles sche kend quhairfor [knew why]!'[41] Many other magical practitioners, however, accepted their familiars' invitations and in these cases their experiences of journeying to the sabbath or fairyland seem to have become an integral part of their relationship with their spirit allies.[42]

Over the past few decades, Continental historians have argued that descriptions of attendance at the witches' sabbath, found in trial records in different parts of Europe throughout the early modern period, were likely to have originated in folk beliefs about travel with the fairies, or into fairyland. They suggest that during the interrogatorial process these fairyland experiences were moulded into sabbath experiences by zealous prosecutors eager to secure convictions of demonological witchcraft.[43] Although there are many differences between British sabbath and fairyland accounts (some of which will be looked at in chapter SIX) there are also enough similarities to make this argument extremely plausible. Early modern accounts in which elements of the stereotypical sabbath merge seamlessly with elements of the stereotypical visit to fairyland, such as those given by Andro Man, Isobel Gowdie and Anne Whittle, are powerful testaments to the truth of this hypothesis.[44] Experiences in both places are characterized by feasting, drinking and making merry with a great company, presided over by one or more supernatural figures variously described as the Devil or the king or queen of the fairies and so on. The festivities associated with visits to fairyland often occurred in great subterranean fairy halls. Argyllshire cunning man Donald McIlmichal (1677), for example, was travelling along a country road at night when 'at ane hill he saw a light not knowin quhair he was. And ther a great number of men and women within the hill quhair he entered haveing many candles lighted, and saw ane old man as seemed to have preference above the rest . . . And saw them all danceing about the lights'.[45] Around the same period the East Lothian 'Fairy Boy of Leith' described a similar event to Captain George Burton, who asked him:

> What company have you there [in the fairy hill]? There are Sir, (said he) a great company both of men and women, and they are entertained with many sorts of Musick besides my drum; they have besides plenty of variety of Meats and Wine . . . I demanded of him, how they got under that Hill? To which he replied, that there were a a great pair of gates that opened to them, though they were invisible to others, and that within there were brave large rooms as well accommodated as most in *Scotland*.[46]

The sabbath was more commonly described as occurring in churches and churchyards, or out of doors. Jonet Howit (Angus, 1661) claimed that she attended a meeting at 'Muryknowes, a litle bewest Halcartoun Miln, and that at this meiting ther wer about twenty persones present with the divill, and that they danced togither and eat togither, having bieff, bread, and ale, and that shoe did eat and drink with them hir selfe'.[47] Helen Guthrie (1661), a witch from the same area, claimed that 'in the church yard of Forfar' she and nine companions 'daunced togither' with the Devil 'in the shape of a black iron hewed man', and that 'Andrew Watson hade his usuale staff in his hand, altho he be a blind man yet he daunced also nimblie as any of the companye, and made also great moviement by singing his old ballards, and Isobell Shyrrie did sing her song called Tinkletum Tankletum'.[48] Such merriment was also a feature of the rarer English sabbath, Elizabeth Style (Somerset, 1665) claiming that herself and several companions 'consumed wine, cakes, and roast meat (all brought by the man in black) . . . danced and made merry . . . and at their parting they said, "A Boy! merry meet, merry part"'.[49]

However, sabbath and fairyland experiences were not only associated with festivity and merriment, they were also sacred events associated with the more serious business of magic. Under the supervision of the presiding supernatural figures, magical skills and magical objects could be acquired and/or communal magical activities performed. Just as we can make a general moral distinction between the harmful magic per-formed by the witch and the good magic performed by the cunning woman, so we can also make a similar distinction as regards the magi-cal activities which took place during their visits to fairyland and the sabbath. Sabbath accounts, for example, usually make reference to the learning and/or performance of harmful magic. In addition to dancing and making merry, Somerset witch Elizabeth Style (1665) and her companions bewitched 'man, woman or child, sometimes by a picture made in wax, which the Devil baptises, sometimes by an apple, dish, spoon, or other thing received from their evil spirit, which they pass on to the party to be harmed'.[50] A group of witches from the Scottish Borders (1634), on the other hand, 'being conveyed by the devil from a meeting they had upon the shoar of Eymouth into a ship wherein George Holdie in Eymouth was with his company . . . cruelly sank and destroyed the ship wherein they perished with the ship and goods'.[51] Alternatively, accounts of visits to fairyland usually make reference to the acquisition of beneficent magical knowledge or skills, and the performance of good magic. In *Daemonologie*, King James undoubtedly referred to the experiences of cunning folk when he claimed that 'sundrie Witches have gone to death with that confession, that they have ben transported with the *Phairie* to such a hill, which opening, they went in, and there saw a faire Queene, who being now lighter, gave them a stone that had sundrie virtues'.[52] That James accurately reflected folk belief is evinced by the confession of Fifeshire cunning woman Alison Peirson (1588), who claimed that she gained knowledge of herbs and healing magic from her visits into fairyland.[53] Similarly, Webster's northcountry cunning man claimed that a fairy woman:

> led him to a little Hill and she knocked three times, and the Hill opened, and they went in, and came to a fair hall, wherein was a Queen sitting in great state, and many people about her, and the Gentlewoman that brought him, presented him to the Queen, and she said she was welcom, and bid the Gentlewoman give him some of the white powder, and teach him how to use it; which she did, and gave him a little wood box full of the white powder, and bad him give 2 or 3 grains of it to any that were sick, and it would heal them, and so she brought him forth of the Hill, and so they parted . . . when he wanted (more powder) he went to that Hill, and knocked three times, and said every time I am coming, I am coming, whereaupon it opened, and he going in was conducted by the aforesaid Woman to the Queen, and so had more powder given him.[54]

As with so many generalizations concerning the practice of magic in early modern Britain, the correlation between bad magic and the sabbath and good magic and fairyland is an overly simplistic one. In many cases the moral ambivalence that we have already observed in both witches and cunning folk was reflected in their magical activities at these events. Some witches claimed to have performed good magic at the sabbath, just as some cunning folk claimed to have performed harmful magic in fairyland. As we have already seen in chapter FOUR, examples of this type of moral overlap can be found in the trial confessions given by Nairnshire witch Isobel Gowdie, at Auldearne, in 1662. Isobel claimed that her sabbath experiences included the learning of maleficent spells and the performance of harmful magic. She described stealing crops from fields, milk from cows and fish from fishing boats; raising winds, killing people with elf-arrows and increasing the sickness of a local minister with whom she and her company had a grievance. However, Isobel interdispersed these descriptions of malevolent magical acts with claims that during these adventures she and her companions performed a complex ritual through which they transferred the sickness from a bewitched child onto a dog or cat, and that the Devil taught them spells with which they could cure broken limbs and fevers.[55]

Scottish descriptions of visits to fairyland and attendance at the sabbath also frequently include references to experiences of 'flight'. The belief that fairies travelled through the air, and that they could carry human beings with them, was an established part of early modern folklore and several contemporary anecdotes relate how ordinary people could find themselves transported in 'fairy whirlwinds'.[56] Not surprisingly, a number of cunning folk claimed that they travelled in this way. Isobel Haldane (Perthshire, 1623) maintained that she was 'lying in hir bed, [when] scho wes taikin furth, quhidder be God or the Deuill scho knawis nocht: wes caryit to ane hill-syde: the hill oppynit and scho enterit in'.[57] Likewise, several decades later when the Fairy Boy of Leith joined the fairies on Thursday evening under the 'great Hill between *Edenborough* and *Leith*' airborne travel with the fairies was often part of the entertainment. The boy claimed that 'many times we are carried to *France*, or *Holland* in a night, and return again; and whilst we are there we enjoy all the pleasures the Country doth afford'.[58] Witches frequently described similar flight experiences. Bessie Flinker (East Lothian, 1661) was 'taken upon the hills by a whirle of wind and masked herselfe, and there daunced with the rest' while John Fian (East Lothian, 1591) claimed that he was 'carried to North Berwick kirk (he being lying in a closed bed in Prestonpans), as if he had been soughing athwart the earth [rushing with a whistling sound above the earth]'.[59] Several sabbath accounts from this period also describe 'animal metamorphosis', that is, the changing of a human into animal form, a process which could also occur outside the sabbath.[60] Renfrewshire witch Marie Lamont (1662), for example, claimed that at the end of a sabbath she and her companions changed into animal form in order to be able to perform maleficent magic: 'The end of their meitting' she confessed 'was to raise stormie weather to hinder boats from the killing fishing; and shee confessed that shee, Kettie Scot, and Margrat Holm, cam to Allan Orr's house in the likeness of kats, and followed his wif into the chalmer, where they took a herring owt of a barrell, and having taken a byt off it, they left it behind them; the qlk herring the said Allan his wif did eat, and yairefter taking heavy disease, died.'[61] Nairnshire witch Isobel Gowdie (1662), on the other hand, sometimes combined animal metamorphosis with flight in order to, like the fairies, gain access to people's houses for the rather more benign purpose of consuming food and ale:

> I haid a little horse, and wold say, 'HORSE AND HATTOCK, IN THE DIVELLIS NAME!' And than we wold flie away, quhair we wold, be evin as strawes wold flie upon an hie-way . . . Quhen we wilbe in the shap of crowes, we will be larger than ordinar crowes, and will sitt upon brenches of treis. We went in the shape of rewkis to *Mr Robert Donaldsones* hous, THE DIVELL, and *Johne Taylor*, and his wyff, went in at the kitchen chimney, and went down upon the crowk. It wes about *Lambes*, in anno 1659; they opened an window, and (we) went all in to the hous, and gott beiffe and drink thair; bot did no more harme.[62]

Other accounts describe animal metamorphosis seemingly undertaken for no other reason than the sheer joy of it. Northumberland witch Anne Armstrong (1673) claimed that while she was at the sabbath she was commanded to sing, while 'they [her companions] dansed in severall shapes first of a haire then of their owne and then in a catt sometimes in a mouse and severall other shapes'.[63]

Fairy Taboos

Witches often seem to have been reluctant to talk about their familiar spirits – both during the course of their everyday lives, and in courts of law. When Elizabeth Bennett (Essex, 1582) was accused of possessing them, she first 'denied the same with many oaths, saying that she was well assured that she had none such'. Under increasing interrogatorial pressure, however, Elizabeth subsequently gave a detailed description of her interactions with several animal familiars on a variety of different occasions.[64] This pattern of denial followed by detailed confession, is scattered throughout witch-trial records from the period and could be seen to support the hypothesis that descriptions of demon familiars found in these records were largely élite in origin. From this perspective, the witch was telling the truth when denying any dealings with spirits, and her fantastic stories about demonaic entities were only fabricated gradually, and reluctantly, in response to the manipulative questioning and emotional intimidation of her interrogators. Nevertheless, it is also equally possible that the witchcraft prosecutors were often right, and that when the accused denied any dealings with spirit familiars she was genuinely trying to conceal beliefs and experiences surrounding her supernatural allies. Furthermore, these lies may not have been rooted purely in fear of legal reprisal, but may also have been rooted in fear of the familiar's wrath. Several confessions describe demon familiars urging the witch to keep their dealings secret. Ellen Greenliefe (Suffolk, 1645) claimed that one of her spirits (which appeared in the form of 'a mole, soft and cold') predicted that she would be arraigned as a witch and 'threatened that if she confessed, he would cause her to put herself to death, when he would have her soul'.[65] Even more dramatically, John Reid (Argyll, 1697) claimed that 'the foul fiend' gave him and his companions 'a morsel of an unchristened child's liver to eat, as a sovereign remedy against confession when apprehended'.[66] Working with the élite-origin-only theory of familiar belief, it would be easy to assume that references to taboos imposed by demons were super-imposed élite rationalizations of the witch's refusal to confess to dealings with familiars. Such explanations, while they may be true in part, completely overlook the fact that in imposing taboos on his human allies, the demon familiar was behaving little differently from the fairy.

For common folk in this period, any contact with the fairies was hedged about by strict taboos. It was believed that any individual who carelessly talked about their dealings with the fairies would almost certainly lose any benefit they may have gained from them. Cunning folk, whose livelihoods often depended on the goodwill of these capricious spirits, were likely to have been particularly careful on this score. Joan Tyrry (Somerset, 1555) claimed that 'she would never again see the fairies after having been made to confess her dealings with them before an ecclesiastical court'.[67] Alice West (Fulham, 1613), on the other hand, who claimed to intercede with the fairies on behalf of her clients, told the latter not to reveal their business to anyone 'for if it were revealed to any save them three whom it did essentially concerne, they should not onely hazard their good fortune, but incurre the danger of the fayries, and so consequently be open to great mishapes, and fearefull disasters'.[68] Some trial records reveal fairy familiars, like their demonic counterparts, verbally setting such prohibitions in place. Edward Cowan and Lizanne Henderson tell us that Donald McIlmichall (Argyll, 1677) 'was made to swear an oath of secrecy by his fairy contacts. He broke his oath by confiding in a friend and was duly punished: "He was engadgeit to conceall them [the fairies] and no to tell other. Bot that he told it to . . . Robert Buchanan once for which he was reproved and stricken be them".'[69] Similarly, Alison Peirson

(Fifeshire, 1588) claimed, rather dramatically, that the fairies told her 'gif scho wald speik and tell of thame and thair doingis, thay sould martir hir'.[70] Bessie Dunlop's claim that Tom 'had forbiddin hir, that, quhair evir sche saw him, or mett with him, sche suld nevir speik to him, unless he spak to hir first' is likely to have been rooted in similar beliefs.[71] Fairy tales from the period and later, also often describe the dire consequences which result from the breaking of fairy taboos.

This reluctance to talk publicly about relationships with familiars may be one of the reasons why the magical use of spirits by cunning folk in Britain in this period remains so hidden from our view. On the one hand, the forceful interrogatorial procedure employed by witchcraft prosecutors undoubtedly acted as an effective tool for breaking through this wall of silence and most of the extant descriptions detailing the relationships between cunning folk and their fairy familiars owe their existence to the efficiency of these coercive interventions. On the other hand, it is also likely that many cunning folk resisted these intrusions, and escaped the law courts with their secrets safely untouched, thus shielding their fairy familiars from the hostile eyes of their early modern persecutors and, by the same token, the fascinated gaze of later centuries.

CHAPTER SIX

Renunciation and Pact

The girl had been so gatless that she had never learnt to spin, so there was nothing for it but to sit and cry. Presently there came a tap-tap at the window, and in came a little black thing, with a long tail . . . 'What are you crying for, my girl?' it says; and after this and that she told it. 'I'll spin the skeins for you,' it said, 'and every day you shall have three guesses at my name, and if you don't guess it by the end of the month, you're mine for ever.'[1]

There was once a poor old fisherman, and one year he was not getting much fish. On a day of days, while he was fishing, there rose a sea-maiden at the side of his boat, and she asked him, 'Are you getting much fish?' The old man answered and said, 'Not I.' 'What reward would you give me for sending plenty of fish to you?' 'Ach!' said the old man, 'I have not much to spare.' 'Will you give me the first son you have?' said she. 'I would give ye that, were I to have a son,' said he. 'Then go home, and remember me when your son is twenty years of age, and you yourself will get plenty of fish after this.' Everything happened as the sea maiden said . . . [2]

In the last two chapters we have seen how encounter-narratives describing the relationships between cunning folk and their fairy familiars closely resemble encounter-narratives describing the relationships between witches and their demon familiars. In both cases the familiar appears spontaneously before the magical practitioner when they are alone and in trouble, or is passed on from another cunning woman or witch. In both cases the familiar takes on a variety of human and animal forms, offers the human magical aid (the moral nature of which reflects the moral disposition of the magical practitioner) and enters into a long-term and usually intimate, working relationship with them which can be characterized by journeys into another place (the sabbath or fairyland) where participants can enjoy feasting, drinking, dancing, music, flight experiences, animal metamorphosis and the learning and performance of magic. Despite this congruity, however, until recently the resemblances between the encounter-narratives of cunning folk and those of witches, and the significance which these resemblances may have for our understanding of popular magic in this period, have been largely overlooked by historians. While this oversight can be attributed to many causes, the most likely must be the distracting effects of what we can term the 'specifically demonological' elements found in the source material.

Any encounter-narrative, whether given by a cunning woman or a witch, was, from an orthodox theological perspective, fundamentally 'demonological' by definition, that is, concerned with spirits not sanctioned as 'good' by the early modern Church and thereby coming under the umbrella definition of 'demon'. Despite having a generally 'demonological' nature, encounter-narratives also contain what can be termed 'specifically demonological elements', that is, elements which refer to specific and very conscious, ritual commitments to the Devil. The most significant of these relate to the 'demonic pact': the bargain made between witch and demon familiar wherein the witch renounces Christianity and pledges her soul to the Devil in return for the familiar's magical aid. In some witch-confessions, these specifically demonological elements seem to be superimposed, rather uneasily, upon a narrative wholly unassociated with such concerns, whereas in others they seem to be deeply woven into the very heart of the witch's story. Since the early twentieth century, when sixteenth- and seventeenth-century witchcraft became the focus of scholarly interest, the derivation of these specifically demonological elements have been a matter of debate. However, until recently, most historians have tended to assume that they were likely to have been rooted in élite rather than popular culture.

There is some support for this view. Throughout the Middle Ages and the early modern period, scholars and ecclesiastics, obsessed with the perceived threat of the Devil and the rise of heresy, formulated complex demonological ideas about the pact and other features of the relationship between a witch and the Devil or demon familiar. Scholars consequently assumed that the appearance of these ideas in witch-confessions was the result of learned influences either during the trial itself and/or prior to the trial. In the former case it was believed that interrogators imposed their élite preconceptions onto the witch's narrative as she stood before them in the courtroom, and in the latter, that the witch herself brought élite ideas to the trial, these ideas having, over a period of many decades, trickled down into the popular imagination through a process of downward filtration. These historiographical assumptions have meant that scholars have only just begun to seriously consider evidence of a relationship between specifically demonological ideas found in witch trials and indigenous folk beliefs. At present, such considerations remain largely at the level of qualifying statements. In 2000, for example, Lawrence Normand and Gareth Roberts put forward the conventional view that 'Notions of convention and band' found in Scottish witch trials 'are more likely to be élite understandings of supposed witchcraft activities than the accused's self-perception' – however they conclude the assertion with the proviso 'though we cannot be sure'.[3] In this chapter we shall go one step further, and illustrate how most of the specifically demonological elements found in early modern witch trials can also be found represented in some form in fairy beliefs of the period. A correlation which suggests that the folkloric contribution to encounter-narratives may have been far greater than is generally assumed.

Renunciation and Pact

By the early modern period learned ideas about the contract made between demon familiar and witch had accreted into a stereotype which would have been familiar to all officials who interrogated magical practitioners on charges of witchcraft or sorcery. The stereotype depicted the demon familiar making a variety of contractual demands in return for his magical services. The two core demands, which together comprised the 'classical' pact, were that the witch renounce her Christianity and that she pledge her soul to him. Other ancillary contractual demands (which were often made at the sabbath) were, among others, that the witch marry him and/or have sexual relations with him; that she serve and worship him; that she allow herself to be re-named by him; that she give him her blood; that she permit herself to be marked by him and that she participate in acts of exhumation and cannibalism.

The contractual element to the witch's relationship with her demon familiar was of intense interest to witchcraft prosecutors. Proving that the alleged witch had made a contract with the demon familiar was unequivocal evidence of her guilt. From a theological perspective, any commerce between a witch and her familiar theoretically involved an implicit or tacit contract, and was therefore enough to condemn her, however prosecutors still took a great deal of trouble to uncover evidence of more explicit negotiations.[4] To have made an explicit contract, the alleged witch would have to have openly and verbally contracted with her demon familiar, freely promising to meet certain demands in return for its help. Hardly surprisingly, descriptions of demonic pacts, containing one or more contractual demands, occur almost universally in confessions containing descriptions of encounters with demon familiars. However, these types of contractual demands, as we shall see, were not the exclusive preserve of the Devil and his cohorts.

Contracting with Fairies

Ideas about contractual relationships between humans and spirits were widely found in popular fairy beliefs throughout early modern Britain. Even the most ordinary type of non-visual relationship between human and fairy was implicitly contractual in nature. The housewife would leave bread and water in the kitchen at night for the fairies to drink in the hope that, in return, the fairies might leave silver in her shoes. Such reciprocity was motivated by fear as well as hope of gain, John Aubrey claiming that 'Countrey-people . . . were wont to please the Fairies, *that* they might doe them no shrewd turnes [my italics].'[5] In the less-commonly experienced 'visual' relationship between human and fairy (the kind of relationship most likely to have been experienced by magical practitioners) the implicit contract found at the core of the ordinary non-visual relationship became concretized. That which was implicit in the 'ordinary' relationship became explicit in the 'extraordinary': the unseen fairy became seen; the unheard voice became heard; and those things which the human ordinarily desired from the fairy in thought, could be verbally demanded for. It is hardly surprising, then, that we should find cunning folk testifying that they believed themselves to have *overtly contracted* with visually-encountered fairies. Tom Reid, for example, constantly made demands of Bessie Dunlop in return for his supernatural aid, demands which ranged from the seemingly innocuous verbal request that she 'trust in him' to more physical attempts to coerce her to accompany him into fairyland.[6] Alison Peirson (Fifeshire, 1588) claimed that the fairies 'wald cum and sitt besyde hir [as she lay sick in bed], and promesit that scho sould nevir want, *gif* [if] scho wald be faithfull and keip promeis [my italics]'.[7] Alternatively, in the following century Webster's northcountry cunning man claimed that a fairy woman told him that '*If* he would follow her counsel she would help him [my italics]'.[8] Rather more dramatically, in a variation on the 'taboo' theme, Elspeth Reoch (Orkney, 1616) claimed that she sacrificed her power of speech in order to avail herself of a fairy's magical skills (in a manner redolent of Hans Christian Andersen's famous 'Little

Mermaid').[9] Some of the invocatory rituals described in magical manuals which betray popular origins also contain contractual elements. One such, described by folklorist Katharine Briggs as 'a pure piece of folk-lore', concludes a description of the long and complex preparations needed to summon a fairy with the exhortation that the invoker 'Then covenant with her for all matters convenient for your purpose and she wilbe always with you of this assure yourselfe for it is proved.'[10] Similarly blatant was the contract made between Joan Willimot (Leicestershire, 1619) and a fairy woman.[11]

Later sources clearly indicate that contractual relationships with visually-encountered fairies were also integral to nineteenth- and early twentieth-century folk belief. In Scotland, the fairy 'Men and Women of Peace' were believed to habitually form 'alliances' with mortals and negotiate to work with them for a prescribed length of time, for an agreed payment, in a manner redolent of the bargains sometimes struck between early modern Scottish witches and the Devil.[12] This contractual theme will also strike a chord in anyone familiar with traditional European folk tales. Time and time again these tales record a suffering human protagonist striking a deal with the supernatural being who offers them help.[13]

Whether it was explicit or implicit, the contract made between human and fairy constituted a series of mutual demands. Most of these demands, as we have seen in previous chapters, were simple and pragmatic: the human, for example, might desire good health, good luck or prosperity; while the fairy, in turn, might desire food and drink, generosity, or respect. Rather more surprising, however, is the fact that we can find the specifically demonological requests that the human renounce their Christianity and pledge their soul featuring among the contractual demands made by the fairy familiar.

The Renunciation

And Thom promeist hir bayth geir, horsis, and ky, and uthir graith, gif scho wald denye hir Christindome, and the faith sche tuke at the funt-stane. Quhairunto sche answerit, 'That gif sche suld be revin at horis-taillis, sche suld nevir do that;' bot promeist to be leill and trew to him in onye thing sche culd do.[14]

The renunciation of Christianity was one of the two core demands which sat at the heart of the stereoptypical pact made between witch and demon familiar and this demand appears in the majority of trial-derived encounter-narratives. Helen Clarke (Essex, 1645), claimed that her famil-iar (in the form of a white dog called 'Elimanzer') 'appeared to her in her house . . . and bade her deny Christ, and shee should never want' while in Suffolk in the same year Joane Ruce claimed that three familiars, called Touch, Pluck and Take, appeared before her in 'the likeness of mice', and spoke to her 'with a great hollow voice, and asked her to deny God and Christ and told her, if she would, she would never want meat, drink, or clothes, or money'.[15] Several hundred miles to the north, Isobel Smith (Angus, 1661) 'confessed covenant and pactione with the divell . . . years agoe, when she dwelt in Hillsyd, the conditiones quherof was: That shee should renunce God and hir baptisme'.[16]

This demand for renunciation, so exclusively associated with the demon familiar, also features in the contractual relationship between human and fairy. As we have already seen in chapter ONE, the distinction between 'Christian' and 'pre-Christian' beliefs was very blurred in the early modern period, particularly on a popular level. On the one hand, many common people, and in particular, popular magical practitioners, saw no inconsistency in juggling their fairy beliefs alongside their Christian beliefs. Katharine Briggs points to this paradox when she argues that early modern witches 'practised their magical rites as many Irish peas-ants do today, side by side with their Christian observances, attempting no rational reconciliation between the two; for it is possible for most people to keep two quite irreconcilable beliefs alive at the same time'.[17] A number of encounter-narratives illustrate the belief that the fairies served the Christian God and were therefore, to all intents and purposes, Christians. Somerset cunning woman Joan Tyrry (1555) claimed that her 'healing of man and beast, by the power of God taught to her by the . . . fairies, be both godly and good' while Perthshire cunning woman Janet Trall (1623) claimed that her fairy familiar told her to 'speak of God, and do good to poor folks'.[18] On the other hand, other encounter-narratives and fairy-anecdotes present us with a slightly more complex picture of the relationship between popular Christianity and fairy belief. Aberdeenshire cunning man Andro Man (1598) claimed that his fairy familiars could appear as, among other forms, both the queen of the fairies and an angel called 'Christsonday', and that the latter familiar worked on his religious conscience by reminding him of the imminence of judgement day, even claiming that Andro Man himself would be one of those to help in this final reckoning of mortal souls. Against this description we then have to set the fact that Andro Man also believed that his fairy familiar had 'a thraw by God' and would be 'cassin in the fyre [on judgement day]'.[19] Bessie Dunlop's fairy familiar, Tom Reid, had a similarly complex char-acter. On some occasions Tom, like Andro Man's Christsonday, took on the role of religious confessor – at one point advising Bessie, with some urgency, to mend her relationship with God. At a subsequent meeting, however, we find him demanding that Bessie renounce her Christian faith in return for his services, promising her 'bayth geir, horsis, and ky, and uthir graith, gif scho wald denye hir Christindome, and the faith sche tuke at the funt-stane'.[20]

Any spirit of pre-Christian provenance which had escaped wholesale assimilation into the Christian pantheon was officially defined as an 'evil spirit' by most contemporary theologians. Such a negative definition was reflected in the fact that fairies, on their part, were often considered hostile towards Christianity. An anecdote recorded in Scotland at the beginning of the eighteenth century describes how a brownie was displeased when his master read the Bible.[21] Alternatively, the Devil told Suffolk witch Mary Skipper (1645) to go to church 'and make a great show, but if she attended diligently he would nip her.'[22] This fairy hostility is described in more detail by Robert Kirk when he claims that the fairies have 'no discernible Religion, Love, or Devotione towards God the Blessed Maker of all. They disappear whenever they hear his name invoked, or the name of Jesus . . . nor can they act ought at that time, after hearing of that Sacred Name.'[23]

Many early modern individuals would have been aware, to a greater or lesser degree, of these mutual hostilities and if they wished to avail themselves of fairy powers they must have circumnavigated this problem in some way. Their solutions may not have differed greatly from those used in later centuries by people who believed in fairies. In the nineteenth century, when at sea, fishermen on the Moray Firth 'would never mention such words as Church or manse or minister. Any utterance suggestive of the new faith would be displeasing to the ancient god of the ocean, and might bring disaster upon the boat'.[24] By their silence the fishermen were, for the duration of their journey, making a superficial show of putting aside their Christian allegiances in return for the protection and goodwill of 'the ancient god of the ocean'. It is not difficult to imagine how in a different century and different context, this and other types of diplomacy towards non-Christian powers could have been interpreted as a betrayal of the official faith.

For many educated people in early modern Britain any dealings with spirits hostile to Christianity were theoretically a betrayal or 'renunciation' of the true faith. The case of Edinburgh cunning woman Jean Weir (1670), illustrates how ideas about renunciation could be woven into a fairy-encounter. Jean was a schoolteacher and therefore more educated than your average popular magical practitioner. The dittays from Jean's trial records state that:

when she keeped a school at Dalkeith, and teached childering, ane tall woman came to the declarant's hous when the childering were there; and that she had, as appeared to her, ane chyld upon her back, and on or two at her foot; and that the said woman desyred that the declarant should imploy her to spick for her to the Queen of Farie, and strik and battle in her behalf with the said Queen, (which was her own words); and that the next day ane little woman came to the declarant, and did give her a piece of a tree, or the root of some herb or tree, as she thought, and told her that als long as she had the samen, she wold be able to doe what she should desyre; and then the said woman did lay ane cloth upon the floor near the door, and caused the declarant set her foot upon the samen, and her hand upon the crown of her own head, and cause the declarant repeit these words thrice, viz. 'All my cross and trubles goe to the door with the;' which accordinglie she did; and that she gave the woman all the silver she hade, being some few turners, and some meall; and that after the said woman went away, the declarant did spin a verie short tyme, and that she did find more yearne upon her pirne, and good yearne, nor she thought could be spun in so short a tyme; which did so affright the declarant, that she did set bye her wheile, and did shut the door, and did stay within her house for the space of twentie dayes or thereby, and was exceedinglie trubled, and weeped becaus she thought what she had done in manner forsaid was *in effect* the renuncing of her baptisme. [my italics][25]

Several Scottish witches describe a ritual act similar to that performed by Jean, involving the symbolic encapsulation of the body between the crown of the head and the sole of the foot, and clearly associate it with the renunciation of Christianity. Marie Lamont (Renfrewshire, 1662) confessed that:

at that tyme the devill bad her betak herself to his service, and it sould be weel with her, and bad her forsak her baptizme, which shee did, delyvering herself wholly to him, by putting her one hand on the crown of her head, and the other hand to the sole of her fott, and giving all betwixt these two into him.[26]

Similar rituals were also practised by cunning folk, particularly in Scotland.[27] Kirk describes how Scottish seers used the following ritual to enable a 'curious person' to gain a glimpse of the fairies: the person 'is to put his foot on the Seers foot, and the Seers hand is put on the Inquirers head, who is to look over the Wizards right shoulder . . . then he will see a multitude of Wights'. Although Kirk does not consider such a ritual to be immoral, he does voice concerns about its implications, noting that it 'hes an ill appearance, as if by this ceremonie, an implicite surrender were made of all betwixt the Wizards foot and his hand ere the person can be admitted a privado to the art'.[28] It is not difficult to see how descriptions of such ceremonies aroused the suspicions of witch-craft prosecutors.

It is possible that many overt renunciations found in confessions for witchcraft mask the more implicit renunciations common to those nego-tiating with the fairies. Whoever recorded the confession of Essex witch Elizabeth Francis (1566), as it appears in a pamphlet, wrote that Elizabeth was advised by her grandmother to 'renounce GOD and His word, and to give of her blood to Satan (as she termed it)'.[29] The bracketed phrase 'as she termed it' strongly suggests that Elizabeth's version of events may have been rephrased into something more demonologically coherent by either the prosecution or the pamphleteer. The argument for the implicit renunciation, of course, also strengthens the case for the explicit. To enter-tain the possibility that some individuals may have openly verbalized the normally tacit renunciation, particularly in the context of a believed visual encounter, is not unreasonable. Fifeshire cunning woman Alison Peirson (1588), for example, claimed that 'thair come ane man to hir, cled in grene clathis, quha said to hir, 'Gif [if] scho wald be faithfull, he wald do hir guid';[30] Alison only needed to say 'yes' and we have, according to prose-cutorial perception at least, an explicit renunciation. A similar interpretative process occurred in Bessie Dunlop's case. Despite the fact that Bessie claimed to have refused to renounce her Christianity, protesting that even if 'sche suld be revin at horis-taillis, sche suld nevir do that', the fact that Bessie promised to 'trow in' Tom and 'be leill and trew to him in onye thing sche culd do' was, in the eyes of her prosecu-tors, tantamount to an explicit renunciation.[31]

The Demand for the Soul

thai war the gude wychtis that wynnit in the Court of Elfame; quha come thair to desyre hir to go with thame: And forder, Thom desyrit hir to do the sam; quha answerit, 'Sche saw na proffeit to gang thai kynd of gaittis, unles sche kend quhairhor!' Thom said, 'Seis thow nocht me, baith meit-worth, claith-worth, and gude aneuch lyke in persoun; and (he?) suld make hir far better nor ever sche was?' Sche answerit, 'That sche duelt with hir awin husband and bairnis, and culd nocht leif thame.'[32]

The second demand at the core of the stereotypical demonic pact was the demon familiar's request that the witch surrender her soul to him in return for his magical services. The demand for the soul, though not so common as the demand for renunciation, still makes a frequent appearance in witchcraft confessions throughout Britain in this period. Lancashire witch Elizabeth Southerns (1612) confessed that she 'was coming homeward from begging' when she met 'a spirit or devil in the shape of a boy, the one half of his coat black and the other brown, who bade this examinate stay, saying to her that if she would give him her soul, she should have anything that she would request.'[33] Sometimes the familiar demanded that the soul be handed over after a specific number of years, or at death, Huntingdonshire witch Anne Desborough (1646) claiming that two spirits in the form of mice called 'Tib' and 'Jone' told her that 'when she dyed, they must have her soule'.[34]

The historiographical assumption that beliefs concerning the familiar's demand for the soul were of learned origin would seem to be corroborated by the fact that this demand almost exclusively appears in encounter-narratives involving demon familiars, and that very few encounter-narratives describe fairies making overt demands for the soul. The following example, found in the confession of Leicestershire cunning woman Joan Willimot (1618), is virtually unique. Joan claimed that:

> (her master) willed her to open her mouth and he would blow into her a fairy which should do her good. And that she opened her mouth, and he did blow into her mouth, and that presently after his blowing, there came out of her mouth a spirit which stood upon the ground in the shape and form of a woman, which spirit did ask of her soul, which she then promised unto it . . . the use which she had of the spirit was to know how those did which she had undertaken to amend.[35]

It would be easy to assume that this description of the fairy's demand for Joan's soul was the result of learned intervention; that Joan's prosecutors, eager to find evidence of the stereotypical demonic pact, inserted the demand for the soul (through suggestion, coercion and so on) into an otherwise benign fairy encounter-narrative. But such an explanation is not the only one.

In the early modern period, beliefs about fairies were closely linked to beliefs about the human soul and this link was most commonly forged in relation to notions surrounding human travel with the fairies or entry into fairyland. Transition into the fairy world was believed to occur either 'in body' or 'in spirit'. In the former case, the physical body either completely disappeared or was replaced with a fairy 'stock'. Nairnshire witch Isobel Gowdie (1662), for example, claimed that when she and her companions travelled with the fairies, they would:

> flie away whair (evir we wold); and least our husbandis sould miss us out of our beddiss, we put in a boosom, or a thrie (leggit stoole besyde thame)

and say thryse over, 'I LAY down this boosom (or stooll) in THE DIVELLIS name, Let it not Steir . . . (Quhill I) com again!' And immediatlie it seimis a woman, besyd our husbandis.[36]

Alternatively, when transition into the fairy world occurred 'in spirit' it was only the spiritual part of the human (which in Christian terms would be called the soul) that went into fairyland, leaving the material body behind: an event which was, as we shall discuss in detail later in chapter TEN, generally associated with trance states. In *Daemonologie*, for example, King James describes how some witches 'sayeth, that their bodies lying stil as in an extasy, their spirits will be ravished out of their bodies, & caried to such places. And for verefying therof, wil give evident tokens, aswel by witnesses that have seene their body lying senseles in the meane time, as by naming persones, whomwith they mette'.[37] Similarly, in 1675 the Synod of Aberdeen recorded that it had received 'divers complaints and reports . . . by several brethren that some under pretence of trances or familiarities of spirits of going with these spirits commonly called the fairies'.[38] This *spiritual* as opposed to *bodily* interpretation of human entry into fairyland corresponds with evidence, most frequently found in Scottish sources, pointing to an association between fairies and the dead. It was commonly believed that some (or all) fairies were souls of the dead, albeit clothed in some type of astral form. After natural death human souls might find themselves in fairyland, or living humans taken into or visiting the fairy realm could find themselves unwilling or unable to leave, resulting in the death of the mortal body.

Throughout the early modern period human presence in fairyland, whether in body or in spirit, was believed to have been actively encouraged by the fairies. Although this fairy enthusiasm was most notoriously associated with the theft of newborn babies, the fairy was also believed to desire adult human company. This desire was prompted by a variety of motives ranging from amorousness to the more practical need for human skills in wetnursing, warfare, sport, music and so on. Nairnshire witch Isobel Gowdie (1662) and Edinburgh cunning woman Jean Weir (1670) both talked of helping the fairies with their fighting skills.[39] On a lighter note, the Fairy Boy of Leith claimed that his drumming skills were enjoyed by the fairies while Argyllshire cunning man Donald McIlmichal (1677) claimed that after entering a fairy hill he met many men and women 'and he playd on trumps to them quhen they danced'.[40] Sometimes the fairy was motivated by darker intentions, plotting to keep the human in fairyland permanently, against their wishes, or to use them as part of their seven-yearly *teind* [tithe] to hell.[41] Although some humans enjoyed their forays into the magical world of the fairies, others, such as Bessie

A late fifteenth-century German woodcut depicting the famous English 'Witch of Berkeley' (who promised her soul to the Devil in return for his magical favours) being carried away by her demonic ally.

A sixteenth-century depiction of a visit to a fairy hill. From *Historia de Gentibus Septentrionalibus* by Olaus Magnus (1555)

Dunlop, were reluctant to embark on such adventures and in these instances the fairies were compelled to actively encourage human entry.[42] Sometimes this encouragement involved coercion or intimidation. Susan Swapper (Wales, 1607) was so frightened when a fairy woman in a 'green petticoat' appeared before her one night saying 'Sue, come and go with me or else I will carry thee' – that she begged her husband to protect her, claiming, 'Here is a thing that will carry me away'.[43] On other occasions, however, the fairies employed more subtle methods, such as enticement, trickery and even bargaining, tempting the human with the delights of fairy revelry, the promise of material gain, or the getting of magical help or knowledge and so on. Bessie herself was prey to such gentler tactics, claiming that the 'gude wychtis' from the 'Court of Elfame' rather politely 'baid hir sit doun, and said, "Welcum, Bessie, will thow go with us?"' – Tom Reid telling her that to do so would 'make hir far better nor ever sche was'.[44]

In the context of the *spiritual interpretation* of entry into fairyland, whichever method the fairy employed to bring the human into their world, and for whatever reason they wanted them there, the fairy would have been, in effect, desiring and appropriating (for a given length of time) the human spirit or soul. In the same context, those individuals who were tempted to enter fairyland voluntarily, for whatever reason, would have been aware that their visit amounted to a temporary, albeit tacit, commitment of their soul to (be used/enjoyed by) the fairies – a transaction which amounted to an implicit contract. Moreover, if the human entered fairyland through some sort of negotiation (and cunning folk, confident and pragmatic about spirits and their ways, were the individuals most likely to do this), then we have something very like an explicit contract for the soul. To compound matters still further, the spiritual interpretation of entry into fairyland was linked to the belief that on death the human soul could find itself permanently in the fairy world and any human who believed themselves to have a relationship with a fairy, even if did not involve visits to fairyland, was likely to have been aware that such a fate was a possibility. It is not illogical to suppose that any prolonged and/or intimate involvement with the fairies, such as that enjoyed by some cunning folk, may have been considered to increase the possibility of such a fate, or to suppose that the issue of the soul's final resting place could have become a 'bargaining chip' in such a context. Even if the spiritual interpretation of entry into fairyland and its associated beliefs were not consciously involved in a cunning man or woman's encounter experience, it is not difficult to envisage how they could have been brought into the equation by an interrogator searching out the stereotypical demonic pact. This explanation would account for the fact that the demon familiar's demand for the soul most frequently occurs in Scottish witch-narratives, for in the latter we find that the witch's interaction with her familiar often pre-dates a sabbath experience, and as we have seen in the chapter FIVE, there are strong links between attendance at the sabbath and visits to fairyland.

'Cold as Clay': Lying with the Devil

> Interrogat, Gif evir sche had bene in suspect place with Thom, or had carnell deil with him? Declarit nocht upoun hir salvatioun and condemnatioun.[45]

A significant minority of witch-trial records, particularly those from Scotland, feature the demon familiar demanding sexual relations from the witch in return for magical favours. Some witches resisted this demand. Jane Wallis (Huntingdonshire, 1646) claimed that 'hee [the Devil] would have lain with her, but shee would not suffer him' although she later admitted that the Devil 'had the use of her body once, twice, and some-times thrice in a week'.[46] Such descriptions often allude to the 'coldness' of the demon familiar. Mary Bush (Suffolk, 1645) claimed that the Devil visited her bed several times a week, but that 'he was colder than man, and heavier, and could not perform nature as man'.[47] In Angus, nearly twenty years later, Isobel Smith claimed that 'whill shee wes alone gath-ering heather hee [the Devil] appeared to hir alone lik ane braw gentleman . . . and that tyme they maid ther covenant, and he kissed hir and lay with hir, as shee thought, and his mouth and breath [were] very cold, and his body lyk clay'.[48] For some witches, sexual relations with the familiar were part of marriage. Ellen Driver (Suffolk, 1645) confessed that many years previously 'the Devil had come to her in the form of a man with cloven feet. He persuaded her to renounce God and the Church, and afterwards he married her'. Ellen claimed that she then lived with him for three years, and bore him two children, both of which were changelings.[49] In Essex in the same year Rebecca West claimed that 'the Devill appeared to her . . . as shee was going to bed, and told her, that he would marry her, and that shee could not deny him; shee said he kissed her, but was as cold as clay, and married her that night, in this manner; he tooke her by the hand and lead [led] her about the chamber, and promised to be her loving husband till death'.[50]

The sexual relationship between a witch and her demon familiar was discussed in theological writings throughout the Middle Ages and early modern period. Some books on witchcraft, such as the influential *Malleus Maleficarum*, were obsessive in their analysis of the carnal relationship between the witch and the Devil or demon familiar, weaving classical beliefs about incubi and succubi into their arguments.[51] As the witch-craze progressed, sexual relations became primarily associated with the sabbath, and were subsequently more of a concern to Continental prosectors than their British counterparts. An examination of fairy beliefs of the period, however, reveals that the tradition of humans having sexual relations with spirits was deeply rooted in contemporary popular belief.

A significant minority of Scottish cunning folk who were brought before the courts on charges of witchcraft and sorcery confessed to such things. The records pertaining to the trial of Andro Man (Aberdeenshire, 1598) state that 'be the space of threttie twa yeris sensyn or thairby, thow begud to have carnall deall with that devilische spreit, the Quene of Elphen, on quhom thow begat dyveris bairnis, quhom thow hes sene sensyn'.[52] Andro Man seems to have been quite willing to oblige his fairy amour, but some cunning folk, like Elspeth Reoch (Orkney, 1616), were far more reluctant. Elspeth claimed that when she was twelve years old, she was waiting by a lochside for a boat to ferry her across when 'thair cam tua men to her ane cled in blak and the uther with ane grein tartane plaid about him. And that the man with the plaid said to her she wes ane prettie'. The young cunning woman then claimed that some time later, when she was in her sister's house after having just given birth to an illegitimate child, the 'blak man' came back to visit her:

> And callit him selff ane farie man quha wes sumtyme her kinsman callit Johne Stewart quha wes slane be Mc Ky at the doun going of the soone. And therfor nather deid nor leiving bot wald ever go betwixt the heaven and the earth quha delt with you tua nychtis and wald never let her sleip persuading hir to let him ly with her wald give you a guidly fe . . . And upoun the thrid nycht that he com to hir she being asleip and laid his hand upoun hir breist and walkint her And thairefter semeit to ly with her.[53]

For some cunning folk, as for some witches, marriage was also part of the bargain; Elizabeth Barton (Kent, 1534), for example, claiming that 'Satan sought to make her his wife'.[54] That the confessions of these magical practitioners were derived from folk belief as opposed to being the result of élite interrogation is supported by other sources. Fairy tales often feature humans lured into fairyland to be bedded by an amorous fairy, or, less romantically, taken to bear or father children to replenish fairy stock.[55] Thomas the Rhymour, the hero of tales and ballads from the Middle Ages onwards, was tempted into fairyland by his love for a fairy woman who asked him to marry her.[56] Similarly, a seventeeth-century pamphlet describing the adventures of the ubiquitous fairy hobman Robin Goodfellow describes how Robin was the result of a union between a fairy man and a mortal woman:

> This same hee fayry did love a proper young wench, for every night would hee with other fayries come to the house, and there dance in her chamber . . . At last this mayde was with childe, and being asked who was the father of it, she answered a man that nightly came to visit her, but earely in the morning he would go his way, whither she knew not, he went so suddainley.[57]

These beliefs are reflected in the fact that Robert Kirk, when describing the moral faults of the fairies, talks about 'the incontinence of their *leannain Sith* [fairy lovers] or succubi who tryst with men'.[58] We also find references to sexual relations and marriage in later fairy beliefs: in nineteenth-century Scotland, for example, it was believed that the fairy folk named the 'Men and Women of Peace' would contract marriages with humans. Several scholars have pointed out the fact that such beliefs have ancient origins, George Kittredge, for example, linking them to an 'old Teutonic belief in elves or trolls or hillmen that woo or abduct mortal women'.[59]

More Demands: Blood and Milk

The demon familiar's contractual demand for blood appears in a large number of encounter-narratives. Blood could be given in a variety of ways. Throughout Britain we find accounts of the demon familiar or Devil 'scratching', 'pricking' or 'nipping' the witch in order to extract a few drops of blood, the wound thereafter becoming the 'Devil's Mark'. In 1644, a Yarmouth witch claimed that she saw a tall man standing in the moonlight at her door and 'he told her, he must first see her hand; and then taking out something like a Pen-knife, he gave it a little Scratch, so that Blood flowed, and the mark remained to that time'.[60] Animal familiars could extract blood in a similiar way. Suffolk witch Thomas Everard (1645) asserted that 'At night, in bed, something like a rabbit asked him if he would love it, and deny God and Christ. On a second occasion, upon giving consent, it scratched him under his ear, and took blood.'[61] Many English encounter-narratives, particularly those from the Home Counties, also describe animal familiars 'sucking' blood from a 'papp' 'dugg' or 'teat' on the witch's body, this event often occurring on a regular basis, as part of the contractual relationship. Ellen Shepheard (Huntingdonshire,

ROBIN GOOD-FELLOVV,
HIS MAD PRANKES AND MERRY IESTS.

Full of honeſt Mirth, and is a fit Medicine for Melancholy.

Printed at *London* by *Thomas Cotes*, and are to be ſold by *Francis Grove*, at his ſhop on Snow-hill, neere the Sarazens-head. 1639.

Frontispiece from the pamphlet *Robin Goodfellow, his mad prankes and merry jests . . .* (1639). This woodcut illustrates contemporary associations between ideas about fairies (and fairy rings), demon familiars, the witches' sabbath and sexuality.

Depiction of a witch feeding her familiars from a pamphlet recording the trial of Elizabeth Stile, Mother Dutten, Mother Devell and Mother Margaret at Windsor in 1579.

1646) maintained that four familiars in the shape of grey rats promised her 'all happinesse' and that in return they demanded, among other things, that 'they must have blood from her, which she granted, and thereupon they sucked her upon and about her hippes'.[62] Some familiars both scratch and suck. Cecil Ewen tells us how Suffolk witch Elizabeth Hubbard (Suffolk, 1645) was visited by:

> 'three things in the likeness of children', which whispering, asked her 'to deny God, Christ, and all his works, and to cleave to them, and she should want nothing'. These imps named themselves Thomas, Richard, and Hobb. They scratched her back to draw blood for sealing the covenant, and 'used to suck on the marks found upon her'.[63]

Demon familiars, however, were not the only spirits to be interested in such things. In later fairy sources there is evidence that some fairies were believed to consume human blood. Walter Evans-Wentz, for example, records a nineteenth-century anecdote from the Isle of Man: 'At night the fairies came into a house in Glen Rushen to bake. The family had put no water out for them; and a beggar-man . . . heard the fairies say, "We have no water, so we'll take blood out of the toe of the servant who forgot our water." And from the girl's blood they mixed their dough.'[64] This belief was also found in Scotland in the period, John Campbell recording that 'the reason assigned for taking water into the house at night was that the Fairies would suck the sleeper's blood if they found no water to quench their thirst'.[65] Although these examples are nineteenth-century Scottish and Manx, there is one relatively early witchcraft confession which suggests that a similar belief was held in early modern Essex. In 1582 Margery Sammon claimed that her mother had given her some animal familiars in a wicker basket (in the form of toads called 'Tom' and 'Robin') and instructed her on how to use them. The trial dittays state that her mother 'bade her keep them and feed them. This examinate [Margery] asking "wherewithal?" her mother answered, "If thou dost not give them milk, they will suck of thy blood".'[66] This witch's warning to her daughter about the dangers of demon familiars sounds little different to warnings likely to have been given by nineteenth-century Scottish or Manx parents to their children about the dangers of the fairies. It is noticeable that in a significant number of trial records the witch seems to express a reluctance to meet her demon familiar's bloodthirsty demands.

In *The Secret Commonwealth*, Robert Kirk provides evidence of a different kind of link between the feeding habits of the fairies and the bloodlust of the demon familiar when he describes 'the damnable practise of Evil Angels, their sucking of blood and spirits out of Witches bodys (till they drein them, into a deformd and dry leanness) to feed their own

Vehicles withal, leaving what wee call the Witches mark behind'.[67] Kirk's claim that the familiar sucks 'blood *and spirits*' out of the witch is pertinent in the light of another passage in which he claims that fairies gained nourishment by piercing animals with elf-arrows and then sucking out 'the aereal and aethereal parts, the *most spirituous matter* for prolonging of Lyfe . . . leaving the Terrestriall behind [my italics]'.[68] Although Kirk only mentions animals being consumed by fairies in this way, earlier in the same passage he claims that humans can also be 'pierced or wounded with those peoples weapon' and contemporary trial records sometimes contain references to humans having been 'elf-shot'.[69] A later Scottish folk tale in which three of four men are reduced to 'bloodless bodies' because the malevolent banshee (a fairy woman) had 'sucked them dry' resonates with Kirk's descriptions of both demon familiar and fairy feeding habits.[70]

Despite the sensationalism of promising the soul, renouncing Christianity and sucking blood, the most common payment given to the English witch's animal familiar (often in conjunction with payment in blood) was ordinary food. Sometimes these familiars demanded what could be seen as some sort of sacrifice, such as a live chicken, however on a daily basis they generally required nothing more than a bowl of bread, milk, ale, water and so on. This tradition is particularly evident in trial records from Essex: Elizabeth Francis (1566) claimed that she had been given a demon familiar called 'Satan . . . in the likeness of a white spotted cat, and [that her grandmother] taught her to feed the said cat with bread and milk', and Elizabeth Bennett (1582) that she possessed two spirits 'one called Suckin, being black like a dog, the other called Lierd, being red like a lion' and that 'many times they drank of her milk bowl'.[71] In the same region, over eighty years later, Margaret Moone (1645) was accused of feeding her 'twelve impes' with 'bread and beere'.[72] The demon familiar did not usually, explicitly, verbally contract for this form of payment, but it seems to have underpinned the witch/familiar relationship, being employed on a continuous basis rather than in exchange for a particular deed done.

In many parts of early modern Britain fairies were fed in precisely the same way. Like the demon familiar they were partial to the odd animal sacrifice, but most commonly expected simple foodstuffs in return for their services and goodwill. Substances such as ale or milk were often poured on springs, trees and rocks etc. sacred to fairies, while bowls of bread, milk or water and suchlike were left in the kitchen overnight for both domestic hobmen and visiting trooping fairies.[73] John Aubrey recorded that the fairies liked a 'messe of milke sopt with white bread'; Robert Burton that they required 'a pail of clean water, good victuals, and the like'; and Reginald Scot that the hobman Robin Goodfellow needed a 'messe of white bread and milke'.[74] This food and drink was not usually verbally contracted for and seems to have been given on a regular basis, as it was to the demon familiar. According to Scot, Robin Goodfellow's messe of white bread and milk was his 'standing fee'.[75]

CHAPTER SEVEN

Demon and Fairy:
The Interface

deliverit the said Elizabeth Dunlop, to be culpable fylit and convict, off the haill pointis above writtin, and of using of Witchecraft, Sorcerie, and Incantatioun, with Invocatioun of spreitiss of the devill.[1]

The last three chapters have looked in some detail at the relationship between popular magical practitioners and their familiar spirits in early modern Britain. We have shown how encounter-narratives given by both cunning folk and witches share the same basic narrative structure and emotional dynamic. We have also seen that even the most specifically demonological features of the relationship between witches and their demon familiars – such as the renunciation of Christianity, the promise of the soul, sexual relations and the giving of blood – can all be found represented in some form in the relationship between cunning folk and their fairy familiars.

This picture enables us to re-evaluate the way we look at witch-trial material in the period. First, it challenges the traditional historiographical view that popular familiar beliefs were predominantly learned in origin. Although it could still be argued that the fairy familiar's resemblances to the demon familiar represented the downward filtration of learned witch beliefs into indigenous fairy lore, in reality such a conclusion would be highly unlikely. While it is true that in early modern Britain there was a constant flow of ideas travelling between learned and popular culture, and that some educated witch beliefs undoubtedly filtered into popular fairy lore, it is not feasible that a downward filtration process of this kind occurring over a couple of hundred years could fully account for the diversity and subtlety of fairy familiar beliefs throughout Britain from the very beginning of this period. It is even more unlikely that beliefs about demon familiars and beliefs about fairy familiars existed simultaneously and completely independently of each other. The only interpretation left before us, therefore, is that a significant proportion of fairy familiar beliefs were indigenous to popular culture. Given the fact that fairy beliefs in general were widespread and deeply held throughout Britain long before the arrival of Christianity, and therefore long before the dissemination and coercive superimposition of learned demonological ideas, we can only conclude that descriptions of encounters with demon familiars found in witch trials were deeply rooted in contemporary folk belief.

The Ambivalent Fairy

The process of fusion between popular fairy familiar beliefs and learned demon familiar beliefs did not only occur in the early modern courtroom. It would have been occurring, to some extent, since Christianity first arrived in Britain many centuries prior to the period of the witch-craze. The longevity of this fusion-process means that in many ways it is fruitless to try and separate fairy familiar beliefs (of popular origin) from demon familiar beliefs (of learned origin). Despite these difficulties it is nonetheless possible to isolate a contemporary 'interface' – a place where the two sets of belief met and transformed into one another. This interface existed in the part of the early modern mind which was concerned with issues of 'morality'.

In the early modern period writers on witchcraft, and most of the lawmen and ecclesiastics who prosecuted witches, shared the opinion that the witch's demon familiar was fundamentally malicious, an inherently evil spirit which either served the Devil or was an incarnation of the Devil himself and who incited and enabled the witch to perform harmful acts of magic towards others. But on a grass-roots level the reality was more complex. Close reading of the narratives given by the witches themselves reveals that, in the majority of cases, the witch's familiar behaved like a morally ambivalent spirit, as opposed to a wholly malevolent one. In this sense it mirrored the nature of the early modern fairy. Although, as we have already seen, some contemporary fairies were believed to be completely good and others were believed to be completely malevolent, the majority seem to have hovered between these two extremes of the moral spectrum and possess the ability to change their moral stature as and when it suited them. It is by looking into these beliefs surrounding the moral ambivalence of spirits and the way the early modern popular mind accommodated this ambivalence, that we can gain insights into the interface between fairy and demon.

In this period it was believed that the fairy's shift from benign to malicious could be prompted by a variety of triggers, the most common of which was the fairy's perception that it had been disrespected or mistreated in some way. As a result of this belief, as we have already seen in chapter ONE, the common folk took pains to avoid fairy displeasure by leaving food and drink out at night for the fairies and so on. Such efforts to please could promote a fairy's shift towards beneficence. Individuals who treated the fairies well could be rewarded with great loyalty. Katharine Briggs wrote of the domestic brownie (as found in both early modern and later sources) that 'Where he was well treated, however, and his whims respected, a brownie would be wholly committed to the interests of his master.'[2] This comment suggests that, like a devoted dog who attacks anyone its owner orders it to, the well-nurtured brownie would conform to its master's desires, whatever their direction. This 'litmus paper' quality of the fairy nature is well expressed in this popular rhyme which, although recorded in the early nineteenth century, is likely to be much older:

> Gin ye ca' me imp or elf,
> I rede ye look weel to yourself;
> Gin ye ca' me fairy,
> I'll work ye muckle tarrie;
> Gin guid neibour ye ca' me;
> Then guid neibour I will be;
> But gin ye ca' me seelie wicht,
> I'll be you freend baith day and nicht.[3]

The rhyme implies that the definition of the fairy was dependent upon the actions of their human allies. In other words, the human could choose to employ the same fairy to either good or evil ends, and it was the moral position of the spirit's user, rather than that of the spirit itself, which determined the latter's moral status at any given time. Many comments in the confessions of cunning folk convicted of witchcraft suggest that something like this may have been the case. Joan Willimot (Leicestershire, 1618) claimed of her fairy familiar that that 'neither did she employ her spirit in anything but only to bring word how those did which she had undertaken to cure'.[4] The fact that Joan pointed out that she had 'only' employed her spirit to perform beneficent acts suggests that Joan may have assumed that, were her intentions less benign, she could have employed the spirit to do harm. Similarly, five years later Perthshire cunning woman Isobel Haldane confessed that although she used the magical skills of her familiar (a man with a grey beard who had facilitated her escape from fairyland) to divine the future, when she was angered she employed the same spirit to malicious ends; threatening her enemies, as we have seen earlier, with the memorable phrase, 'He that delyveret me frome the ffarye-ffolk sall tak amendis (on) thé!'[5] It is notable that in many witch-narratives, the familiar, rather than offering its services specifically to do harm, offers to serve the witch in more general terms. For example, it might promise 'to do what she would command', 'do for her what she would have him to do'; tell her that 'she should have anything that she would request' or offer to 'lerne her to ken and sie ony thing she wald desyre'.[6] The demon familiar's offers of freedom from want, or a living, or even riches, just like similar offers from the fairy, were not in themselves morally questionable. In order that the human might achieve those ends the familiar or fairy put its powers at their disposal and it is possible that immorality only entered the equation if the witch or cunning woman chose to employ those powers in a negative way.

However, defining a spirit by the moral status of its human 'master' would not have been a simple matter in the early modern period for, as we have seen earlier, many cunning folk were considered as guilty of ambivalence as their supernatural allies. Although some had a reputation for being wholly malevolent or wholly good, the majority seem to have been considered ambivalent, performing both good and bad acts in varying proportions. The magical practitioner's moral definition at any given time would therefore have depended upon the way their actions were interpreted both by themselves and others, and these interpretations would have been very subjective. A magical act which was considered good by one individual may have been considered bad by another. Agnes Sampson, for example, was sentenced to be burnt as a witch in Edinburgh in 1591, however she had clearly been practising as a midwife and cunning woman and was locally known as the 'wyse wyff of Keyth'.[7] When a woman came to Agnes complaining that a man had 'done her great wrong' Agnes claimed to have obliged her by employing maleficium against the man. It is highly likely that although Agnes's legal prosecutors condemned the act, others in her community – including of course the client – may have judged the act differently, bearing in mind that it was performed in a culture where the ancient form of justice, 'revenge', was still considered honourable despite the available arms of the law and the 'turn-the-other-cheek' ministrations of the Church.[8] As we have seen previously, a more straightforward and self-centred ambivalence was modelled by Orkney cunning woman Jonet Rendall (1629), who claimed that her familiar spirit, whom she called 'Walliman', told her that 'thair was nather man nor beast seik that wer not deadlie be the hand of God bot she getting almiss and praying to Walliman he would haill thame, and if she got no almiss he wald be angrie and mak thair beastis die'.[9]

Throughout their working life such a magical practitioner would have moved up and down the good/bad continuum depending on how their acts were judged by their neighbours and overlords. When seen to perform beneficent acts, they would have been defined in those instances as a 'good cunning woman' and when seen performing maleficent acts, as a 'bad cunning woman'. The distinction between 'bad cunning woman' and 'witch' must have been a small one, if it existed at all. When neighbour-hood tensions and political forces brought such a magical practitioner under suspicion it would have been easy to transform them into the stereo-typically evil witch.

The intricate way in which relations between cunning folk and their community could deteriorate is illustrated by the chain of events which gradually soured the friendship between Essex cunning woman Ursula Kemp and her neighbour, Grace Thurlow, in the latter years of the sixteenth century.[10] Despite the fact that Ursula was obviously a tricksy character (the trial records state that she had a 'naughty name') Grace had, at one time, great faith in the former's healing powers, and asked for her help when her son was ill and she herself became lame. The relationship, however, was underpinned by tensions, with Grace offending Ursula by not employing her as a lying-in maid after the birth of her new baby and Ursula offending Grace by refusing to nurse the baby (who later died) when Grace went back to work. These tensions finally came to a head when Grace refused to pay Ursula for some healing services and Ursula, in response, 'seeing nothing [was] to be had of the same Grace, fell out with her and said, that she would be even with her; and thereupon she [Grace] was taken lame [again], and from that day to this day hath so continued'.[11] When Ursula was subsequently tried as a witch, Grace was among her accusers, retrospectively attributing many of her past misfor-tunes to Ursula, including the sickness of the child she had temporarily cured, the death of her new baby, and her lameness.

The fear and resentment of neighbours seems to have also been instru-mental in Bessie Dunlop's transformation from cunning woman to convicted witch. Bessie's trial records state that two gentlemen, Henry Jameson and James Baird, asked her if she could find out who had stolen their 'plew-irnis, fittick and musell'. After consulting with Tom, Bessie told the two men that 'Johne Blak and George Blak, smythis, had stollin the samin; and that the cowtir and fok were lyand in his awin hous, betwix ane mekle ark and ane grit kist'.[12] The business of accusing people was a touchy business, frequently laying cunning folk open to the resentment of those whom they accused and indeed, in Bessie's case, the indignant blacksmiths were so outraged at her slanders that they retaliated by apprehending her and taking her to the Lord of Glasgow – the first stage on her journey towards the Edinburgh Assizes and eventual execution on Castle Hill.

Just as the cunning woman's moral status shifted up and down the good/bad continuum, so did the moral status of their fairy familiars. A good cunning woman's spirit would have been seen as a fairy familiar employed to do good and a bad cunning woman's spirit as a fairy familiar employed to do harm. The distinction between 'fairy familiar employed to do harm' and 'demon familiar' would have been as fine as the distinction between bad cunning woman and witch. Whatever the definition of a given spirit on a popular level, however, if and when circumstances conspired (through inter-personal enmity, community scapegoating or élite religious/political motivations etc.) to bring its human ally to the dock and define her as a witch before a prosecuting élite, the fairy's transformation into the wholly malicious stereotypical witch's familiar could easily have become complete.[13] The magical practitioner's perception of themselves and their fairy helpers could also then have shifted according to community or prosecutorial perception. Such a shift is suggested in the plaintive comment made by Leicestershire cunning woman Margaret Flower (1618). In reference to a confused meeting with her three familiars (named Rutterkin, Little Robin and Spirit) and a fourth spirit in the middle of the night in Lincoln jail, Margaret claimed that 'she never mistrusted them nor suspected herself till then'.[14] Essex witch Rebecca Jones (1645) seems to have undergone a similar shift in perception. Her confession reads: 'About twenty-four years since, being servant with John Bishop of Great Clacton, there knocked at the door a handsome young man (*whom she now thinks was the Devil*) [my italics].'[15]

Early modern popular (and to a lesser degree élite) culture was still considerably influenced by a magical, essentially monist, conception of life, and therefore people would have been more comfortable with the idea of ambivalence in both people and spirits than contemporary Christian teachings might suggest. Pragmatic individuals would have accepted that certain spirits and magical practitioners had the capacity to act in ways which could deliberately or arbitrarily help or harm them, and would have attempted to manipulate the latter in whatever way was necessary to ensure that they would be the recipient of good rather than bad fortune. To the popular mind the ambivalence of the fairy or magical practitioner may not have seemed that different to that modelled by the Christian God (and his entourage), whose capacity to punish an individual if they did not conform to his laws (that is, if they sinned), must often have seemed as great as his capacity to bestow blessings.[16] Indeed, Angus witch Isobel

Smith's claim, in 1661, that the Devil met her 'alone lik ane braw gentleman, when shee *desyreing either God or the diwell* to reweng hir one James Gray [my italics]', clearly illustrates that Isobel considered the Christian God just as capable as the Devil of exacting her revenge.[17] As we shall see in later chapters, this 'amoral conception of God' was also shared by some learned magicians.[18]

The same capacity for contradiction that enabled an individual to feel comfortable negotiating with a spirit capable of evil also enabled them to make use of a spirit which was theoretically hostile to Christianity, while still believing themselves to be a Christian. Such a paradox was inadvertently supported by Church and State. Most theologians officially condemned fairies as demons and yet at the same time fairy belief was often tolerated on a parish level. An Elizabethan statute made the invocation of evil spirits – for any purpose – a felony and this was reinforced (to include, among other things, the keeping and feeding of familiar spirits) in 1604. In some courtrooms, however, especially at the beginning of the period, those who supposedly confessed to such things were allowed to walk free.[19] Even as late as 1670 a contemporary lamented that some Cornish witches 'the assizes being over, are freed, although that about their familiarity with rats and cats and other things were plainly proved against them'.[20] It is clear that Bessie Dunlop mistakenly believed that she would be treated with similar leniency. Although she knew that she might get into trouble for keeping company with Tom (presumably being to some degree aware of Tom's ambiguous status in the eyes of the law), she nevertheless believed him when he assured her that she only need get good testimonies (affayis) from her neighbours and all would be well.[21] Many other trial records reflect these contradictions. Alongside standard renunciations of Christianity it is not uncommon to find detailed Christian prayers or charms (usually of Catholic origin) which the witch or cunning woman claims to have used for healing purposes, sometimes believing that they had been taught them by a familiar spirit. We also find angels and demon familiars serving the queen of the fairies: fairies and demon familiars serving God and/or urging the witch to a better Christian faith; demon familiars who are called 'Daniel the Prophet' or 'Jesus'; and others who are invoked by calling 'Come Christ' or who recite 'Amen, Amen' during an invocation.[22]

The mental outlooks which generated such ideological hybridizations can only be surmised. The evidence suggests that for those with an obscure grasp of Christian teaching the cosmos would have been peopled by a medley of supernatural figures of both Christian and pre-Christian origin, with little or no discrimination being made between them, either morally or ontologically. Of those individuals who were conscious of the official antipathies between fairy and Church many are likely to have mastered the arts of diplomacy, using, and in effect pledging alleigance to, both 'sides' either consecutively or at the same time. Northamptonshire witch Agnes Wilson (1612), when asked by an interrogator 'how many gods she did acknowledge' answered 'two, God the father, and the Devil'.[23] A similarly flexible pragmatism was modelled by lettered Edinburgh cunning man Thomas Weir just before his execution in 1670: convicted of witchcraft, Weir 'would not hear any minister pray to and for him, telling, his condemnation was sealed, and now since he was to goe to the devil, he would not anger him'.[24] The religious confusions wrought by the Reformation would only have served to encourage such duplicity. In such an unsettled climate it is easy to see how some individuals, struggling to survive in a harsh world, could have clung to any supernatural agency which promised to improve their condition, not caring to question too deeply into their provenance or moral status.[25] It would have been hard for recently widowed Suffolk witch Mary Skipper (1645), for example, to quibble over the moral shades of a demon familiar who, although it asked her to sign a covenant with blood, also promised to 'pay her debts, and carry her to heaven'.[26] Another Suffolk widow, Joane Ruce (1645), would have to have been very sure of her religious convictions to refuse her demon familiars' promises that she should 'never want meat, drink, or clothes, or money' – particularly in the light of the fact that the spirits claimed that 'they were more able to save her soul than God'.[27] Other men and women did not need pseudo-Christian inducements to encourage them to accept the familiar's offer of help – the immediacy of their need was motivation enough. As Robert Burton observed 'If a man fall into a ditch, as he prosecutes it, what matter is it whether a friend or an enemy help him out? and if I be troubled with such a malady, what care I whether the Devil himself, or any of his Ministers, by God's permission, redeem me?'[28] When Scottish cunning woman Agnes Sampson (East Lothian, 1591) met her demon familiar soon after the death of her husband, she was in such haste to alleviate the suffering of herself and her fatherless children that 'Before she knew what spirit it was she consented [to make a demonic pact]'.[29] Similarly, although Bessie Dunlop was scared of Tom Reid and resisted his attempts to make her renounce her Christianity and abandon her family – she was in desperate straits and his offer of help was irresistible. You can almost hear the weary desperation in her voice as she finally accepted his aid, saying that she 'wald trow in *ony bodye* [who] did her gude [my italics]'.[30] A cunning woman such as Bessie, stepping out from this ambiguous world of folk belief into the reductionist glare of the law courts would have had little chance of escaping the charge of covenanting with Satan. Even if she did not already consider herself to be negotiating with a fairy which could be a familiar which could be a devil which could be *the* Devil, it would not have been too difficult for an angry community or zealous prosecutor to persuade her that it was so.

PART II

Anthropological Perspectives

INTRODUCTION TO PART II

In Part I we have looked closely at popular familiar beliefs in early modern Britain. Through a detailed analysis of encounter-narratives found in witchcraft and sorcery trial records we have suggested that beliefs about demon familiars were rooted in a coherent and widespread matrix of popular beliefs surrounding the use of fairy familiars by cunning folk. We have gone on to argue that in many cases a witch convicted of using a demon familiar may have been a cunning woman using a fairy familiar which had been effectively 'demonized' either by her neighbours, her élite prosecutors or in some cases, herself.

These findings can help us to discard the outdated 'élite-origin-only' theory of the demon familiar's genesis and corroborate the growing acknowledgement among historians that there was a strong folkloric component to familiar beliefs in the period – however can they do any more than this? Any analysis of the popular component of early modern witch-trial records is inherently compromised by the fact that confessions were influenced by judicial interrogators: the effects wrought by zealous 'witch-finders' like Matthew Hopkins, John Stearne and Brian Darcey (who all extorted large numbers of confessions reflecting, to a greater or lesser degree, their own demonological preoccupations) are too significant to be overlooked. As we have seen in earlier chapters, attempts by scholars to pick apart individual trials have shown how difficult it is to untangle the voice of the suspect from that of the interrogator. In the majority of cases, it is largely impossible to separate the two.[1] Given these problems, the question we now face is not whether fairy beliefs contributed to ideas about demon familiars in this period, but how we can assess the extent of this contribution.

It is possible to shed further light on this subject by turning to anthropological perspectives. While early modern familiar beliefs were, as we have already seen, partly rooted in fairy beliefs, the latter, in their turn, were rooted in the animistic religions of Europe's pre-Christian peoples. Although we can gain few direct insights into these indigenous beliefs, the religious and magical world-view of pre-Christian Britons being largely lost to us, we can compensate by making use of cross-cultural comparisons.[2] Anthropological studies of recent and contemporary non-European tribal cultures provide a wealth of first-hand and, relatively speaking, 'objective' accounts of magical belief and practice surrounding familiar spirits largely uninfluenced by Christian ideology. Although these findings come from societies which are geographically and temporally distinct from early modern Britain, they can still be used to gain insights into our subject.

Relatively few historians of early modern British magic and witchcraft have used anthropological material as an analytical tool, despite the fact that when it has been used, the results have contributed hugely to debate in the field. The works of Alan Macfarlane and Keith Thomas, published in the early 1970s, remain influential. By drawing comparisons between the magical beliefs and practices of cunning folk and witches in early modern England and those of magical practitioners from a number of recent and contemporary tribal societies (with particular emphasis on the southern Sudanese Azande tribe), Thomas and Macfarlane revealed the types of emotional and societal dynamics which may have lain beneath the activities of cunning folk and witches and provided compelling evidence to suggest that there was a genuinely popular basis to witchcraft accusation in England in this period.[3]

Across the Channel, meanwhile, Continental historians have used anthropological perspectives to explore the folkloric roots of the more specifically demonological elements of European witchcraft. Over forty years ago the most prominent of these, the Italian scholar Carlo Ginzburg, published his analysis of a series of witch-trial records from Friuli in Northern Italy, in which he argued that the successive groups of Friulian peasants accused of convening at witches' sabbaths and practising witchcraft over the period 1575–1675 were in fact members of a local agrarian cult, of pre-Christian origin, whose essentially beneficent folkloric magical practices were being demonized by witchcraft interrogators.[4] In his follow-up book, *Ecstasies* (1989), Ginzburg considerably widened the scope of his research. Tracing belief motifs, myths and rituals from throughout Europe back through recorded history and into prehistory, he concluded that the folkloric beliefs and rituals of the Friulian Benandanti were evidence of the survival of pre-Christian Eurasian shamanistic visionary traditions.[5] Ginzburg went on to claim that similar shamanistic traditions did not only survive into sixteenth- and seventeenth-century Friuli, but were widespread on a popular level throughout early modern Europe, and that they fused with élite demonological ideas to create the stereotype of the witches' sabbath. Although elements of Ginzburg's work have been disputed by scholars (much of this focusing on his attempts to illustrate the continuity of secret ecstatic cults from prehistory through to the early modern period), the import of his basic hypothesis cannot be discounted and it has single-handedly eliminated the 'élite-origin-only' theory of the sabbath. Since Ginzburg's pioneering work other Continental scholars have taken up the baton, developing his ideas and applying his findings to regional studies. This line of research has proved particularly fruitful with regard to Eastern Europe, where a rich store of relatively recent folk traditions associated with shamanistic beliefs and experiences (such as those pertaining to the Hungarian *táltos*, Romanian *călusari* and Croatian-Slovenian *kresniks*) have made the links between early modern witchcraft and prehistoric shamanism easy to forge.[6]

Scholars in this field unanimously acknowledge that descriptions of encounters between cunning folk or witches and individual spirit-helpers or 'familiar spirits' are also, like descriptions of sabbath experiences, likely to have derived from pre-Christian shamanistic visionary traditions. Gábor Klaniczay claims that:

> The initiatory vision, the appearance of fellow magicians, superhuman beings or angels to the would-be magician at a certain age in dreams (or, more accurately, when he first falls into trance) the obligatory character of the calling to exercise his functions, his eventual resistance to this calling and the futility of this resistance – all these characteristics bring to mind shamanism.[7]

Despite such acknowledgements, however, scholars working in this field have tended to reflect Ginzburg's emphasis on the shamanistic identity of the communal sabbath/fairyland/spirit world experience, paying particular attention to fertility-related rites, trance-fighting traditions and so on. Consequently, the connections between familiar-encounters of the type common to Britain (that is, the solitary encounter with an individual spirit) and shamanism have received less attention.

In Part II we will be contributing to this field by exploring the shamanistic identity of early modern familiar belief in some detail, in a specifically British context. We will look at some of the ways in which beliefs surrounding popular magical practitioners and familiar spirits found in early modern Britain resemble beliefs surrounding shamans and their familiar spirits found in a selection of traditional animist cultures. The information collected will serve two purposes. First, it will corroborate the conclusions reached in Part I, by supporting the view that there was a folkloric component to early modern familiar beliefs and giving us a better idea of the possible extent of this folkloric component. Secondly, it will provide us with a theoretical platform from which, in Part III, we can begin to look at the experiential nature of the familiar-encounter.

In our use of anthropological material, we will not be attempting to provide evidence of historical contiguity between European witch beliefs and pre-Christian European shamanism, as attempted by Ginzburg et al., nor will we be attempting to reconstruct the animist traditions of pre-Christian Britons. Instead, we shall be working with the considerably simpler cross-cultural comparative approach as modelled in the works of Keith Thomas and Alan Macfarlane. The premise upon which the comparisons will be based is the following: if an early modern familiar belief can be found to resemble a familiar belief found in a traditional non-European animist culture then this resemblance will be seen to support the likelihood that the former was rooted in pre-Christian British animism, that is, that it was of folkloric origin. The use of such a general premise, however, is not without its dangers. A correlation drawn between an individual British familiar belief and a similar belief from any given animist society signifies little in isolation, in the sense that it is possible to cross-culturally reference almost any belief, however idiosyncratic, if the net is spread wide enough. On the other hand, the argument for the animistic origin of an individual British familiar belief becomes very compelling if the latter can be simultaneously cross-referenced with a number of similar beliefs from a number of different animist cultures. From this perspective, the limitations of using a broad comparative premise can be offset by drawing on an equally broad spectrum of anthropological material.

Taking these issues into consideration, our cross-cultural comparisons will be drawn within the following parameters: (1) The use of anthropological sources will be restricted to material relating to traditional tribal societies from Siberia and the Americas, with occasional reference to societies existing outside these locations. This wide geographical and cultural canvas provides enough scope for multiple cross-referencing without being too diverse or unmanageable. These sources also benefit from being relatively unmined by scholars exploring European witchcraft beliefs. The material used will date primarily, although not exclusively, from the late nineteenth and early twentieth centuries, by virtue of the fact that it reflects Siberian and Native American cultures before they were too heavily influenced by Christianity, or had developed the self-consciousness which emerges as a result of being 'looked at' by the modern world. (2) The term 'shaman' will be employed in a general sense. The origins of this word are disputed, but the most universally accepted explanation is that it derives from the language of the Tungus-speaking peoples of Siberia, where it is used, in the words of scholar of religion Graham Harvey, to denote 'a communal leader chosen and trained to work for the community by engaging with significant other-than-human persons'.[8] Over the past century the term has been taken up by both academics and popular writers alike, and applied to a diverse range of tribal magical practitioners, with widely differing magical practices, from all over the world. While it has been argued that this indiscriminate use of the term 'shaman' has rendered the word almost meaningless, in the absence of any viable alternative, it will still be used here. Despite its dilution, the term is unique in that it is distinct from other, equally generalized, names such as 'witch-doctor', 'sorcerer' or 'magician', in that it specifically denotes a tribal magical practitioner who works with the help of spirits. (3) Unlike early modern encounter-narratives, shaman encounter-narratives will not be dated. Unless otherwise stated, the reader can assume that the overwhelming majority of the latter derive from anthropological studies undertaken in the first half of the twentieth century, with a small minority of references falling a decade or two on either side of this period. Where possible, shamans will be defined by both geographical location and tribe or, where the latter is not available, by indigenous group. Although the anthropological material used is historical, shamans shall be referred to in the present tense, reflecting the fact that traditional shamanism is still extant in many parts of the world today. (4) Anthropological studies designate the shaman's familiar spirit in a variety of ways: the terms 'guardian spirit', 'helping spirit', 'assistant spirit', 'familiar spirit' and so on being largely interchangeable. In order to distinguish the familiar spirits used by shamans from those used by cunning folk and witches the former shall be denoted by the term 'helping spirits'. (5) This comparison will not be covering 'spirit-possession'. Beliefs concerning possession are a significant part of many shamanic traditions and, as is to be expected, also feature in the magical world-view of cunning folk and witches. However, while spirit-possession is a relevant subject, it can be seen as distinct from the experiences of meeting spirits face to face as described in early modern and shaman encounter-narratives.

CHAPTER EIGHT

The Shaman's Calling

All tribal shamans operate within an animist belief system, that is, a belief system built upon the assumption that the cosmos, and all worldly phenomena, are imbued with an immaterial animating force. This force can be conceived of in many ways: as 'essence', 'consciousness', 'spiritual energy', 'soul' and so on. It can also be seen to manifest as autonomous conscious beings or 'spirits'. Individuals living in animist cultures believe that humans can communicate with these spirits in order to influence their lives and the world around them. Although this communication can theoretically be undertaken by any individual, it is the magical practitioner, whom we shall here term shaman, who possesses the skill to encounter spirits regularly, at will, and who takes on the obligation to do so for the benefit of his community.

Despite the fact that the late nineteenth- and early twentieth-century Siberian and Native American shamans we shall be looking at here come from very different social contexts and geographical locations from the cunning folk and witches of early modern Britain, in many respects their roles in their respective communities are startlingly similar. Like the cunning man or woman, the shaman's magical activities usually supplement a more ordinary profession. Like them, he comes to the role either by heredity or accident; like them, his skills are primarily employed in healing, with a strong secondary emphasis on divination; and finally, like them, his magical expertise is dependent upon intimate and long-term relationships with particular supernatural entities, or, as we shall term them here, 'helping spirits'.

The Appearance of the Spirit

Like the encounter between cunning folk or witches and their familiars, the encounter between the shaman and his helping spirit is primarily a visual one although, as we shall see in later chapters, non-visual auditory encounters with spirits may play a key role in the magical activities of both shamans and their early modern counterparts. Helping spirits usually appear in the form of humans, animals, or less commonly, human/animal hybrids, inanimate objects, or natural phenomena. Human forms can range from the beautiful, tall or imposing to the ugly, small or ordinary. We hear of 'two great hill spirits, tall, tall as a tent'; a 'cute little spirit' sitting in a rotten tree trunk: a 'lovely girl in fine clothes'; a girl spirit who was 'lame and fat'; and a small man who was 'about four feet high . . . dressed in blue'.[1] Animal forms are equally varied. In Siberia, for example, we hear of helping spirits in the form of whales, seals, polar bears, wolves, ravens, owls, gulls, ducks, squirrels and dogs, while in North America we find them in the form of horses, buffalos, grizzly bears, cougars, deer, eagles, robins, mountain lizards, snakes, fish, rabbits, foxes and so on. As in early modern Britain, the size of the spirit does not necessarily relate to its power. Shamans of the North American Paiute tribe, for example, like the witches of England's Home Counties, particularly prize spirits in the form of small rodents such as the mouse or the 'packrat', believing that they are particularly skilled at 'stealing' away disease.[2] Alternatively, North American Quinault shaman Sammy Hoh valued his helping spirit in the form of a mole for its digging abilities, telling anthropologist Ronald Olson that when he was attacked by another shaman, who had sent a spirit to 'block the path' and prevent his (Sammy's) return from a journey into the spirit worlds, 'he was fortunate in having Mole for a spirit, who was of course able to burrow under any obstruction'.[3]

Many descriptions of helping spirits found in shaman encounter-narratives are as closely observed and specific as those of British familiars. The following account given by North American Zuni shaman Palowahtiva, is redolent of Bessie Dunlop's detailed description of Tom Reid. The shaman saw:

> the form of a little old man, dressed in the most ancient costume of my people. White was his apparel, with leggings of knotted cotton, soft and in figures, fringed down the front of the leg, with embroidered breech-clout, and embroidered wide-sleeved cotton coat; and his hair was as white as snow and very long, falling down either side of his head in front, and done up in a strange old-fashioned knot behind. His face was surely pleasant, but

very old, and he was short, not as high as the lower part of the window. Though so very old, he walked with an easy and majestic tread, noiselessly, more so than the wind.[4]

The shaman's helping spirit also shares the early modern familiar's capacity to shapeshift. A shaman from the Siberian Gold tribe claims of his spirit that 'Sometimes she comes under the aspect of an old woman, and sometimes under that of a wolf, so she is terrible to look at. Sometimes she comes as a winged tiger.'[5] Like cunning folk and witches, shamans can also possess a number of helping spirits simultaneously. One Canadian Netsilik shaman, named Iksivalitaq, possessed seven helping spirits which included 'the spirit of Big Mountain, the ghosts of three dead men, one of them his grandfather, and the spirits of a sea scorpion, a killer whale and a black dog without ears'.[6] Like early modern familiars, the shaman's supernatural helpers are often believed to be the spirit of a dead man or woman, frequently a relative who had themselves been a shaman. The Canadian Caribou shaman, Aggiartoq, claimed that his dead mother and an unnamed human skeleton became his helping spirits, while his fellow shaman Kinalik claimed that her dead brother was her main protecting spirit and that he 'had often come to visit her by gliding through the air with his legs and head down. But as soon as he landed on the ground he was able to walk like an ordinary man.'[7]

Like their early modern counterparts, shamans can also receive their helping spirits from other magical practitioners, again often family members. Anthropologist Ronald Olson claims that among the North American Quinault Indians, 'A man controlling a score of spirits need not go on a vision quest for each one. Some came to him after the death of relatives who had controlled them' while the Canadian Iglulik shaman, Aua, claimed that his conversion to Christianity caused him to pass on his spirits to his sister: 'I am a Christian' he said, 'and so I have sent away all my helping spirits; sent them up to my sister in Baffin land.'[8] Others receive their helping spirits from more powerful supernatural beings with whom they have a more distant working relationship, in much the same way as cunning folk and witches sometimes received their familiar spirits from the fairy king or queen, or the Devil. Scholars of shamanism often identify two overlapping categories of helping spirit. Nevill Drury claims:

Firstly, there are the spirits which are substantially under the shaman's control, and which serve as familiars. But there are also other spirits, thought of more as guardians and helpers, who are available when the shaman needs to call on their aid. These may be minor deities, or the spirits of deceased shamans: entities who maintain a certain independence in their particular realm and who are not automatically subject to the control of the shaman.[9]

Such beliefs are reflected in an encounter-narrative given by a shaman from the Siberian Gold tribe, in which a spirit in the form of a beautiful woman appears before the shaman, during a long sickness, and says to him, 'I am the Ayami of your ancestors, the shamans. I taught them shamanizing. Now I am going to teach you . . . I shall give you assistant spirits. You are to heal with their aid, and I shall teach and help you myself.' The assistant spirits, as did the Ayami, appeared before the man in a variety of animal forms.[10] A Siberian Avam Samoyed shaman, on the other hand, claimed that while he was seriously ill with smallpox he travelled into a spirit world which he described as 'the middle of a sea' where he met 'the Lady of the Water' and her husband, 'the Lord of the Underworld', who gave him 'two guides, an ermine and a mouse, to lead him to the underworld'.[11]

The shaman's first encounter with his helping spirit is either deliberately cultivated or spontaneous. In tribal societies the deliberately cultivated initial encounter is based upon the rationale that an individual can only become a shaman if he obtains one or more spirit-helpers, and that therefore an aspirant shaman needs to work at magical techniques believed to encourage the appearance of such spirits. A survey of anthropological sources suggests that in tribal societies far more emphasis is placed on the deliberately cultivated initial encounter than was the case in early modern Britain, although how far this difference is rooted in culture, as opposed to the divergent circumstances under which information about these magical traditions has been gathered, is hard to determine. The nature of these invocatory practices will be examined in more detail later in this chapter.

Despite the fact that deliberately cultivated initial encounters with helping spirits are widespread, for many shamans the intial encounter is spontaneous and in this respect it resembles the initial encounter between cunning folk or witches and their familiars. The Danish explorer Knud Rasmussen, who travelled widely among the Inuit or 'Eskimo' peoples of the North American Arctic and Greenland in the early twentieth century, claimed that among the Polar Inuit 'It is not every one who can become a magician, for it is not every one whom the spirits will serve; a special predisposition is necessary, and a sort of call. If a man, walking about alone, hears a sound which may emanate from a spirit, or sees a spirit in the flesh, he feels himself called to be an Angakoq [shaman].'[12] Like his early modern counterparts, the shaman is usually alone at the time of his first meeting, and undergoing a period of intense physical and/or psychological stress. Often it is the naturally-occuring pressures of life which generate these stresses. The anthropologist Waldemar Bogoras, for example, claims that among the Siberian Chukchi 'some great misfortune, dangerous or protracted illness, [or] sudden loss of family or property' can bring an individual into contact with spirits.[13] As in early modern Britain, bereavement is often a powerful trigger. The following description of the first encounter between Guatemalan shaman Gabriel Mir and his helping spirit, from ethnopsychologist Holger Kalweit, is typical:

> Gabriel Mir was thirty-two years old when he suffered a whole string of catastrophic misfortunes. His wife and five children died in an epidemic and he himself lay ill for several months, escaping death by a hair's breadth. He had very little food, was unable to look after himself, and depended on the occasional help given by his neighbors. Too weak to rise to his feet, he chewed coarse grain and drank the rain water dripping down from the roof of his dwelling. One night a small gnome, no more than four feet tall and dressed in blue, appeared to him. Gabriel took him to be San Antonio, whose picture hung over the altar in his house. 'I come to impose on you,' said the gnome. 'You have been ill, my son. You have been close to La Gloria.'[14]

The Greenlandic Inuit shaman Autdaruta's description of his first encounter with his helping spirits is less detailed, but follows the same basic format. Autdaruta claimed that after the death of his father, he was wandering alone in the hills, grieving, when 'I saw two men coming towards me. They were inland-dwellers. "We were sorry for you, because you were an orphan; so we have come to help you," they said, and so they became my first helping spirits. Then I began to be a magician, but did not speak to any one about it.'[15] Alternatively, the helping spirit which appeared before Tak, a North American Quinault shaman, was moved by her poverty. Ronald Olson tells us: 'Tak was an old Queets woman who lived at the village of na'uḳalxʷ (big village) at the mouth of the Clearwater. Her guardian spirit was a dwarf. When it came to her it said, "I heard that you are a poor woman and that the people make fun of you because you have no property. I am going to help you."'[16] Among the South American Araucanians, on the other hand, a shaman-to-be often encounters his helping spirits through a sudden illness. Scholar of religion Mircea Eliade recounts how a fisherman's daughter claimed 'I was gathering shells from the reefs, when I felt something like a blow on the breast, and a very clear voice inside me said: "Become a machi! [shaman] It is my will!" At the same time violent pains in my entrails made me lose consciousness.'[17] Like the early modern familiar, the shaman's helping spirit offers the suffering individual comfort and promises to put an end to their misfortunes – often making it clear that this cessation of suffering will come about when the individual begins to 'shamanize', that is, gain helping spirits and earn a living as a magical practitioner. The rather rough comfort offered to 'Scratching-Woman', a male shaman from the Siberian Chukchi tribe, was associated with just such a promise: 'Cease being such a weakling' his helping spirit said, 'Be a shaman and be strong, and you will have plenty of food!'[18] Similarly the spirit which appeared to the Siberian Gold shaman described earlier concluded her offer of assistant spirits and healing skills with the promise that, as a result, 'Food will come to us from the people.'[19] Just as the acceptance of aid from an early modern familiar initiated an individual's transformation into a cunning woman or witch, so the acceptance of aid from a helping spirit heralds the beginning of an individual's career as a shaman.

However emotionally charged the initial encounter, the relationship between shaman and helping spirit is often accompanied by the type of hard-headed business transactions found in early modern descriptions of the demonic pact. The shaman/spirit alliance is seen as a contractual one, in which the spirit offers the shaman-to-be the benefit of his magical powers only if he agrees to fulfil certain conditions. Anthropologist William Lyon claims that among the Canadian Ojibwa 'The powers one receives [from the helping spirits] are "always contingent upon the fulfillment of obligations that took a variety of forms."'[20] Holger Kalweit describes this contractual relationship in more detail:

> we are here confronted by a sort of spiritual division of labor: the spirit beings grant the wishes of the shaman by healing through him, undertaking exploratory flights to obtain visions of the future, observing and reporting on the actions of an enemy and, in extreme cases, causing the death of a competitor. The shaman, for his part, during the illness leading to his initiation had to promise his protecting spirit that he would act as an agent of healing – and this is a promise he must keep if he doesn't want to attract the wrath of his spirit companion.[21]

In some instances, something approaching the explicit pact is found in shamanic narratives. The anthropologist Ioan Lewis writes that 'Amongst the [Siberian] Tungus, some emphasis is given to the idea that a contractual relationship binds the shaman and the spirits which he incarnates. This conception of an agreement of compact . . . is stressed amongst the Eskimos.'[22]

Like cunning folk and witches, many shamans establish their contractual relationships with spirits willingly, or at least with willing resignation, while others are reluctant to accept their calling. Sometimes this reluctance is based on fear. William Lyon tells us that among the Omaha Indians of the North American Plains it was believed that 'One of the most important aspects of their training involves teaching them [aspirant shamans] to stand their ground when a spirit appears rather than running away in fear.'[23] The Omahan shaman, 'Small Fangs', laments that 'Supernatural beings are like that. If you're not frightened of them the first time they may give you a power. But I ran away and my running from them hurt them.'[24] Similarly, Ronald Olson notes that among the North American Quinault Indians 'The [first] vision [of the familiar] itself was terrifying in nature, and the faint-hearted usually ran away'.[25] Shaman encounter-narratives also describe helping spirits plaguing resistant shamans, haunting their homes, making them sick and otherwise disrupting their lives in a manner very similar to the ways in which early modern familiars pursued reluctant cunning folk and witches. Shamans subjected to these pressures usually maintain that it is only by relenting and giving in to the persistent spirit's demands that they get any peace. The Siberian Yakut shaman, Uno Harva, claimed:

> I became ill when I was twenty-one years old, and began to see with my eyes and hear with my ears things others could neither hear nor see. For nine years I fought against the spirit, without telling anyone what had happened because I feared they might not believe me or make fun of me. In the end I became so ill that I was close to death. So I began to shamanize and very soon my health improved.[26]

One of the main reasons why shamans try to resist their calling is a reluctance to take on the responsibilities that being a shaman entails, and an unwillingness to relinquish the comforts of ordinary life. For many shamans, like those of the North American Paviotso tribe, this reluctance is also connected to the fact that being a shaman makes you permanently susceptible to accusations of witchcraft.[27] For those prospective shamans who are Christians, or Christian converts, resistance to the shamanic vocation can take the form of an inner struggle very redolent of the struggles of conscience experienced by cunning folk and witches when propositioned by their familiars. In the early twentieth century a young woman called Nelly Lawrence from the South American Yamana tribe, who had recently converted to Christianity, told the local missionary father, Martin Gusinde, that she:

> was walking one day with her little daughter in the forest when she heard break from the trunk of a tree a loud 'Pah!' 'I looked around,' she told him, 'and saw a cute little spirit in that rotten trunk who beckoned to me in a friendly way. I did not realise that it was an apparition, but took it for an ordinary soul. But an uncanny fear unstrung my limbs, and as though in a

coma, I dragged myself on. Overcome then by a fatigue that was irresistible, I flung myself onto my bed, where I dreamed; and again there was that spirit before me, smiling in the friendliest way. It loaded me with presents: furs, baskets, necklaces and so on; even gave me a special song. And when, later, I woke with heavy senses, that song continued to sound for a long time within me.' For many days the woman was faint and ill, feeling weak and helpless; but then she was visited by a female shaman who, when served a cup of tea, started back in horror. 'Why,' she asked, 'do you hand me this disgusting beast?' Terrified, Nelly Lawrence replied, 'But I gave you a cup of tea!' The shaman left, greatly troubled for her friend, but in a dream then realised what had happened to her. The apparition had thrown a leather noose around the woman's neck and a heavy cloak was upon her shoulders and was killing her because she had not begun to shamanize. 'It was that cloak,' the afflicted woman told Gusinde, 'that had been so greatly oppressing and exhausting me that frequently I fell down.' The shaman sent for her and, in a violent scene, tore from her throat and back those invisible things, the gifts, even the song, and so saved her life.[28]

This description is so similar to the vivid narrative given by Essex witch Elizabeth Bennett, in 1582, that it merits reproducing the latter account here. Elizabeth described how she was plagued by two spirits, one 'black like a dog' and the other 'red like a lion', and how she drew on her Christian convictions when attempting to resist their oppressive attentions. Her trial confession reads:

this examinate was coming from mill, [when] the spirit called Suckin came unto her and did take her by the coat, and held her that she could not go forward nor remove by the space of two hours, at the which (this examinate saith) she was much amazed. And she saith, that the spirit did ask her if she this examinate would go with it, whereat this examinate said, 'In the name of God, what art thou? Thou wilt not hurt me?' At the which speech it said, 'No.' And this examinate saith, that she then prayed devoutly to Almighty God to deliver her from it, at which time the spirit did depart from her until she had gone a good way; and being come within 30 or 40 roods of her house, this examinate saith, that the said spirit came again unto her and took her by the coats behind, and held her fast, whereat this examinate saith, that she desired God to deliver her from that evil spirit, and then that did depart to the well. And this examinate saith, that within one hour after, the same spirit came again unto her, she being a-sifting of her meal, and saith, the same remained with her until she had laid her leaven, and then departed. The said examinate saith, that the next day, she being a-kneading of her bread, the spirit came again unto her, and brought the other spirit with it called Lierd, and that one of them did ask her why she was so snappish yesterday. To that this examinate saith, that she made answer, 'I trust I am in the faith of God, and you shall have no power over me,' at which words, this examinate saith, the said spirits departed. Then she this examinate saith, that she being a-making of a fire in her oven, the said spirits came again unto her and took her by the leg; this examinate feeling it to take her by the leg saith she said, 'God and the Holy Ghost deliver me from the evil spirits,' at which words, this examinate saith, that the said spirits did depart, to her thinking. But this examinate saith, that within half an hour after, she having a fire fork in her hand and being a stirring of the fire in the oven, the spirit called Suckin came unto her and took this examinate by the hips, and said, 'Seeing thou wilt not be ruled, thou shalt have a cause,' and would have thrust this examinate into the burning oven, and so had (as this examinate saith) but for the forsaid fork. But this examinate striving and doing what what she could to her uttermost, the said spirit burnt her arm, the which burning is apparent and evidently to be seen; and when it had thus done it did depart.[29]

The Working Relationship

Like the cunning woman or witch, once the shaman overcomes the surprise, joy, fear, or resistance stimulated by the initial encounter with a helping spirit and has made some kind of contractual agreement with it, the two then embark upon a working relationship which can survive for many years. Like the cunning man or woman, the shaman's primary function in his community is that of healer, and he employs his helping spirit to diagnose illness, divine outcomes and prescribe cures in a manner startingly similar to that of his early modern counterpart. It can be the spirit's offer of healing skills which entice the individual into becoming a shaman in the first place. Dick Mahwee, a North American Paviotso shaman, claimed that:

> A man dreams that a spirit of deer, eagle or bear comes after him. The spirit tells him that he is to be a doctor. When a man first dreams this way he does not believe it. Then the dream comes again. He dreams this way for a long time. The spirit tells him to collect eagle feathers, wild tobacco, a stone pipe, a rattle, and other things. When he gets these things he becomes a doctor.[30]

Guatemalan shaman Gabriel Mir was less eager to accept his helping spirit's offer to help him become a healer:

> The gnome pointed to an invisible person whom Gabriel was to heal. Gabriel resisted, saying that he neither could nor would heal anybody . . . Thereafter the shining gnome appeared to him every night for a whole week and taught him various methods of healing . . . Gabriel then began to work

as a healer. During his healing rituals he always spoke in the plural because he and his heavenly protector were effecting the cure together. San Antonio always remained close to Gabriel, prescribed medicinal herbs and even medicines that had to be obtained from the chemist.[31]

Many shamans, like Gabriel Mir, verbally discuss diagnoses and cures with their helping spirits in a manner which closely resembles the way early modern cunning folk like Bessie Dunlop worked with their famil-iars. Mircea Eliade describes how, among the Californian Achomawi, the practising shaman 'loses himself in meditation and talks *sotto voce*; he is conversing with his *damagomi*, his "powers" [helping spirits], to discover the cause of the illness. For it is really the *damagomi* that make the diag-nosis.'[32] Such was also the case for the Siberian Sagay shaman, Kyzlasov, who claimed of his helping spirits that, 'it is through them, that when I hold the pulse of a sick person, it becomes clear to me, what is wrong with him'.[33] Anthropologist Frances Densmore describes how North American Ute shaman Pagitsh, whose helping spirit appeared in the form of a little green man about two feet tall, claimed that when he performed healing rituals inside a tent: 'throughout his treatments the little green man stayed outside the tent, and he could see him and hear what he said, every phase of the treatment being according to his direction'.[34] The shaman supple-ments the use of spirits in healing with a variety of other methods, many of which are similar to those employed by cunning folk and witches: herbal medicine, magical amulets, chants, charms, the laying on of hands, massage, manipulation, the transferral of sickness onto an animal or the shaman himself and so on. The sucking out of sickness and the removal of 'arrows' inflicted by evil spirits or other magical practitioners also feature in both early modern and shaman encounter-narratives. As we shall examine in chapter NINE, many shamans also resembled the cunning man or woman in that their healing rituals also involved sending, or accompanying, their helping spirit into spirit worlds.

Like the cunning man or woman, the second most common use to which the shaman puts his helping spirit is that of divination. The lat-ter's divinatory skills are often highly prized, indeed some scholars suggest that, in Siberia at least, these skills were historically as highly valued and sought after as those of healing.[35] With the aid of their spir-its, shamans can divine future events, such as predicting the likely outcome of a patient's illness or whether a certain venture, such as a hunting trip, battle, or journey, will meet with success or failure. These divinatory powers frequently incorporate 'remote viewing' skills through which a shaman can locate lost or stolen goods, identify criminals, describe the condition of persons distant, or chart the position of fish shoals or animal herds and so on. A North American Shivwits Paiute shaman, for example, who went by the name of Mapitcabï, specialized in locating stolen property and when undertaking a quest he would concentrate 'without singing, while his ïnïpits [spirit helper] guided him to the place where the goods were concealed'.[36] Canadian Ojibwa shaman Kimvuanipinas, on the other hand, claimed that when he was asked to find some lost horses and a lost bag he 'went outside and started to pray. As I prayed, I started to talk, you know – started to know where these things are. I continued to pray . . . and then he [the spirit] shows me where those horses are – where a lost bag was . . . Just the other side of Eliceborg in the Valley, the second house – that's where his horses were, in a barn.'[37] Other shamans use their spirits to gain news of sick persons. One eye-witness account describes how the North American Menominee shaman, Onawabano, asked his spirit to 'fly to the Carp [River] to see if his [the client's] mother was still alive. The spirit was absent about five minutes. He told Muk-kud-de Wi-kan-a-we that his mother was better; she had already taken the broth of a grey duck and that she was going to recover. These spirits seem to be obliged to answer any question.'[38] Shamans can supplement the use of spirits in divination with a variety of other methods, many of which are similar to those used by cunning folk and witches, such as reading the bones of animals; analysing dreams; watching the behaviour of a flock of birds, the way coals burn on a fire, the pattern a bunch of sticks makes as it falls to the ground, the way a ball of chewed tobacco floats in a cup of water and so on.

Like cunning folk and witches, shamans can also employ their helping spirits in a wide variety of pursuits above and beyond the core matters of healing and divining. Almost anything of human concern, from agriculture and hunting to love or war, can be resolved with the help of a powerful spirit. Among the North American Maidu it is believed that 'Every shaman must have one or more of these [ku'kini] as his guardian spirit or spirits, and they aid him in *all that he does* [my italics]' – while North American Ojibwa chief Charles Kawbawgam claimed that '[a novice shaman] sees the spirit before him in the shape of a man, saying: "Whenever you need help, you will see me."'[39] Such flexibility on the part of the helping spirit means that, like the early modern familiar, it is sometimes employed to perform mundane or frivolous activities. The anthropologist Roland Dixon recounts how one North American Maidu shaman 'resolved to acquire the spirit of the honeybee. This he did, and then was able to secure whiskey in unlimited quantities, as the bee could insert its proboscis through the corks of bottles, or through the closed bung-holes of barrels, and suck out the liquor, which it afterward put into other receptacles for the Indian's use. The bee could also enter anywhere, as it could unlock all doors by inserting its proboscis.'[40]

Invocations

The relationship between shamans and their helping spirits is, like the relationship between cunning folk or witches and their familiars, based upon a series of frequent visual encounters. Like their early modern counterparts, some helping spirits reserve the right to appear unbidden before the shaman from time to time, but more commonly they appear in response to an invocation or conjuration. While the invocatory techniques employed by cunning folk and witches are largely lost to us, in large part because the latter's familiar-encounters often took place when they were alone, or unobserved, the invocatory techniques employed by shamans have been closely described in many eye-witness accounts.[41] The early anthropologists and missionaries who first documented the activities of tribal shamans, tended to associate spirit conjuration with dramatic public 'séances' and as a consequence the image of a mesmerized tribe gathering around an exotically-dressed performing shaman has entered into the modern western imagination. But this stereotypical image is only part of the picture. On a day-to-day basis public séances are usually low-key affairs. Among the traditional Siberian Evenk, for example, most invocations occur at any time of the day and involve only a prayer, followed by singing and drumming.[42] More specific to the discussion here, however, is the fact that shamans often invoke helping spirits when alone, or in some other way separated from the body of the tribe, in a manner redolent of the circumstances in which many cunning folk and witches encountered their familiars. The classic 'vision quest' of the Native American shaman necessitates the cultivation of solitude for several days, weeks, or even months, in order to encounter helping spirits.[43] Less dramatically, the shaman might sit or lie in his hut alone, or separated from his companions by a skin-hanging, while he performs his invocations. Ronald Hutton notes that 'Among the Turdic-speaking groups who became the Khakass nation, a great kam would sometimes perform for up to six hours, but more usually the practitioner would leave the company and return with an account of a spirit-journey undertaken in solitude.'[44]

Whether solitary or public, the shaman's invocations can vary widely in character. Sometimes they are 'extreme', in the sense that they involve overtly ritualistic or demanding procedures, often incorporating asceti-

Three helping spirits drawn by the Canadian Iglulik shaman, Anarqâq, in the early twentieth century. From left to right: 'Nuvatqik', who could shapeshift between human and dog form; 'Sangungajoq', the spirit of a dead man from the Adelaide Peninsula and 'Uvliaq', a spirit which the shaman inherited from his uncle.

An eighteenth-century depiction of a North American Ojibwa shaman healing the sick. The shaman sits in a tent, alone with his patient, while he calls up his helping spirits or 'Manitou'.

cisms (such as fasting, self-immolation, or subjection to extremes of heat, cold or solitude); the use of rhythmic sound (such as chanting, banging drums or shaking rattles); prescribed movements and the use of hallu-cinogens and similar. At other times these invocations are 'minimalist' in the sense that they are barely perceptible to an onlooker and can some-times seem to involve little more, to external perception, than a verbal request for the spirit's presence. Rasmussen claims that among the Polar Inuit 'A magician does not always require spirit songs and vehement conjurations in order to call up spirits; in a less serious case [of healing] he may content himself with placing a person on his back on the sleeping-place, binding a seal-leather thong round his head, and pulling it up and down, saying: '*qiláka nauk?* – where are my spirits?'[45] Similarly, Frances Densmore noted that when North American Ute shaman Pagitsh wished to talk with his helping spirit he 'sat outdoors in the early morning before sunrise. He sat facing the east and smoked. No ceremonial act was connected with this and he had no drum or rattle, neither did he sing. Sometimes it was not even necessary for him to smoke in order to talk with the little green man.'[46] Rasmussen, again, describes an Inuit shaman who 'sits for a while in silence, breathing deeply, and then, after some time has elapsed . . . begins to call on his helping spirits'.[47] For some shamans, the appearance of spirits can also occur as part of the daily round, in the seeming absence of any invocatory techniques at all. In these cases, the initial spontaneous encounter may become an ongoing feature of the shaman's relationship with his spirits. The Canadian Netsilik shaman, Anarqaoq, had such a powerful imagination that it 'peopled the whole of nature with fantastic spirit creatures that came to him either while he slept, or even when fully awake and engaged in his normal occupations'.[48] It is highly significant that the majority of information about the invoca-tory methods of shamans come from external observers, rather than the shamans themselves. Encounter-narratives taken directly from shamans seldom contain detailed references to these methods. In the majority of cases we find the shaman stating simply that he 'called on', 'asked', 'demanded' or 'went with' his helping spirits. In this sense his encounter-narratives are wholly congruent with those of cunning folk and witches.

Intimate Relationships

Like relationships between cunning folk or witches and their familiars, relationships between shamans and their helping spirits can continue for many years; exhibiting a complex tension between numinous intensity and down-to-earth mundanity and embracing the full gamut of human emotions. Holger Kalweit claims that this relationship is 'often no different from his [the shaman's] relationship with his fellow beings. It frequently resembles a marriage and displays the whole spectrum of human emotions such as love, hate, jealousy, distrust, obedience, fear, longing, quarrels, etc.'[49] An account given by the Inuit shaman, Alualuk, who rejected his helping spirits when he converted to Christianity, is a testament to the depth of affection and companionship which such relationships can sustain. Alualuk lamented that after his conversion, 'He often felt lonely without the spirits, because he missed their friendship and company. The spirits, too, were sad and lonely because they had to be without him. He pitied them.'[50] However, the shaman/spirit alliance could simultaneously incorporate the banality and bickering often characteristic of long-term human intimacy. In reference to shamans from the Californian Achomawi tribe, Mircea Eliade writes that 'The dialogue between the shaman and his "powers" is sometimes amazingly monotonous. The master complains that the *damagomi* has kept him waiting, and the *damagomi* offers excuses: it had fallen asleep beside a stream, etc. The master dismisses it and summons another.'[51] The comments of contemporary Native American shaman Brooke Medicine Eagle show a similar impatience with tardy spirits. She complains, 'Running off the mountain, with her hair flying, is this friend of mine [that is, her familiar]. She's always late. She is a very high person, but she is very unstable.'[52] North American Wintu shaman Nels Charles, on the other hand, became anxious because his spirits were losing their efficacy, claiming that 'My power is not so strong as it used to be. My power is not so great because my spirits worry. They don't know what to do with themselves . . . My spirits aren't sure whether they can cure a sick person and they are weakened by not being sure'.[53] Some encounter-narratives describe helping spirits, in their turn, getting angry with the shaman if he fails them in any way. The Polar Inuit shaman, Otaq, claimed that 'Once I was very ill, and then I lost a great deal of my magic power. My helping spirits began to despise me, they despised me because I fell ill.'[54] Similarly, the spirits which formerly belonged to the shaman Alualuk were not only 'sad and lonely' as a result of his conversion to Christianity, but were also, in some cases, 'angry and even offended' and 'tried to get their own back on him at every opportunity'.[55] Ronald Hutton articulates these contradictions when he points out that among traditional Siberian cultures some spirits were regarded with 'respect, affection and solicitude' while others were seen as 'groups of efficient but untrustworthy thugs. Those serving a single shaman would commonly quarrel amongst themselves, and would punish with death any human master or mistress who shirked the duties of the shamanic vocation.'[56]

The relationship between shamans and their helping spirits, like those between cunning folk or witches and their familiars, can also be expressed on a sexual level and sometimes involve marriage. Among the Siberian Eskimos, for example, it is traditional for shamans to consent to marry their helping spirit and even produce children by them. The man from the Siberian Gold tribe, who we met earlier, describes how his seduction by a spirit was an integral part of his becoming a shaman. The beautiful female spirit who appeared to him during his long sickness (possessing 'magnificent' hair which was 'decorated with small plaits and hung down her shoulders') said to him '"I love you. I have no husband now. You will be my husband and I shall be a wife unto you. I shall give you assistant spirits. You are to heal with their aid".' The spirit's seduction, however, like that of many early modern demon familiars, was coercive, for when the already-married shaman tried to resist her proposal the spirit concluded "If you will not obey me, so much the worse for you. I shall kill you."'[57] A similarly close relationship between spirit-marriage and healing powers is illustrated in an anecdote from Central India. Worried parents from the village of Bungding, on the boundary between Ganjam and Koraput, were told that the intermittent sickness of their teenage daughter, Sondam, was caused by a spirit who wanted to marry her. The girl's father said to the spirit:

> 'Why do you keep on troubling this girl? She may die if you don't leave her alone.' But the tutelary [spirit] said, 'No, I am pleased with your daughter. I have given her a lot of wine to drink and I am going to marry her. Then if anyone feels ill and she sends for me, I will tell her what is the matter, and help her cure the patient. I insist on marrying her. Give me a she-goat and I will come into the house.'[58]

The anecdote goes on to describe how a child was born of their union in the spirit world, and how the tutelary spirit brought the baby to the shamaness to suckle.

Consumed by Spirits

Some aspects of the shaman's relationship with his spirit helper are reminiscent of the ways in which early modern witches and, less frequently, cunning folk, exchanged their blood in return for the familiar's magical services. In many traditions the shaman's relationship with his helping spirits is intimately tied up with the destruction and/or consumption of his physical body.[59] The belief that the process of becoming a shaman involves being bodily consumed by the spirits, for example, is central to North American and Siberian shamanism. Waldemar Bogoras states that in North America, 'To enter into contact with the spirits or to obtain guardian spirits, the aspirant withdraws into solitude and subjects himself to a strict regime of self-torture. When the spirits manifest themselves in animal form, the aspirant is believed to give them his own flesh to eat.'[60] Similarly the Siberian Tungus shaman Semyon Semyonov claimed that 'my ancestors made me into a shaman . . . They cut the flesh off me. They separated my bones and counted them. My flesh they ate raw.'[61] These experiences of being consumed, like the early modern witch's experience of being suckled by her animal familiars, are generally not considered painful. The Greenlandic Inuit shaman, Autdaruta, recounted with surprise that when a polar bear crunched him up 'limb by limb, joint by joint . . . strangely enough it did not hurt at all'.[62]

Just as the English witch believed that allowing the animal familiar to consume her blood gave her access to the spirit's magical powers, many North American and Siberian shamans believe that in order to gain access to supernatural power they must allow themselves to be bodily consumed by the spirits or 'spirit-hardened'.[63] Autdaruta claimed that after being eaten by the polar bear, 'From that day forth I felt that I ruled my helping-spirits. After that I acquired many fresh helping-spirits and no danger could any longer threaten me, as I was always protected.'[64] This 'spirit-hardening' process could be repeated many times, each time further increasing the shaman's strength. The Greenlandic Inuit shaman, Qangatse, claimed that he invoked a spirit which is 'like a dog to look at . . . It will take me and eat me, press me, and grind me up, limb for limb . . . But it will throw us up again, just as we were before it ate us, and then we will have become greater magicians than we were before. This monster has often eaten me like that, that I might grow greater in my magic power.'[65]

Unlike similar narratives given by cunning folk and witches, descriptions of bodily consumption by spirits given by shamans do not usually emphasize the value of blood over that of other body parts (flesh, bones, skin and so on), although in a rare account, the Siberian Tungus shaman, Ivan Cholko, claimed that 'a future shaman must fall ill and have his body cut in pieces and his blood drunk by evil spirits'.[66] Almost all tribal societies, however, share the more general belief that spirits, and in particular spirits of the dead, drink human and animal blood and these ideas provide much of the rationale behind traditions of animal and human sacrifice.[67] A North American Quinault shaman claimed to possess a helping spirit in the form of a snake which 'sucks the blood and poison out of people'.[68] Similarly, in the middle of a healing ritual, one Californian Achomawi shaman clearly attributed just such a blood lust to his helping spirits when he lamented that 'I hear my *damagomi* [helping spirits] quarreling. They all want me to give them something to drink. They have worked well for me. They have helped me. Now they are all hot. They're thirsty. They want to drink. They want to drink blood.'[69] In order to fulfil his spirit's request the shaman sucked what he called the 'bad blood' out of his patient's body. Alternatively, some Siberian shamans drink the blood of sacrificed animals on behalf of their thirsty spirits.[70] Taken together as a whole, these aspects of shamanism strongly suggest that early modern beliefs concerning the giving of blood as part of compact with demon familiars or fairies were rooted in this bedrock of ancient belief concerning the process of interchange between the physical body of the human and the supernatural power of the spirits.[71]

CHAPTER NINE

Spirit Worlds and High Gods

The helping spirit, like the early modern familiar, can live in very close proximity to its human ally. The Canadian Iglulik shaman, Aua, for example, claimed that one of his helping spirits, who assumed the likeness of a little woman 'no taller than the length of a man's arm', appeared to him for the first time when he was in his house, and then 'placed itself in a corner of the passage, invisible to others, but always ready if I should call it'.[1] Helping spirits can also live inside 'fetish' objects belonging to the shaman such as clothes, rattles, crystals, stones, pebbles or wooden figurines.[2] The majority, however, like the majority of early modern familiars, live elsewhere in the rarified atmospheres of what can be loosely termed 'spirit worlds'.

Descriptions of these spirit worlds found in shaman-narratives bear many resemblances to those described by cunning folk and witches. Tribal cosmologies from throughout the world, however culturally distinct, seem to share the concept of a fundamentally three-tiered universe: the 'upper' world, associated with the sky and space; the 'middle' world, associated with the surface of our earth and the human realm; and the 'lower' or 'under' world, associated with subterranean places and often described as the 'land of the dead'. Given the ubiquity of such beliefs, it is likely that the notion of a three-tiered universe possessed by early modern cunning folk and witches owed as much to the perceptions of their tribal ancestors than to Christian teachings about heaven, earth and hell. This likelihood is supported by the fact that although contemporary theologians identified fairyland with either hell or purgatory (depending on their religious perspective), the fairy realm described by popular magical practitioners and represented in folk tales of the period, bore far more resemblance to the underworld (and, less frequently, the upper world) of the tribal shaman than it did to the lower worlds of the Christian cosmology.

Like fairyland, the shaman's underworld is conceived of as subterranean and is sometimes characterized by dim light.[3] Just as cunning folk and witches could enter into fairyland by going into a hill or beneath a lake, so the shaman often visits the underworld by 'descending' in some manner: down a hole in the ground, beneath the sea or through the back of a cave and so on. The Polar Inuk, Osarqaq, explained to Rasmussen that the spirits who lived in the lower worlds 'were as invisible as the human soul; and their houses went straight down into the earth, so that no one could find them. They only allowed themselves to be seen by persons who were alone, and then their appearance and conversation were like a human being's. When you found their houses, a hole in the earth would be the entrance to them.'[4]

Like fairyland, the shaman's underworld is inhabited by both spirits of non-human origin and souls of the dead. Like many cunning folk and witches, on their return from visiting these realms shamans often claim to have met deceased friends and relatives there and to have observed them living lives very similar to those they enjoyed when alive. A South American Guajiro shamaness claimed that she 'saw many dead people there [in the underworld]. Some I knew, sisters and other relatives as well . . . Many of the dead wanted to talk to me, but my spirit forbade me to answer . . . The dead look like people here. They live the way people used to live on earth, and the place we went to in the Beyond is just like here.'[5] The landscape of the lower spirit world, and the appearance and lifestyle of its inhabitants, reflects the cultural origin of its human visitors. In fairyland we find the fairies and the dead dressed in waistcoats and hoods, sitting at tables illuminated by candles, and drinking ale and eating bread; in the Arctic underworld the spirits live in skin huts, wear furs, eat seal and walrus and sport in a landscape of ice and snow, while in the North American underworld the dead wear buffalo skins and beaded moccasins, ride horses, and live in tepees.

Like cunning folk and witches, shamans can make contact with their helping spirits in either the human realm or in the spirit worlds. As we have already seen, the shaman frequently uses a variety of invocatory methods to 'call' his spirits to him, however his helping spirits, like their early modern counterparts, are often equally keen to lure the shaman into their own realms. The encounter-narrative of the North American Zuni shaman 'Palowahtiva' closely resembles Bessie Dunlop's description of the entreaties of Tom Reid. The shaman claims:

I saw a broad-shouldered, god-sized man coming toward me, he having opened and passed through the door. I did not know him. He was dressed in the ancient costume of my people. He came toward me, holding in one hand, which was extended toward the door, a riata (lasso), as though he had led a horse behind him. Then he stood over me, and looked down at me and smiled . . . Then he said to me, "Would you like to go with me?" And I looked at him and said, "Why not?"'[6]

Similarly, the following description given by a Californian Achomawi shamanness called 'Old Dixie', resembles the interaction between English witches and their insinuating animal familiars: 'my first *damagomi* [helping spirit] came to find me. I still have it. It is a little black thing, you can hardly see it. When it came the first time it made a great noise. It was at night. It told me that I must go to see it in the mountains.'[7] Just as shamans frequently attempt to resist the call to become a shaman, so they can also, like cunning folk and witches, attempt to resist the helping spirit's invitation to 'go with' them (Old Dixie claiming, for example, that she was 'very frightened. I hardly dared go'). As a consequence helping spirits are often compelled to use all their arts of persuasion, and if this fails, coercion to achieve their end. It is not uncommon for them to punish shamans with sickness when they refuse to journey. One South American Guajiro shamaness, named Graziela, claimed: 'I do not like traveling to these distant places. My spirits often invite me to go there, but I prefer not to go with them. Sometimes I say to them, "I do not want to go with you." Whenever I turn down such an invitation I develop a fever and become very ill . . . I receive many invitations.'[8] In Part I we surmised that the reluctance expressed by some cunning folk and witches at the idea of accompanying their familiar into fairyland or to the sabbath may have been connected to fears associated with the separation of the soul from the body. This theory becomes even more likely when it is examined in relation to shamanism – for the shaman believes that every time he takes a journey into the spirit worlds he hazards the safety of his soul.

Hazarding the Soul

Everything that concerns the soul and its adventure, here on earth and in the beyond, is the exclusive province of the shaman. Through his own preinitiatory and initiatory experiences, he knows the drama of the human soul, its instability, its precariousness; in addition, he knows the forces that threaten it and the regions to which it can be carried away.[9]

Historians have traditionally assumed that the appearance of beliefs concerning the soul in early modern witch trials is attributable to the influence of learned Christian thinking, however shamanic encounter-narratives suggest that these beliefs may have owed as much to pre-Christian animism as to Christianity. The concept of a spiritual self or soul is not exclusive to developed religions. The idea that there is a part of the human which can survive after the death of the body is a very ancient one and found in primitive theologies right across the globe.[10] The Victorian anthropologist, Edward Tylor, claimed that 'The conception of the human soul is, as to its most essential nature, continuous from the philosophy of the savage thinker to that of the modern professor of theology. Its definition has remained from the first that of an animating, separable, surviving entity, the vehicle of individual personal existence.'[11] In other words, the idea of 'soul' or 'spirit' held by the shaman and his community differs little in fundamentals from the more complex theologies of the soul found in developed religions. In both belief systems the soul is immortal and without it the body dies; the soul separates from the body on physical death and travels to inhabit a spiritual realm; and the soul is the most important part of a man, defining and vitalizing him. No Christian theologian could dispute the assessment of the soul's importance given by the Utkuhikhalingmiut Inuk, Ikinilik, who claimed that 'The only thing of value in a man is the soul. That is why it is the soul that is given everlasting life, either in the land of the Sky or in the Underworld. The soul is man's greatest power; it is the soul that makes us human, but how it does so we do not know. Our flesh and blood, our body, is nothing but an envelope about our vital power.'[12] Nor could the theologian dispute the ubiquitous tribal belief, expressed here by an Iglulik Inuk, that the soul should be esteemed because it facilitates consciousness after physical death:

> Among us, as I have already explained to you, all is bound up with the earth we live on and our life here; and it would be even more incomprehensible, even more unreasonable, if, after a life short or long, of happy days or of suffering and misery, we were then to cease altogether from existence. What we have heard about the soul shows us that the life of men and beasts does not end with death. When at the end of life we draw our last breath, that is not the end. We awake to consciousness again, we come to life again, and all this is effected through the medium of the soul. Therefore it is that we regard the soul as the greatest and most incomprehensible of all.[13]

This dichotomy between body and soul is fundamental to the shaman's concept of journeying into spirit worlds. The soul needs to be able to detach itself from the body in order to travel into these realms and as a consequence, when the helping spirit invites or coerces the shaman to visit his world, he is in effect inviting or coercing the shaman's soul. In Burma it is said that a male 'nat' or helping spirit is attracted to a shamaness by his 'love for her beautiful soul'.[14] Some shaman-narratives describe spirits specifically inviting the shaman's soul to journey. The following account from a South American Yamana shaman (which also sounds remarkably similar to Bessie Dunlop's description of how a group of spirits attempted to persuade her to 'go with thame' into fairyland) is representative: 'when strolling, musing, in the forest, one may suddenly find oneself in the midst of a large company of spirits, little people, very like men; and passing into a deep sleep, one then will see them sitting about a fire, keeping warm, talking quietly. In a friendly way they will invite one's soul to join them.'[15] Yamana animal spirits can be just as keen. A shaman, for example, might find that 'Around him crowds an immeasurable company of herrings, whales, swordfish, vultures, cormorants, gulls, and other creatures. All are addressing him in flattering terms, respectfully, in the most friendly way . . . They are inviting his soul to join them. And it does so, following them, presently, out onto the high seas.'[16]

In some cases the separation of the soul from the body is conceived of as a physical process. Among the Iglulik Inuit of Northern Canada at the beginning of the twentieth century, it was customary for a novice shaman to retire behind a curtain with the shaman who was initiating him and submit 'to the extraction of the "soul" from his eyes, heart and vitals, which would then be brought by magic means into contact with those beings destined to become his helping spirits, to the end that he might later meet them without fear'.[17] Other shamans believe that to accept an invitation to the spirit world will result in their death. A North American Paviotso shaman who had fearful dreams in which his deceased brother, a former shaman, kept appearing in an effort to pass onto him his magical power, complained that he 'did not like the dreams. He was afraid that his brother was trying to get him away [so he would die]'.[18] Mexican farmer Don Soltero Perez had a similar fear, but in his case his journey to the underworld would have resulted in death if he had refused to become a shaman. He claimed that the spirits of 'enanitos', or dwarf-sized rain deities (one of which later became his helping spirit), stole his spirit and took it to the caves underground where they lived. The enanitos 'wanted Don Soltero to become a healer and told him they would not allow his spirit to return to his body unless he agreed to their request'.[19] In a variation on this theme a shaman named Tarendu, from the Central Indian town of Pattili, claimed that when he refused a proposal of marriage from a beautiful girl spirit she 'caught hold of me and took me to the Under World, where she shut me up in a stone house and gave me nothing to eat. I grew thin as a tamarind leaf, and then she took me to the top of a high date palm and shook it until I was so terrified of falling that I promised to marry her after all. Her name was Sirpanti.'[20] When Tarendu finally agreed to the marriage, the event marked the beginning of his career as a shaman.

These fears surrounding the loss of the soul are closely connected to the belief, found in tribal societies throughout the world, that serious cases of sickness can be caused by soul theft, that is, by the soul being stolen from the body by spirits and taken into the underworld. Unless the soul can find its way back, or be retrieved, it remains trapped there and the body dies. In a classic 'shamanistic' diagnosis, the North American Twana shaman, Tyee Charley (who gained his healing powers from a helping spirit in the form of a mountain-marmot), claimed that a man's mental illness was due to the fact that 'the little-earths (. . . dwarfs) got him, they got him there [while fishing on the canal], they took his shɑl'ɛ' [soul], and that's what makes him act crazy and talk as if he was out of his head'.[21] Echoes of this primitive association between sickness and 'soul theft' can be detected in early modern folk belief. Those who were mentally or physically ill were sometimes described as 'fairy-taken', meaning that their souls had been taken away by the fairies. Similarly, sickly or deformed children were often defined as 'changelings' – inferior replicas left by the fairies in exchange for the original healthy children which were spirited away into fairyland. Later folk tales such as *Ethna the Bride* and *The Smith and the Fairies* also reflect these beliefs.[22] The reluctance expressed by some cunning folk and witches at the idea of travelling into fairyland or to the sabbath is likely to have been rooted in this primeval fear that the soul could get stuck in the spirit world, thereby presaging physical death. That Bessie Dunlop, for example, believed that to accept Tom's invitation into Elfame might lead to such an end is suggested by the fact that her refusal emphasized '[that] sche duelt with hir awin husband and bairnis, and culd nocht leif thame'.[23]

Despite such fears, in the majority of instances the shaman, like the cunning woman and witch, believes that his journey into the spirit world will only be a temporary one, during which the soul will be separated from the body for a short period. These temporary journeys are undertaken for a variety of reasons. Like many visits to fairyland or the sabbath, they can involve an element of pleasure; feasting, playing games, making music, dancing and so on. Rasmussen reported that in the early twentieth century the Canadian Iglulik believed that the 'greater among the angakoqs, or wizards, often go up on a visit to the People of Day [the dead] just for pleasure . . . It is said that there is great rejoicing in the Land of Day, when a wizard comes on a visit.'[24] However these visits are also, like their early modern equivalents, undertaken with more serious intentions. With the assistance of helping spirits, who act as guides, the shaman enters into spirit worlds in order to perform magical activities or to gain knowledge

from or propitiate more powerful spirits or deities. The two most important magical activities traditionally performed during these visits or
'journeys' are those of retrieving the souls of the sick and escorting the
souls of the dead from the human realm to their final resting place in the
underworld. The North American Twana shaman we saw earlier, who
attributed a man's mental illness to the fact that his soul had been stolen
by dwarf spirits, concluded his diagnosis by stating, 'And now I'm going
to go down there and get him back from those little-earths.'[25]

For reasons which are as yet unclear, we seldom find direct reference
to beliefs surrounding 'soul retrieval' or 'soul escort' in early modern
descriptions of sabbath or fairyland experiences – although vestiges of
such beliefs can be found in traditional British folk tales.[26] Associated
beliefs, however, are more clearly evident. The cunning woman's role as
a messenger between the dead and the living, as illustrated by Bessie
Dunlop when she brought information about the deceased Tom Reid and
the Laird of Auchinskeyth back to their respective families, is also – by
virtue of his unique access to the land of the dead – part of the shaman's
remit.[27] Mircea Eliade describes how a Siberian Gold shaman, on
returning from a funerary journey into the underworld, 'gives a long
account of all that he has seen in the land of the dead and the impressions
of the dead man whom he escorted. He brings each of the audience greet-
ings from their dead relatives and even distributes little gifts from them.'[28]
Shades of shamanic traditions involving travel into spirit worlds in order
to engage in battle with malevolent beings (hostile souls of the
dead/spirits/shamans etc.) to magically protect the interests of the tribe,
can also be found in the encounter-narratives of Scottish magical practitioners such as Isobel Gowdie and Jean Weir.[29] Other correspondences
are stronger. Like some cunning folk and witches, shamans can journey
into spirit worlds in order to receive healing objects. While an early
modern cunning man from the North of England returned from his visits
to a fairy hill with magical healing powder, Mexican shaman Don Soltero
Perez returned from the spirit world with 'three healing stones' which he
found 'in his pocket upon returning to his body; one was shaped like a
cannon, the second like a doll, and the third like a duck.'[30] Similarly,
shaman-narratives which describe travel – often in the company of a
helping spirit – into spirit worlds in order to gain advice or favour from
more powerful supernatural beings or deities can sound very similar to
sabbath and fairyland experiences which describe meetings with the Devil
or fairy king and queen. A Canadian Tsimsyan man from the Gyilodzau
tribe, named Qamkawl, claimed that in the spirit world he met 'a very
bright man' who asked him:

"Where are you from, and what do you want?" "Oh! supernatural One, I have come to get halaeit power, to cure my people." The bright man said, "Come with me, I will take you to my father. He may help you." The Gyilodzau followed this shining man, who led him to a large house. A number of people sat about . . . The Gyilodzau man was seated near the big chief . . . The people in the house began to sing . . . A live drum then ran out and began to beat itself with one of the beaters. Everything seemed to be alive. The Gyilodzau heard the singing and the dancing. The great chief arose and rubbed the Gyilodzau-man's eyes . . . He could no longer see.[31]

As a result of this journey the man became a powerful shaman. Similarly, an Arctic encounter-narrative describes how, after undertaking a long and hazardous journey into the spirit world, a shaman manages to gain an audience with Erlik, the King of the Dead. Mircea Eliade tells us that after the shaman has shared wine with the king, and offered him gifts of garments and furs, the king 'becomes benevolent, blesses him [the shaman], promises that the cattle will multiply, etc. The shaman joyously returns to earth, riding not a horse but a goose . . . The shaman rubs his eyes as if waking. Asked: "How was your journey? What success did you have?" he answers: "The journey was successful. I was well received!"'[32] Like some cunning folk and witches, shamans can enter spirit worlds in the company of others at specific times of the year in order to perform ritual magical acts. In Mexico it is believed that some healers 'die twice a year. Their spirits go to a cave of the enanitos [rain deities] where they receive further instruction in healing. The first annual death occurs in October or November, after the end of bog rain fall. All the curanderos [healers] "die" at the same time and remain dead for half an hour or an hour while their spirits attend the great assembly of cunanderos and enanitos.'[33]

Like the sabbath and fairyland experiences of Scottish cunning folk and witches, the journeying experiences of shamans can also involve magical flight. Among the North American Hopi, shamans are believed to have the power of 'flying, and instantaneously transporting themselves long distances', while among the Greenlandic Inuit they can, with the aid of their helping spirits, 'fly to the moon and back'.[34] Like comparable early modern flight experiences, the airborne journeys of the shaman can be depicted with great precision and realism. The shaman described in a Siberian ritual song as descending to earth 'at such speed that the wind passes through him' enjoys sensations similar to those experienced by East Lothian witch John Fian (1590) when 'soughing [rushing] athwart the earth', while the Alaskan Tikerarmiut shaman Asetcuk's ability 'to fly with one knee drawn up and arms outstretched' while circling houses to 'peer in through the skylights' is reminiscent of the airborne agility of Nairnshire witch Isobel Gowdie (1662).[35] The link between travel into spirit worlds and animal metamorphosis, seen in the early modern period, is also a widespread shamanic theme. Eliade tells us that during the shamanic séance 'Chukchee and Eskimo shamans turn themselves into wolves; Lapp shamans become wolves, bears, reindeer, fish; the Semang *hala* can change into a tiger, as can the Sakai *halak* and the *bomor* of Kelantan.'[36]

Whatever the exact nature of his supernatural adventures and whether or not they involve travel into other worlds, the shaman, like the cunning woman and the witch, is reluctant to talk about his experiences. Rasmussen claimed that many of the Inuit shamans he met denied they had any knowledge of spirits, even making a mockery of such beliefs. In the case of the Caribou Inuk, Igjugârjuk, however, this scepticism turned out to be a front, for Rasmussen reports that the shaman 'who had so vehemently asserted that he was no magician, and knew nothing of the past history of his people, soon changed over when he found that he could trust me, and realized that I was earnestly interested in such matters'.[37] As in early modern Britain, maintaining silence about such things is associated with the acquisition, or retaining, of magical power. A Greenlandic Inuit boy named Qalanganguasê, for example, was told by his spirits, 'Take care to tell no tales! Then the lower part of your body will receive strength and nothing shall be impossible to you!'[38]

The Ambivalent Shaman

Some tribal societies possess decisive concepts of the wholly 'good' or wholly 'bad' shaman (with 'witch' figures merging into the figure of the 'bad' shaman). In the majority of cases however, the shaman, like his early modern counterpart, is considered to be morally ambivalent – capable of performing both helpful and harmful magic. Indeed, in *Shamanism in Western North America*, anthropologist Willard Park incorporates the ability to perform witchcraft into his basic concept of shamanism, claiming that the 'power' possessed by the shaman 'is generally manipulated in such a way as to be a matter of concern to others in the society. Accordingly, the practice of witchcraft may be as important a part of shamanism as the curing of disease or the charming of game in a communal hunt. We will designate by the term of shamanism, then, all the practices by which supernatural power may be acquired by mortals, the exercise of that power either for good or evil, and all the concepts and beliefs associated with those practices.'[39] As a consequence of such beliefs, the shaman, like the cunning man or woman, is an easy target for accusations of witchcraft. Among the North American Seminole 'Most suspect [of poisoning] are shamans who are known to have healing powers because such persons are also capable of knowing how to harm people with their powers. Therefore, a shaman who loses a patient is bound to come under suspicion of witchcraft.'[40] Similarly, shamans from the North American Kawaiisu tribe are reluctant to try and cure patients who are near death for fear of being accused of witchcraft should the patient die.[41] There is no doubt that some shamans, considering themselves to have been wronged in some way, are sorely tempted to wreak magical revenge on their enemies. North American Wintu shaman Nels Charles stated, 'If a person abuses me I musn't wish him to be sick, or die, or have bad luck. That would ruin me.'[42]

Like cunning folk and witches, shamans who wish to perform malevolent magic can do so with the assistance of their spirit-helpers. Among the Californian Achomawi, as we have already seen, the shaman summons his helping spirits or 'damagomi', as he calls them, to diagnose the causes of sickness and prescribe cures; however he can just as easily despatch them to cause sickness and death. Eliade claims that when the Achomawi shaman 'wants to poison someone he sends a *damagomi*: "Go find So-and-so. Enter him. Make him sick. Don't kill him at once. Make him die in a month".'[43] Many sources indicate that – as was the case with cunning folk and witches – the shaman's use, or alleged use, of spirits to perform harmful magic, was rooted in inter-personal tensions. One account, recorded by anthropologist Asen Balikci, describes how a Canadian Netsilik shaman, named Tavoq, was jealous of his neighbour, Angutitak, who was a fine hunter, and 'scolded him repeatedly'. Balikci tells us that 'Angutitak, a quiet and fearful man, never answered, until one day he accused Tavoq of being a mediocre and lazy hunter. Tavoq avenged himself by dispatching his *tunraq* [helping spirit] to raise a snowstorm just at the moment when Angutitak was stalking caribou.'[44] The use of spirits to harm can also be linked to tensions between tribes. Among the traditional Siberian Evenk, fierce rivalry among clans meant that 'sickness in one was commonly ascribed to the work of an evil spirit sent by a shaman in another'.[45] As we saw in the previous chapter, helping spirits can also be malevolent on their own account, and not just at the behest of their human ally. A Siberian Sakha shaman claimed that when he converted to Christianity and abandoned his vocation as a shaman, his spirits 'blinded him in revenge'.[46] Helping spirits used by shamans from the Canadian Kwakiutl tribe have a similar capacity for malevolence – the anthropologist Ivan Lopatin stating that: 'The spirits when fed, employed, and entertained by the shaman brought the people no harm; so the shaman rendered great service to the people by keeping hungry and idle spirits from troubling them.'[47]

The Demonization

When Victorian anthropologists and missionaries first came across non-European tribal societies, they interpreted the shaman's experiences of encountering helping spirits and travelling into spirit worlds in much the same way as early modern ecclesiastics and witchcraft prosecutors interpreted the encounter-experiences of cunning folk and witches. In both cases the experiences were 'demonized'. Mircea Eliade states that 'nineteenth-century observers and ethnographers often saw shamanism as demonic: for them, the future shaman undergoing initiation could only be putting himself at the disposition of the "devil."'[48] He then goes on to cite a Victorian description of a Siberian Yakut initiation ceremony in which the observing anthropologist states that the instructing shaman urges the novice to 'renounce God and all that he holds dear, and makes him promise to devote his whole life to the "devil," in return for which the latter will fulfil all his wishes. Then the master shaman teaches him the places where the demon lives, the sicknesses that he cures, and the way to pacify him'.[49] Such a description would have come only too naturally to an early modern witchcraft interrogator.

In tribal cultures undergoing Christianization, some shamans seem to experience a conflict between their traditional animism and the newly-introduced Christianity in the same way that cunning folk and witches experienced conflict between their folkloric beliefs and the orthodox teachings of the Church. Both can claim that their spirit-helpers are hostile towards Christianity, and in both cases the sacrament of baptism seems to be axiomatic in this context. The Greenlandic Inuit shaman, Autdaruta, described how, 'When I made up my mind to journey to the West coast to be baptized, they [his familiar spirits] appeared to me and urged me not to do so. But I did what I willed, all the same. Since then they have not shown themselves to me, because *I betrayed them by my baptism* [my italics].'[50] The way shamans describe their relationships with their helping spirits gradually corroding under the influence of Christian teaching also mirrors the breakdown of the relationship between cunning folk or witches and their familiars. We have already seen how the certainty and persuasiveness of witchcraft interrogators and suspicious neighbours could weaken a magical practitioner's faith in her own world-view, persuading her to doubt the integrity of her relationship with her familiar and eventually seek solace in the rejection of the spirit and anticipation of salvation on the scaffold. The following account from Rasmussen, which describes the experiences of an Inuit shaman, illustrates how the latter can undergo surprisingly similar doubting processes:

> it was plain to see that he was an honest man, earnestly believing in his powers and those he had invoked. But, he informed us, from the moment he first listened to the words of the stranger priest, his helping spirits seemed to have deserted him; doubt entered into his mind, he felt himself alone and forsaken, helpless in face of the tasks which had called forth his strength in earlier days. At last he was baptized, and since then, his mind had been at rest.[51]

However, other shamans do not find the conversion to Christianity so peaceful. Old allegiances die hard. The sufferings experienced by the Inuit shaman, Alualuk, for example, may have been experienced by those few cunning folk and witches who were lucky enough to be able to resume a normal life after having repented of their dealings with familiars. On their first meeting Alualuk told Arctic explorer Steffanson that he had 'half a dozen helping spirits with which he was able to cure illnesses and even reawaken the dead', however when Alualuk met the explorer again some time later, he told him that he:

> had become a Christian and sent all his helping spirits away. He admitted that he was now as helpless against the powers of the Beyond as any ordinary mortal and that he felt unwell and weak without his spirits, who had formerly supported him whenever he needed them. He often felt lonely without the spirits, because he missed their friendship and company. The spirits, too, were sad and lonely because they had to be without him. He pitied them. Some spirits, however, were angry and even offended. That is why they tried to get their own back on him at every opportunity. He had to be always on the alert, pray regularly, and follow the Christian commandments, so that the Church and Jesus Christ would protect him against the attacks of his former helpers.[52]

For many shamans, however, as for many cunning folk and witches, the juxtaposition of animist and Christian beliefs do not create such conflicts: old and new faiths exist alongside each other in a reasonably amicable fashion, often fusing together almost seamlessly to create hybrid belief and ritual. The following chant sung by Mesoamerican Mazatec shaman María Sabina is very redolent of early modern charms, effortlessly combining Christian and pre-Christian elements: 'Oh most holy Mary, oh

Jesus, Legendary healing goddess am I . . . Eagle woman am I, Important eagle woman am I, Clock woman am I, Whirling woman of the whirlwind am I, Yes, Jesus Christ says . . . '[53] An account of a spirit-journey to the Upper World made by the North American Slave shaman, Tinite, betrays a similarly harmonious fusion. The shaman's dead father 'appeared to him as an angel with wings and carried him in spirit up through a hole in the sky to heaven . . . He also gained control over the sun which is the father of all and sees everything, the wind which [is] the spirit of all and pervades everything, and the earth which is the mother of all and touches everything.'[54]

The ease with which many shamans fuse animist beliefs with the theistic teachings of Christianity is not as incongruous as it may at first appear. Most tribal belief systems contain some concept of a supreme spirit or deity. This spirit is seldom represented in imaginal form, few rituals are performed for it, few temples or priests are devoted to its worship and it is usually conceived of as remote and mysterious. Although on a day-to-day basis the shaman is primarily concerned with his helping spirits and other lesser supernatural entities, there is no doubt that he considers the supreme spirit to be the ultimate authority. The Alaskan Inuit shaman Najagneq, for example, talked of a 'great spirit' called Sila who:

> is not to be explained in simple words. A great spirit, supporting the world and the weather and all life on earth, a spirit so mighty that his utterance to mankind is not through common words, but by storm and snow and rain and the fury of the sea; all the forces of nature that men fear . . . When all is well, Sila sends no message to mankind, but withdraws into his own endless nothingness, apart. So he remains as long as men do not abuse life, but act with reverence towards their daily food. No one has seen Sila; his place of being is a mystery, in that he is at once among us and unspeakably far away.[55]

The shaman's inherent belief in the presence of a remote and all-powerful 'great spirit' can make it relatively easy for him to accommodate the notion of an omnipotent, inscrutable Christian God, and assimilate this God into his animist cosmology without unduly disturbing the hierarchy of spirits already existing there. Similarly, the spiritual entourage of the Christian God – Jesus, the saints, the apostles, angels and so on – and his spiritual enemies – the Devil and his demons – can be spliced into these pre-existent spirit-hierarchies with the minimum of disruption. This process of assimilation gives us an insight into the way pre-Christian and Christian beliefs may have interacted in the early modern popular mind. The animist belief systems which lay at the root of the fairy faith would almost certainly have included concepts of a supreme spirit, and an amalgamation between these concepts and concepts of a Christian God would have been occurring on a cultural level since Christianity first arrived in Britain. Given the fact that even by the early modern period the Christianization of the rural British peoples was often only superficial, it is possible that the concept of an omnipotent God held by many cunning folk and witches owed as much to inherited notions of a tribal supreme spirit than to the patrician God of the Hebrews.

PART III

The Experiential Dimension

INTRODUCTION TO PART III

The information presented in Part II has provided us with an overview of the main similarities between beliefs about helping spirits held by early twentieth-century Siberian and Native American shamans, and beliefs about familiar spirits held by early modern British cunning folk and witches. Of necessity, this overview has been brief. It is important to remember that there are significant areas of difference between the two sets of belief which have not been covered: shamans from these societies, for example, put far more emphasis on the public séance; the deliberately sought after initial encounter; escorting the dead to spirit worlds and retrieving souls than cunning folk and witches. Against these differences, however, can be set the fact that there are many similarities which have either not been addressed, or have only been mentioned in passing: beliefs surrounding spirit possession, exorcism, animal metamorphosis, the feeding of spirits and spirit flight, for example, are rich and complex areas of correspondence which remain relatively unexplored in the British context.

Despite such limitations, these anthropological comparisons are nevertheless sufficient to support and develop the conclusions drawn in Part I. They clearly illustrate that animist beliefs about helping spirits, as found in the aforementioned tribal societies, and early modern British beliefs about familiar spirits are very close, to the extent that even elements of familiar lore most commonly assumed by historians to have been of learned origin, such as the selling of the soul and the pact, are to be found present in some form in descriptions of relationships between shamans and their spirit-helpers. These similarities cannot be attributed to the transhistorical and transcultural diffusion of early modern European familiar beliefs out into Siberia and the Americas; therefore the only plausible explanation is that they represent the survival of indigenous pre-Christian animist beliefs in Britain in this period. This conclusion not only supports the hypothesis that descriptions of familiar-encounters found in the trial records of cunning folk and witches contained a popular folkloric component, but also indicates that this popular component may have been significant. While it is still important to acknowledge that learned thinking and popular Christian beliefs moulded notions about familiars in early modern Britain, it is now possible to argue that the downward filtration of élite ideas about the stereotypical demon familiar was working in tandem with an upward filtration from below of dynamic and coherent popular folk beliefs.

While supporting and clarifying the conclusions drawn in Part I, these anthropological perspectives also act as a platform from which we can progress onto an entirely different debate. The cunning folk and witches who were interrogated in early modern courts of law were not only providing us with a catalogue of contemporary *beliefs* about familiars, they were also describing their *experiences* of meeting them. Because historians of British witchcraft and magic have traditionally dismissed encounter-narratives as largely, if not exclusively, élite fictions, they have seldom given serious consideration to the fact that these narratives may have been describing genuine experiences, which occurred in historical time and space. As we shall see later, the growing Europe-wide acknowledgement that there was a folkloric component to popular familiar beliefs, and the rich body of work by Continental scholars into the experiential dimension of witch beliefs have, until very recently, not significantly influenced this prevailing attitude.

The comparisons drawn here between the encounter-experiences of cunning folk, witches and shamans, present us with the opportunity to tackle this overlooked subject with some precision. For over a century, scholars from a wide range of disciplines have been intrigued by the experiential dimension of the tribal shaman's beliefs concerning encounters with helping spirits and journeys into spirit worlds, and as a consequence there exists a large – and still fast-growing – body of diverse research on the subject. This research can be usefully mined in order to provide us with fresh perspectives on the British encounter-narrative. To use this material to understand the nature and significance of the familiar-encounter as an *experience*, then, will be our task in Part III.

CHAPTER TEN

Phantasicks and Phantasms

Confessions recorded in British witchcraft and sorcery trials give the impression that when cunning folk and witches described their encounters with familiar spirits, they believed themselves to be describing real experiences – distinct historical events which had occurred at specific moments in time. Most of the learned men who interrogated these magical practitioners were of the same opinion (although their interpretation of the significance of these events may have differed from that of those who claimed to have experienced them), and they took a great deal of time and trouble to prove that these events did indeed take place. Although Continental scholars have been exploring the experiential dimension of witch beliefs for nearly half a century, historians of British witchcraft and magic have been more interested in the influence of demonological ideas on encounter-narratives than in the reality or otherwise of the familiar-encounter as a historical event or psychological experience. Consequently, many questions about the ontological nature of the British familiar-encounter remain unresolved. While the latter automatically discount the interpretation adopted by most early modern witchcraft prosecutors – that is, that actual events took place in which cunning folk or witches communicated with the Devil in human or animal form – they seldom devote any time to providing alternative interpretations. Most consider questions of ontology to lie outside their field. Keith Thomas asserts, for example, in relation to the conjuration of spirits by both élite and popular magicians, that 'It is best left to the psychologist to determine just what happened at these spirit-raising sessions'.[1] It is also frequently maintained, quite justifiably, that for the purposes of historical analysis attempts to assess ontology are not necessary. Comments such as the following, made recently by Frederick Valletta in reference to the encounter-experiences and other supernatural events described in mid seventeenth-century

English pamphlets, are standard: 'Their contribution to historical knowledge is not whether they might be true or not, or whether contemporary people believed them; their importance lies in what they have to tell us about the beliefs and superstitions of the time.'[2] A similar type of rationale, but with a different emphasis, can be found in Owen Davies's recent analysis of the encounter-experiences of sixteenth-century Bavarian cunning man Chonrad Stoeckhlin: 'Whether he [Stoeckhlin] made up the stories of his soul journeys, or whether he really experienced some form of altered state of consciousness, is not important because the purpose of his stories was primarily to legitimate his claim to special knowledge, and that is precisely what he achieved.'[3]

Despite such statements, scholars often make passing comments which reveal their personal opinions as to what was actually going on during a familiar-encounter. Most of these comments pertain to the general view that the encounter, if not wholly a fiction created in the courtroom, was likely to have been a mixture of fact (involving remembered events involving 'real' humans and animals) and fantasy (involving fiction, distorted memory, suggestion, self-delusion, hallucination and so on). The wide variety of interpretative options available, and the lack of consensus reached among scholars in this area, is illustrated in the following passage by Marion Gibson. After paraphrasing a famous witch trial in which Lancashire woman Alison Device (1612) confessed to having met a familiar in the form of a black dog while walking through the Forest of Pendle and to having commanded the familiar to lame a pedlar who had refused to sell her some pins, Gibson concludes that:

> Readers of such a story will divide into two main groups: those who accept that the magical details in the story are probable, and those who do not believe in magic. There will be further divisions within the second group: for example, those who suggest that the talking dog was an hallucination of Alizon's, those who believe that she was pressed by the prosecuting authorities into creating a folktale-like story, those who read her story as a voluntary adoption of the powerful mythic status of the witch. Some will see the whole story as a fiction, while others contend that the pedlar really did fall ill, or that Alizon really saw a (mute) black dog.[4]

The Shaman's Encounter: real or imagined?

While questions surrounding the ontology of the early modern familiar-encounter have been largely overlooked by scholars, similar questions surrounding the spirit-encounters of the tribal shaman have received a wholly different fate. In the hundred years or so since shamanism first became a subject of interest to western scholars, there has been increasing interest in the ontological nature of the shaman's encounter experiences. Although it is acknowledged that shamans can sometimes interpret a confrontation with a 'real' animal or object as an encounter with a spirit, scholars generally agree that in the overwhelming majority of cases the shaman's spirit-encounters and his associated experiences of travelling to spirit worlds are historical events of a 'visionary' nature. In basic psychological terms this means that the shaman enters into an altered state of consciousness, commonly described as some kind of 'trance' or 'ecstasy', during which his sensory experience is drastically altered and as a result he is able to perceive imaginal psychic phenomena not visible to a man in his normal state of consciousness. This perceived link between shamanism and trance-induced visionary experience is now so strong that scholars in the field increasingly cite the ability to enter trance as one of the defining characteristics of the shaman. The anthropologist Michael Harner, for example, describes the shaman as 'a man or woman who enters an altered state of consciousness – at will – to contact and utilize an ordinarily hidden reality in order to acquire knowledge, power, and help other persons'.[5] These psychological perspectives on shamanism can be used to gain insight into the encounter-experiences of early modern cunning folk and witches.

The Reality of the Sabbath

The ontological nature of the sabbath experience has long been a subject of heated debate. Early modern scholars and lawmen, particularly those from the Continent where sabbath experiences were more prevalent and the issue given more importance, could not agree whether the descriptions of attending the sabbath or visiting fairyland given by witches and cunning folk related to real or illusory events. On one side of the fence were those who believed that these were empirically real events; they maintained that men and women gathered 'in body' in the company of the Devil or the king and queen of the fairies and other spirits at specific times and in specific geographical locations. On the other side were those who believed that these experiences were illusory ones. The 'illusory' camp did not challenge the reality of the Devil, they merely maintained that he assumed an illusory form and manufactured the events of the sabbath as a means through which he could bring the magical practitioner under his influence. This view was summed up, in 1597, by James VI in

Daemonologie: 'it is verie possible to the Devils craft, to perswade them to these meanes. For he being a spirite, may hee not so ravishe their thoughts, and dull their sences, that their bodie lying as dead, hee may object to their spirites as it were in a dreame, & represente such formes of persones, of places, and other circumstances, as he pleases to illude them with?'[6] Other early modern thinkers remained undecided and chose to sit on the fence. With regard to the nocturnal journeying of the 'Fairy-Boy of Leith', for example, Richard Bovet claimed with circumspection: 'What this manner of Transvection was, which the boy spoke of, whether it were corporeal, or in a dream only, I shall not dispute, but I think there be some relations of this kind that prove it may be either way, & therefore that I leave to the reader to determine.'[7] This ambiguity is sometimes found expressed during the witch trials themselves. In relation to the nocturnal gatherings of a group of witches near Taunton, Somerset, in 1664, the records cover all options by stating that 'They [the witches] are carried sometimes in their bodies and their clothes, at other times without, and Examinate thinks their bodies are sometimes left behind. Even when their spirits only are present, yet they know one another.'[8]

Like their early modern counterparts, twentieth-century scholars have also troubled themselves over the reality of the sabbath experience and they too have veered between the 'real' and the 'illusory' sides of the fence. In the 1920s, British scholar Margaret Murray claimed that witches' sabbaths were empirically real historical events, representing the survival of pre-Christian fertility rites throughout early modern Europe.[9] Subsequent scholars rebuked Murray's theories, revealing the flaws in her presentation of evidence. In 1975, the most vehement of Murray's critics, Norman Cohn, helped to shift the balance of scholarly opinion away from the perception of the sabbath as a historical event by arguing that the early modern notion of the sabbath was rooted in collective fantasies about religious heresy, perpetrated by the ruling élite as a method of social control.[10] In other words, it was predominantly an élite fiction. The year 1989 saw something completely new brought to the debate when Carlo Ginzburg published his pioneering work, *Ecstasies*.[11] In this book Ginzburg offered an interpretation of the ontological nature of the sabbath which diverged from the polarized views of both Murray and Cohn. Ginzburg argued that descriptions of attendance at the sabbath (along with affiliated descriptions of spirit-related experiences, including visits to fairyland) found throughout early modern Europe, were in fact evidence of the survival of ritual trance experiences derived from pre-Christian Eurasian shamanism. Ginzburg's theory has since been backed up by other scholars who have uncovered evidence of popular shamanistic visionary traditions in different parts of early modern Europe.[12] As a result of Ginzburg's work many scholars now accept that there was likely to have been an experiential component to sabbath beliefs in this period, although they might disagree as to its extent.

The Reality of the Familiar

Continental scholars researching the folkloric roots of the European witch's sabbath generally maintain that associated beliefs surrounding encounters with solitary spirits, usually described as the Devil, were also sourced in 'shamanistic' trance experiences. Gábor Klaniczay claims that the 'initiatory vision' of the Central European cunning man, which occurs 'when he first falls into trance', is characteristic of shamanism; Wolfgang Behringer that the angel-encountering adventures of the Bavarian cunning man, Chonrad Stoeckhlin, were an expression of his 'shamanistic abilities'; and Éva Pócs that 'Contacting the supernatural through trance techniques in order to accomplish community tasks was common among mediators connected with the system of witchcraft. This activity was aided and abetted by a helping spirit and corresponds to the criteria that are generally accepted for shamanism.'[13] However, these clear correlations between the familiar-encounter and the visionary or trance experience have not been followed up by historians of British witchcraft and magic. Despite their general acknowledgement that fantasy is likely to have played a role in the formation of many encounter-narratives, only a small number of the latter categorically state that the narrative may have been rooted in a specific visionary event occuring at a particular time and in a particular geographical location. Consequently, claims such as the following, made by Malcolm Gaskill in relation to Ely witch Margaret Moore: '[her encounter-narrative did not] necessarily originate at the time of her examination: long before she could have believed that she had actually seen the spirits and given her soul to the Devil'; or the following, made by Peter Maxwell-Stuart with regard to Bessie Dunlop: 'Essentially, therefore, one might say that Elizabeth experienced a visual hallucination with attendant auditory phenomena' – appear sensational by virtue of their rarity.[14] In most works by historians in the British field the visionary element of the encounter-narrative remains unemphasized and unexplored, general terms such as 'fantasy' or 'imagination' being usually listed in passing, alongside a number of other factors, as possible factors in the genesis of a given narrative. In some analyses the fantasy element is dispensed with altogether. In reference to a pamphlet account of an English witch trial James Sharpe recently claimed that 'we are left wondering how accurately the authors are reporting the words of the alleged witches: it is possible that the accounts of familiars is in large measure a fabrication. But at the very least the pamphlet demonstrates how the ideas of the familiar were in circulation.'[15] Similarly, in a recent examination of fairy-encounters described in Scottish witch trials, Diane Purkiss claimed of the accused that 'Scrabbling frantically for an answer, women probably told their interrogators [fairy] stories that they had heard, changed to the first person, and stories that they had told as pastimes, not meaning to be believed.'[16]

One of the reasons why scholars underplay the visionary dimension of the encounter-experience is because its existence is not well supported by source material. On the one hand, occasional references linking the familiar-encounter and trance experience can be found in early modern trial records. The Aberdeenshire divines who tried Patrick Ellis, of Auchindoir, in the seventeenth century accused him of 'being a seducer under pretence of lying in a trance or [and?] having converse with familiar spirits', a statement backed up by Robert Kirk's claims that Scottish seers used ointments which 'cast them in a trance'.[17] Similarly, records from a witch trial held in Somerset in 1664 state that a woman named Alice Duke 'confesseth that her Familiar doth commonly suck her right Breast about seven at night, in the shape of a little Cat of dunnish colour, which is as smooth as a Want, and when she is suckt, she is in a kind of trance'; while fellow witch Christian Green, who possessed a familiar spirit in the form of a hedgehog, similarly stated that 'she is usually in a trance when she is suckt'.[18] Fulham cunning woman Alice West, on the other hand, who claimed to be 'familiarly acquainted with the king and queene of fairies', stated that the royal couple had 'appeard to her in a vision'.[19]

Although these references are suggestive, they are proportionally insignificant, only appearing in a tiny number of examined trial records from the period and can easily be offset by the number of equally scarce – but equally persuasive – references which suggest that no visionary dimension was present at all. Some trial records, for example, indicate that in England 'real' animals were believed to function as familiar spirits. The keeping of pets was widespread in the period, and Essex witch Joan Upney's claim, in 1589, that her youngest daughter 'would handle them [her toad familiars], and use them as well as herself' while her eldest daughter could 'never abide to meddle with her toads', vividly describes the feelings which clammy amphibians can evoke in the squeamish.[20] This seeming realism is supported by the comments of élite observers such as Dr Harvey, physician to Charles I, who claimed that 'being at Newmarket, he called on a reputed witch, and ingratiating himself by pretending to be a wizard, persuaded her to introduce her imp, which she did by calling a toad from under a chest and giving it milk'. After sending the witch out on an errand, Harvey seized the animal, slit it open with his dissecting knife and demonstrated it to be 'nothing but a plain natural toad'.[21] In addition to these references to the materiality of the familiar, the case for its visionary status is further weakened by the fact that, while references to the visionary status of the familiar-encounter are rare, overt references to trance states in relation to mental illness, sickness, demonic possession or psychic attack by witches are frequently found in trial records throughout the period.[22] Despite such comments, the over-whelming majority of trial records contain no reference to the ontological status of the familiar-encounter. This omission is likely to reflect the fact that ecclesiastics and prosecutors were more interested in the content of the magical practitioner's narrative, than in analysing its ontology. The interest in the supernatural experiences of Scottish seers expressed by several notable minds in the later seventeenth century, including English natural philosopher Robert Boyle, diarist Samuel Pepys and antiquarian John Aubrey, provide us with a fascinating exception to this rule.[23]

However, the general lack of reference to visionary experience or trance states in early modern encounter-narratives is misleading. Perspectives gained from research into shamanism indicate that this lack of reference cannot be taken as evidence that visionary experience or trance did not occur. While accounts of shamanic séances recorded by external observers often describe the shaman entering into trance states before he communicates with spirits, descriptions of encounters with spirits given by shamans themselves (which were, like the narratives given by cunning folk and witches, retrospective), rarely make reference to them. The shaman does not objectify his experience from a modern psychological perspective: for him, it is the experience that counts. As Holger Kalweit explains: shamans 'are not sufficiently aware of the mech-anisms involved in the transformation of their consciousness or, for that matter, the psychic principles of intercourse with their spirit partners, for their reports to satisfy our scientific and analytical curiosity. The shaman is deeply and unconsciously rooted in his traditional culture and looks upon contact with a spirit being as a relatively normal occurrence. In consequence, he feels no need to search for complicated explanations.'[24] Often, it is only the anomalies that appear in the shaman's narrative which give us any indication that we are dealing with a trance-induced visionary experience and not a real event. Again, Kalweit remarks that 'Helping spirits frequently manifest themselves in a very direct and sudden way. That is why descriptions of shamanic experiences often strike us as vague, disconnected and inconsistent; there seems to be no gradual change from normal consciousness to the trance state. The above narratives therefore

Both of these depictions of familiars share a similar mix of naturalistic and fantastical detail. On the left, a demon familiar from an English witchcraft pamphlet (Chelmsford, 1566), and on the right, the helping spirit called Nujaliaq, or 'hair woman', drawn by the Canadian Iglulik shaman, Anarqâq.

A depiction of a shaman's flight to the spirit world, with the aid of his helping spirits, by the Canadian Utkuhikhalingmiut artist, Jessie Oonark (1908–1985). Until she settled in Baker Lake in 1958, Jessie led the traditional nomadic life of her Inuit forefathers.

The Witches' Sabbath, by Hans Baldung Grien (1510) incorporates some of the bizarre and dramatic elements characteristic of sabbath accounts; elements which make it easier for historians to accept that such accounts may have been associated with visionary experience. Ideas surrounding flight to the sabbath on the backs of animals, for example, (see top centre) come from the same reservoir of human experience as those surrounding the shaman's animal-assisted flight to the spirit world (see *Flight of the Shaman*, left).

Source: Photograph copyright 2005 Museum of Fine Arts Boston.

give us the impression that an actual material being has been manifested, which is characterized by so many unrealistic elements that we are unable to consider it to be part of the external world.'[25]

The role of anomalies as indicators of trance experience is one of the reasons why historians have traditionally been more open to defining the visit to the sabbath or fairyland as a visionary experience, rather than the familiar-encounter. Descriptions of the former often contain such a vivid and bizarre combination of elements that we can be in no doubt that the experiences described occurred in a dramatically altered state of consciousness. Nairnshire witch Isobel Gowdie claimed, for example, that herself and some companions:

> went be-east *Kinloffe*, and ther we yoaked an pleughe of paddokis [plough of frogs]. THE DIVELL held the pleugh, and *Johne Younge* in *Mebestowne*, our Officer, did dryve the pleugh. Paddokis did draw the pleugh, as oxen; qwickens [dog-grass] wer soumes [traces], a riglen's horne [a half-castrated ram] wes a cowter [coulter] and an piece of riglens horn wes an fok. We went two severall tymes about; and all we of the COEVEN went still up and downe qith the pleughe, prayeing to THE DIVELL, for the fruit of that land, and that thistles and brieris might grow ther.[26]

The signature of the visionary experience is also written boldly through the encounter-narrative given by Aberdeenshire cunning man Andro Man in 1598, whose trial dittays read that 'the elphis will mak the appeir to be in a fair chalmer, and yit thow will find thy selff in a moss on the morne; and that thay will appeir to have candlis, and licht, and swordis, quhilk wilbe nothing els bot deed gress and strayes'.[27]

Descriptions of encounters with familiars generally contain far fewer anomalies and more naturalistic detail than those of sabbath or fairyland experiences. We can see how the prosaic realism of Bessie Dunlop's encounter-narrative may have fooled the nineteenth-century historian, Robert Pitcairn, into thinking that Tom Reid may have been a real man, that is, 'some heartless wag, acquainted with the virtues and use of herbs'. Bessie provides an incredibly thorough description of Tom's clothing and appearance, word-for-word accounts of their conversations and detailed recitations of the herbal cures which Tom dispensed with the precision of an apothecary. Encounter-narratives also frequently contain accurate descriptions of the place and time at which spirits were encountered, a realism which could be seen to support one historian's recent claim that 'English meetings with the fairies, like those confessed to by John Walsh, were usually conducted corporally and not spiritually.'[28]

The magical practitioner's corporal presence, however, does not pre-suppose that of the familiar. Despite the pervading realism of most encounter-narratives, many still contain enough anomalies, or just plain 'oddness', to indicate that the experiences described may have been visionary ones. The prosaic conversation between Bessie Dunlop and Tom Reid, for example, abruptly came to an end when Tom, as Bessie put it 'gait in at ane naroware hoill of the dyke nor ony erdlie [earthly] man culd haif gane throw'.[29] Suffolk witch Anne Hammer (1645), on the other hand, claimed that 'In the likeness of a black man, the Devil, used to come in at the key hole', while Leicestershire cunning woman Joan Willimot (1618) claimed that when her fairy familiar first appeared it 'came out of her mouth' and 'stood upon the ground in the shape and form of a woman'.[30] Huntingdonshire witch Jane Wallis (1646) was approached by a 'man in blacke cloaths' whom, she noticed, had 'ugly feete, and then she was very fearfull of him for that he would seem sometimes to be tall, and sometimes lesse, and suddenly vanished away'.[31] Devon witch Temperance Lloyd (1682) met a similarly uncanny-looking familiar when she was walking along the street, and 'knelt down to the Black Man or Devil, who sucked the teats in her secret parts. The Black Man was "about the length of her arm and his eyes were very big"'.[32] Berkshire witch Elizabeth Style (1579) came across her familiar when she was walking in the woods 'sitting . . . under the body of a tree, sometimes in the shape of an ape, and otherwhiles like a horse', while young Agnes Brown (1566), from Chelmsford, was churning butter when her neighbour's familiar appeared 'like a black dog with a face like an ape, a short tail, a chain and a silver whistle (to her thinking) about his neck, and a pair of horns on his head'. The familiar was also unfeasibly acrobatic, for Agnes went on to say how 'I was afeared, for he skipped and leaped to and fro, and sat on the top of a nettle'.[33] Yorkshire witch Margaret Waite (1622) claimed that her familiar was 'black of colour, rough with hair, the bigness of a cat, the name of it unknown' but prefixed this unremarkable description by claiming that it was a 'deformed thing with many feet', while Suffolk witch John Bysack (1645) claimed to have encountered his familiar when it 'came in at the window in the shape of a rugged sandy-coloured dog' and 'in a great hollow voice, asked him to deny God'.[34] More flamboyantly, a familiar spirit in the form of a child appeared before Ely witch Adam Sabie (1647) in a 'flame of Fyor', while Lancashire witch James Device (1612) claimed that when he first refused to surrender his soul, his familiar, which appeared in the form of a brown dog, gave 'a most fearful cry and yell and withal caused a great flash of fire to shew about him'.[35] Intriguingly, Huntingdonshire witch Elizabeth Weed (1646) and her familiar sealed their covenant in her bedroom late at night with only the 'light of the Spirit' to see by.[36]

Many cunning folk and witches expressed palpable fear at the uncanny nature of their familiar's appearance. Essex witch Rebecca Jones (1645) claimed that her familiar was dressed 'in a ragged suit and having such great eyes, that she feared him', while her fellow countrywoman Elizabeth Bennett, who was tried at St Osyth in 1582, claimed that her demon familiar unnerved her so much that 'her eyes were like to start out of her head' and that she beseeched him 'In the name of God, what art thou? Thou wilt not hurt me?' It seems that in this case Elizabeth's fears may have been justified, for on another occasion when she was 'coming from [the] mill, the spirit called Suckin came unto her and did take her by the coat, and held her that she could not go forward nor remove by the space of two hours, at the which she was much amazed'.[37]

The signature of the visionary experience can also be traced in the number of encounter-narratives in which the familiar appears and disappears quite suddenly. Essex witch Elizabeth Francis (1579) claimed that she was walking alone when 'suddenly in the way she heard a great noise' and 'there appeared unto her a spirit of white colour, in seeming like to a little rugged dog, standing near her upon the ground, who asked her whither she went'.[38] Similarly, Essex witch Joan Prentice (1589) maintained that her demon familiar, who appeared before her in the form of a ferret, 'vanished out of her sight suddenly' while Devon witch Susannah Edwards (1682) claimed that her familiar spirit 'instantly vanished away' when she cited the Lord's name.[39] The visionary nature of other familiars is suggested by the fact that they could be visible to their human allies, but invisible to anyone else. Bessie Dunlop claimed that she alone could see Tom Reid at Edinburgh market.[40] Similarly, when Essex witch Joan Cunny's grandson (1589) took, on her orders, one of Joan's demon familiars to help him procure some firewood, the spirit apparently 'went unseen to anybody but the boy'.[41]

It is also not uncommon to find anomalies recorded in association with the familiar's voice. Joan Cunny felt it significant to point out that her two spirits, Jack and Jill, would 'familiarly talk with her when she had anything to say or do with them' and that when they did so it was 'in her own language'.[42] Other demon familiars were less easy to understand. Faversham witch Joan Cariden (1645) claimed that the Devil visited her 'in the shape of a black rugged dog, crept into her bed, and spoke in mumbling language'; the fairy familiar possessed by Leicestershire cunning woman Joan Willimot (1618) came to her 'in the form of a woman, mumbling, but she could not understand what it said'; and the Devil who came to Norfolk witch Mary Smith (1617), spoke to her with a 'low, murmering and hissing voice'.[43] The familiar in the form of a white spotted cat inherited by Essex witch Elizabeth Francis (1566) spoke to her 'in a strange hollow voice, but such as she understood by use'.[44]

Huntingdonshire witch Jane Wallis (1646), on the other hand, claimed that when she met the Devil he 'was not as her husband, which speaks to her like a man, but he as he had been some distance from her when he was with her'.[45] Other witches have described the demon familiar's voice as 'a hollow shrill voyce'; a voice that was 'low but big'; 'a hollow Solemn Voice' or a voice that was 'hough and goustie'.[46]

Trance-Inducing Techniques

Narrative anomalies are the not the only indicators that an encounter with a familiar may have been a visionary experience. References to the use of physical and psychological methods known to induce trance states, and to the physical behaviours which naturally accompany these states can also be helpful indicators. We have already seen in chapter NINE how the shaman employs a variety of invocatory techniques in order to envision spirits, which can include asceticisms, music, chanting, dance, seated and lying meditations, the use of hallucinogens etc. Some of these techniques are performed in public, some in private; some are extreme or visually dramatic, others are minimalist and barely perceptible to the observer. Whatever their nature, however, all of these techniques encourage the cultivation of some form of 'monotonous focus', whether the attention be fastened onto sound, movement, physical sensation or visual objects. Monotonous or sustained focus, as psychologists have shown, is remarkably effective at altering or 'destabilizing' ordinary states of consciousness and precipitating trance states in which visionary experiences might occur.[47]

Descriptions of witches' sabbaths, particularly those from the Continent, often contain references to music-making, singing, dancing and theatricals, and it is possible that these descriptions bear testament to the fact that in this period people came together and ritualistically employed these types of overt invocatory techniques in order to attain trance states, although such an assertion is controversial.[48] Generally undisputed, however, is Ginzburg's claim that references to the extreme physical rigidity or 'catatonia' characteristic of some deep trance states can be found in sabbath accounts from throughout early modern Europe. An account given by an old woman from the Scottish Island of Tiree to seventeenth-century Scottish clergyman John Fraser is representative. The woman (whose destination was fairyland in all but name) claimed that she had been to 'heaven' and 'kindly entertained with Meat and Drink, and that she had seen her Daughter there, who Died about a year before'.

The clergyman, unconvinced, asked her children 'if she [the old woman] fell at any time in a Syncopa [faint], which they told me she did, and continued for a whole night, so that they thought she was truly Dead, and this is the time she alleaged she was in Heaven; the Devil took an advantage in the Ecstasy, to present to her fancy a Map of Heaven as if it had been a Rich Earthly Kingdom'.[49] Nairnshire witch Isobel Gowdie's claim that when she went on her fairyland and sabbath adventures she left a 'fairy stock' beside her husband in bed, also indicates that she underwent her experiences in a catatonic trance.[50] Such accounts are supported by several comments in *Daemonologie*, King James VI claiming on one occasion that while the senses of magical practitioners are 'dulled, and as it were a sleepe' the Devil conjures 'such hilles & houses within them, such glistering courts and traines . . . And in the meane time their bodies being senselesse.'[51]

While it is relatively easy for historians to acknowledge that accounts of fairyland or sabbath experiences may contain references to ritual techniques and behaviours associated with trance, it is more difficult for them to draw the same conclusions about descriptions of familiar-encounters. Although Robert Kirk claimed that the Scottish seer could perceive spirits in a state of dramatic excitement, or be 'put in a rapture, transport, and sort of death, as divested of his body, and all it's Senses; when he is first made participant of this curious body of knowledge', such references are an exception to the general rule.[52] Unless the description of a familiar-encounter is associated with sabbath or fairyland experiences it does not usually contain references to the more dramatic physical behaviours associated with trance, nor does it describe lengthy and elaborate overt ritual conjurations of the type found in the magical grimoires favoured by learned magicians and literate cunning folk. In the majority of cases, cunning folk and witches are described as being alone and quietly going about their daily business when they meet their familiar spirits. Even encounter-experiences directly witnessed and recorded by observers seldom mention any unusual behaviour on the part of the protagonist.

This lack of reference to the more dramatic indicators of trance states, however, is wholly congruent with shamanic encounter-narratives and does not mean that trance states did not occur. As we have seen in chapter EIGHT, many shaman-narratives describe the use of minimalist ritual to invoke helping spirits and scholars of shamanism have long recognized that such rituals can mask the use of powerful consciousness-altering techniques. The anthropologist Gerardo Reichel-Dolmatoff, for example, describes the complex physical and mental effects induced by the South American Tukano shaman's deceptively simple 'knee-hugging' position:

To the casual observer it may simply seem to be a resting position, but the Tukano shamans explain that the person who takes this posture, far from being relaxed, is in great tension and concentrating intensely on perceiving either external sensations or internal voices. To this position and state of acute perception are to be added the following further factors; first; hugging of the knees causes the thighs to exert pressure on the thorax, thereby substantially controlling respiration, which slows down considerably; and secondly, in many cases the person concentrates his sight on a luminous point, for example, a torch. I have seen Tukano shamans sitting in this position for long intervals and fixing their eyes on the intensely red light of a resin-covered torch set in the middle of an otherwise dark house.[53]

The shaman's invocatory techniques can be so minimalist and internalized that they can be performed while the shaman seems, to an external observer, to be maintaining his normal state of consciousness and pursuing his everyday activities. Such skills are usually associated with a high level of both natural skill and conscious application. Scholar of shamanism Roger Walsh claims that the novice shaman's task of learning to see the spirits involves two stages: 'The first is simply to catch an initial glimpse of them. The second is to deepen and stabilize this glimpse into a permanent visionary capacity in which the spirits can be summoned and seen at will.' The possession of such a capacity means that shamans 'may become less dependent on their external aids. They may then be able to enter and remain in altered states without the aid of drumming or other techniques.'[54] Such a skilled shaman would be telling the truth, then, when he claimed that he just 'asked' his helping spirit to come and speak with him when he needed magical aid. Scholar and practising twenty-first century shaman Gordon MacLellan puts it another way: 'Shamans work with trance – and ecstasy', he claims, but trance is not necessarily of the '"all fall down and twitch convincingly" school of magic (although it may be): it can just as easily involve a shaman sitting down and having an apparently rational conversation with her client while still looking into the spirit world.'[55]

If we bring this understanding of shamanic trance states to our analysis of early modern descriptions of familiar-encounters, then we can draw some clear conclusions. Scattered comments from élite writings of the period suggest that, among the educated at least, it was believed that individuals could work to develop and enhance their visionary capacities. The sixteenth-century Swiss physician, Philippus Paracelsus, claimed famously that: 'Everyone may educate and regulate his imagination so as to come thereby into contact with spirits, and be taught by them.'[56] That similar beliefs may have also existed on a popular level is suggested by Robert

Kirk's claim that the perception of a spirit will continue 'so long as they [the seer] can keep their eye steady without twinkling. The hardy therefore fix their look that they might see the longer, But the timorous see only glances, their eyes alwayes twinkling at the first sight of the object.'[57] The following seventeenth-century account of a popular invocatory ritual clearly illustrates how a seemingly simple activity could mask a powerful contemplative technique aimed at developing sustained 'monotonous focus'. An English clergyman recounts how:

> It was my happe that since I undertooke the Ministerie, to question an ignorant soule, (whom by undoubted report I had knowne to have been seduced by a teacher of unhallowed arts to make a dangerous experiment) what he saw, or heard, when he watcht the falling of the *Ferne-seed* at an unseasonable and suspitious houre. Why (quoth he) (fearing (as his briefe reply occasioned me to conjecture) lest I should presse him to tell before company, what he had voluntarily confessed unto a friend in secret, about some foureteene years before) doe you thinke that the devill hath ought to doe with that good seed? No: it is in the keeping of the *King of Fayries*, and it I know will doe me no harme, although I should watch it againe.[58]

The 'ignorant soul' was, like the shaman, unlikely to have objectified the psychological mechanisms behind his invocatory technique. He would have concentrated on the fern seed without entertaining theories of 'monotonous focus' and 'psychic destabilization'. Like the shaman, however, his resolve and commitment to the task in hand may have been enough to achieve the desired results. That unlettered common folk were capable of such skills was also intimated by the sixteenth-century German magician, Cornelius Agrippa, in his influential *Three Books of Occult Philosophy*. Agrippa concludes a description of the ritual means through which to invoke familiar spirits by emphasizing that 'especially to be observed [during the ritual] is this, the singleness of the wit, innocency of the mind, a firm credulity, and constant silence; wherefore they [the spirits] do often meet children, women, and poor and mean men'.[59]

It is virtually impossible for modern readers to ascertain whether trance-inducing techniques and the enthusiasm and resolve necessary to bring them to effect, are hidden between the lines of any given early modern encounter-narrative. In the light of the evidence presented here, however, it can be argued that the mundane circumstances in which cunning folk and witches encountered their familiar spirits do not negate the possibility that these encounters may have been undergone in states of trance. The intense interest in the spirit-encountering experiences of Scottish seers displayed by a handful of British scholars in the late seventeenth century has left us with a collection of contemporary observations which support this conclusion. In the Scottish Highlands some seers were reputed to go about their daily lives while being in almost constant contact with spirits: James Mack-coil-vic-Alaster claimed to perceive two ghosts called 'Brownie' and 'Meg Mullach' and 'sometimes many more' spirits almost continuously, while John McGrigor, who practised near Inverness, claimed that he would not advise any man to learn the second sight because 'once learned he would be never a minute in his life, but he would see inumerable men & women night & day round about him; which perhaps he would think wearisome & unpleasant'.[60] External indicators that such a seer was encountering spirits could be minimal. Although Scottish observer Martin Martin claimed that the seer's visionary experiences were habitually accompanied by strange behaviour, the behaviour he describes is relatively 'normal' compared with the dramas of catatonia or frenzy:

> the vision makes such a lively impression upon the Seers, that they neither see nor think of anything else, except the vision, as long as it continues: and then they appear pensive or jovial, according to the object which was represented to them.
>
> At the sight of a vision, the eye-lids of the person are erected, and the eyes continue staring until the object vanish. This is obvious to others who are by, when the persons happen to see a vision, and occurred more than once to my own observation, and to others that were with me.[61]

The strange behaviours which the Scottish Lord of Tarbott claimed to have twice witnessed first hand were even less dramatic. In the first instance, a local seer, who was digging out a track near Ullapool, merely stopped his digging to 'stare a little strangely' when he encountered a vision of a spirit army, while in the second, a seer who sat 'in a corner of the great chimney' at the house of William McLeud, merely looked 'oddly' when he observed the spirit of a dead man sitting in his (Tarbott's) chair.[62] One of the most powerful testaments to the external composure maintained by the popular magical practitioner when undergoing visionary experiences comes down to us from the clergyman George Hickes. Hickes visited Janet Douglas, a teenage seer from the Western Highlands of Scotland, when she was being held in custody in Edinburgh, and asked her:

> if the second sight came upon her sleeping or waking, she answered never sleeping, but alwaies when she was awake . . . Then I asked her if she was wont to have any trouble, disorder, or consternation of mind <be>fore, at, or after the second sight came upon her, to which she answered never, never, but was in the same temper at those, as at all other times. Then I asked her, if the second sight never left any weariness or faintness upon her, or list-

In this woodcut a Lapp cunning man is depicted lying in a trance, on behalf of a client, in order to gain knowledge of persons distant. His familiar spirit, led by a 'demon' (top and bottom right respectively), brings tokens back from the journey in order to prove to the client that the errand has been fulfilled. From *Historia de Gentibus Septentrionalibus* by Olaus Magnus (1567).

A North American Cheyenne Ledger drawing, from the late nineteenth century, depicting a visionary experience. According to anthropologist Piers Vitebsky, the drawing depicts a 'dreamer rising from his body', presumably in order to journey to the spirit world. The figure on the right may be a spirit, inviting the dreamer to journey, while the insect-like creatures along the top could represent either helping spirits or animal metamorphosis.

Source: Buffalo Bill Historical Centre, Cody, Wyoming.

lessenesse to speak, walk, or do other busieness, to which she answered, no, adding that she was then alwayes as before.[63]

Such examples make it clear that we cannot assume that because an individual claimed to have been sitting by the fire, carrying butter to market, leading a cow to pasture, ploughing a field, gathering sticks or waiting for a ferry to come in at the lochside when they encountered their familiar, that they had not spontaneously encountered a visionary entity. And we cannot assume that because a magical practitioner claimed that they just 'asked' or 'demanded' or 'inquired after' their familiar when they needed magical aid, that they did not invoke this visionary entity through the deliberate employment of trance-inducing techniques.

The perspectives presented in this chapter suggest that familiar beliefs in early modern Britain were likely to have possessed an experiential dimension. They suggest that although élite interventions and retrospective fiction-making on the part of the accused undoubtedly played a large role in shaping encounter-narratives, we cannot preclude the possibility that some descriptions of familiar-encounters were, like some descriptions of attendances at the sabbath and visits to fairyland, depictions of coherent and vivid visionary events which occurred at specific times and in specific geographical locations prior to the trial scene. The structure and content of these visionary events make it possible to argue, as Ginzburg and others have done in relation to the European sabbath, that although these visionary experiences were clearly influenced by Christian beliefs, they are likely to have been rooted in the shamanistic beliefs and practices of pre-Christian Britain. This 'shamanistic' inheritance may in part be attributed to the profound longevity of certain cultural elements, inherited pre-Christian cosmologies, mythic images and ritual techniques handed down through the generations through oral transmission and through which process the shaman's helping spirit transmuted into the early modern familiar, and his subterranean world of the dead into the fairy Elfame or Christian purgatory. Evidence of historical contiguity, however, is not wholly necessary to support the perspectives presented here. The resemblances between early modern and shamanic encounter-experiences can also be attributed to the physical structure of the human mind. Mircea Eliade argues that shamanism is, at root, a psychological tendency rather than a religious belief: 'We have termed the ecstatic experience a 'primary phenomenon' . . . because we see no reason whatever for regarding it as the result of a particular historical moment, that is, as produced by a certain form of civilisation. Rather, we would consider it fundamental in the human condition.'[64] Similarly, in reference to the ideas of Piers Vitebsky, Ronald Hutton recently claimed that 'the traits which underpin Siberian shamanism occur naturally in individuals throughout humanity, although they are given different cultural expression at particular times and places'.[65] The uncanny similarity between the encounter-experiences of early modern cunning folk and witches and those of nineteenth- and early twentieth-century Siberian and Native American shamans are therefore wholly in keeping with the transhistorical and transcultural congruity of shamanistic experience.

From this perspective, Britain's rich collection of regionally variant but essentially synonymous encounter-narratives, recorded in places as far apart, and culturally distinct, as Cornwall, Essex and the Orkney Isles, can be seen as testament to the fact that coherent and vigorous 'shamanistic visionary traditions' existed in many parts of Britain during the early modern period.

CHAPTER ELEVEN

Psychosis or Spirituality?

As we have seen in chapter TEN, although most historians now acknowledge that there was likely to have been a visionary, or as it is often termed, 'hallucinatory', element to some familiar-encounters in early modern Britain, this dimension of familiar belief has not yet been examined in any detail. This lack of scholarly attention can, in part, be attributed to the long-standing historiographical tendency to 'pathologize', and thereby dismiss as unimportant, the visionary dimension of the familiar-encounter. Robert Pitcairn, the nineteenth-century scholar who transcribed Bessie Dunlop's trial confession, supposed that 'With regard to the *guilt* of this unlucky woman, there can hardly be two opinions. She was certainly the dupe of her own overheated imagination, already well stored with such fancies, before her first interview with Thom Reid; who (if not entirely the phantom of a disordered brain) may not unlikely have been some heartless wag, acquainted with the virtues and use of herbs, and who possibly may have played off this too fatal joke on his unhappy victim.'[1] Similarly, in the 1920s, George Kittredge claimed that witches 'may even imagine themselves to hold intercourse with Satan, for they share the current superstitions and are not very strong in their wits', while John MacCulloch claimed that the 'hallucinations' of spirits described by both witches and cunning folk were 'The boastings and ravings of half-crazy and self-conscious as well as self-deluded persons'.[2] In 1959, Katharine Briggs maintained that Isobel Gowdie's encounter-narratives were 'strange, mad outpourings', while ten years later Barbara Rosen stated that in Joan Prentice's encounter-narrative: 'an extremely detailed and accurate observation of the behaviour of ferrets co-exists with senile fantasy'.[3] Even as recently as 1981, Christina Larner dismissed the encounter-narratives found in witch trials as relating only 'to dreams, nightmares, and collective fantasies'.[4] In the last two decades or so, as a result of changing perspectives in the field of witchcraft studies, historians are increasingly hesitant to employ pathological explanations in relation to both encounter-narratives and witch beliefs in general.

The way historians have traditionally pathologized the visionary experiences of early modern cunning folk and witches is little different from the way scholars have traditionally approached the visionary experiences of the tribal shaman. In the early decades of Western psychiatry, visionary waking states were predominantly associated with mental illness, particularly that of schizophrenia, and consequently the majority of Victorian and early twentieth-century anthropologists and missionaries dismissed the encounter-experiences of the shaman as symptomatic of mental illness. As Shirley Nicholson points out, historically scholars claimed that shamans 'suffered from chronic mental illness. That is, that the bizarre experiences that they report were nothing more than the ravings of florid psychotics, and that the "primitive" societies in which they lived were too ignorant to recognize such psychopathology and instead institutionalized it into a religious social role'.[5] Even as late as 1956, French anthropologist George Devereux stated categorically that 'there is no reason and no excuse for not considering the shaman as a severe neurotic and even as a psychotic'.[6] Advances in psychology, ethnography, comparative religion and other related fields since the 1950s have since rendered such simplistic diagnoses untenable, and scholars of shamanism are now far more circumspect about pathologizing unusual states of consciousness. Roger Walsh describes how until quite recently 'Western psychology and anthropology recognized only a very limited range of normal states – mainly our normal waking, dreaming and nondreaming sleep states' but that 'In recent years this view has changed dramatically. It has become clear that the range of potential healthy states of consciousness is considerably broader than previously imagined.'[7] Contemporary scholars are now more likely to make a distinction between the visionary who is mentally ill and the visionary who is mentally healthy. Interestingly, most put the shaman into the second category and maintain that although during their initiation some shamans may undergo episodes of mental illness – which can resemble those of schizophrenia – these episodes are generally temporary. While the visionary experiences of the schizophrenic are random and autonomous, breaking down the individual's sense of identity and contributing to an overwhelmingly negative emotional experience, the shaman learns to control his visions, and the emotional states which accompany them, and through these efforts develops a strong sense of identity and positivity. The schizophrenic's experience, claims Roger Walsh, is 'very different from the shamanic journey. The shaman's experience is coherent, meaningful, and consistent with the purpose of the journey. In addition the shaman has good control of his experience, heightened concentration, and a clear, coherent sense of identity'.[8]

Although it is a relatively new development in modern psychiatry, the distinction between the visionary who is mentally ill and the visionary who is mentally healthy was widely upheld in early modern Britain. On the one hand, commentators were quite capable of pathologizing the experiences of cunning folk and witches in a manner very similar to that of modern historians. The following psychological analysis of the witch drawn by seventeenth-century essayist Joseph Addison, for example, is little different from those given by historians like Pitcairn or Rosen. Addison claimed that, 'When an old woman begins to dote, and grow chargeable to a parish, she is generally turned into a witch, and fills the whole country with extravagant fancies, imaginary distempers, and terrifying dreams. In the mean time the poor wretch that is the innocent occasion of so many evils, begins to be frighted at herself, and sometimes confesses secret commerces and familiarities that her imagination forms in a delirious old age'.[9] Addison's opinion, however, unlike those of his modern successors, was not a majority view. In the early modern period the overwhelming majority of people, whether young or old, rich or poor, sane or insane, believed in invisible spirit worlds. Although not composed of matter in the same way as mortal men, the spirits which inhabited these worlds were still believed to possess some kind of ontology and therefore those exceptional individuals who had the capacity to perceive them were not insane, they were perceiving 'real' entities. For Robert Kirk, therefore, although visions of spirits could be experienced by the mentally ill, they could also be experienced by the mentally healthy. In the *Secret Commonwealth* he claims that (having performed an invocation correctly) a novice Scottish seer will see 'a multitude of Wights like furious hardie men flocking to him hastily from all quarters, as thick as atomes in the air; which are no nonentities or phantasms, creatures, proceeding from ane affrighted apprehensione confused or crazed sense, but Realities, appearing to a stable man in his awaking sense and enduring a rational tryal of their being'.[10] Kirk also claims that when a seer first gains the second sight he 'is put in a rapture . . . when he is first made participant of this curious piece of knowledge: But it maketh no wramp or strain in the understanding of any; only to the Fancy's of clownish and illiterat men it creats some affrightments and disturbances'.[11] The magical practitioners who underwent these experiences were, according to Kirk, 'for the most part candid, honest and sociable people'.[12] Similarly, seventeenth-century Scottish traveller Martin Martin claimed that when he was in Scotland he heard tales of spirit-encounters from persons 'of as great Integrity as any are in the World'.[13] The men who interrogated East Lothian cunning woman Agnes Sampson (1591) maintained that she was 'most remarkable, a woman not of the base and ignorant sort of Witches, but, Matron-like, grave and setled in her answers, which were all to some purpose', and this despite the fact that Agnes claimed to have conversed with the Devil in the form of a dog and a man.[14] The seventeenth-century Scottish seer, James Mack-coil-vic-Alaster, was also considered to be 'a very honest man & <of right> blameless conversation' while the impression gained from reading the trial confession of Bessie Dunlop is that of a sane, intelligent and compassionate individual with scruples and integrity.[15] A similar picture is to be gained several hundred miles south of the Scottish border. One of the men assigned to 'watch' Essex witch Margaret Moone (1645), who was accused of possessing no less than 'twelve imps', claimed that when she made her confession she 'spake very plainly and very intelligently, discoursing of some things done long before, her memory serving her very exactly'.[16] Further south still, Devon witch Temperance Lloyd (1682) and her companions stood, in the words of Cecil Ewen, 'on a gallows ladder with the halter round the neck ready for swinging off, answering questions politely and firmly', while in 1616 Alexander Roberts claimed of witches in general that 'neither be they overflowed with a blacke melancholique humor, dazeling the phantasie, but have their understanding cleer, and wits as quick as others'.[17] While the visionary experiences described by the victims of witchcraft often sound distressing and eerily fantastic, thereby resembling the out-of-control experiences of psychosis, those described by cunning folk and witches frequently sound so calm and ordered that, as we saw in chapter TEN, some historians have assumed that the entities encountered were real people or animals.[18] Indeed it is possible that the palpable 'sanity' of the popular magical practitioner sometimes prejudiced them in the courtroom. Sir Francis North, who was present at the trial of Temperance Lloyd and her companions in Exeter, in 1682, suggested that the jury was ready to believe that the witches' familiar-encounters were the effects of 'confederacy, melancholy, or delusion', a conclusion which would have increased their chances of acquittal, but lamented that the witches had 'a great deal of skill to convict themselves. Their descriptions of the sucking devils with saucer-eyes were so natural that the jury could not choose but believe them'.[19]

If we take the view, then, that the cunning folk and witches of early modern Britain who envisioned familiars were not necessarily mad or mentally unstable, then we find ourselves confronting a more subtle question. If the visionary familiar was not a 'phantom of a disordered brain', then what was it? If cunning folk and witches were, as we have seen previously, 'honest and sober' and 'grave and setled', and were, not-

withstanding their subtle profession and their entanglement in neighbourly tensions, in all other respects leading relatively unremarkable
lives, than how and why were they having these unusual and highly
complex visionary experiences? And if the friends and neighbours of
these individuals did not define these experiences as symptoms of mental illness, then how did they define them?

In recent years, the few historians of British witchcraft and magic who
have attempted to address these issues in any detail have predominantly
employed psychoanalytic perspectives. Lyndal Roper and Diane Purkiss,
working with what we can term here 'collaborative retrospective fiction'
theories, have argued, with great ingenuity, that the fantasy elements of
encounter-narratives, if they existed at all, were the result of intimate
negotiation: a strangely creative fusion of ideological preconceptions and
emotional responses exchanged between interrogator and suspect during
the long questioning process. They have claimed that these fantasy
elements were strongly rooted in the life experiences of the accused,
reflecting profound anxieties surrounding poverty, sickness, childbirth,
parenting and relationships – and that the encounter-narrative acted as a
vehicle through which repressed emotions and memories surrounding
taboo issues such as infanticide and maternal envy could be expressed.[20]
In a recent analysis of the encounter-narrative given by Orkney cunning
woman Elspeth Reoch (1616), in which Elspeth claimed to have enjoyed
sexual relations with a fairy man, Diane Purkiss identifies a number of
stresses which may have lain behind Elspeth's story, including those
surrounding teenage pregnancy, pre-marital sex, childbirth, the coming
to sexual maturity and incest.[21] Malcolm Gaskill, on the other hand,
considers that bereavement-grief, the need to escape poverty and the
desire for power, may have lain behind Ely witch Margaret Moore's
description of encountering four familiar spirits in the form of her dead
children, claiming that: 'it was (and remains) common for poor and otherwise oppressed people to fantasize about the reversal of their predicament
– Margaret Moore's specific fantasy, as we have seen, concerned resisting
the domination of death and poverty.'[22] While such psychoanalytic explanations are valuable and certainly contain elements of truth, by themselves
they can, en masse, become reductionistic. To explain a fantasy solely in
terms of the emotional distress which lies behind it can reduce it as effectively as a simplistic pathological explanation. If we focus too closely on
encounter-narratives as conduits for repressed emotion, or vehicles
through which 'poor or otherwise oppressed people' can 'fantasize about
the reversal of their predicament' then it is all too easy to close our minds
to other possibilities.

What is markedly absent from analyses of the experiential dimension of British encounter-narratives is a comparative religious approach. There has been little attempt to analyse the 'fantasies' of cunning folk and witches in relation to visionary experience as it is found in magical belief systems and developed religions throughout the world, including Christianity. One of the reasons for this oversight may be the fact that many scholars, as we have seen in chapter TEN, remain undecided as to whether encounter-narratives predominantly refer to visionary experience or fiction. It is also possible that the early modern encounter-narrative has been inadvertently 'secularized' in an unconscious reaction to the ideological excesses of Margaret Murray, and the imaginative abandon with which neo-pagan movements have 'spiritualized' beliefs and practices associated with pre-modern witchcraft and magic. It is also possible that in a secular age, dominated by the psychoanalytic paradigm, historians are wary of adopting the controversial and unquantifiable terms and perceptual frameworks necessary for an analysis from a comparative religious viewpoint. Bearing these problems in mind, in the remainder of this book we will be drawing on a variety of comparative religious perspectives to help us to gain some insight into the visionary familiar-encounter. These perspectives will complement, rather than contradict, psychoanalytic viewpoints and give us the opportunity to look at our subject matter from a new angle. We will start this process by returning to shamanism.

The Spirituality of the Shaman

Scholars of shamanism increasingly acknowledge that many shamans are not only sane, but that they are somehow 'more than sane': possessing mental faculties which are not only healthy but are in fact superior to those possessed by the average man. They often emphasize the fact that the shaman is universally respected for his wisdom.[23] Roger Walsh claims that 'Shamans are often outstanding members of the community and may display considerable intellectual, artistic and leadership skills and make significant contributions to their community'; Swiss anthropologist Alfred Metraux that the shamanic vocation 'attracts a certain élite of intelligence and character'; and Marjorie Balzer that 'Within their own cosmological-philosophical systems, [Siberian] shamans were and still are respected as wise spiritual advisors and keepers of a huge range of sacred knowledge, not just religious ballet masters or charlatan actors.'[24] Similarly, Knud Rasmussen was consistently impressed by the shamans whom he encountered on his journeys through Arctic America in the early twentieth century. After a conversation with one of them he was moved to write that the shaman's words 'come as an echo of the wisdom we admired in the angakoq [shaman] we met at every stage of the journey in the inhospitable regions of King William's Land, in Aua's snow-palace at Hudson Bay or in the circle of the Caribou Eskimo Igjugârjuk'.[25] Shamans created the same impression in nineteenth-century North America. When the Cheyenne shaman 'Porcupine' spoke 'all other listened, for his mind was stored to fullness with wisdom appertaining to old time Indian social relations and spiritual lore'.[26] Similarly, in the 1940s Mackenzie-Yukon shaman Thekenendatetco was equally revered, it being claimed that 'His wonderful deeds are manifold. He is very old, but will never die; he hears and knows everything and all Indians must obey his will.'[27]

The respect and even reverence in which many shamans are held is no doubt in large part attributable to the fact that they are believed to possess technologically effective magical powers: in a world without doctors, they can bring a sick child back from the brink of death; in a world without policemen they can track down the whereabouts of a valuable stolen horse, identify the thief, and intimidate him into making a confession; in a world without modern science, they can predict and manipulate the coming of rain, the growing of seeds or the track of an arrow. The respect in which shamans are held, however, may not only be accorded them in admiration of their technological skills as doctors and policemen.

The tendency of Victorian and early twentieth-century scholars and missionaries to pathologize the visionary experience of the shaman was symptomatic of a generally reductionist attitude towards 'primitive' religions, an attitude which was rooted in a form of 'cultural evolutionism'. These early scholars assumed that the existence of tribal peoples, and by the same token, the religico-magical belief systems they developed to help themselves deal with this existence, was wholly centred around material concerns: the search for food and shelter, the fight against death and sickness, the strengthening of communal bonds and the need for protection against aggressors and so on. The seminal Victorian anthropologist, Sir James Frazer, worked with this assumption when he portrayed tribal magico-religious belief systems as basically amounting to an amalgamation of cause and effect magical technologies designed to meet basic survival needs.[28] In the century following Frazer's work, scholars have increasingly recognized the limitations of such perspectives. In the 1960s, the prominent scholar of religion, Ninian Smart, was eloquent in his dismissal of the Frazerian view:

Frazer's theory neglects the perception of the numinous to which we referred earlier. Religion, and man's relationship to deities, are not simply means to centain ends. They are not simply instruments whereby men promote the solidarity of the tribe and the security and fertility of the food supply. It is true that these last concerns are quite obviously of the greatest importance to people struggling in a difficult environment, and it would be surprising if these concerns did not appear in a fairly central way in religious rituals and beliefs. But also men have seen the world transfused with significances of a different order.

For the primitive, as indeed for many folk who have a strong religious sense, the world is not just a beautiful or ugly place, a difficult or easy habitat, a place for living in: they have also seen it as an awe-inspiring, sacred, holy environment, in which the forces of the unseen shine through the visible environment and in which terror and love, and hate and favour, the ghostly and the demonic, the spirit world and the shining glory of deities are perceptible to the inward eye. It is a world of strangeness, it is uncanny, but it is also familiar and peopled with beings not totally dissimilar from ourselves. In brief, the world provides the material for religious experience as well as for ordinary perception and technological manipulation.[29]

In the decades since Smart wrote these words, there has been an increasing awareness among scholars that tribal magical belief systems, like developed religions, constellate around a experiential core: what Smart calls a 'perception of the numinous', or what is more conventionally described as 'religious', 'spiritual', or 'mystical' experience. Until relatively recently such experiences have been identified and defined by western scholars according to criteria laid down by the traditional Christian mystical, or, as we shall call them here, 'contemplative', traditions. In recent decades, however, owing to advances in the study of ethnography and comparative religion, and in the psychological and scientific study of consciousness, the general conception of what constitutes a 'mystical experience' has opened up considerably and scholars now concur that the range of experiences which come under this umbrella term are far wider and more various than previously thought. As a consequence, the term 'mystical' can now be loosely applied to almost any altered state of consciousness which occurs to a 'healthy' mind and which involves the experience of a 'reality surpassing normal human understanding or experience, especially a reality perceived as essential to the nature of life'.[30] As a result of these findings, it is now universally acknowledged that the tribal shaman's experiences of encountering helping spirits and travelling to spirit worlds can be defined as 'mystical' and the shaman as 'mystical adept'. This elevated view of shamanism was first introduced into mainstream thought by Mircea Eliade, in his influential *Shamanism: Archaic Techniques of Ecstasy* (1964). Although scholars have since criticized Eliade's work, in particular his romanticism and 'ascensional emphases', few contemporary scholars would question his once-revolutionary assertion that 'shamanism represents the most credible mystical experience of the religious world of primitives, and within this archaic world fulfils the same role as does mysticism in the official faith of the great historical religions from Buddhism down to Christianity'.[31]

There are many different kinds of experiences which come under the umbrella term 'mystical' and in order to be able to gain a perspective on, or 'categorize', the visionary experiences of the shaman we can turn to the work of American psychologist Ken Wilber. After examining a wide range of the world's spiritual traditions, Wilber concluded that although these traditions recorded access to many different types of altered states of consciousness, beneath their varied descriptions it was possible to identify a finite number of 'recognizable deep structures'.[32] Wilber also claimed (as paraphrased by Roger Walsh) that these 'deep structures emerge in a set sequence during spiritual practice and that this same sequence is found across different traditions and practices' raising the possibility of the existence of a universal 'sequence of development or emergence of transpersonal states'.[33] As a result of these observations Wilber devised a theoretical model which maps out ten basic groups of states or levels of consciousness – ranging from the 'personal' (levels 1–6) to the 'transpersonal' or 'transcendent' (levels 7–10) – the last four levels marking a sequence of development in the emergence of mystical states which reflects the hierarchical placing of mystical experience in world religions.[34] Identified as (in ascending order) the *psychic*, the *subtle*, the *causal* and the *absolute*, these last four groups of states are progressively more difficult to access.

Psychic   This level marks the very beginning of transcendence, that is, an awareness which extends beyond the experience of the sensations, thoughts and emotions which characterize the 'personal' states of consciousness.[35]

Subtle   The overwhelming majority of mystical experiences accessed by humans are on this level. According to Walsh, subtle experiences comprise 'those faint images and sensations that tend to emerge when the more raucous mental contents are stilled; as, for example, in meditation. The experiences that arise may be with or without form. Formless experiences comprise pure light or sound. Experiences with form may comprise all manner of images, including vast scenes of worlds of extraordinary richness and complexity. Archetypal figures . . . may arise, such as images of saints, angels, or Buddhas'.[36] However they manifest, subtle level experiences give 'illumination and rapture and initial transcendental insight'.[37]

Causal   These states are only occasionally accessed by mystics. Unlike subtle states, causal level experiences are characterized by a lack of phenomena in the field of awareness. They are simple awareness itself. These states provide 'an unlimited consciousness of unity which pervades everywhere'.[38]

Absolute In many traditions this level is believed to be the 'ultimate' or 'absolute' realization. Here, phenomena may reappear, but 'Consciousness or Spirit alone is now seen to manifest and express itself in and as all the levels and worlds and beings of the universe'.[39]

In his penetrating study *Spirit of Shamanism*, Roger Walsh argues that according to Wilber's classification, the characteristically visionary trance experiences of the shaman bear all the hallmarks of subtle-level mystical states, although he suggests that in some instances these states may evolve to higher levels.[40] The shaman's conviction that his experiences of meeting spirits and travelling to spirit worlds are 'real', is wholly congruent with the fact that although subtle-level visionary experiences are likely to be linked to the imaginative faculty, they are qualitatively different from normal fantasy and dream, being characterized by a high level of autonomy and realism. The quality of this realism is evocatively described by the Swiss psychologist, Carl Jung, who experienced first hand these types of visionary phenomena: 'I would never have imagined that any such experience was possible,' he claimed, 'It was not a product of imagination. The visions and experiences were utterly real; there was nothing subjective about them; they all had a quality of absolute objectivity.'[41] Similarly, the shaman's ability to 'conjure' spirits and voluntarily enter into spirit worlds is wholly congruent with the fact that subtle-level states can be induced at will and entered into with specific intention. The visionary journeys of the shaman, as Roger Walsh notes, 'are remarkably rich and highly organised. They involve several senses, including auditory, visual and body sensations . . . They are coherent and purposeful, reflecting both the shamanic cosmology as well as the purpose for which the journey is undertaken.'[42] The shaman's belief that it is through communicating with helping spirits and travelling into spirit worlds that he gains his magical powers is congruent with the fact that in spiritual traditions throughout the world these preliminary levels of mystical experience are associated with the acquisition of 'miraculous' or, in more secular terms, 'parapsychological' abilities. Finally, and most significantly, the references to profound emotion and understanding found in some shaman encounter-narratives are congruent with the fact that subtle-level visionary experiences can be the gateway to 'illumination and rapture and initial transcendental insight'. As we shall examine in more detail in chapter TWELVE, the differences between modern western and tribal mentalities have historically made it difficult for scholars to acknowledge the spiritual dimension of the shaman's encounter-narratives. A significant minority of these narratives, however, evocatively describe the intensity of feeling and depth of perception recognizable as the hallmarks of mystical experience from spiritual traditions throughout the world. Ninety-year-old Blackfoot shaman 'Smoking Star' (1922), for example, told the anthropologist Clark Wissler that:

> Four times in my life the Smoking-Star has stood before me. All visions are sacred, as are some dreams, but when a vision appears the fourth time, it is very holy. Even a shaman may not speak of it freely. Many times have I gone to lonely places and cried out to the powers of the air, the earth, and the waters to help me understand their ways. Sometimes they have answered me, but all the truly great mysteries are beyond understanding.[43]

Similarly, in the early twentieth century the famous North American Oglala Sioux shaman, Black Elk, claimed that:

> I was standing on the highest mountain of them all, and round about beneath me was the whole hoop of the world. And while I stood there, I saw more than I can tell and I understood more than I saw; for I was seeing in a sacred manner the shapes of all things in the spirit, and the shape of all shapes as they must live together like one being. And I saw that the sacred hoop of my people was one of many hoops that made one circle, wide as daylight and as starlight, and in the centre grew one mightly flowering tree to shelter all the children of one mother and one father. And I saw that it was holy.[44]

Comparable experiences are described by shamans from the North American Arctic. Although in the following passage the Alaskan Inuk, Najagneq, laments the fact that 'true' shamans no longer exist, it is clear that he upholds the classical spiritual tradition of his forefathers:

> I have searched in the darkness, being silent in the great lonely stillness of the dark. So I became an angakoq, through visions and dreams and encounters with flying spirits. In our forefathers' day, the angakoqs were solitary men; but now, they are all priests or doctors, weather prophets or conjurers producing game, or clever merchants, selling their skill for pay. *The ancients devoted their lives to maintaining the balance of the universe; to great things, immense, unfathomable things* [my italics].[45]

Other shamans express the joys of classical mystical 'bliss' or 'rapture', the Canadian Iglulik shaman, Aua, telling Rasmussen that when he first became a shaman 'I felt a great, inexplicable joy, a joy so powerful that I could not restrain it, but had to break into song, a mighty song, with room for only one word: joy, joy! . . . And then in the midst of such a fit of mysterious and overwhelming delight I became a shaman . . . I could see and hear in a totally different way.'[46]

From this perspective the shaman's visionary experiences not only give him the technical magical abilities necessary to minister to his people as a healer and diviner, but they simultaneously give him the existential insights necessary to act as spiritual consoler or priest. For a community largely concerned with the mundane business of finding and preparing food and maintaining safety and shelter, the shaman's accounts of his personal visionary odysseys both inform, inspire and comfort. He speaks to his tribe of that *mysterium tremendum et fascinans*:[47] he charts the hidden landscapes of the spirit worlds and describes the character and activities of the invisible beings who live there; he sheds light on the profound mysteries of human existence: love, death, suffering, time and man's place in the wider scheme of creation. His visionary experiences shape tribal ritual, ethics and mythology in the same way that the visions of Christian contemplatives such as Moses or St John have shaped the nature of Christian belief and worship. It is hardly surprising to find that by virtue of these experiences the shaman, like mystics from spiritual traditions throughout the world, is believed to transform into a 'spiritualized', or more 'god-like', human being. 'The shamans and mystics of primitive societies,' writes Mircea Eliade, 'are considered – and rightly – to be superior beings; their magico-religious powers also find expression in an extension of their mental capacities. The shaman is the man who knows and remembers, that is, who understands the mysteries of life and death.'[48] The North American Apache shaman who claimed grandiosely that 'I am all powerful. I will never die. If you shoot me, the bullet will not enter my flesh, or if it enters it will not hurt me . . . My power is like that of a god' – was merely expressing an accepted belief.[49]

As far as the shaman is concerned, all of these supernatural powers and experiences are contingent upon the aid of his helping spirits. Helping spirits can either directly impart knowledge and power to the shaman or enable him to gain it by guiding – and in some cases carrying – him to spirit worlds. When there, they can negotiate (and sometimes battle) with spirit-beings on the shaman's behalf and if necessary 'merge' with him, enabling him to assume their powers and capacities.[50] The following passage from Rasmussen dramatically sums up the helping spirit's axiomatic role in Arctic shamanism:

> . . . it is not enough for a shaman to be able to escape both from himself and from his surroundings. It is not enough that, having the soul removed from his eyes, brain, and entrails, he is able also to withdraw the spirit from his body and thus undertake the great 'spirit flights' through space and

through the sea; nor is it enough that by means of his quamaneq [powers] he abolishes all distance, and can see all things, however far away. For he will be incapable of maintaining these faculties unless he has the support of helping and answering spirits . . . But he must procure these helping spirits for himself; he must meet them in person . . . He cannot even choose for himself what sort he will have. They come to him of their own accord, strong and powerful.[51]

The appearance and acquisition of helping spirits is associated with a process of profound psychological transformation. The Iglulik Inuk, Aua, who so eloquently described the joys of mystical rapture to Rasmussen also claimed that '[when I became a shaman] I could see and hear in a totally different way. I had gained my enlightenment, the shaman's light of brain and body, and this in such a manner that it was not only I who could see through the darkness of life, but the same bright light also shone out from me, imperceptible to human beings but visible to all spirits of earth, sky and sea, and these now came to me to become my helping spirits.'[52] If we place the visionary experiences of shamans on Wilber's subtle level of mystical states, then the helping spirit can be seen to perform the function of a 'spiritual guide'. From this perspective, the spirit's ability to perform magical acts for its human ally can be interpreted as the process through which a visionary entity facilitates the understanding and deployment of mystical knowledge and power. Similarly, its ability to act as a guide or host in spirit worlds can be interpreted as a process through which a visionary entity enables the shaman to access and negotiate mystical states of consciousness.

This brief examination of the ontological status of the shaman's visionary experience enables us to examine the familiar-encounters of popular magical practitioners in early modern Britain from a new perspective. If the visionary experiences of the shaman can be defined as 'subtle-level mystical experiences', then can we make the same claims for the visionary experiences of cunning folk and witches? If the shaman's helping spirit can be defined as an 'envisioned spiritual guide', then can we make the same claim for the early modern familiar? From a broad theoretical standpoint, the latter's encounter-experiences and magical activities so closely resemble those of the shaman that it would be deeply illogical to dismiss such a possibility out of hand. And yet, focusing in more closely, to conceive of the bereaved Bessie Dunlop bickering with the impeccably-dressed but rather bossy ghost, Tom Reid, or the poverty-stricken Joan Prentice, sitting in her chamber in the almshouse at Sible Hedingham with a small, disobedient ferret boldly sucking blood from her cheek, as undergoing 'subtle-level mystical experiences' which confer 'illumination and rapture and initial transcendental insight', demands a great shift in perspective.[53] In order to be able to make this shift we will return to the early modern period to see if there is any evidence to support this view.

CHAPTER TWELVE

The Unrecognized
Mystics

'not witchcraft, not superstition, not demonolatry, but wise, priestly and prophetic'.[1]

Historians have long recognized that the magical beliefs and practices of learned magicians in early modern Britain possessed a spiritual dimension and that this dimension was rooted in mystical experience. Keith Thomas writes that the learned magician sought to understand the mysteries of God's creation through 'revelation', claiming that this type of 'spiritual magic' was:

> a religious rite, in which prayer played an essential part, and where piety and purity of life were deemed essential . . . Spiritual magic or theurgy was based on the idea that one could reach God in an ascent up the scale of creation made possible by a rigorous course of prayer, fasting and devotional preparation. For many, this was no mechanical manipulation of set formulae, but a humble supplication that God should extend to them the privilege of a unique view of his mysteries . . . At this level the practice of magic became a holy quest; the search for knowledge, not by study and research, but by revelation.[2]

Scholars of Continental witchcraft and magic often acknowledge that the beliefs and practices of popular magical practitioners also possessed a spiritual dimension in this period – Wolfgang Behringer, for example, claiming that the shamanistic visionary experiences of Central European cunning folk can be described as a 'type of religious expertise'.[3] Scholars in the British field, however, seldom make such elevated claims on behalf of their popular magical practitioners, despite the fact that such claims, as we shall see later in this chapter, would be well-supported by comments found in contemporary élite writings. This is not to say that the value and efficacy of the British cunning man or woman's magical activities is not acknowledged. No historian working today would dispute the accuracy of George Gifford's claim, in 1587, that 'many in great distress have been relieved and recovered by sending unto such wise men or wise women, when they could not tell what should else become of them and all that they had'; nor would they challenge Keith Thomas's assertion that common folk 'went to sorcerers for help and advice, and whether their trouble was physical or psychological they gained comfort and assistance'.[4] It is now de rigueur for historians to acknowledge that the magical cures of cunning folk were effective on many levels. The successful cure of a physical ailment, for example, could have been achieved through the use of herbal remedies (or other physical cures which had a genuine curative effect) or as a result of the self-healing facilitated through the use of non-invasive medical techniques (the healing methods of cunning folk being generally less invasive than those of contemporary doctors). By the same token, charms, prayer and ritual could have been very effective in curing the psychosomatic dimension of disease through auto-suggestion, while divinatory technologies (such as mirror-gazing or the sieve and shears) may have worked on a psychological level to disclose the wishes or suspicions of the client or to intimidate the guilty. The effectiveness of these grass-roots healing skills were often acknowledged by élite observers in the period, one noting that 'there are diverse and sundry kinds of Maladies, which though a man do goe to all the physitions that can be heard of, yet he shall find no remedy: wheras sometimes they are cured by those which are called cunning folkes'.[5]

Despite approbation such as this, the magical beliefs and practices of cunning folk and indeed popular magic in general in Britain during this period, emerge from the history books as a confection of largely 'Frazerian' technologies. This effect, which must be unintentional, is the unavoidable result of discussing these beliefs without reference to their experiential dimension. Without an experiential dimension any set of magical beliefs, however sophisticated, becomes little different from a scientific procedure – a manufactured means through which to manipulate nature and the objects within it. From this perspective, the cunning man or woman, however skilled, possesses a status on a par with a doctor or a constable, and the esteem in which they are held is consequently attributable to their possession of superior technological and perhaps 'people' skills, without them needing to have had any recourse to spiritual revelation. Keith Thomas intimates as much when he claims of the cunning man that:

usually the precise source of the wizard's skill seems to have been left conveniently undefined. He owed his reputation to his technique and knowledge ('his cunning'), rather than to any special holiness of life . . . In rare cases he might purport to employ a familiar spirit, who could charitably be regarded as a good angel, but he did not usually have any other spiritual pretensions. It was the clergy who forced him into the posture of the divine healer by their refusal to allow that magical powers might have a theologically neutral staus. The cunning man who acquired a reputation as a demi-god sometimes did so in order to throw off the label of devil-worshipper.[6]

Other scholars support Thomas's position, usually through implication or omission. Christina Larner, for example, implied that popular magical traditions in early modern Scotland had little or no spiritual dimension when she wrote that during the Reformation there was a movement – both among the urban and peasant laity – away from 'animist beliefs to a *more spiritual* form of religion [my italics]'.[7] Similarly, Alastair McIntosh, in a review of a collection of papers given at a symposium on the seer in Oxford in 1987, writes that 'it emerges strikingly from these papers that the seer's role *is by and large an adjunct to the spiritual or religious.* The seer makes prognostications on matters generally mundane rather than ethereal and may also manipulate psychodynamic processes, usually as understood in terms of a parallel spirit world [my italics].'[8] Stephen Wilson's recent panoramic study *The Magical Universe: Everyday Ritual and Magic in Pre-Modern Europe* (2000), implies the same by virtue of the fact that it contains no examination of an experiential dimension.[9] The equivalent is true of Owen Davies's recent study of English cunning folk. Although Davies discusses an experiential dimension in relation to more learned magical practitioners, through an in-depth examination of a wide range of contemporary magical manuals allegedly used in the conjuration of spirits, the overall emphasis of his work supports his perception that, in general, cunning folk were concerned with the application of 'practical magical solutions to resolve everyday problems' and that they left little record of their 'thoughts and experiments' because occult philosophies 'just did not interest many of them'.[10] Diane Purkiss, one of the few British historians to pay any serious attention to the fairy-encountering experiences of cunning folk and witches, does not analyse these experiences in relation to any spiritual significance, but defines them as 'fantasies of the dispossessed' coming from 'the deeps of misery'. The 'fairy religion', she suggests, was a 'supernatural refuge'; a 'compensatory fantasy that allowed them [cunning folk and witches] to experience in imagination the splendour and specialness denied them in life'.[11]

The factors which have inhibited, and still inhibit, historians from recognizing the spiritual significance of popular magical traditions in early modern Britain are in many ways the same as those which have historically prevented scholars from recognizing the spiritual significance of tribal shamanism. We have already seen how a disinterest in, or unfamiliarity with, the study of altered states of consciousness has fostered the tendency to 'pathologize' the spirit-encounters of both shamans, cunning folk and witches. Alongside this tendency to pathologize, we can identify other, more subtle inhibitory factors.

Literate and Non-Literate Minds

Tribal shamanism, like early modern magical traditions, operates within predominantly non-literate cultures. The mystical or contemplative traditions which stand at the core of the world's great historical religions, on the other hand, have evolved out of cultures which have been literate for thousands of years. Despite the fact that contemplatives universally lament both the futility and the danger of trying to describe their spiritual experiences, every developed religion possesses a formidable canon of mystical literature: sacred texts, often thousands of years old, which detail spiritual practices, discuss their relation to ritual, doctrine and ethics and describe the lives and teachings of mystics themselves. These traditions are closely linked to philosophical and scientific traditions, having made significant contributions to the development of discursive thought, and both theoretical and practical science. In this way, the spiritual experiences of the traditional religious mystic, inexpressible and incomprehensible as they are, are thrown into relief by the written word. It is only by merit of such written proof that scholars have acknowledged that the magical beliefs of learned magicians in early modern Britain possessed a mystical dimension. Élite magic, although theoretically heretical, was underpinned by an established literary tradition. Although this tradition is small (in comparison with those of orthodox religions), of labyrinthine genesis and sometimes questionable authenticity, it still represents a body of written evidence of considerable antiquity. In this literature learned magical practitioners specifically state spiritual motives and describe mystical experiences.

Any mystical dimension to popular magic in this period, however, would have possessed no such legacy. The beliefs and practices of cunning folk and witches were, like those of shamans, rooted in the animism of pre-literate cultures and as such would have been passed down through the centuries by a process of imitation and word of mouth. These types of orally-inherited mystical traditions might be thousands of years old and yet not have a shred of literary evidence to show for themselves.

The zeal of both early modern witchcraft prosecutors and modern anthropologists has meant that some of the visionary experiences of cunning folk, witches and shamans have been preserved on paper, however the presence of this usually unsympathetic third party means that these experiences have come down to us distorted. Material relating to cunning folk and witches, moreover, has been subject to far more distortion than material relating to shamans. Although the records of shamanic trance experiences made by early anthropologists were influenced by factors such as disdain, disapproval, pity and the zealous desire to convert, these observers were not recording these experiences with the intention of proving heinous crimes against humanity. Although not always objective (particularly in the early years), many at least attempted to describe shamanic beliefs and experiences for their own sake, without an agenda. As a consequence, some of these encounter-narratives, as we have seen in chapter ELEVEN, contain the recognizable hallmarks of classic mystical experience.

The men who questioned cunning folk and witches, on the other hand, were looking for evidence of maleficent witchcraft and association with the Devil. Even those interrogators who favoured leniency were looking to quash false accusation or establish mental instability rather than reveal the existence of spiritual insight. The magical practitioners who were interrogated by these men were being forced to divulge information under conditions of extreme stress. Often exhausted and scared, their overwhelming concern would have been to defend themselves against their aggressors. An insight into the courtroom experiences of the popular magical practitioner can be gained from the following comments, made by a contemporary critic of the Elizabethan justice system:

> a man standing at the bar for his trial upon life and death, feared on the one side with terror of what may happen unto him, and on the other side astonished with the sight of such a court and company set against him . . . especially if he be bashful and unlearned, in so short a time as there is allotted to him for answering of his life, without help of a lawyer . . . that may direct, counsel or assist him in such an agony; how can he see all the parts or points that may be alleged for his defence, being never so innocent?[12]

Even if the accused had the courage to speak for themselves they may not, in some cases, have been given the opportunity. Twenty-year-old Mary Spencer, for example, who was tried for witchcraft at Lancaster in 1634, claimed that 'she would have answered [the charges brought against her] for herself, but the wind was so loud, and the throng so great that she could not hear the evidence against her', while at the trial of Wiltshire cunning woman Anne Bodenham in 1653, John Aubrey observed that 'the spectators made such a noise that the judge could not hear the prisoner nor the prisoner the judge, but the words were handed from one to the other by Mr R. Chandler, and sometimes not truly reported'.[13] This was certainly not the kind of environment to encourage eloquence and articulation over such a subtle matter as spiritual motivation or experience. Moreover, to these circumstantial difficulties must also be added the fact that mystical experiences are notoriously difficult to talk about, even under sympathetic conditions. In relation to the shaman's frequent reluctance to talk about his altered states of consciousness, Holger Kalweit explains that 'It is not that the shaman considers it sacrilegious to talk of such matters to strangers or the uninitiated, nor that he cannot remember what he experienced in his trance; the reason is much more likely that he simply cannot find words to describe what he has seen.'[14]

The absence of a written mystical canon is not the only factor which has obscured the spiritual dimension of popular magical traditions in Britain in this period. Cunning folk and witches, like tribal shamans, inhabited a culture immersed in nature and informed by animist beliefs and therefore possessed very different frames of reference to those of people living in Britain today. Such cultural divides can be very difficult to bridge. In reference to the shaman, for example, Kalweit claims that 'the anthropologist who studies the world of the shaman is all too often faced by an impenetrable web of cosmological theories and cultural characteristics, which prevent him from understanding their psychic origin and background. This, we believe, is why we are unwilling to acknowledge the mystical inspiration of the shaman and to put him on a par with other religious mystics.'[15] In some ways, the lives of cunning folk and witches are less comprehensible to the modern western mind than the lives of tribal shamans, for we are more ready to accept our 'differentness' to the shaman, and therefore make allowances for it, than we are to accept our differentness to the cunning woman or the witch. For many people, scholars and lay alike, familiarity with the élite culture of early modern Britain – the culture of Shakespeare, Elizabeth Tudor, Francis Bacon and Christopher Wren – can coax us into forgetting about how starkly the daily lives and mental climates of the majority of the population differed from those of both educated people in the period, and people today.

To some degree this difference is attributable to the gulf which exists between the literate and the non-literate mind. Despite the fact that Protestantism and its emphasis on reading the Bible in the vernacular may have served to encourage popular literacy, during this period of British history the vast majority of ordinary people remained illiterate or partly literate. Anthropologists have shown that without recourse to the written word human cultures primarily express themselves through imagery, whether in the form of art, mythology or magical belief and ritual. This 'imaginal language' can be highly sophisticated and express complex ideas and states of mind, much of it being employed metaphorically and symbolically. The encounter-experiences of both cunning folk, witches and shamans are narrated in this imaginal language and this presents real problems for the scholar looking for evidence of mystical experience. In relation to the experiences of the shaman Holger Kalweit remarks that:

> Part of the difficulty of proving that shamanic vocation involves a mystical experience is due to the fact that tribal terminology only approximates the classical characteristics of the phenomenology of enlightenment. Moreover, all tribal cultures express psychic experiences within a framework of cultur-ally conditioned metaphors or as personified energies in the form of gods, spirits, animals and so on. In order to make it all understandable, the abstract life of the psyche is concretized and expressed as myth, so that in many cases only a pale glimmer of the original experience shines through this veil of mental constructs.[16]

The art historian, Ananda Coomaraswamy, has argued that the rise of rationalism and literacy has caused modern western man to gradually lose the ability to think in images, and that this 'imaginal illiteracy' prevents him from fully deciphering primitive visual mythology. 'To have lost the art of thinking in images', he claims 'is precisely to have lost the proper linguistic of metaphysics and to have descended to the verbal logic of "philosophy."'[17] From this perspective, to have lost the art of thinking in images is synonymous with a reduction in the capacity to recognize descriptions of mystical states. The mythologist, Joseph Campbell, shares Coomaraswamy's view and doubts whether the average anthropologist, being 'professionally bound to the concepts of positivistic science would be able to recognize and follow a truly mystical and transtheological state-ment, even if he heard one'.[18] The anthropologist, and indeed anyone raised in the modern western world, approaches primitive visual mythology much as they would a foreign language. Even in the early modern period itself, the gulf between the learned and the unlearned mind inhibited the attempts of some educated men to understand the experien-tial dimension of popular magic. Hilda Ellis Davidson laments the superficial and ultimately sceptical assessment of the faculty of second sight given by Samuel Johnson in eighteenth-century Scotland, claiming that: 'sensible, downright and honest as it is, [it] shows the difficulties confronting a learned man from a predominantly literary background who sets out to explore evidence which his education and scale of values prevent him from fully appreciating. The kind of proof he and his contemporaries sought was simply not available, and many others since Johnson have been similarly frustrated.'[19]

Christian Preconceptions

Even if we can resist the tempatation to pathologize visionary states and can negotiate the obstacles presented by the absence of a written tradition and the gulf between the literate and non-literate mind, our ability to recognize the spiritual significance of the visionary experiences of early modern cunning folk and witches is inhibited by yet another factor – our own inherited, and largely unconscious, Christian preconceptions.

The stereotypical Christian contemplative is an individual cut off from the common run of humanity. His search for divine revelation necessitates a frugal, largely solitary, highly-disciplined life, absorbed in ritual, silent prayer, intellectual discourse and public service. The descriptions we have of the lives of early modern cunning folk and witches evoke a very different picture: they lived in the heart of their communities, often as members of large families living in cramped living conditions. Their lives were dominated by the drudgery of survival and their magical exploits centred around the attempts to secure the money, food and goods necessary to stave off hunger and privation. Their magical beliefs and techniques were devoid of intellectualism or urbane ritual and their visionary experiences occurred in fields, bedrooms, kitchens or by roadsides.

Cunning folk and witches differed from the Christian contemplative in character as well as lifestyle. For the contemplative, the search for divine revelation is inextricably linked to the search for moral perfection. In order to know God, he strives to become like God, who is morally perfect. 'Sinful' emotions such as hatred, anger, pride, envy, and the thoughts and actions which are rooted in them, are resisted and hopefully eliminated, while the Christian virtues of humility, compassion, kindness, temperance and so on are cultivated in their place. As a consequence of this equation, the divine revelations experienced by the contemplative are seen to be authenticated by the exhibition of specific moral qualities: saints and holy men, in effect, are characterized by 'goodness'. Cunning folk and witches, on the other hand, seem to have been less inhibited by such ethical prescriptions. While they could, like any individual, aspire to cultivate the virtues of the contemplative, they could also be openly and unapologetically volatile, proud, manipulative and, most notoriously, morally ambivalent. Part of this moral ambivalence can be attributed to the prevailing moral climate as opposed to any out-of-the-ordinary malevolence on the part of the magical practitioner. Although in this period the Church encouraged its congregation to strive for Christian virtues, the British authorities, meanwhile, had no compunction in chopping individuals into quarters and scooping out their intestines while they were still conscious, burning them alive at the stake or mounting their heads upon sticks in public places and leaving them to rot because they dared to express political or religious views divergent from the official norm. The British people, meanwhile, legally carried daggers, and often swords, around with them both day and night and had no qualms about using them if they quarrelled with a neighbour or were attacked by the many thieves and vagabonds which roamed the streets. Conditions of life were difficult; food, possessions and good health were scarce, and the human capacity for benevolence was often pushed to its limits. In such a climate, as in similar climates in parts of the world today, you had to fight hard for survival, and as a consequence, reactions to perceived wrongs were far more aggressive than would be considered appropriate in Britain today.

Even if we take this moral relativism into account, there is no doubt that the alleged behaviour of some witches and cunning folk was considered, even by the standards of the time, to have overstepped common moral boundaries. While some of those accused of committing maleficium were undoubtedly innocent (she confessed that 'she never hurt anybody but did help divers that sent for her which were stricken or forespoken') and others were perhaps only guilty of minor transgressions ('being demanded what mischiefe he caused . . . he answered never any, onely hee sent his beare Spirit to provoke the Maid-servant of Mr. *Say* of *Molmesworth* to steale victualls for him out of her Masters house'), a proportion are likely to have been truly culpable in intent, if not in actuality.[20] Although it could be argued that perhaps historian Owen Davies goes too far when he claims that 'in general' cunning folk were 'commercially hard-nosed, possessed a cynical streak, and were rather too prone to unscrupulous activities', there is clearly no doubt that many cunning folk and witches were quite capable and ready to use their magical powers (or perceived magical powers) to intimidate, deceive or harm others and their possessions, both on their own behalf or at the request of a client.[21] Given the fact that the lives and characters of these popular magical practitioners seem so riddled with human contradiction it is hardly surprising that many of us, conditioned as we are by Christian notions of the serene cloister and moral perfection, assume that there was no spiritual dimension to their vocation.

These assumptions can be challenged, however, by returning to shamanism. Shamans generally present the same complexities of lifestyle and character as cunning folk and witches: they too live in the hearts of their communities, are often members of large families living at subsistence level and are largely concerned with the use of magic to maintain physical survival. They too freely express the full gamut of human emotions and behaviour, including moral ambivalence. While the shaman is quite capable of being 'good', in the Christian sense of the word, he is also equally capable of being 'bad' and employing his powers to intimidate, deceive or hurt others, either on his own or on another's behalf. Descriptions of shamans found in anthropological literature tend to focus on their strength of will or wisdom, as opposed to their 'goodness'. Shamans from the Taulipang tribe in Venezuela were, for example, described as 'generally intelligent individuals, sometimes wily but always of great strength of character, for in their training and the practice of their functions they are obliged to display energy and self-control'.[22] The mystical quest undertaken by the shaman can be informed by very different aspirations and ethics from that of the Christian mystic. Mythologist Joseph Campbell, for example, claims the aim of the shaman is to achieve 'virtue' but that the term bears little resemblance to its Christian meaning: 'Our usual association of the spiritual life with "virtue" in the modern sense of the word as referring to "moral excellence and practice"', he claims, 'breaks down here. If applied at all to the spirituality of the shaman, "virtue" must be read in the earlier and now archaic sense of the word as referring to "the supernatural influence or power exerted by a divine being." The elementary mythology of shamanism, that is to say, is neither of truth and falsehood nor of good and evil, but of degrees of power.'[23]

Subterfuge and Spirituality

A lack of consideration for this radical difference in perspective is responsible for some of the errors of judgement made by western scholars attempting to understand shamanism. Scholars have often been shocked for example, by the fact that a wide range of shamans from many different parts of the world use deception and theatricality in their magical work. These controversial 'tactics' can take many forms. A Kwakiutl shaman from the Vancouver area of Canada, for example, learns:

> a curious mixture of pantomime, prestidigitation, and empirical knowledge including the art of simulating fainting and nervous fits, the learning of

sacred songs, the technique for inducing vomiting, rather precise notions of auscultation and obstetrics, and the use of 'dreamers' that is, spies who listen to private conversations and secretly convey to the shaman bits of information concerning origins and symptoms of the ills suffered by different people. Above all, he learned the *ars magna* of one of the shamanistic schools of the Northwest Coast: the shaman hides a tuft of down in a little corner of his mouth, and he throws it up, covered with blood, at the appropriate moment – after having bitten his tongue or made his gums bleed – and solemnly presents it to his patients and the onlookers as the pathological foreign body extracted as a result of his sucking and manipulations.[24]

The shaman's overt employment of theatricals and subterfuges have, in the past, led scholars to dismiss him a quack – an opportunistic trickster whose magical activities and reputation are founded on elaborate falsehoods. The reality, however, is more subtle. The shaman sees no contradiction between the employment of theatricality and deception and the genuine performance of effective magic; in other words, deception is seen as an integral part of an effective ritual, whether it is intended to help or to harm. That this can indeed be the case is supported by the fact that psychologists have observed that many of the shaman's subterfuges inspire a strong placebo response, in both clients and observers.[25] Knud Rasmussen claimed that 'It is difficult indeed for the ordinary civilized mentality to appreciate the complexity of the native mind in its relations with the supernatural; a "wizard" may resort to the most transparent trickwork and yet be thoroughly in earnest.'[26] The Alaskan Inuit shaman, Najagneq, 'frequently employed deceptions to protect himself from his neighbors by playing on their superstitions, and he was not afraid to admit that he had made an art of pulling their legs'. When he was asked, however, whether he really believed in any of the powers to which he pretended, he returned an unequivocal 'yes'.[27] As a result of meeting shamans like Najagneq, Rasmussen drew up a model of shamanic thinking which effectively articulates the complexities and contradictions integral to the shamanic vocation.[28] The model is comprised of four levels, listed here in ascending order:

4. The *exploitative* level, concerning those spooks and powers deliberately invented by the shaman to impress and intimidate the uninitiated.

3. The *socio-historical* level, concerning the 'mythological image of the shaman' created by his own theatricals and 'sleight of hand' illusionism.

2. The *psychological* level, concerning those 'personal guardians, helpers, and familiars who capture and bind the imagination'. Also

associated with the acquisition of occult powers. Although coloured by cultural and personal elements, it can open up to the metaphysical level.

1. The *metaphysical* level, concerning profound transcultural and transpersonal realizations.

Rasmussen claimed that shamans can operate on all four levels of shamanic thinking *at the same time*. In other words, a shaman can employ the deceptions and superficialities of the exploitative and socio-historical levels while also being capable of acquiring the superior faculties and insights associated with the psychological and metaphysical levels. The contradictions embodied by Najagneq provide a good example. At first glance, this aggressive and intimidating shaman could not be further from the stereotype of the 'good' Christian contemplative. We have already seen how he admitted to deceiving and manipulating his neighbours, however his moral ambivalence does not end here. Najagneq was imprisioned on charges of killing no less than seven or eight members of his village and at one point was alleged to have 'turned his house into a fort and waged war single-handed against the rest of his tribe'.[29] Despite evidence of deceit and aggression, however, Najagneq's descriptions of encountering familiars and going on journeys to the spirit world are clearly related to psychological level mystical experiences, and some of his comments also suggest that he may have experienced the profound transcultural and transpersonal experiences of the metaphysical level. As we saw earlier, Najagneq claimed that true shamans were devoted to 'maintaining the balance of the universe; to great things, immense, unfathomable things'. With similar delicacy, he painted the spirit Sila as:

> A strong spirit, the upholder of the universe, of the weather, in fact all life on earth – so mighty that his speech to man comes not through ordinary words, but through storms, snowfall, rain showers, the tempests of the sea, through all the forces that man fears, or through sunshine, calm seas, or small, innocent, playing children who understand nothing . . . All we know is that it has a gentle voice like a woman, a voice so fine and gentle that even children cannot become afraid. What it says is: *sila ersinarsinivdluge*, 'be not afraid of the universe.'[30]

Rasmussen's model of shamanic thinking lends support to the hypothesis that there was a mystical dimension to the vocation of cunning folk and witches. The activities and experiences of both can be easily identified on the first three levels of Rasmussen's model. Like the shaman, for example, they could use theatricals to impress and intimidate their clients. As we have seen in previous chapters, early modern trial records contain references to the drawing of circles in the ground, the use of staffs, candles, stones and other ritual objects, the recitation of charms and prayers, the laying on of hands and the performance of elaborate physical rituals. Even if, in comparison to the sophisticated ritual activities of the élite magician, these theatricals were simply employed, they would still have served to impress the popular magical practitioner's largely illiterate rural clientele.

Cunning folk, as we have seen earlier, also used their psychological knowledge to both intimidate the guilty and prompt their clients into identifying criminal suspects, while there is additional evidence that some, in an attempt to convince clients of their magical prowess, resorted to overt fraudulence. One of the most notorious of the latter was Fulham cunning woman Alice West, who was arraigned on various charges in 1613. The pamphlet which records her activities, states that:

> Shee had by the porch and doore to her house a little closet, where she might heare every word spoken at the doore. When a young fellow came to know what success hee should have, at what trade he should best thrive, or when any maid came to know where anything was lost, or when any woman came to know whether her husband should burie her, or shee him, or in the like kind, shee would send one to the doore by sundrie interrogatories to understand their businesse . . . Which no sooner in her closet she heard, but she would straight come to the doore, give them entertainment, bid them welcome, and tell them that the queen of fayries had told her their businesse, and so recite to them particularly every thing that shee had evesedropt in her closet: which gave such credit to her profession that the simle people did simply beleeve that it should happen . . . by which subtletie shee purchast to herselfe great opinion of her skill and many large summes of monie.[31]

Despite the complexity of her deceptions, Alice West, like the shaman Najagneq, still believed in the integrity of her own magical powers. The author of the pamphlet describing Alice's activities qualifies his general tone of censure by admitting that 'to give the greater grace to these fraudulencies, she hath the opinion [ie: believed herself] to he halfe or the greatest part of a witch: without which, it were impossible that by any outward management, shee could goe through so many things as shee hath done, but especially in and so neere London, where the people for the most part assume to understand most things, nay to know all'.[32] In addition to acknowledging Alice's self-belief, the author also brings attention to her 'Robin Hood style' moral ambivalence, claiming 'nor hath she laid traines for prentises, maides, and the simple sort of people, but she hath fetcht off usurers and misers, as finely as they fetch off young heires that are newly come to their lands'.[33]

While we can place the deceptions and theatricality of cunning folk and witches on the exploitative and socio-historical levels of Rasmussen's model of shamanic thinking, we can also place their visionary experiences of encountering familiars and journeying into fairyland, and the acquisition of magical knowledge and skill which occurs during these experiences, on the psychological level. Evidence of their attainment of the transpersonal and transcultural realizations of the metaphysical level remains, as it must with the shaman, speculative. However the fact that many cunning folk and witches habitually functioned on the psychological level does present a strong theoretical likelihood that some of them moved on to experience the spiritual revelations of higher mystical states. From this perspective, we can argue that whatever fraudulences cunning folk and witches employed and whatever the extent of their moral ambivalence, these factors do not negate the possibility that there was a spiritual dimension to their vocation.

Such a conclusion is further strengthened by the fact that theatricals, deceptions and moral ambivalence lived quite comfortably alongside spiritual experience in élite magical traditions of the period. Theatrical English magician Alexander Hart, for example, was said to have 'sat like an alderman in his gown' when in consultation, while literate Scottish cunning man Thomas Weir (East Lothian, 1670) always wore a cloak, which was 'somewhat dark', and carried a staff which was 'carved with heads like those of satyrs'.[34] Similarly, scholars frequently point out that élite practitioners could be morally ambivalent: while they could perform magic to heal the sick, find lost goods, identify criminals, predict the future, uncover treasure and ensure success in business and so on, they could also perform magic to gain control over the minds of others, create illusions, raise the dead and gain revenge on enemies.[35] These ambivalent activities reflected ambivalent motivations. While magicians could adopt lives of prayer and piety, through which they made 'humble supplication that God should extend to them the privilege of a unique view of his mysteries' – they could simultaneously lust after power, sex and worldly wealth.[36] Such contradictions can clearly be seen in the life of Thomas Weir. Throughout his life Weir was widely considered to be an exceptionally religious man, who feared God 'in a singular and eminent way; making profession of strickness in piety beyond others'.[37] However, this piety did not protect Weir against charges of witchcraft, and in 1670 he was burnt at the stake on Edinburgh's Castle Hill, having confessed to adultery, incest and other 'flagittious and horrid sins' and after refusing to repent of his deeds or renounce the Devil.[38] Unless, as Weir's prosecutors suggested, Weir's piety was an elaborate and long-standing hoax, we can only assume that his complexities of character were genuine. If we can accept that literate cunning men and élite magicians could, like shamans, grapple with a contradictory mix of pecuniary motives and desires for revelation, then we should also entertain the possibility that the same was true of their less educated counterparts.

Psychic vs. Spiritual

Another reason why it is difficult for the modern western mind to recognize the mystical dimension of early modern popular magic is an inherited, and again largely unconscious, mistrust of what can be termed here 'psychic' experiences and powers. The precise meaning of the word 'psychic' in this context is as difficult to determine as that of the words 'mystical' or 'spiritual'; however, as an umbrella term it can be used to denote a wide variety of supersensory experiences, which include those involving visionary entities and worlds, and a wide variety of extrasensory abilities such as clairvoyance, telekinesis and telepathy. Psychic powers and experiences can be defined as mystical in the sense that they can be automatically gained as a result of accessing certain transcendent states, and can be placed on Wilber's subtle level of mystical states and on Rasmussen's psychological level of shamanic thinking. According to this definition, many of the experiences and activities of cunning folk and witches, and tribal shamans, can be defined as 'psychic'.

Psychic powers and experiences feature strongly in mystical traditions throughout the world. In Christian contemplative traditions they have always been treated with extreme caution. The writings of medieval mystics abound with warnings about the ways in which the Devil can corrupt the mystical adept by tempting him to employ his psychic experiences and powers for malevolent or self-gratifying ends. These writings also warn the adept that even if he resists such temptations, more subtle ones lie in store. Certain psychic experiences and the powers gained therefrom are to be avoided and resisted because they are, either with or without the Devil's involvement, 'distractions' from the true spiritual path. The contempt with which some prominent contemplatives view the visionary experience is illustrated by a passage from the classic medieval mystical treatise, *The Cloud of Unknowing*, in which the anonymous author claims that disciples 'will sometime with the curiosity of their imagination pierce the planets, and make a hole in the firmament to look in thereat. These men will make a God as them list, and clothe Him full richly in clothes . . . These men will make angels in bodily likeness, and set them about each one with diverse minstrelsy, far more curious than ever was any seen or heard in this life . . . Now truly all this is *but deceit*, seem it never so holy [my italics].'[39] Being enticed by beautiful visions or terrified by nightmarish entities; being able to traverse through the barriers of time and space; being curious about these visions and these powers and spending time and attention exploring them further – all this distracts the mystic from his one-pointed focus on God.

Despite the fact that they are viewed with such mistrust, psychic experiences and powers have nevertheless consistently played a positive role in Christian spirituality. Miracles such as turning water into wine and multiplying loaves and fishes were an important feature of Christ's ministry. Similarly, Christ, the saints and the apostles were all marked out for their healing abilities. The prophesies and visions of Samuel, Elijah, Elisha, Joseph, and St John were integral to the development of Christian thought and imagery, as were the divinatory skills of St Columba and St Francis of Assisi's ability to talk to animals. In addition, as we shall examine in more depth later, experiences of visionary worlds and beings could also be seen as valuable mystical aids. Most writers on Christian mysticism bridge these apparent contradictions by asserting that although psychic powers and experiences are to be mistrusted, their presence does not always preclude spirituality. The scholar of religion, Alan Watts, writes that 'People who are in touch with this [the psychic] world, however, are *not necessarily* spiritual people; they may have unusual faculties of perception and be familiar with the beings and ways of a more glorious world than our own, but this is a matter of faculty and knowledge, not of spirituality [my italics].'[40] By the use of the words '*not necessarily*', Watts is claiming that although an individual can be in touch with this world and not be a 'spiritual person', you cannot assume that a person is not spiritual because they are seen to be in touch with the psychic world. The Jesuit priest and scholar of east-west mysticism, William Johnston, makes a similarly small but significant qualification when he claims that:

The world of the mystic and the world of the psychic explorer, it is true, have much in common and they overlap. Both are inner mansions of hypnagogic imagery, unconscious locution, exquisite symbolism and violent upheaval. But whereas the interest of the psychic explorer lies in this world itself, the mystic is passionately in love with a reality that lies beyond consciousness. His main interest is in something or someone he loves but can never fully grasp. For him expansion of mind and states of consciousness are unimportant consequences of his great love. *Yet the dividing line is fine.* Jung and Huxley, both psychic explorers, were also deeply religious men. And Poulain, primarily a theologian, was also an acute psychological researcher [my italics].[41]

The phrase *'yet the dividing line is fine'* is important. It could be argued that the reason the Christian Church drew this dividing line between the 'psychic' and the 'spiritual' in the first place was as much to do with concern over the Church's institutional authority than concern about mystics being distracted from their spiritual path. In the early modern period, the Church could not deny that psychic powers and experiences could be sent by God. However, in a period of history when so many people, as we have seen previously, held such unorthodox and ambiguous views concerning the spiritual forces which governed the cosmos, many must have professed psychic experiences and powers which, even if not specifically associated with immoral activities, would have been hard to square with Christian doctrine and would therefore have been seen to challenge the authority of the clergy or the saints. It is hardly suprising to find that the mistrust of psychic powers and experience, so strong a feature of Christianity, is also found in some form in all of the world's developed religions, further corroborating the likelihood that this mistrust is historically linked to fears surrounding the loss of authority.

Over the past century, research in the fields of ethnography, psychology and comparative religion has revealed that in tribal magico-religious belief systems no dividing line is drawn between the 'psychic' and the 'spiritual'. No such line is needed. The two are harmoniously combined. The psychic powers and experiences of the shaman do not challenge the established tribal belief system because they are integral to that belief system. Psychic experiences are a gateway, rather than an obstacle, to spiritual experience, and the shaman's descriptions of these experiences provide his community with an authentic, rather than alternative, vision of the universe and the spiritual forces that govern it. The development and employment of psychic powers is seen as a raison d'être, rather than a distraction – a vitally important means through which spiritual powers can be seen to intervene for good in the lives of men. The process of acquiring psychic powers is inseparable from the process of acquiring spiritual insight and understanding. An encounter with a spirit or a journey into the spirit world, therefore, cannot only achieve a desired prediction, or medical diagnosis, but can simultaneously be experienced as a moving and personally enriching event. The encounter-narratives given by individuals such as Smoking Star, Najagneq and Igjugârjuk, for example, put us in no doubt that psychic powers and experiences do not necessarily prevent shamans from accessing profound mystical states. From this perspective, the fact that early modern cunning folk and witches had experiences and possessed powers which could be defined as 'psychic' does not preclude the possibility that their vocation possessed a spiritual dimension.

Cunning Folk and Spiritual Status

If we successfully relinquish some of the preconceptions identified in this chapter, then we can go on to fully appreciate the significance of comments, found scattered throughout contemporary élite writings, which allude to the spiritual status and function of some popular magical practitioners in early modern Britain. Many of these comments suggest that common folk did not only esteem the latter's magical skills, but they also believed them to possess a divine origin. One of the characters in George Gifford's *Dialogue Concerning Witches and Witchcrafts* claimed of one cunning woman's skill that 'It is a gift which God hath given her. I think the Holy Spirit of God doth teach her' and goes on to assert that by virtue of this gift she 'doth more good in one yeere then all these Scripture men will doe so long as they live'.[42] That such comments accurately reflected popular belief is corroborated by contemporary observers: the Staffordshire gentleman who, as late as 1680, claimed that 'white' witches had 'as many followers as the greatest divines'; the man who claimed, after seeing Wiltshire cunning woman Anne Bodenham at work, that she was 'either a witch or a woman of God'; the gaoler of Canterbury castle who, in 1570, released a cunning woman imprisoned on charges of witchcraft because 'he believed that she did more good by her physic than the preachers of God's word'.[43]

While these comments suggest that, in the eyes of the common folk at least, the ministry of the cunning man or woman was often seen as little different from that of the priest or holy man, others spiritualize the former's status even further. Reginald Scot complained that after the Reformation cunning folk took on the role previously played by the Catholic saints.[44] Scot's opinions are echoed in Keith Thomas's assertion that some popular magical practitioners were visited in such huge numbers that 'the process was much the same as that which had, in the Middle Ages, enabled the shrines of saints to attract great concourses of people, once they had obtained their initial reputation for healing. In their own communities the cunning folk were often feared and respected.'[45] Cunning folk were not only compared to saints, however. They were also compared to Christ himself. Scot, again, complained that:

> we flie from trusting in God to trusting in witches, who doo not onelie in their coosening art take on them the office of Christ in this behalfe; but use his verie phrase of speech to such idolaters, as com to seeke divine assistance at their hands, saieng; Go thy waies, thy sonne or thy daughter, &c. shall doo well, and be whole.[46]

The fact that some cunning folk were seen to be closer to God, or more 'god-like' than ordinary men is a strong indicator that they were believed to possess the numinosity of the contemplative or shaman – the transformed, semi-divine nature which was the mark of the mystical adept. In 1618, Cambridge theologian William Perkins observed that the common people 'honour and reverence' cunning folk, and that the cunning man 'is so deare unto them, that they hold themselves and their country blessed, that they have him among them; they flie unto him in necessitie, they depend upon him as their God'.[47] Approaching a century earlier, English statesman and humanist Sir Thomas More claimed that 'in such wise witches . . . have many fools more faith a great deal than in God' while the sixteenth-century cunning man, Robert Allen, was actually designated the title 'the god of Norfolk'.[48] Such comments led Keith Thomas to conclude that people who sought help from cunning folk 'did not regard the wizards as ordinary men'; that they honoured them 'no less than demi-gods'; and that they 'were more likely to believe that the cunning folk were taught by God, or that they were helped by angels, or *even that they possessed some divinity of their own* [my italics].'[49]

The fact that some cunning folk were believed to possess a spiritual status and function in early modern Britain supports the view that their visionary experiences could be interpreted as expressions of a popular mysticism. We can only begin to understand this mysticism, however, by appreciating the role that envisioned familiar spirits played in this context. In the next chapter, then, we will explore the significance of the familiar as 'spiritual guide'.

CHAPTER THIRTEEN

Greedigut and the
Angel Gabriel

Over the past century an increasing number of psychologists and scientists have been turning their attention to the study of visionary phenomena and although research in this area is still in its infancy, it can be examined for insights into the psychological processes through which early modern familiars may have functioned as spiritual guides. Of particular relevance in this context are the works of pioneering Swiss psychologist Carl Jung (1875–1961), who combined perspectives from psychiatry, religion and western magical traditions to develop a profound theory of mind which placed great emphasis on the therapeutic benefits to be gained through interaction with autonomous envisioned entities.[1] Also of value are the works of psychologists such as James Hillman, Thomas Moore and Mary Watkins, who have engaged with Jung's ideas and developed the field of imaginal psychology.[2] While there is no scope here to go into any of these theories in any detail, it will be useful to outline some basic psychological perspectives which will help us to understand the nature and function of the familiar.

There are three basic hypotheses which can be used with regard to both the early modern familiar and the shaman's helping spirit.[3] The first, which we cannot discount, but which we can put aside for the purposes of this discussion, is the 'spiritist' hypothesis; that is, the traditional belief that these envisioned spirits are souls of the deceased which exist in a 'realm of the dead'. The second, which has until recently been the preferred choice for historians and anthropologists wishing to understand both early modern familiars and helping spirits, is the 'psychodynamic hypothesis'. According to this view the envisioned spirit is an image which the psyche projects from the 'personal unconscious' (that is, thoughts and feelings of which the individual is not normally aware) to compensate for unfulfilled needs, the classic example being the imaginary friend envisioned by the lonely child. This compensatory principle may also manifest in other ways: an individual holding repressed aggression might find themselves confronting a violent entity; a powerful person with hidden vulnerabilities, an entity which is delicate and gentle; a person with suppressed sexual feelings, a handsome young man; and a person given over to melancholy, a playful child. The psychodynamic hypothesis has a wide application and can be used, in whole or in part, by those who define the encounter with the envisioned spirit as symptomatic of either pathology, mental health or mystical experience. The third option is the 'transpersonal hypothesis'. According to this view, although the early modern familiar or helping spirit may be constructed out of personal psychic projections, which may or may not fulfil a compensatory function, they can either simultaneously or separately be characteristic phenomena of a 'suprapersonal' realm of consciousness, or in Jungian terms, the 'collective unconscious' – a realm which has a significance and reality above and beyond the personal. Those who employ the transpersonal hypothesis tend to put the experience of encountering autonomous visionary entities fully in the mystical realm.

Whether we define the early modern familiar according to the psychodynamic or the transpersonal hypothesis, from both perspectives the envisioned spirit is created, in part or in whole, out of 'personal psychic projections'. As a result it possesses physical and psychological characteristics specifically recognizable to the individual who encounters it and these characteristics enable the visionary and the envisioned to enter into easy communication. Simultaneous with being recognizable, however, the spirit is also 'other', in that it has a direct link with a part of the psyche which is hidden from the visionary; a part which, from the psychodynamic perspective, would be defined as the personal unconscious and from the transpersonal, as the personal and/or collective unconscious. Whether it has personal or transpersonal origins, the dual nature of the envisioned spirit enables it to act as a link between known and unknown parts of the mind. The way in which such a link may work is still a matter of theoretical speculation. Psychologists often work with metaphors such as 'doorways' and 'vehicles', that is, the envisioned entity can be seen as a 'doorway' through which previously unconscious thoughts, feelings and perceptions can travel through to the conscious mind, or as a 'vehicle' with the help of which the conscious mind can access and manage previously unattainable or hard-to-negotiate altered states. This dual nature of the envisioned spirit means that it is experienced by the visionary as recognizable and intimate in a very personal and human way and yet simultaneously numinous and 'other'. By virtue of their unique and powerful functions, envisioned spirits in their role as 'spiritual guides' are found in the majority of the world's mystical traditions. Envisioned spirits defined as 'deities' (as opposed to some kind of lesser spirit-being or soul of the dead), but which perform a fundamentally helpful function, would in this context come under the definition of spiritual guide.

These three hypotheses can also be applied to experiences of encountering spirits which are primarily auditory, as opposed to visual. In these cases an individual hears, or becomes aware of, a voice or internal intellectual communication that they identify as belonging to a specific supernatural entity, but the experience is not accompanied by a visual representation. From a psychological perspective, these auditory phenomena possess the same dual nature as the envisioned entity; acting as conduits through which unconscious elements of the personal/transpersonal psyche can be communicated to the conscious mind through the medium of language. Visionaries from both tribal and developed religions describe experiences of communicating with spirits which are both visional (usually incorporating an auditory element) or auditory only, and we find a similar distinction being made by some cunning folk and witches.[4] It is possible that this auditory dimension played a more prominent role in the relationship between popular magical practitioners and their familiar spirits than is generally supposed, although there is no scope to go into this issue here.[5] Auditory phenomena are also closely connected to the process of prayer. From this perspective, a Christian contemplative at her prayers who hears the voice of Jesus (whether through her 'bodily ears' or, more profoundly, through the 'ears of her soul') in response to her supplications, could be said to be communicating with her spiritual guide.[6]

Despite the fact that early modern familiars can be seen to come under the definition of 'spiritual guide', academic historians seldom draw attention to the fact that familiars may have performed this function in Britain during this period. Similarly, most of the educated lawmen and ecclesiastics who actually interrogated cunning folk and witches did not elevate demon or fairy familiars in this way. This oversight could be attributed, in part, to the fact that the subject itself is obscure – the experiential dimension of mystical traditions being largely inaccessible to any but practising adepts. More pertinent to the discussion here, however, is the fact that both the modern western mind (however secular, and however uninterested in mysticism), and the early modern élite mind, inherit Christian preconceptions about the moral nature, visual appearance and behaviour appropriate to a spiritual guide. Both find it difficult to imagine Greedigut drinking from the same cup as the Archangel Gabriel.

Despite expressing a profound mistrust of visionary experience,

Christian mystical literature has consistently described how visions of 'sacred beings' – variously defined as angels, saints, the Virgin Mary, Christ, or even God – can aid the spiritual aspirant on their mystical journey. Jewish and Christian thought has termed such experiences as the 'encounter model' of revelation: experiences in which, according to theologian Keith Ward, 'a personal Spirit is encountered in an experience of peculiar urgency and intensity' and which 'provides a sense of experienced unity with a reality of great, even unsurpassable worth, a disclosure of transcendent spiritual reality in some way underlying the realm of sense experience'.[7] Old Testament figures such as Abraham, Jacob, Samuel and Joseph all claimed to have gained wisdom from such visionary beings, while in the New Testament Zacharias and the Virgin Mary received comfort and prophesy from the Archangel Gabriel. Records of the lives of Christian saints also frequently make reference to guidance gained from encounters with envisioned deities and other sacred beings.

In European Christian traditions, some of the most vivid and sophisticated descriptions of the integration between encounters with envisioned entities and spiritual life can be found in the writings of medieval (and to a lesser extent, early modern) contemplatives, and consequently it is to these writers that we shall turn for examples of the nature and function of the stereotypical Christian spiritual guide. These medieval sources also have the advantage of being relatively close, in geographical and temporal terms, to the visionary experiences of British cunning folk and witches. Many of our examples will be drawn from the autobiography of the fifteenth-century mystic, Margery Kempe. A fervent contemplative, whose spiritual experiences were personally authenticated by the widely respected anchoress, Julian of Norwich, Kempe nevertheless differed from most of the contemplatives who wrote about their vocation by virtue of the fact that she was uncloistered, of relatively low birth, illiterate, married and a mother many times over (having given birth to at least fourteen children). As a consequence, Margery's descriptions of both her outer and inner lives are closer to the experiences of cunning folk and witches – in both style and content – than most medieval mystical writings.

Suprisingly, scholars of British witchcraft and magic have seldom discussed the visional experiences of cunning folk and witches in the context of medieval or early modern visionary mysticism, despite the fact that several Continental scholars, including Gábor Klaniczay (*The Uses of Supernatural Power*), Carl-Martin Edsman (*A Swedish Female Folk-Healer from the Beginning of the 18th Century*) and Wolfgang Behringer (*Shaman of Oberstdorf*) have drawn attention to this line of inquiry in their respective fields.[8] As we have seen previously, the former have been generally reluctant to acknowledge that the early modern encounter-

narrative was a description of a visionary 'event' – a specific psychological process which occurred in the past at a particular time and place –
and tend to favour explanatory hypotheses of the 'collaborative retrospective fiction' type. Adherence to this paradigm also makes it difficult
for scholars to understand why early modern ecclesiastics and legal interrogators, whose mental worlds in so many ways resembled our own, were
so ready to believe that the familiar-encounter and the sabbath/fairyland
experience was an actual 'event', whether defined as 'real' or a visual illu-
sion produced by the Devil. Marion Gibson, for example, concludes her
claim that the encounter-narratives given by English witches were 'about
cooperation, co-authorship and negotiation' with the bemused observation that 'Oddly, all sides agree that there is a story to be told'.[9] The
educated interrogator's participation in this conspiracy of belief, however,
becomes more understandable when we recognize that the religious beliefs
and practices of the early modern Christian community, both pre- and
post-Reformation, would have been influenced by – either positively, or
through reaction against – the contemplative traditions of medieval
Europe. The writings and reputations of contemplatives acted as raw
material, providing inspiration and guidance for both the educated lay
reader, and for theologians and ecclesiastics who formulated doctrine and
liturgy. As a consequence, the men who wrote about popular magic and
witchcraft and who interrogated cunning folk and witches would have
been acquainted with the visionary dimension of religious experience and
would have understood, to a greater or lesser extent, its inherent
complexity and dynamism. Without the benefit of modern comparative
religious and psychological perspectives, these men would have categorized any elements of these experiences which did not conform to
Christian stereotypes as 'of the Devil', but they would not have questioned
the experiences themselves, nor their capacity to be used as a resource for
mystical knowledge and power. Modern historians, on the other hand,
who possess the enlightened perspectives with which to acknowledge the
role which cultural ideas play in shaping religious beliefs, do not always,
in their turn, possess the familiarity with visional mystical states necessary to recognize the experiential dimension of popular encounter-
narratives. Both sides, for different reasons, can miss the significance of
the experiences which cunning folk and witches describe.

Mystical writings reveal that the visionary experiences of European
medieval contemplatives rivalled those of early modern cunning folk and
witches in variety, intensity and realism. The contemplative's experience
could be simple, involving a solitary envisioned entity, or elaborate, in
which the adept, often in the company of an envisioned guide, witnessed
complex sequences of events or narratives inspired by Christian iconog-

raphy and scripture. The latter could include seminal episodes from the life of Christ, such as the crucifixion or the nativity, or involve joyful experiences of being transported by angels or other sacred beings, to heaven. These visionary experiences were 'vibrant, in technicolor and stereo sound'; pervaded with a combination of intense realism and numinosity, and interactive, in the sense that the visionary could participate in the events witnessed.[10] They could occur in company or in solitude, and could be encouraged through focused meditation or encountered spontaneously.[11] Since the time of St Augustine theologians have analysed the nature of, and made distinctions between, the different kinds of visionary (and auditory) phenomena which can be experienced by contemplatives, although unfortunately there is no scope here to enter into the complexities of these categorizations.[12] For the purposes of the present discussion, it is sufficient to note, as scholars such as Klaniczay have pointed out, that to some degree the visionary capacities of medieval saints and mystics can be seen as expressions of the perennial 'shamanistic tendencies' of the psyche, informed and moulded, in these instances, by a Christian context.[13]

Believe Not Every Spirit

Although encounters with envisioned entities played a prominent role in medieval European mysticism, contemplatives were consistently wary of these experiences, for not all spirits were believed to be of divine origin. Adepts received careful instruction in how to make the all-important distinction between 'good' and 'bad' spirits. Good spirits come from, or are manifestations of, God; they dispense wisdom and aid the progression towards higher mystical states. Bad spirits come from, or are manifestations of, the Devil; they encourage evil thoughts and desires, and distract the individual from their spiritual path. An often-quoted passage from the first Epistle of St John (chapter 4, verse 1) advises the spiritual aspirant to 'believe not every spirit, but try the spirits whether they are of God'. Similarly, the fourteenth-century English contemplative, Walter Hilton, cautions that 'if a spirit such as an angel appears to you in bodily form to comfort and guide you' you need to determine its origin by treating it with 'reserve' – both while it is manifest, and afterwards – while you 'test the reactions of your soul'. If the encounter with the angel enables you to 'pray more fervently and devoutly, and to think more readily of spiritual things' then, according to Hilton, you can conclude that 'the spirit comes from God'.[14] Such subtle distinctions were often very hard to make and even the greatest contemplatives found the task difficult. The sixteenth-century Spanish mystic Teresa of Ávila often questioned whether her visions of spirit worlds and spirit beings were of divine or demonic origin, despite the reassurances of others, once claiming that after praying to God on the matter 'He gave me to understand that when so many people of such quality had told me that my visions were of God, I should be wrong to disbelieve them.'[15]

Some cunning folk and witches fretted over the origins of their familiars in much the same way. Cornish cunning woman Anne Jefferies (1645), who was renowned for her fairy-derived healing skills, was 'not a little troubled' when ministers 'endeavoured to persuade her' that her fairies were 'evil spirits'. One night, when Anne was sitting in company before the fire, the fairies repeatedly called to her to go and speak with them. After their third request, against the advice of her companions, Anne went to her chamber:

> After she had been in her chamber some time, she came to us [her companions] again with a bible in her hand, and tells us, that, when she came to the fairies, they said to her, What! has there been some magistrates and ministers with you, and dissuaded you from coming any more to us, saying, we are evil spirits, and that it was all the delusion of the devil? Pray desire them to read that place of scripture in the 1st epistle of St. John, chap. 4, ver. 1. "Dearly beloved, believe not every spirit, but try the spirits, whether they are of God, &c." This page of scripture was turned down to in the said Bible.[16]

Other cunning folk, such as Janet Trall (Perthshire, 1623) and Joan Tyrry (Somerset, 1555) also clearly believed that their familiars came from God, though they were less lengthy and articulate in their justifications.[17] Some magical practitioners, conversely, such as Essex witch Elizabeth Bennett (1582), interpreted their familiars as demonic and struggled to resist their influence.[18] Overall, however, the wide variety of familiars used by popular magical practitioners and the equally wide variety of tasks in which these familiars were employed, suggests that the criteria which many of these practitioners used to distinguish the origin and moral disposition of a spirit, if indeed they bothered to make such distinctions at all, were not as finely nuanced nor as ethically precise as those employed by the contemplative. As we saw in chapter TWELVE, many cunning folk and witches operated out of a fundamentally monistic and animistic belief system. They therefore did not believe it necessary to be morally pure – in the Christian sense of the term – in order to enter mystical states and gain mystical knowledge and power, and they did not believe it necessary that their familiar spirit exhibit, or promote, moral purity in order to facilitate this transcendence. As we have seen in chapter SEVEN, the popular magical practitioner was, like the shaman, far more interested in a spirit's *usefulness* than in its moral disposition. Pragmatic and expedient, they interacted with a spirit if it was able to give them the magical knowledge and ability necessary to alleviate their personal suffering and help them to survive in a harsh and mysterious world. As a consequence of this practical imperative and its accompanying monist world-view, cunning folk and witches did not, in psychological terms, so vigorously resist or repress psychic projections which did not precisely conform to a Christian ideal of goodness or propriety, and this is one of the reasons why we find such a complex and fantastic array of familiars described in early modern trial records. Like the helping spirits of the shaman, these familiars exhibit the full gamut of human and animal characteristics as derived from the experiences and observations of their creators.

The Prosaic and the Sacred

Cultural relativism is also responsible for the differences in visual appearance between Christian spiritual guides and early modern familiars. In the Christian tradition, envisioned guides and sacred beings, both as described by contemplatives and as portrayed in iconography and imagery, are usually depicted as men, women, or elderly bearded sages and are either noble and/or beautiful. Although there are some exceptions, they generally possess a calm quasi-regal demeanour and their moral purity and spiritual status is signified by rich apparel, incandescence and illumination. Some early modern familiars conformed to this Christian stereotype in part or in whole. Those encountered by Scottish cunning women Bessie Dunlop and Isobel Haldane (1623), for example, appeared in the form of ageing bearded sages, while others, such as those described by East Lothian witch John Fian (1591) and Orkney cunning woman Jonet Rendall (1629), appeared shining with light or dressed in white.[19] Other familiars, like those encountered by Agnes Sampson (East Lothian, 1591), Ross-shire witch Donald Mair and Huntingdonshire witch Jane Wallis (1646), inversely echoed the stereotype by conforming to Christian ideas about the Devil being a tall, frightening man in black, or possessing cloven, hairy feet and a fearsome demeanour.[20] It is not difficult to perceive how these quasi-regal familiars could have been invested with the 'numen' of sacred beings. Other familiars, however, had an altogether different demeanour: appearing in the form of a 'little man' or a 'halfling boy', often with ragged clothes, or assuming an unremarkable animal guise such as a 'meickle brown dog', 'grey kitten', 'dunnish-coloured ferret', 'white cat', 'mole' or 'snail'. The names attributed to such familiars, such as 'Tewhit', 'Greedigut', 'Vinegar Tom', 'Jack', 'Robin' and so on, were equally prosaic.[21] According to Christian writers, spirits which appeared in the form of animals, unless those animals were doves, lambs or eagles and so on, were of the Devil. Zurich pastor Ludwig Lavater, in his polemic titled *Of Ghostes And Spirites Walking By Nyght* (published in English in 1572), claimed that 'popishe writers teach us . . . [that if spirits] appeare under the forme of a Lyon, beare, dog, tode, serpent, catte, or blacke ghost, it may easily be gathered that it is an evill spirit . . . [while] good spirits do appeare under the shape of a dove, a man, a lambe, or in the brightnesse, and clere light of the sunne'.[22]

However the visual forms assumed by these early modern familiars were wholly congruent with their origin. The representations of fairy and demon familiars found in early modern encounter-narratives reflect the animist culture of the rural village, as opposed to the theistic culture of the cloister or oak-panelled study.[23] We have already seen how, among the common folk of this period, the assortment of spirits which came under the umbrella term of fairies – bizarre and sometimes ridiculous-looking as they were – possessed the numen of sacred beings, and as such were objects of devotion. In Wales fairies were held in an 'astonishing reverence' and people dared not 'name them without honour'; while in England, according to one late sixteenth-century commentator, 'The opinion of faeries and elfes is very old, and yet sticketh very religiously in the myndes of some.'[24] That this devotion was not only reserved for the beautiful and/or noble fairy monarchy and other spirits who conformed in some way to stereotypical Christian notions about sacred beings, is suggested by contemporary descriptions of relationships with fairy familiars. We have seen, for example, how in 1664 a group of Somerset witches claimed to have made 'obeysance' to a 'little Man in black Clothes' whom they called 'Robin'; how Bessie Dunlop reverenced the 'stout woman [that] com in to hir [while she was in labour], and sat doun on the forme besyde hir, and askit ane drink at hir' as the fairy queen; and how the spirits 'of God' so vehemently and piously defended by Cornish cunning woman Anne Jefferies in 1645, were 'of a small stature, all clothed in green'.[25] Additional support for the view that such prosaic-looking beings could be reverenced as sacred by common folk in the early modern period, can be found in later British fairy beliefs. On the Scottish Borders in the nineteenth century it was believed that a domestic brownie called the 'Wag-at-the-wa' lived in the hearth and could be invoked by swinging the pot-hook, or crook. A contemporary anecdote records how an old woman stormed out of a neighbour's house

Saint Anthony Tormented by Demons by Martin Schongauer (1470–75) illustrates how malevolent spirits were often visualised as, and depicted in, animal forms in Christian traditions. The famous Desert Father, widely considered to be the founder of Christian monasticism, was reportedly attacked by demons in the form of wild beasts.

in disgust when she observed a young lad sitting by the hearth 'idly' swinging the pot-hook, claiming that 'she wouldna abide in the hoose where sic mookerie was practised'. The old woman's strength of feeling comes across as little different to that which would be experienced by a devout Christian who entered a church to find a boy 'idly' playing about with the Communion cup.[26] Such devotion is particularly suprising to modern western eyes, when we find out that the being who occasioned such reverence was, as described by folklorist William Henderson, a 'grisly old man, with short crooked legs, while a long tail assisted him in keeping his seat on the crook. Sometimes he appeared in a grey mantle, with the remains of an old "*pirnicap*" on his head, drawn down over that side of the face which was troubled with toothache, a constant grievance of his; but he commonly wore a red coat and blue breeches, both garments being made of "familie woo".'[27]

The animistic culture of the early modern village is also responsible for the fact that familiars were often envisioned in animal form. Like many of their 'humanoid' counterparts, animal familiars were often not remarkable in any way: neither exotic nor intimidating, they generally resembled small mammals, and less frequently, birds or insects, and were described with vivid realism. In order to gain some insight into how these envisioned animal familiars could have possessed the numen of a sacred beings we need to move more deeply into an understanding of how animals in general were experienced in early modern Britain. We have seen earlier that the milk, meat, eggs, hides and fleeces derived from animals were of paramount importance to the largely self-sufficient rural population in this period. By virtue of necessity, therefore, most people would have possessed animals of some description and it would have been an everyday occurrence to encounter chickens, geese, pigs, mules, cows and goats in streets, fields, gardens and back yards. In the countryside the lives of most people were punctuated by animal-related activities: taking animals to and from pasture, walking them to and from market and in and out of barns. Milking, shearing, birthing and slaughtering would have been ongoing, as were the domestic processes which transformed milk into butter and cheese, fleeces into breeches and shawls and carcasses into leather jerkins, salt-meat, rush-lights and twine. In a time without the luxury of central heating, the body heat of animals would have been a valuable commodity, and for this reason many kept their livestock close – either in stables adjoining the main body of the house, or, in the case of the very poor, in the main living area separated from the human inhabitants by nothing more than a low wall. Keith Thomas notes that in Wales 'there was a tradition that cows gave better milk if they could see the fire', and that in the late seventeenth century an observer claimed, with 'some exaggeration', that '"every edifice" was "a Noah's Ark", where cows, pigs, chickens and the human family all lay together promiscuously'.[28] Even in eighteenth-century Lincolnshire the owners of geese treated their birds 'with great kindness, lodging them very often in the same room with themselves'.[29] Dogs and cats were also commonplace, their numbers not only attributable to their reproductive skills, but also to their invaluable role in keeping down vermin and, in the case of dogs, guarding property and hunting small game. A foreign visitor to England in 1602 was astonished at how many 'peasants' were able to hunt: 'they keep big fine dogs, at little expense, for with a little money they can procure the heads, entrails and feet of lambs and calves [to feed them with]'.[30] Seventeenth-century author Daniel Defoe claimed that in London during the Plague, 40,000 dogs were destroyed (a figure which translates into two dogs per household), and 'five times as many cats, few houses being without a cat, some having several, sometimes five or six in a house'.[31]

Much of domestic life took place at ground level. The hearth, whether in the middle of the room or to one side with a chimney, would have been built on the bare earth; people would have squatted on the floor or sat on a low stool to tend the fire, cook food, spin wool and perform other domestic tasks; they would have crouched by the riverbank to wash their clothes and scour pots; they would have thrown blankets or straw mattresses down by the hearth at night to sleep on. Living at this level, dogs, cats, chickens and resident pigs would have been encountered eye to eye, as would the toads and snails which encroached across the damp earth floors at night, and the many mice and rats which crept in to scavenge for scraps. Suffolk cunning man John Bysack (1645), who claimed that 'he used to arise from his bed, make a fire, and lay down by it to allow the snails to suck his blood, excusing himself to his wife by saying that it eased him from pain which troubled him', was likely to have been drawing on impressions gained from real life, whether the experience described was a visionary one or not.[32] The following passage from the early seventeenth century, though penned by prosperous English gentleman Nicholas Breton, is evocative of the interdependence between animals and humans which existed in all walks of rural life:

> We have again in our woods the birds singing; in the pastures the cow lowing, the ewe bleating, and the foal neighing . . . Again we have young rabbits that in a sunny morning sit washing of their faces . . . we have besides tumblers for our conies and greyhounds for our courses, hounds for our chases, hawks of all kind for the field, and the river and the wood . . . hay in the barn, horses in the stable, oxen in the stall, sheep in the pen, hogs in the stye, corn in the garner, cheese in the loft, milk in the dairy, cream in the pot, butter in the dish, ale in the tub, and Aqua Vitae in the bottle, beef

in the brine, brawn in the souse, and bacon in the roof, herbs in the garden, and water at our doors.[33]

The lives of common people were so intertwined with those of their animals that, as one late seventeenth-century gentleman observed, they made 'very little difference between themselves and their beasts'.[34] Animals were in many ways, as Keith Thomas notes, 'subsidiary members of the human community, bound by mutual self-interest to their owners, who were dependent on their fertility and wellbeing'.[35] The common people would have been surrounded by the smell of animals, the noise of animals, the fur and the faeces of animals. But just as significantly, they would have been surrounded by the 'animal-ness' of animals; the eager curiosity of the dog, the lazy grace of the cat, the stealth and skill of the rat, the grumpy good nature of the oxen, the noisy assertiveness of the crow. The uninhibited nature of the animal, so true to itself, so unrestricted by societal values of good and bad, kind or unkind, appropriate and not appropriate – would have been intimately woven into an individual's impressions of 'what life was' and 'how one could be'. Given the ubiquity and value of the animal, it is not surprising that, in psychological terms, some of these impressions were used by the early modern popular psyche to craft envisioned familiars – and that these familiars were imbued with the numen of sacred beings and duly reverenced. Earlier in this book we have seen how the tribal shaman, who is similarly intimate with and dependent upon the animal world, can also value and reverence the most humble of beasts. In North America, Paiute shamans prize helping spirits in the form of mice and rats, because they are skilled at stealing away disease, while those from the Quinault tribe favour moles, because they are skilled at digging beneath obstructions.[36] Hares can also be prized in this way, anthropologist R. F. Fortune reporting that among the North American Omaha in the early twentieth century the envisioned jackrabbit was valued because 'The peculiar powers of the jack-rabbit are its elusiveness before its enemies. It has great swiftness and ability to dodge and elude pursuit. So the person who has the jack-rabbit as his patron [helping spirit] trusts that he shall be given these powers of escape from his enemies when hard pressed in war.'[37] From such a perspective, it does not seem so strange that Essex witch Joan Cunny (1589) should kneel down before two familiars who appeared 'in the similitude and likeness of two black frogs'; that Huntingdonshire cunning man John Winnick (1646) should fall down on his knees and worship as 'a God' a familiar 'having pawes like a Beare, but in bulk not fully so big as a Coney'; or that Essex witch Rebecca West (1645) and four companions should have 'together spent some time in praying unto their familiars' who appeared variously in the form of dogs, kittens and white, grey and black 'imps'.[38]

Coercive Devotions

Although the early modern familiar differed from the Christian guide in visual appearance and moral nature, in other ways it resembled its orthodox counterpart very closely. The primary function of both, whether appearing in the form of an angel 'in shining and clear light', a 'beauteous, and most amiable [Christ]', 'a mole, soft and cold', or a 'blak, roch man' – was to help the visionary.[39] For the cunning woman or witch, whose main aim (once they had agreed to become a magical practitioner) was to perform magical functions for – or in some cases against – their community, the familiar provided them with the magical knowledge and information they needed to effect cures, divine the future, locate lost goods and so on. For the contemplative, by contrast, whose primary aim was union with God, the guide nourished their devotion by encouraging them to 'pray more fervently and devoutly, and to think more readily of spiritual things' and had the ability to 'transform and quicken' their heart to a 'deeper desire for virtue'.[40] Although this distinction between functionality and spirituality can be identified clearly on a theoretical level, in reality the distinction was very fine.

Like familiars, Christian guides could dispense advice on a wide variety of matters, some of them very practical in nature. Richard Kieckhefer, for example, describes how in medieval Europe: 'Christ appeared frequently to Bridget of Sweden to instruct her regarding her personal life: he advised her to move to Rome, for example, and instructed her how to deal with her daughter Catherine . . . When Jane Mary of Maillé received a vision of the Virgin, it was to instruct her that she should wear humble clothes in imitation of Christ . . . Saints and angels at times brought similar messages.'[41] Similarly, despite being wary of the spiritual corruptions associated with the deployment of mystical knowledge and power, many contemplatives attempted to prompt their guides, through the process of prayer, to employ their supernatural abilities for the benefit of others. They often interceded with Christ on behalf of the dead (their descriptions of the demeanour and location of deceased souls in many ways resembling those which cunning folk and witches gave of the dead who lived in fairyland).[42] Some also gained knowledge of the future through prayer. In the early fifteenth century the Bishop of Worcester, Thomas Peverel, claimed that 'he had been warned by a holy man, who had understood by revelation that . . . [he] would be dead within the space of two years', while a Dominican anchorite at 'Lynne', in Norfolk, accurately predicted to Margery Kempe, before she set out on her long pilgrimage to Jerusalem, that 'when all your friends have forsaken you, our Lord shall cause a broken-backed man to escort you wherever you wish to go'.[43] Margery herself was frequently petitioned to pray for the sick and dying and claimed that during her prayers Christ would inform her as to whether the sick individual would live or not, on one occasion claiming that a friend of hers 'was very ill, and many people thought she would die. Then, while this creature [Margery] was praying for her, our Lord said, "She shall not die these ten years, for after this you will celebrate together and have excellent talks, as you have had before." And so it was, in truth; this holy woman lived for many years afterwards.'[44]

Although the process through which Margery Kempe obtained healing predictions from Christ could be seen as little different from the way cunning folk such as John Walsh (Dorset, 1566) or Agnes Sampson (East Lothian, 1591) obtained healing predictions from their familiar spirits, Margery, and most of her educated contemporaries, would have conceived of these processes as being inherently different. As a good Christian, when Margery wished to obtain knowledge or guidance from sacred beings she did so through prayer. Cunning folk and witches on the other hand, although they sometimes claimed to have prayed to their familiars in order to obtain their help, were more likely to have elicited spirit-aid through the performance of some kind of invocation, whether in the form of a simple verbal request or an overt ritual conjuration. Agnes Sampson, for example, 'charged' her familiar 'to come and speak to her' when she wished to receive predictions about the fate of the sick.[45] In reality, as scholars of comparative religion frequently point out, the dividing line between conjuration and prayer is a fine one: prayer can be a thinly-veiled form of request or demand, while invocatory rituals can be performed in a spirit of supplication.[46] In psychological terms, both conjuration and prayer incorporate physiological and mental techniques capable of inducing altered states of consciousness which can be defined as mystical. Despite this area of overlap, however, the cunning woman or witch's tendency to favour conjurative over supplicatory methods of accessing spirit-aid betrays the predominantly pre-Christian origins of her beliefs and practices. Like tribal shamans, many cunning folk and witches saw no inconsistency in revering their familiars as sacred beings and yet simultaneously demanding that they give them magical knowledge and power and verbally challenging them if they did not meet their expectations. Similar dichotomies were also to be found in élite magical traditions of the period. Learned wizards could quite happily make devotions to sacred beings until their knees were 'horny with praying' and yet go on to magically conjure them up the next – these magical traditions combining, in the words of Richard Kieckhefer, 'a mixture of magic and devotion that assumes no incompatability between the two, and in the mind of the practitioner there presumably was no incongruity'.[47] For the élite magician, like the shaman and by implication, the cunning woman or witch, the desire to manipulate sacred beings in order to acquire psychic power was inseparably intertwined with the yearning for mystical experience and spiritual transformation. There is no reason to assume that the popular magical practitioner did not believe, like the learned magician, that 'Religious perfection would bring magical power.'[48]

Intimacy and Comfort

Although early modern encounter-narratives indicate that the interactions between popular magical practitioners and their familiars could range between the extremes of 'coercion' and 'devotion', they also suggest that on a day-to-day level these relationships were defined by high levels of intimacy: frequent, neighbourly exchanges which could range from the simple giving of comfort to the intensity of a sexual encounter. These intimacies, which have in the past been viewed with condescension and bemusement by some historians, take on an altogether new significance if we view them as indicative of the profound closeness which can develop between a mystical adept and their envisioned guide.[49]

In religious traditions throughout the world, interaction with sacred beings is characterized by varying degrees of both familiarity and reverence. Despite their spiritual power and numinosity, in medieval Britain saints were 'first and foremost perceived as friends and helpers'.[50] The devotional text, the *Golden Legend*, claims that when individuals pray to the saints they pay 'the debt of interchanging neighbourhood', while Julian of Norwich wrote of St John of Beverley that 'our Lord shewed him full highly, in comfort to us for homeliness; and brought to my mind how he is a kind neighbour, and of our knowing'.[51] For some medieval Christians the relationship with Christ or God could also assume this neighbourly, intimate quality and for the contemplative this quality could be experienced very directly. We find references to 'how homely our Lord was in her soul'; how 'in us is his [Christ's] homeliest home'; how the '[contemplative is on] such homely terms with God by love and homely conversation'; and how the two can share 'terms of homely familiaritie'.[52] There are many passages in *The Book of Margery Kempe* in which

Margery talks with Christ in the human, intimate manner redolent of the way cunning folk and witches talked to their familiars, scholar Anthony Goodman claiming that 'The entities of the Godhead and other sacred beings conversed with her soul as clearly and plainly as one friend spoke to another.'[53] Margery's conversations with Christ often focused on spiritual anxieties, but they could also extend to travel plans, clothes, sexual relations with her husband, neighbours, and eating habits or health. On one occasion, while at prayer, she 'lay still, not knowing what she might best think of. Then she said to our Lord Jesus Christ, "Jesus, what shall I think about?"' Our Lord Jesus answered in her mind, "Daughter, think of my mother, for she is the cause of all the grace that you have."' On another occasion Margery claimed that 'Our Lord, of his mercy, visited her so much and so plentifully with his holy speeches and his holy dalliance, that many times she did not know how the day went.'[54] Thirteenth-century Belgian contemplative Marie D'Oignies, on the other hand, cuddled and played with an envisioned Christ in a manner very similar to the way witches like Essex witches Joan Prentice (1589) and Rebecca West (1645) interacted with their animal familiars. Marie claimed that 'sometimes it seemed to her that for three or more days she held Him close to her so that He nestled between her breasts like a baby, and she hid Him there lest He be seen by others. Sometimes she kissed him as though He were a little child and sometimes she held Him on her lap as if He were a gentle lamb.'[55]

The writings of medieval mystics also stress the importance of the envisioned guide's capacity to give comfort in times of both physical and psychological distress. For educated and cloistered contemplatives this distress/comfort dynamic was often played out in an intellectual arena: spiritual comforts being received in response to concerns about the understanding and interpretation of mystical texts and experiences and the rights and wrongs of the spiritual path. For individuals like Margery Kempe, however, who were not materially provided for by an ecclesiastical institution, such elevated concerns were interdispersed with the more prosaic problems related to material survival. Margery frequently describes the ways in which Christ comforted her when she was distressed about her poverty and although these accounts usually refer to Christ speaking 'in her soul', as opposed to appearing in a vision, they are very redolent of descriptions detailing the initial encounter between a popular magical practitioner and their familiar spirit. On one occasion, when Margery was 'thinking and concentrating as to where she could get her living, inasmuch as she had no silver to keep herself with, our Lord answered to her mind and said . . . do not be afraid, daughter, for money will come to you, and I have promised you before that I would never fail

The Annunciation from Albrecht Dürer's Small Passion series (1510) depicts the Angel Gabriel in stereotypical form. Like many familiars, the angel came with comfort and predictions, in this case regarding the birth of a child: 'Fear not, Mary' he urged 'for thou hast found favour with God. And, behold, thou shalt conceive in thy womb, and bring forth a son'.

A woodcut from a pamphlet relating to the trial of three witches in Chelmsford in 1589, depicts the intimacy between Joan Prentice and her familiar, who appeared in the form of a ferret. The latter climbed onto her lap and urged 'fear me not, my coming unto thee is to do thee no hurt . . . if thou wilt have me do anything for thee, I am and will be always ready at thy commandment'.

you.' On another, Christ told her 'good daughter, I pray you, love me with all your heart, and I shall give you goods enough to love me with . . . And I shall provide for you, daughter, as for my own mother and as for my own wife.'[56]

Margery's claim that 'Many times, when this creature would say her prayers, our Lord said to her, "Daughter, ask what you wish, and you shall have it"' is even more reminiscent of the comforts offered by the demon familiar.[57] Similarly unspecific beneficence on the part of an envisioned deity was recorded by the twelfth-century English contemplative, Christina of Markyate, who describes a vision in which she travels above the clouds and 'saw the queen of heaven sitting on a throne and angels in brightness seated above her . . . [then] the queen turned to one of the angels standing by and said, "Ask Christina what she wants, because I will give her whatever she asks."'[58]

From this perspective, we can re-evaluate the stereotypical initial encounter between a popular magical practitioner and their familiar. These often occurred when the practitioner was suffering the severe physical and psychological stresses caused by poverty, sickness, bereavement and so on. We can interpret the familiar's offer of help, and the magical practitioner's acceptance of this help, not as a retrospective fiction, created out of learned ideas about the manipulative insinuations of the Devil, but as a psychological event: an event which consisted of a genuine and therapeutic emotional exchange occurring on a profound psychological level. The familiar's gently probing enquiries of 'What aild her?' and 'why make you such great dule and fair greting [weeping]' and his promises that the suffering individual 'suld never want'; that he would 'bring her victuals'; that he should 'do her good'; that she should 'have all happinesse'; that 'she should live gallantly' and that 'it sould be weel with her' could have been experienced as a form of spiritual solace.[59] Similarly, when the Devil appeared before Devon witch Temperance Lloyd (1682) as she was struggling to carry a pile of sticks and sighed '"This poor woman has a great burthen"' and before Scottish witch Bessie Wilson (1661) with the memorable words 'thee art a poor puddled (overworked) body', Temperance and Bessie may have been genuinely moved by his compassion.[60] From the same perspective, Edinburgh cunning woman Jean Weir (1670) may have experienced therapeutic relief when she recited three times, at the behest of her fairy familiar, 'All my cross and trubles goe to the door with the', and Bessie Dunlop have been deeply fortified by Tom Reid's exhortations to 'tak ane gude hart to hir, for nathing suld ail her' as she laboured to give birth to a child.[61]

Christian mystical literature reveals that spiritual guides could be equally effective when the individual's distress was caused by an event occurring on a visionary level. In the following account a guide, in the form of an envisioned Christ, protects Teresa of Ávila from being battered to death by an angry crowd. In psychological terms, the guide is enabling the saint to negotiate an altered state of consciousness which is experienced so negatively and powerfully that it threatens to overwhelm her:

> Whilst I was at prayer, I saw myself in a large field alone, and around me was a crowd of all sorts of people that hedged me in on every side. They all seemed to be carrying weapons with which to attack me . . . In fact, I could not escape in any direction without running the risk of death, and I was quite alone, without anyone to take my part. I was in great spiritual distress and did not know what to do, when I raised my eyes to the sky and saw Christ – not in heaven, but far above me in the air – holding out his hand toward me and encouraging me in such a way that I no longer feared all these people, and they could not harm me, try though they might.[62]

Some of the encounter-narratives given by cunning folk and witches suggest that familiars could perform similar functions. As we have seen earlier, Perthshire cunning woman Isobel Haldane (1623) was 'lying in hir bed, scho wes taikin furth, quhidder be God or the Devill scho knawis nocht; wes caryit to ane hill-syde: the hill oppynit, and scho enterit in. Thair scho stayit thrie dayis, viz. fra Thursiday till Sonday at xij houris. Scho mett a man with ane gray beird, quha brocht hir furth agane.' Subsequent to this event Isobel referred to her saviour as 'He that delyveret me frome the ffarye-ffolk'.[63] Similarly, Fifeshire cunning woman Alison Peirson (1588), whose magical practice was facilitated through frequent contact with the fairies, was at times overwhelmed by the negative intensity of her visionary experiences. Alison claimed that 'thay [the fairies] come verry feirfull [fearsome] sumtymes, and fleit [frighten] hir verry fair, and scho cryit quhene thay come' – but that she was protected from their worst effects by her familiar, deceased cunning man William Simpson (who lived with the fairies), who 'speikis and wairnis hir of thair [the fairies'] cuming and saulsis [saves] hir'.[64]

Sexual Intimacies

The overtly sexual nature of some relationships between cunning folk or witches and their familiars can also be re-evaluated if we define the familiar as an envisional spiritual guide. The concept of the 'sexual transmaterial union with God' is found in spiritual traditions throughout the world and in all periods of history, from tribal shamanism to the great world religions, and has been defined as 'a universal symbol of mankind'.[65] Christian mystical literature contains many accounts of sexualized relations and/or marriage between female contemplatives and Christ, taking place on both an external ritual and an inner experiential level (sometimes including accounts of 'miraculous conception'). Despite their elevated sub-text, some of these narratives contain as much realism and detail as those of cunning folk and witches. The thirteenth-century Flemish contemplative, Hadewijch of Brabant, claimed that 'he [Christ] came in the form and clothing of a man . . . wonderful and beautiful, and with glorious face, he came to me as humbly as anyone who wholly belongs to another . . . he came himself to me, and took me entirely in his arms, and pressed me to him; and all my members felt his in full felicity, in accordance with the desire of my heart and my humanity.'[66] Margery Kempe's account of her marriage to Christ is similarly detailed. Her description of the large crowd (including a careful identification of many of those present), and of the bridegroom's offers of comfort (sitting incongruously alongside his emphasis on the conditional and contractual nature of the marriage vows), is redolent of early modern encounter-narratives detailing sabbath experiences where witches seal their alliance with the Devil through sexual relations.

> And then the father took her by the hand [spiritually] in her soul, before the Son and the Holy Ghost, and the Mother of Jesus, and all the twelve apostles, and St Katherine and St Margaret and many other saints and holy virgins, with a great multitude of angels, saying to her soul, 'I take you, Margery, for my wedded wife, for fairier, for fouler, for richer, for poorer, provided that you are humble and meek in doing what I command you to do. For, daughter, there was never a child so kind to its mother as I shall be to you, both in joy and sorrow, to help you and comfort you. And that I pledge to you.'[67]

From this perspective, when Orkney cunning woman Elspeth Reoch claimed that the Devil 'com to hir she being asleip and laid his hand upoun hir breist and walkint her And thairefter semeit to ly with hir', and when Essex witch Rebecca West (1645) claimed that the Devil 'married her that night, in this manner; he tooke her by the hand and lead [led] her about the chamber, and promised to be her loving husband till death', these women were not expressing interrogatorial preconceptions, or cathartically releasing repressed or forbidden sexual desire, but were drawing on a metaphor for mystical union, and giving voice to 'a universal symbol of mankind'.[68]

The Experience 'for its own sake'

Accounts of the pleasures which could be derived from the 'sexual trans-material union with God' are indicative of the primary role which 'mystical joy', that is, the profound pleasure to be attained through certain forms of mystical experience, plays in spiritual traditions throughout the world. Although medieval Christian writers often warned against seeking mystical joy as an end in itself, claiming that it could be a distraction from the adept's primary aim, 'union with God', there is no doubt that such joy was highly valued, both as an indication of God's favour and as a fore-taste of the eternal bliss to be enjoyed in heaven. Such experiences went a long way towards leavening the suffering and loneliness which could accompany the spiritual vocation. For contemplatives who possessed a rich imaginal life, mystical joy could be synonymous with visionary experience. For one, a vision 'filled my heart full of the greatest joy'; for another it prompted 'a new spiritual joy and a new spiritual comfort, which was so marvellous that she could never tell of it as she felt it'; while another claimed of such an experience that 'My spirit was filled with great bliss at the sight of such glory.'[69] On other occasions this joy was expressed through metaphor and imagery. Accounts of the pleasures of heaven, for example, are illustrative. The fourteenth-century French contemplative, Flora of Beaulieu, claimed to have been guided by an angel to a heaven which possessed the same celebratory, semi-formal and pervasively numinous atmosphere as an early modern sabbath or fairy court: 'she [Flora] had a vision of the angels and saints in heaven, who were celebrating a great feast that was not on the liturgical calendar of the Church militant below. There was much singing and other solemnity. She asked her angelic escort what the feast was, and he answered, "Have you not heard that there will be joy in heaven whenever a sinner repents of his past life?"'[70] The heavenly festivities experienced by fourteenth-century German contemplative Christina Ebner, on the other hand, were conducted with rather less solemnity. She 'saw that Christ was preparing a special celebration, and was inviting all his saints to it. She beheld a dance in heaven, in which God and Mary took part along with the saints. Their proximity to God reflected their level of spiritual attainment, with Mary as the closest of all. Whenever the Lord raised his foot, he emitted a great flame.'[71]

As we explored in chapter TWELVE, it is difficult to find references to the spiritual dimension of the cunning woman or witch's vocation because the conditions in which their testimonies were taken down were not conducive to the expression of mystical sentiment. Furthermore, the images and metaphors which these primarily illiterate men and women used to describe their spiritual experiences were often very different from those used by contemplatives, even ones of relatively humble origin like Margery Kempe. Despite such difficulties, however, we can still make reasonable suppositions. Visits to fairyland and attendance at the sabbath were often, like the contemplative's journey to heaven, described as pleasurable, and this pleasure could have had as much to do with mystical joy as with the satisfactions of, as has been recently suggested, 'a compensatory fantasy that allowed them to experience in imagination the splendour and specialness denied them in life'.[72] Fifeshire cunning woman Alison Peirson (1588) claimed that although the fairies could be very frightening, she had 'mony guid feindis' in the fairy court and saw 'pypeing and mirrynes and gude scheir' when she was there; Somerset witch Elizabeth Style (1664) and her companions attended a sabbath where they 'consumed wine, cakes, and roast meat (all brought by the man in black), and they danced and made merry'; East Lothian cunning woman Agnes Sampson (1591) met the Devil on a boat off the North Berwick coast where he 'caused her drink wine and gave her other good cheer'; Renfrewshire witch Marie Lamont and her companions (1662) described how 'the devill was in the likeness of a meickle black man, and sung to them, and they dancit; he gave them wyn to drink, and wheat bread to eat, and they warr all very mirrie'; and Aberdeenshire cunning man Andro Man described how 'thay will have fair coverit taiblis [in fairyland] . . . and that thay have playing and dansing quhen thay pleas; and als that the quene is verray plesand'.[73] Nairnshire witch Isobel Gowdie (1662) claimed that at the sabbath she and others 'haw werie great pleasour in their carnall cowpulatioun with him [the Devil] . . . and they will haw a exceiding great desir of it with him . . . He is abler for ws that way than any man can be'.[74] Other narratives hint at the less dramatic, but perhaps no-less-intense, joys that could be shared with the solitary familiar. Bessie Dunlop describes how Tom Reid's comforts and counsel left her feeling 'sumthing blyther'.[75] Many descriptions of the conversational, blood-sucking, bed-sharing intimacies of English witches and their animal familiars also intimate a tender numinosity.[76] That such exchanges could be synonymous with mystical joy is articulated with rare delicacy in an encounter-narrative given by Ely cunning man Adam Sabie (1647), who claimed to have experienced a twelve-year-long relationship with a familiar in the form of a child. It is also possible that this narrative alludes to the 'sweet tastes' characteristic of some meditative states:[77]

[He claimed that his familiar] remained in his Body the space of 12 years & divers tyme doth speake to this ex[amina]t & doth feed this ex[aminan]t & comes & give this ex[aminan]t a prick upon his lip which when this ex[aminan]t sucketh he receiveth greate Nurishment w[h]ich this ex[aminan]t Conceaveth preserveth his life & the said spirit speakes unto hime & saith Adam I am thy god and feare not . . . for all thy wrongs shal be righted.[78]

King James VI's claim, in *Daemonologie,* that those people 'whome these kinde of Spirites [the fairies] carryed awaie, and informed, they were thought [by the common folk] to be sonsiest [wisest] and of best life' also suggests that, for the popular magical practitioner, the envisioned familiar could be a gateway to both wisdom and mystical joy.[79]

The fact that the familiar could be a 'gateway to mystical joy', however, is not incompatible with the fact that its function was a primarily a pragmatic one. Spiritual aspirations aside, one of the core motivations for entering into an alliance with a spirit-helper was to ensure physical survival and wellbeing through earning a living (or supplementing an existing living) as a magical practitioner. To this end, cunning folk and witches communicated with their familiars and travelled with them into spirit worlds with specific and very practical objectives in mind: the acquisition of cures or predictions, the performance of maleficium, the getting of information concerning the whereabouts of criminals or lost goods and so on. As we have seen earlier, this balance between utility and spiritual experience is also a feature of shamanism. Although the shaman communicates with his helping spirits and travels with them into spirit worlds in order to attain magical knowledge and power on behalf of his community, the process of seeking out this knowledge and power can bring him into contact with the pleasures of mystical joy. The following invocatory chant, used by the Canadian Iglulik shaman, Aua, when he needed assistance from one of his helping spirits, illustrates the close links between the magical use of envisioned guides and religious ecstasy:

> Joy, joy,
> Joy, joy!
> I see a little shore spirit,
> A little aua,
> I myself am also aua,
> The shore spirit's namesake,
> Joy, joy![80]

Aua claimed that he would repeat this chant many times 'until I burst into tears, overwhelmed by a great dread; then I would tremble all over, crying only: "Ah-a-a-a-a, joy! joy!'[81] Scholars tell us that the yearning for such experiences can drive shamans to seek them out 'for joy alone' and for their 'own sake', and that among the Inuit peoples of Northern Canada at the turn of the nineteenth century it was believed that the more powerful shamans 'often go up on a visit to the People of Day [to the spirit world], just for pleasure' and that 'there is great rejoicing in the Land of Day when a wizard comes on a visit.'[82]

Given the horrors of the British witch-craze: the scapegoating, the intimidation, the humiliating trials, the suffering of both those accused of witchcraft and those who believed themselves to have been the victims of witchcraft, it is redemptive to think that at the core of all this human fear and pain we can find treasures as simple, and yet profound, as 'comfort' and 'joy'. From such a perspective it is easier to understand why the relationship between a cunning woman or witch and her familiar could often last for decades, surviving marriages, bereavements, the rearing of whole families and the ever-present threat of accusations of demonological witchcraft. We can also understand why a magical practitioner might be motivated to stay loyal to their familiar until the very end, despite being threatened with hellfire and brimstone by the whole weight of Church, community and State. Why Wiltshire cunning woman Anne Bodenham (1653) at 'eighty years of age . . . deprived of food and sleep, kept up her spirits, bravely cursing the hangman to the last'; why Essex witch Alice Nokes (1579) claimed, when being reprimanded before a church congregation, that 'she cared for none of them all as long as Tom [her familiar] held by her side'; why an unnamed Cambridgeshire witch (1653), being 'on the point of execution . . . declined to renounce the faithful friend of threescore years [that is, her demon familiar], and "died in her obstinacy"'; and why so many magical practitioners stood up in courtrooms across the length and breadth of Britain and 'persisted in telling long and involved stories about fairies' – despite the fact that in doing so, they often knowingly condemned themselves to death.[83]

CHAPTER FOURTEEN

The Freedom
of Magic

This book began by asking a number of questions. Were the descriptions of encounters with familiar spirits given by magical practitioners in early modern Britain fictions, or were they descriptions of genuine experiences? If they were fictions, how and why were they fabricated? If they were real experiences, what was the origin and nature of these experiences? And what relevance do these encounter-narratives have for our understanding of popular culture in early modern Britain?

As a result of our enquiries, we can now assume with reasonable certainty that at her trial in Edinburgh in 1576, Scottish cunning woman Bessie Dunlop was describing a visionary experience; and that this experience was an expression of a vigorous popular visionary tradition rooted in pre-Christian shamanistic beliefs and practices. We can also assume that her visionary encounter-experiences came under the definition of lower-level mystical states and that through them she may have gained access to more profound levels of spiritual experience.

Although we can now offer up these kinds of explanations for Bessie's experiences, most of us living in Britain today are still imaginatively a great distance from them. Unless we are familiar with the study or experience of visional mystical states, Bessie Dunlop's experiences must remain completely foreign to us. The scholar Roger Walsh claims that shamans (and therefore by the same token early modern cunning folk and witches) are individuals who possess an enhanced visionary capacity, or what has been termed a 'fantasy-prone' personality. Such capacities are not confined to animistic cultures, however, and recent psychological studies suggest that around 4 percent of the current western population may be fantasy-prone.[1] In the great timescale of biological evolution, the four hundred year span between ourselves and Bessie Dunlop is not a long one, and the number of people who possessed enhanced visionary capacities in early modern Britain is unlikely to differ considerably from the number who possess them in Britain today. And yet if this is so, where are these visionaries? Who are the people who are having these experiences? It is likely that every single person in the crowded Edinburgh courtroom on November 5, 1576, believed that Bessie's Dunlop's encounter with Tom Reid had taken place, though their definitions of Tom's ontological status may have differed. And yet over the past century, most historians have looked on descriptions of spirit-encounters such as Bessie's with such unfamiliarity and bemusement that they have often resorted to claiming that these experiences did not happen, or that they were symptomatic of mental illness or elaborate fiction-making during the trial process itself. What has caused such a great differential between Bessie's world and ours?

Conditions for Visionary Experience

Allace! Haif I nocht grit caus to mak grit dule? ffor our geir is trakit; and my husband is on the point of deid, and ane babie of my awin will nocht leve; and myself at ane waik point: haif I nocht gude caus thane to haif ane fair hart?[2]

Some of the answers to these questions may lie in the fact that while the structure of the human brain may not have changed significantly in the last four hundred years, living conditions and ways of thinking have changed dramatically. Throughout history it has been recognized that certain conditions of body and mind induce altered states of consciousness which can be defined as 'mystical' and 'visionary'. For people living at subsistence level in undeveloped cultures many of these conditions are more naturally present than they are in the modern developed world, and this may be one of the reasons why popular magical practitioners in early modern Britain were more likely to experience visions than people living in Britain today.

Throughout the sixteenth and seventeenth centuries the majority of the population were underfed and overworked to a degree unimaginable to most people in twenty-first-century Britain. Their major preoccupation was the production of food and they worked long and hard throughout the year to grow crops and raise livestock. Often, however, these efforts were not enough. For many, chronic undernourishment since childhood would have been periodically compounded by periods of acute shortage and famine, brought about by poor or failed harvests. In addition to this, women's bodies were subjected to almost constant childbearing, Barbara Rosen claiming, in relation to witchcraft beliefs, that women like Bessie Dunlop were 'ill-nourished, over-worked and almost continually pregnant and nursing'.[3] As we have seen in earlier chapters, depriving the body of food and pushing it to the limits of its endurance are very powerful ways of inducing altered states of consciousness, and for this reason they are two of the most frequent ritual asceticisms traditionally practised by mystical adepts in both tribal and developed societies throughout the world. In psychological terms, these asceticisms severely disrupt normal physiological functioning to the extent that they can 'destabilize' the ordinary state of consciousness, precipitating those unusual experiences traditionally defined as mystical.[4]

While the harsh conditions of subsistence level living endured by the early modern poor would have had very definite effects on their physiology, they would also have had very definite effects on their hearts and minds. Undernourishment and over-exertion, combined with poor sanitation and limited medical services, meant that disease and death were ubiquitous, and the close-knit, communal nature of early modern village life ensured that the misfortunes of others was frequently witnessed first hand. It is difficult for many in the modern western world to imagine the kinds of mental and emotional states generated by the persistent experience of, and witnessing of, acute suffering. Barabara Rosen, again, emphasizes that 'Precious brewings and bakings are lost; treasured livestock suffer from inexplicable sicknesses; crippling diseases strike; and over and over again, children scream and suffer helplessly and die. There are very few literate people today who can enter into an existence in which one bears ten children and watches five of them die in infancy.'[5] It is often argued that people living in these kinds of conditions develop a resilience to suffering; in response to high infant mortality, for example, they would be 'slower to acknowledge the individuality of their children'.[6] Despite evidence of this resilience, however, there are also many indications (which can be corroborated by observation of peoples in present-day undeveloped countries) that these sufferings were nevertheless felt very keenly. According to Frederick Valletta, the Buckinghamshire rector and physician Richard Napier (1590–1634) 'often included "grief" in the lists of symptoms of his patients, sometimes for the death of a relation months or even years previously . . . In addition the Bills of Mortality for London between 1647 and 1659 list 222 recorded deaths from "grief".'[7] Witch-trial records, as we have seen, frequently refer to the anxiety and grief caused by sickness and bereavement. The distress felt by Ely witch Margaret Moore (1647) at the loss of three children, and her fear for the life of her remaining child, echoes painfully through her confession, in which she claims that 'she hard ye voyce of hir Children whoe had formerly died Calling unto hir'. The trial records state that they called:

> Mother Mother to which the said Margeret answered sweet Children where are you what would you have with me & thay demanded of hir drincke w[hi]ch the said Margeret Answered that she had noe drincke then theire Came a voyce which the said Margeret Conceaved to be hir third Child & demanded of hir hir soule, otherwise she would take a-way the life of hir 4th child which was the only Child she had left to which voyce the said Margeret made answer that rather then shee would lose hir last Child she would Consent unto the giving a-way of hir soule & then a spirit in the liknes of a naked Child appeared unto hir & suckt upon hir Body.[8]

Proximity to sickness and death prompts profound mental and emotional states. Overwhelming feelings of anger, helplessness and despair can combine with the intense need to find remedy, explanation and solace. Such powerful experiences force the mind beyond its normal parameters, opening it up to new ways of seeing and generating those kinds of extra-ordinary emotions and psychic experiences traditionally associated with the supernatural or the mystical. It is hardly surprising, therefore, that suffering stands at the experiential heart of developed religions and animistic belief systems alike. 'All true wisdom', claimed the Canadian Caribou shaman, Igjugârjuk, 'can only be attained through suffering. Suffering and privation are the only things that can open the mind of man to that which is hidden from his fellows.'[9] Similarly, William Johnston concludes a discussion about suffering in Christianity and Buddhism by stating that 'So we end with an awful paradox. From the viewpoint of science and common sense, sickness and death are great evils to be conquered. And here we find religions claiming that they are conditions for true healing and that they lead to life . . . What heals is love, which is most dramatically expressed in suffering.'[10] The fact that cunning folk and witches often encountered envisioned familiars subsequent to a bereave-ment is also congruent with modern psychological research into the common phenomenon of 'grief hallucination'. In 1985, for example, one American study reported that out of a random sample of 46 widows, 61 percent had experienced hallucinations of their deceased spouses and that for nearly half of these the hallucinations were recurrent.[11] Studies from other countries corroborate these results.[12]

The devastating effects of deprivation and suffering were not the only conditions of early modern living which were conducive to visionary expe-rience. Some recognition must also be given to the effects of darkness and illiteracy on the imagination. Electrical lighting is so powerful and efficient that it enables modern men and women to have almost complete immunity from both the practical and psychological effects of darkness. An immediate escape from the fears which breed as we lie in our beds or walk down deserted country lanes is but the flick of a switch away. Even when lights or torches are not being used, there is the psychological security, gained from past experience, of knowing that if one were to be turned on everything would appear just as it does during the day. In the early modern period, however, there was not the immediate comfort of the light switch, nor the remembered comfort of having used one in the past. The reed candles used by the poorer folk were too precious and difficult to light to be used casually and in any case the illumination they shed was dim, flickering, and of little use in banishing the shadows shifting in the corners of barns or behind whispering hedgerows. This scarcity of artificial lighting meant that a significant proportion of waking and working life would have been spent in darkness or in the semi-darkness of dawn and twilight. Animals could not be left hungry and corn could not be left to rot in the fields because the light was fading or the sun not yet risen, consequently the early modern poor would have lived much of their lives under the powerful thrall of darkness, and their perception of the world and its inhabitants would have been sculpted by its mystery.

This susceptibility to the effects of darkness would also have been accompanied by highly developed imaginative faculties. Without recourse to the leisure aids available to those living in a highly literate, technologically-advanced world, such as books, televisions, radios, and so on, people living in early modern Britain would have created their own entertainment, and a large element of this would have been the listening to, and telling of, stories and ballads. Unlike watching television, an occupation in which the imagination lies dormant and the mind becomes a passive recipient of images – listening to stories and ballads directly and powerfully stimulates the imaginative faculties. Although people in this period were almost constantly employed in practical (and often communal) tasks, many of these tasks would have been monotonous enough to allow the mind some imaginative freedom. Long days or evenings spent busy with the spindle, the needle or the blade, would have been seasoned and leavened with 'old wives trattles about the fire': tales and ballads of Thomas the Rhymour, Robin Goodfellow, Tom Thumb, King Arthur and Robin Hood; heroic tasks, fantastic voyages, humorous adventures and great loves, all played out against the backdrop of colourful and fantastical worlds. Just as the blind person develops exceptional powers of hearing and touch to compensate for their lack of vision, so children, denied the visual stimulation of television or the written word, would have developed an exceptionally vivid and muscular imagination. This imagi-

Death and the Child, from Hans Holbein the Younger's Dance of Death series (1523–26), takes us inside a poor man's cottage and shows us the all-too-familiar tragedy of a mother losing a child to malnutrition or disease.

The harsh lives of the poor were leavened by a rich imaginal heritage. This pamphlet titled *The History of Tom Thumbe . . .* (1621) is one of the earliest known printings of a British fairy tale. In the early modern period popular fairy lore was almost exclusively oral.

nation would have been strengthened by prodigious skills of concentration and memory. Without any other distractions, even the very young would have been accustomed to sitting through the slowly-unfolding narrative of a long story or a many-versed ballad.

To these environmental and circumstantial factors can be added the physical and mental effects of consuming 'mind-altering' substances. Beer, which is known to produce hallucinations, particularly in the undernourished, was drunk in large amounts by both adults and children and was generally stronger than it is today.[13] Hallucinogenic moulds also periodically entered the food chain. Some historians have, controversially, linked outbreaks of mass hysteria, such as those associated with the witch-craze, with the mould ergot which grew on rye, a grain which was the staple diet for many people in early modern Britain.[14] Psychoactive agents could also be found in commonly occurring plants and fungi such as Amanita muscaria ('fly agaric'), Psilocybian Mushrooms ('magic mushrooms'), mandrake, henbane, hemp, datura and could even be extracted from toad skins. Whether these powerful substances were used consciously and ritually, cannot be proven. However reports of the use of 'flying ointments' and magical potions used by witches throughout Europe were widespread enough to become part of the stereotypical picture of the witch, particularly on the Continent, and it is likely that these reports were based on some kind of ritual activity.[15]

While the physical and psychological effects of early modern living conditions were generally conducive to visionary experience, to these effects can be added one further factor, the burning taper which sets the whole pile of combustibles alight – a belief in the reality of spirits. In Britain today questions surrounding the existence, nature and significance of spirits have, for many people, ceased to be of any significant import. In general the whole idea of spirits is so irrelevant and de-potentiated that the experiences of those who consider themselves to have encountered spirits is of little relevance to those around them, including the institutions which govern society. The situation was very different in early modern Britain. The overwhelming majority of the population, both rich and poor, believed in the existence of spirits and the activities of the supernatural beings of all types were considered to be of great religious and political significance. Although a learned judge or priest may have disagreed with the common man as to the definition, status, or role of a particular spirit, they would not have denied its existence. To do so would, in the words of Katharine Briggs, have been 'no better than atheism'.[16] For the common man, as we have seen throughout this book, fairies and ghosts often stood centre stage. Eighteenth-century journalist John Addison claimed bemusedly that during the time of his forefathers,

'There was not a village in England that had not a ghost in it; the churchyards were all haunted; every large common had a circle of fairies belonging to it, and there was scarce a shepherd to be met with who had not seen a spirit.'[17] Consequently, encounters with spirits of all kinds were frequent topics of conversation. In response to Ludwig Lavater's polemic on the existence of spirits, Angevin lawyer Pierre Le Loyer claimed in 1605 that 'Of all the common and familiar subjects of conversation . . . that are entered apon in company of things remote from nature and cut off from the senses, there is none so ready to hand, none so usual, as that of visions of Spirits, and whether what is said of them is true. It is the topic that most people readily discuss and on which they linger the longest because of the abundance of examples, the subject being fine and pleasing and the discussion the least tedious that can be found.'[18] Children would have been particularly impressionable. In his *Discoverie of Witchcraft* Reginald Scot claimed that 'in our childhood our mothers maids have so terrified us with an ouglie divell having hornes on his head . . . and they have so fraied us with bull beggers, spirits, witches, urchens, elves, hags, fairies . . . Robin good-fellowe, the spoorne, the mare, the man in the oke, the hell waine, the fierdrake, the puckle, Tom thombe, hob gobblin, Tom tumbler, boneles, and other such bugs, that we are afraid of our owne shadowes.'[19] Studies into Victorian and early twentieth-century folk beliefs indicate that such fears survived into more recent times, a nineteenth-century Scottish clergyman recounting, for example, how as a child, 'Every bush was suspected of harbouring some malignant spirit, and every rustle among the branches sent a shock through my nervous system from the effects of which, in spite of my philosophy, I sometimes feel I have not yet quite recovered. Even now I cannot pass through a dark wood late at night without recalling these boyish experiences, and, "Glowran" round wi' anxious care, Lest bogle catch me unaware'.[20] Not having the benefit of a 'philosophy' which rendered the causes of their fears non-existent, most men and women in early modern Britain would have carried their childhood apprehensions of spirit-malevolence into their adult lives. An insight into how the world may have been experienced by common folk in this period can be gained from Swedish linguist Kai Donner's accounts of an evening spent with a group of Siberian Samoyed Eskimos in the early twentieth century. Donner describes how, for a brief while, he was able to suspend his objectivistic and materialistic mind-set and enter into the very different reality of his companions:

> . . . darkness descended. The fire had slowly gone out and the age-old trees of the forest made contours against the starry heavens like large powerful

shadows. The snow lay softly on the barren earth and nature in its unending loneliness seemed to lie in a half slumber. The men had told their old legends of dead heroes and the shamans had talked with the spirits of the heavens and with those of the underworld. I had forgotten all that made me a man of civilisation; I was thinking neither of Christianity nor of other teachings but rather I was completely involved in childlike admiration of what I saw and heard.

I suddenly felt like a child and, as in childhood, I imagined that every object had its spirit, that water and air were populated by mysterious invisible beings who, in inexplicable fashion, ruled the course of the world and the fate of men. In the untouched wilderness and its infinite silence, I was encompassed by the traditional mysticism and religious mysteries through which faith touches so many things.

After several of these meetings I naturally became inured and did not let myself be so completely captivated but even today, because of what I have seen and heard, I have retained a deeper understanding of what and how these children of the wilderness feel and think. Their religion has become alive for me and I think that such understanding and knowledge could be and is useful in many ways. One can scarcely get to the bottom of a problem in any other way no matter what aspect of life might be involved.[21]

The early modern fascination with, and fear of, spirits would have extended to those individuals who fraternized with them. Many of the tales and anecdotes told around hearths in the cottages and farmhouses of early modern Britain would have described the activities and experiences of cunning folk and witches: miraculous cures and malevolent magical attacks; encounters with black-clothed devils, beautiful fairy queens, mischievous hobgoblins and well-dressed, gentlemanly ghosts; tales of miraculous flights through the air, transformations into animals, lavish feasts, high-spirited festivities and secret journeys into the hearts of hills. To the impressionable child, with an inescapable future already mapped out by the dictates of toil and domesticity, the drama and the numinosity of the magical practitioner's activities and experiences would have stimulated many things: the desire for power and prestige, the yearning for adventure, for meaning, and the ineffable lust for self-transformation. Against such a backdrop it is not difficult to see how those individuals who possessed an enhanced visionary capacity could sometimes find that circumstances conspired to transform their inherent belief in, and fascination with, such things into something more experiential. For Bessie Dunlop, this crucial moment occurred around noon, on the road between her house and Monkcastle as she drove her cattle to pasture. Labouring along the road, worrying about her husband who was 'on the point of deid' and her newborn baby who would 'nocht leve [live]', it is not difficult to imagine how, during an unguarded moment, her mind slipped its normal constraints and she unexpectedly found herself experiencing a powerfully realistic waking vision. And it is also hardly surprising, given her cultural inheritance, that she knew exactly what to do with it.

Visionaries – Ancient and Modern

The perspective on the visionary experiences of cunning folk and witches presented in this book is greater than the sum of its parts. Not only does it give us a window into the spiritual life of ordinary people in early modern Britain, but it also gives us an insight into the spiritual lives of people living in Britain today. The dramatic technological and cultural changes which have taken place in the western world over the last two hundred years have weakened the institutional and ideological power of Christianity, and at the present time Britain's 'official' faith has lost its grip on the hearts and minds of many ordinary people. Some of the latter remain nominal Christians, others reject religion altogether and become atheists or agnostics while others turn to alternative world faiths. A wide range of people, both with or without religious belief, also gain comfort and guidance from philosophical systems and modern therapeutic psychologies. More relevant to our discussion, however, is the huge and growing appetite for belief systems and ritual practices which can be described as 'magical', and which generally combine, in varying degrees, both influences from the past and the present, and from both European and non-European cultures. There are, for example, the many traditions which come under the umbrella term 'neo-paganism': Hermetic and Thelemic magic, Druidry, Wicca, Goddess spirituality, Hedge Witchcraft, Tantric magic and so on. There are also the traditions which come under the term 'neo-shamanism' – most notably 'core-shamanism' which draws primarily on classical shamanic traditions and 'North European paganism', which draws inspiration from a reconstructed Norse shamanic tradition. Spiritualism, astrology and many types of alternative medicine and healing also have their roots in magical theory and practice, while a wide range of psychological therapies employ mental and physical techniques historically associated with magic, such as visualization, hypnosis and affirmation. Other therapies, like analytic psychology, draw directly and openly from western magical traditions, to the extent that their founders have been defined as 'magicians'.[22] The contemporary popularity of magical belief and practice is borne out by the fact that there are substantial numbers of alternative or 'new age' practitioners to be found in virtually every town in Britain.

In addition to the popularity of magic as a quasi-religious or therapeutic construct, however, there is also a huge cultural emphasis on magic as an imaginative preoccupation. Much bestselling popular fiction, whether intended for adults or children, involves or centres on magical themes. Classic works such as the *Lord of the Rings* trilogy, the Narnia adventures or, more recently, the Discworld and Harry Potter series are ubiquitous, and magical lore also plays an integral role in the hugely popular science fiction genre. Television programmes made for children frequently work and re-work stories of magical power and witchcraft, while adult documentaries and films on the subject continue to draw large audiences. Although it may seem as if magical beliefs are being re-discovered in response to the decline of Christianity, in reality they have never really left us. Recent research by historians such as Owen Davies establishes what folklorists have long known, that magical belief and practice remained remarkably strong and widespread in rural Britain until the early twentieth century.[23] The apparent demise of magic has, in effect, been simultaneous with its re-emergence.

Why is magic currently enjoying such widespread popularity? Since the arrival of Christianity in Britain nearly 2000 years ago, until the present, educated, literate people have frequently belittled magic, both as it is found in our own past and in contemporary tribal cultures, considering it to be the preserve of the unlettered, the gullible and the 'primitive'. If magical beliefs are so risible then why are they of such interest to a society which enjoys the benefits of unsurpassed quantities of rationalist-based education, material prosperity and sophisticated medical care, and which is so technologically advanced that it can send probes to Mars, clone an animal and split the atom? Why does a society in which the majority of men and women have the unprecedented freedom, for the first time in history, to explore their spirituality through any one of the world's great developed religions, philosophical systems and therapeutic psychologies, still remain fascinated by the most 'primitive' spiritual traditions of them all? Although there is no scope in the present discussion to go into these issues in any detail, we can shed a little light on them by returning, for the last time, to the visionary experiences of early modern cunning folk and witches.

The Freedom of Magic

In this book we have looked closely at the encounter-narratives of individuals like Bessie Dunlop and have concluded that, as descriptions of visionary experiences, these narratives are testaments to the fact that popular magical belief and practice possessed an experiential dimension in Britain in this period, and that this dimension possessed a spiritual significance. If we draw back, however, and look at early modern culture through a wider lens, this popular spirituality, and the magical beliefs and practices which supported it, all but disappears. From this wide-screen perspective, Christianity fills the frame. The historical dominance of the orthodox faith is still evident to this day in the churches which stand in every village and town in the land: in the gravestones and tombs carved with prayers; the stained glass windows and wall paintings; the carved fonts, pulpits and rood screens; the statues, silver chalices and candlesticks. The message of Christianity is spelt out in prayer books for pious Catholics, prayer books for pious reformers, Bibles in Latin, Bibles in English and in the private devotion found in letters and journals. These visible trappings of faith are supported by the documentary evidence of a widespread early modern ministry: the ritual performance and administering of the sacred sacraments, the vivid and emotional celebration of seasonal rituals at Christmas, Easter, Lammas and so on, and the pastoral care and provision for the poor and the sick.

The institution, the teachings, the sheer physical presence of medieval and post-Reformation Christianity in Britain was so ubiquitous that it is difficult to see how magical beliefs and practices of pre-Christian origin could have retained enough influence and coherence to inspire and inform a popular mysticism – a mysticism unsupported by societal organizations and which was upheld by no sacred buildings, no visible iconography, no sacred books, no formalized doctrine or cosmology and no institutionalized ritual or pastoral care. It is hard, despite the compelling evidence presented by the encounter-narratives of cunning folk and witches, to envisage how such formless and invisible constructs could have challenged the Christian Church for the hearts and minds of ordinary people. This challenge becomes far more comprehensible, however, when we take into account the fact that magical beliefs and practices held an incredibly powerful ace up their collective sleeve. An oral legacy.

A legacy as old as mankind and woven out of infinitesimal threads. A complex inheritance of magical beliefs and practices worked together over millenia to form vivid and charismatic mythological and cosmological tapestries. While Christianity in this period also possessed a rich legacy, this legacy was, by comparison, relatively recent, relatively foreign and most importantly, rested primarily in the hands of the clergy and literate laymen. The custodians of magical beliefs and practices, however, were the common people themselves. Magical beliefs were passed on by word of mouth: behind ploughs, at spindles, on river banks and by hearths; magical rituals were performed in kitchens, in bedrooms, by roadsides and on hillsides under cover of darkness. People did not perform these rituals because some institution or figure in authority compelled them to do so – they performed them because they believed them to work. While it has long been recognized that the widespread use of magical spells and charms in this period are indicative of how seriously practical magical technologies were taken, the perspectives drawn in this book enable us to recognize that the encounter-narratives of cunning folk and witches are indicative of how deeply experiential magical techniques, and the animistic mythologies and cosmologies which informed them, were also impressed upon the common mind. Earlier we have seen how historians have argued that one of the reasons why magical beliefs were so popular among ordinary people in this period was because they offered immediate methods of practical self-help which were an effective alternative to those offered by the Church.[24] It is likely that it was this same 'self-helping' or 'self-empowering' quality of magical belief and practice which was of value in the realm of the early modern imagination and ultimately, in the realm of mystical experience. These beliefs provided the 'fantasy-prone' common man with a far more expansive, self-determining framework of ideas through which he could enable and rationalize his visions than that made available through the Church. Under Catholicism, the visionary experiences of Christian sacred beings and sacred places would have been hedged about with moral prohibitions and queried for authenticity by religious authorities who really preferred qualified individuals, such as the clergy, to have such spiritual encounters. Similarly, although Protestantism was fuelled by the ardent belief that a man had the right to take his spiritual experience into his own hands, its high moral tone and fervent condemnation of anything magical would have combined to have an equally prohibitory effect on the imagination.

Visionary experiences informed by magical belief and practice, by contrast, were relatively unpoliced and were far less inhibited by doctrinal and ethical restrictions. A man could go his own way. As we have seen in previous chapters, no fairy was too little, too ugly, or too hairy to be effective; no 'devil' too mischievous, aggressive or lascivious to be an agent of magical empowerment; and no spirit world too wild, dangerous or compelling to be an opportunity for exploration and joy. Historians are fond of emphasizing that Protestantism brought unprecedented freedom to the spiritual lives of common people in the early modern period, Christina Larner claiming, for example, that the Reformation and Counter-Reformation in Scotland were characterized by 'an entirely novel shift from the idea that the religious life was to be lived only by religious specialists to the assumption that each individual was personally responsible for his own salvation'.[25] However novel such an idea was to Christianity, however, the perspectives drawn in this book suggest that magical belief and practice, as preserved through oral traditions, had been providing ordinary people with this kind of freedom and personal responsibility for many thousands of years prior to the arrival of the orthodox faith.

The self-reliance and self-determination inherent to early modern magical belief and practice would have been similar to that traditionally enjoyed by shamans throughout the ages. Shamanism, according to Ioan Lewis, 'celebrates a confident and egalitarian view of man's relations with the divine, and perpetuates that original accord between God and man which those who have lost the ecstatic mystery can only nostalgically recall in myths of creation, or desperately seek in doctrines of personal salvation'.[26] Within such an egalitarian partnership, the shaman possesses a high level of autonomy and freedom. Michael Harner claimed, for example, that 'Shamanism ultimately is only a method, not a religion with a fixed set of dogmas. Therefore people arrive at their own experience derived conclusions about what is going on in the universe, and about what term, if any, is most useful to describe ultimate reality.'[27] Similarly, at their most basic, early modern magical beliefs and technologies were tools which an individual could use in whichever way they wished: whether to secure a bet, brew a barrel of beer, find a lost purse, cure a sick child or seek to maintain 'the balance of the universe' and be privy to 'immense, unfathomable things'.[28] From this perspective, the persistence of fairy beliefs into the early modern period (and on into the early twentieth century) was not only, as some social anthropologists and historians have argued, a consequence of their ability to 'help to enforce a certain code of conduct' such as good housewifery, neighbourliness and responsible parenting, but was also a testament to their enduring role as imaginal raw material for popular visional mysticism.[29]

It is likely that magical beliefs and practices are currently enjoying a renaissance in modern Britain for similar reasons. The decline of Christianity is leaving not only a cultural vacuum, but also a cultural confusion. No one has a prerogative on the truth, but anyone can claim to have found it. Every man and woman has innumerable religions, psychologies, philosophies and rationalisms at their fingertips, all of which claim to possess the answers to the big existential questions. In the midst of such uncertainty, many choose to return to the simplicity and dependability of their own thoughts and experiences. 'We no longer require,' says scholar of shamanism Nevill Drury, 'a formal religious framework or belief system based on some form of empty inherited doctrine. Our religion, once again, has become based on what we can feel, what we can know.'[30] Under these conditions, the need for an 'experience-derived' method of explaining the universe and living life has never been greater and therefore it is hardly surprising that the self-empowering beliefs and technologies of magic have found themselves once again playing a leading role. 'I would like to challenge you to do your own research,' urges the author of a modern magical manual, 'come to your own insights, and to construct your own working hypothesis as you go along . . . you, and you alone, are responsible for what happens.'[31] Surely at no time since the sixteenth and seventeenth centuries have we been in a better position to enter into, and enjoy, the visionary experiences of women like Bessie Dunlop. Or been in a better position to recognize their significance as an unsung dimension of Britain's native spiritual heritage.

NOTES

Preface

1 It is also possible that Bessie was tortured, although the nature and extent of torture-use in this period of Scottish history is hard to establish. See Maxwell-Stuart 2001 for an overview of the subject.

2 This description of the events leading up to and during Bessie's appearance at the Edinburgh assizes is based on information found in Bessie's trial records and more general evidence about the legal process in sixteenth-century Scotland. Legal procedure in this period was inconsistent and convoluted, and there is much about it that still remains obscure. Elements of the description given here can, therefore, only be speculative.

3 Pitcairn claims that 'Lyne or Linne, in Ayrshire, was a six-merk land, lying in the barony of Dalry, the property of the family of Lord Boyd' (Pitcairn 1833: I ii 49).

4 Throughout the record a number of words are used to denote the asking of questions, the most frequent of these being 'interrogat', 'demandit' and 'inquirit'. For the purposes of readability, I have substituted the word 'asked' in all these cases, although the blandness of this word does not adequately express the tenor of the questioning, which is likely to have been more aggressive.

5 The Battle of Pinkye, where the Scots suffered a thorough and humiliating defeat at the hands of the English, was fought near Edinburgh on September 10, 1547, thirty years before Bessie's trial.

6 Pitcairn notes that 'There is probably a clerical omission in this part of the Record, for no notice is taken of the second meeting' (Pitcairn 1833: I ii 52).

7 'Fourth' (Pitcairn 1833: I ii 52, note 15).

8 There is a possibility that Bessie's accusers were brought to the assize court in Edinburgh so that they could cross-examine and be cross-examined by Bessie. Ultimately, however, Bessie's conviction may have had little to do with the Blacks, and more to do with Tom Reid, in whom her various interrogators seemed to show an inordinate interest. Once Bessie had confessed to having a relationship with Tom Reid, and Tom had been defined as a 'spirit of the devil', she was guilty according to the law and only an extremely indulgent panel of judges could have saved her from the death penalty.

9   These spaces denote blanks left in the sixteenth-century text.

10   The records are silent as to the reaction of the Reid family to Bessie's arrest. On the one hand, it was very likely that Tom Reid the younger (who was in the service of the laird of Blair) did believe that Bessie had been in contact with his father, for it was common belief in the period that the dead could communicate unfinished business to the living through cunning folk. It is also noteworthy that Bessie seems to have helped various members of the Blair family and that it was a 'James Blair' who secured Bessie's release from a previous confinement in Irvine tollbooth. On the other hand, by advancing so deeply into the personal lives of the Reid family and, by implication, their noble employers, Bessie was treading on dangerous ground and her interventions could have been seen as troublesome or threatening.

11   Two words omitted and two words inserted here. Pitcairn's original text reads: 'and sche gaif hir; quha alsua tauld hir, that that barne wald de, and that hir husband suld mend of his seiknes' (Pitcairn 1833: I ii 57).

12   This reference could be a misspelling of Beith, near Dalry, however there is no reason to doubt that the spelling is accurate, and that Bessie did travel to Leith, a port near Edinburgh. During her confession Bessie describes attending Edinburgh market, despite the fact that the capital city was over sixty miles from her home, and references to experiences in Dumbarton and other places a good distance from Lyne suggest that Bessie was well travelled.

13   Two words omitted here. Pitcairn's text reads: 'Neuir save anis that sche had gane afeild with hir husband to Leith, for hame bringing of mele, and ganging afeild to teddir hir naig at Restalrig-loch, quhair thair come ane cumpanye of rydaris by, that maid sic ane dynne as heavin and erd had gane togidder; and incontinent, thai raid in to the loich, with mony hiddous rumbill' (Pitcairn 1833: I ii 57).

14   Candlemas: February 2nd, the Feast of the Purification of the Virgin Mary and the presentation of Christ in the Temple. The day on which the church candles are blessed. In Scotland it is one of the four quarter days.

15   Affayis: testament of good character.

16   The next three entries relate to the confession which took place in Edinburgh on September 20th, 19 days before her appearance at the assizes.

17   Phrase omitted here. Pitcairn's text reads: 'and being inquirit, Quhow oft Thom Reid come to hir, or sche inquirit quhow thai callit him?' (Pitcairn 1833: I ii 57).

18   Passage omitted here. Pitcairn's text reads 'VERDICT. And immediatlie efter the chesing and swering of the saidis persones of Assyis, as use is, the said Elizabeth Dunlop, being on pannell, accusit be dittay oppinlie red in jugement, of the crymes above writtin; the samin persounes removit thame selfiss furth of Court, and altogidder convenit, and ressownit on the pointis of the said dittay; and being rypelie awysit thairwith, and resolvit thairin; re-enterit agane to the said Court of Justiciarie'. Just prior to this passage the jury is listed as 'Andro Craufurd of Baithlem, Hew Hommyll in Kilburne, Thomas Gawand thair, Cuthbert Craufurd in Kilbirnie, Hew Dunlop of Crawfeild,

Henrie Clerk in Cokeydaille, Johnne Knok in Kilcuse, James Aitkin in Balgrene, Johnne Or in Barnauch, Thomas Caldwell in Bultreis, James Harvye in Kilburnie, Robert Roger thair, Johnne Boyde in Gowanlie, Johnne Cochrane in the Manys of Bar, Thomas Stewart of Flafwod. Several of the men come from Bessie's locality. (Pitcairn 1833: I ii 58).

19   Bessie's confession may have resembled that of East Lothian cunning woman Agnes Sampson who was burnt on Castle Hill fifteen years later. According to an observer, Agnes 'deit maist penitentlie for her sinnis, and abusing of the simple people renuncet the devil, quhom sche oftentymes callit "Fals decever of God's pepill": and had hir only refuge to God's mercie in Christ Jesus, in quhom alane sche was assurit to be saif, as that theif quha hang at his right hand' (Normand 2000: 246). On the other hand, Bessie may not have been so compliant. Her long confinement, her separation from her loved ones, the reluctance or inability of her friends to save her, the fear of imminent death and maybe even the belief in the integrity of her magical activities and the injustice of her sentence, may have worked together to fuel the fires of anger and defiance. In this case, Bessie's final moments may have resembled those of Edinburgh cunning woman, Jean Weir, who was executed in the Grassmarket nearly a hundred years later. Jean resolved to 'die with *all the shame she could*' and to this end she 'cast away hir mantell, hir gown-tayle, and was purposed, as was sayde, to cast off all hir clothes before all the multitude; bot Baylie Oliphant, to whom the business was intrusted, stoped the same, and commanded the executioner to doe his office.' But Jean did not give up her efforts, for when the executioner 'was about to throw hir ovir the leather, she smote the executioner on the chieke' and continued to resist him until the very end (Law 1818: 28–9).

CHAPTER ONE   **A Harsh and Enchanted World**

1   Pitcairn 1833: I ii 52.
2   Although the distinction between 'the common people' and 'the élite' suffices for this discussion, it is a simplistic one and belies the existence of a complex stratified society. At the bottom of the social hierarchy were beggars, paupers, cottagers and labourers; above these were the slightly more prosperous farmers, tradesmen and freeholders; above these the professional persons such as lawyers, clergymen, merchants and officials and above these, the landed gentry and aristocracy. And at the zenith, rested the royal family. This intricate stratification saw élite and popular cultural elements interrelating in complex ways. As Robin Briggs reminds us, in relation to witch trials: 'It is mistaken to think of simple oppositions between popular and learned culture . . . Judges, clerics and peasants shared much of their cultural experience, while their ideas were always interacting' (Briggs 1996: 28).
3   Folklorist Katharine Briggs eloquently describes this symbiotic relationship between magical mentalities and harsh living conditions, claiming that the early modern period was 'a time of eager intellectual curiosity and of alert

senses. People listened better than they do today, and looked better. They were far more callous to some things and more sensitive to others. There were many more superstitions, and yet people lived closer to realities than we do. Death and pain were not hidden as they are now, and most people were religious' (Briggs 1959: 6).

4 Thomas 1991: 46. Thomas is the first to admit that the distinction is simplistic. Later anthropologists recognize that in primitive cultures magical belief is intricately bound up with what can be defined as religious beliefs concerning 'transcendent realities' such as gods and spirits. One such anthropologist explains the interrelation between primitive magic and religion thus: 'Magical dogma asserts that the material characteristics of a particular reality are essential to its intrinsic character. It does not necessarily assert that no partly transcendent reality is also disclosed in it. A sickness which is held to be sent by the ancestors is no less magically conceived because of its theistic reference. It is magically conceived because it asserts that the ancestors have directly determined the material facts, as well as the intrinsic character of the event' (Wilson 1945: 73). One of the aims of this book is to compile evidence to show that fundamentally religious notions concerning 'transcendent realities' (that is, familiar beliefs) were an intrinsic part of popular magical belief and practice in early modern Britain.

5 See Duffy 1992.

6 Thomas 1991: 84 & Duffy 1992: 579.

7 Larner 1981: 140.

8 Black & Thomas 1903: 114.

9 Pitcairn 1833: I ii 52.

10 Ibid.: I ii 52.

11 Ibid.: I ii 56.

12 Historians have criticized Thomas's psychological reductionism and sociological functionalism. Thomas has acknowledged these criticisms and admitted that he did not pay enough attention to, among other things, 'the symbolic or poetic meanings' of magical rituals (see Ginzburg 1991: 4–6 and Barry 1996: 1–45).

13 Thomas 1991: 39.

14 By the laws of inversion, the rites and ritual objects of Catholicism could be used not only for good, but also for harm. It was commonly believed, for example, that prayers recited backwards could create maleficent effects. Similarly malevolent use could be made of holy objects. In 1543, moved by animosity towards a young woman called Elisabeth Celsay, Joanna Meriwether of Canterbury 'made a fire upon the dung of the said Elizabeth; and took a holy candle and dropt upon the said dung. And she told the neighbours that the said enchantment would make the cule [buttock] of the said maid to divide into two parts' (Ewen 1933: 447).

15 Thomas 1991: 52.

16 Ibid.: 70. Despite the high-mindedness of reformers, Protestantism did not completely free itself of magical elements. Some lay people, cunning folk

and even Anglican clergy employed Protestant prayers and rites magically. In addition, some Protestant officials (such as churchwardens) and clergy saw no inconsistency in resorting to cunning folk (see Thomas 1991: 318–32).

17 The controversial conclusions of French historian Jean Delumeau, para-phrased by Christina Larner 1985: 117.

18 Larner 1981: 140.

19 Thomas 1991: 191.

20 Larner 1981: 172–3.

21 Thomas 1991: 195.

22 Ibid.: 194.

23 Ibid.: 192.

24 Ibid.: 191 & 192. Such irreverence could also be expressed through humour. After hearing a sermon on the text, *Thou art Peter and upon this rock I will build my church*, a sixteenth-century tailor went on to an alehouse and 'taking a full pot in his hand in jesting manner pronounced these words: "Upon this rock I will build my faith". And there being in the company one whose name was Peter he applied the matter unto him, saying, "Thou art Peter", and then, taking the pot he said, "But upon this rock I will build my church"' (Thomas 1991: 192).

25 Ibid.: 196 & Norden 1967: 411.

26 Thomas 1991: 197.

27 The use of the term 'fairy' was widespread in the period, being a blanket term for a diverse group of spirits. Many other terms, often regional, were also employed to signify fairy-type spirits such as 'elves', 'faunes', 'puckrels', 'brownies', 'siths', 'Robin Goodfellowes', 'good people', 'good neighbours', 'subterraneans' and so on.

28 Pitcairn 1833: I ii 52–3 & 56–7.

29 The three most popular contemporary theories as to the nature and ontology of the types of spirit covered by the term 'fairy' were summed up by the anonymous seventeenth-century author of *A Discourse concerning Devils and Spirits*: 'Many have insisted upon the Natures of these Astral Spirits: some alledging, That they are part of the faln Angels, and consequently subject to the torments of Hell at the last Judgment: Others, That they are the departed souls of men and women, confined to these outward Elements until the Consummation: Lastly, others, as Del rio, Nagar the Indian Magician, and the Platonists affirm, That their nature is middle between Heaven and Hell; and that they reign in a third Kingdom from both, having no other judgment or doom to expect for ever' (Latham 1930: 41).

30 Stuart 1841: 120.

31 Law 1818: lxxvi.

32 Latham 1930: 45; Hunter 2001: 150.

33 Sanderson 1976: 58.

34 Black and Thomas 1903: 113.

35 Latham 1930: 47.

36 Briggs discusses the distinction between solitary and trooping fairies at length in *The Vanishing People* (see Briggs 1978).
37 Briggs 1959: 171; Kirk 1976: 49–50; Beaumont 1705: 396.
38 Thomas 1991: 728.
39 Burton 1896: 1 212.
40 Hole 1977: 47.
42 Pitcairn 1833: I ii 57 & 53.
42 Briggs 1959: 112.
43 Rosen 1991: 214.
44 Thomas 1991: 725–6.
45 See Cowan 2001, Maxwell-Stuart 2001, and Purkiss 2001.
46 Sharpe 2001: 58.
47 Stuart V1 & 1: 159.
48 Sanderson 1976: 51.
49 Latham 1930: 31 & Thomas 1991: 726.
50 Scot 1972: 121; Latham 1930: 31–2.
51 Aubrey 1972: 203 & Bovet 1975: 124.
52 Webster 1677: 302 & Latham 1930: 33.
53 Latham 1930: 33.
54 Halliwell 1845: 186.
55 Pitcairn 1833: III ii 602–12. In 1975 Nairnshire became part of the newly created 'Highland Region', however the term is retained here for easier geographical reference.
56 Briggs 1959: 12.

CHAPTER TWO **Cunning Folk and Witches**

1 This gender bias reflects the fact that most of the information we have about British cunning folk in this period comes from witch-trial records. The question as to why women were more likely to be accused of witchcraft than men remains a matter of debate among historians. The fact that fears about witchcraft were predominantly played out in a domestic sphere, and were consequently more closely related to the activities and concerns of women is likely to be significant in this context.
2 Owen 2003: 119–61.
3 See Macfarlane 1991 and Thomas 1991.
4 See Owen 2003.
5 See Maxwell-Stuart: 2001. Also relevant here are Hilda Ellis Davidson's *The Seer in Celtic and Other Traditions* (a collection of papers given at a symposium on the seer in Oxford in the 1980s) and the assortment of writings and letters on the subject of Scottish seers and other supernatural curiosities derived from the pens of a variety of seventeenth-century scholars and clergymen, published under the title, *The Occult Laboratory: Magic, Science and Second Sight in Late Seventeenth-Century Scotland* (see Davidson 1989 and Hunter 2001).

6 Thomas 1991: 293–4.
7 Macfarlane 1991: 117–18.
8 Scot 1972: 3; Burton 1896: II 7.
9 Thomas 1991: 295.
10 Larner 1981: 79.
11 Rosen 1991: 22; Thomas 1991: 307.
12 This can be clearly seen in Bessie Dunlop's trial records, which state that she was arraigned for 'Sorcerie, Witchcraft, and Incantatioune, with Invocatioun of spretis' and so on.
13 See Sharpe 1996.
14 Purkiss 1994: 145–76; Roper 1994: 19–20.
15 Gibson 1999: 35.
16 Ibid.: 25 and 34.
17 Pitcairn 1833: I ii 53.
18 Thomas 1991: 6; Picard 2000: 77–8.
19 Thomas 1991: 14.
20 Hole 1953: 79–98.
21 McPherson 1929: 243.
22 Burton 1896: II 7.
23 Pitcairn 1833: I ii 54.
24 Ibid.: II 536.
25 Thomas 1991: 211–12.
26 Pitcairn 1833: II 536.
27 Ibid.: I ii 54.
28 Normand 2000: 265–6.
29 Ewen 1933: 451.
30 Guiley 1989: 346.
31 Normand 2000: 266.
32 Stuart 1841: 120.
33 Levack 1992: 357.
34 Pitcairn 1833: II 537.
35 Halliwell 1845: 297; Thomas 1991: 219. The breath could be used as a healing aid in other ways. Rutland cunning man William Berry, for example, invoked a healing fairy by breathing *into* a woman's mouth (see Rosen 1991: 377).
36 Levack 1992: 360. Such repetition of ritual actions was common. While Janet Dickson ran 'thrise about the said thorn withershines' and Andro Man cured Alexander Simpson by putting him nine times forward through a hesp of 'unvatterit' yarn, Perthshire cunning woman Isobel Haldane (1623) described yet another variation on the theme. In an attempt to cure a sick child she made: 'thrie severall caikis, everie ane of thame of ix curneis [handfulls] of meill [meal], gottin fra ix wemen that wer maryit madynnis; maid ane hoill in the crowne of everie ane of theme, and pat ane bairne, throw it thrie tymeis, "in the name of the father, Sone and Halye Goost," to wemen that pat the saidis bairnes thryse throw bakward, wfeing the saidis wordis' (Pitcairn 1833: II 538).

37 Thomas 1991: 217.
38 Pitcairn 1833: I ii 54–5.
39 Davenport 1646: 3.
40 Pitcairn 1833: I ii 55.
41 Ibid.: I ii 55.
42 Ibid.: I ii 55.
43 Thomas 1991: 278.
44 Ibid.: 253–5.
45 Ibid.: 262.
46 Macfarlane 1991: 125.
47 Thomas 1991: 262.
48 Sanderson 1976: 67–8.
49 Pitcairn 1833: I ii 56.
50 Normand 2000: 233.
51 Sanderson 1976: 74.
52 Hunter 2001: 149.
53 Thomas 1991: 709.
54 Sanderson 1976: 61.
55 Normand 2000: 262.
56 Thomas 1991: 278.
57 In an age when so much depended on the success of the annual harvest, it is hardly surprising that cunning folk found themselves asked to predict the weather or give advice on how to secure a good crop. Andro Man advised anxious farmers to 'lay the harrowis on the land befoir the corne be brocht furth, and hald aff the crawis quhill ane rig be brockin . . . [then] say ane oration, quhilk thow hes perquier, nine sindrie tymes, and that being done, the cornis sall cum saiff to the barne that yeir' (Stuart 1841: 122).
58 Rosen 1991: 375.
59 Gifford 1603: 10.
60 Valletta 2000: 112.
61 Thomas 1991: 220.
62 Heywood 1888: 266.
63 Levack 1992: 353.
64 Rosen 1991: 142.
65 Ibid.: 87.
66 Levack 1991: 408.
67 Ewen 1933: 448.
68 Rosen 1991: 97.
69 Ewen 1933: 200–1. In Windsor in 1579, where four witches were accused of multiple murder, one of their company, 'Mother Dutten', allegedly 'made four pictures of red wax, about a span long, and three or four fingers broad [of the victims] . . . and the said Mother Dutten, by their council and consent, did stick an hawthorn prick against the left sides of the breasts of the images, directly there where they thought the hearts of the persons to be set whom the same pictures did represent, and thereupon within short space, the said four persons, being suddenly taken, died' (Rosen 1991: 87).

70 See Trevor-Roper 1969 and Cohn 1993.
71 See Macfarlane 1991 and Thomas 1991.
72 Rosen 1991: 120–1.
73 Ewen 1933: 313.
74 Ibid.: 193.

CHAPTER THREE **The Magical Use of Spirits**

 1 Rosen 1991: 78–82.
 2 Macfarlane 1991: 25.
 3 Macfarlane 1991: 24. Another example can be found in the case of Essex witch Joan Waterhouse, 1566. The indictment does not mention familiars, merely stating that Joan was 'indicted for witchcraft . . . she bewitched Agnes Browne of Hatfield Peverel, spinster, so that she lost the use of her right arm and leg'. However, the pamphlet which detailed the activites of Joan and her mother Agnes stated that Joan employed the services of a familiar in the form of an 'evil-favoured dog with horns on his head' (see CAR 1985: 46 & Rosen 1991: 78).
 4 Sharpe 2003: 227.
 5 Briggs 1996: 28. In his introduction to *A Witchcraft Reader* in 2002, Darren Oldridge sums up academic opinion as regards the sabbath in the following way: 'Carlo Ginzburg and Éva Pócs argue in this book that the origins of the sabbat can be found in folk beliefs. On the opposite extreme, some historians have argued that *all* the elements in witchcraft accusations should be regarded as learned fantasies . . . The majority of historians occupy ground somewhere in between' (Oldridge 2002: 3).
 6 Sharpe 1996: 7.
 7 See Oldridge 2000; Valletta 2000; Miller 2002.
 8 See MacCulloch 1921 and Briggs 1959.
 9 Thomas 1991: 727; Russell 1972: 52.
10 Purkiss 1996: 135 and 159–62; Purkiss 2001: 85–157; Wilby 2000: 283–305.
11 Sharpe 2003: 228.
12 See Henderson 2001 and Maxwell-Stuart 2001.
13 Oldridge 2002: 10. For Continental studies in this context see Henningsen 1990; Klaniczay 1990; Pócs 1989 & 1999; Behringer 1998; Edsman 1967.
14 Thomas 1991: 680. Thirty years later James Sharpe echoed that: 'The precise reason for the prominence enjoyed by familiars in accounts of English witch-craft remains elusive' (Sharpe 1996: 71).
15 Sharpe 2001: 61–2.
16 Thomas 1991: 317.
17 Davies 2003: 95.
18 One of the reasons for this oversight may be a general disinterest in spirit-conjuration. Another may be that references to cunning folk in witch-trial records are often missed among all the furore about witches and demono-logical stereotypes. Scholars who have looked for cunning folk in witch-trial

records have generally, in the opinion of this author, underestimated the numbers of those charged with witchcraft who were likely to have been working as cunning folk (see Macfarlane 1971: 127–8 & Davies 2003: 168). The arguments about familiars developed in this book support the view that many of those convicted as witches were, in fact, performing the role of cunning women, albeit cunning women who swayed towards the 'dark-side'.

19 See Beaumont 1705.
20 See Sanderson 1976; Law 1818: lxxvi.
21 Webster 1677: 300.
22 Scot 1972: 3.
23 See Kittredge 1956: 23–40; Murray 1921: 19–27; Ewen 1929: 2–5; Ewen 1933: 26–30.
24 Ibid.: 70.
25 Thomas 1991: 307.
26 Rosen 1991: 53–4.
27 Larner 1981: 138–9.
28 Pitcairn 1833: II 543.
29 Ewen 1933: 451.
30 Normand 2000: 245.
31 Beaumont 1705: 185.
32 Valletta 2000: 112.
33 Rosen 1991: 7.
34 Ibid.: 84.
35 Ibid.: 57–8.
36 Ibid.: 58.
37 Pitcairn 1833: I ii 51& 58.
38 Black 1903: 113–14.
39 Stuart 1841: 120.
40 Pitcairn 1833: I ii 51–8; Ibid.: I ii 161–3; Stuart 1841: 119–25; Normand 2000: 231–46; Rosen 1991: 376–8.
41 Pitcairn 1833: III ii 602–16; Black & Thomas 1903: 103–11.

CHAPTER FOUR **Human and Spirit: The Meeting**

1 Smallhead and the King's Sons, Jacobs 1994: 136–7.
2 The Frog Prince, Grimm 1996: 1.
3 A description of the classic spontaneous fairy-encounter can be found in the famous ballad about Thomas the Rymour, which was well-known in the early modern period (see Halliwell 1845: 58).
4 Kinloch 1848: 132; Rosen 1991: 186; Ibid.: 358; Howell 1816: 855.
5 Pitcairn 1833: I ii 51; Kinloch 1848: 112; Normand 2000: 243; Halliwell 1845: 297 and Latham 1930: 175.
6 Howell 1816: 840.
7 Hole 1977: 39.
8 Rosen 1991: 377.

9 Davenport 1646: 12–13.
10 Stuart 1841: 120; Pitcairn 1833: I ii 57.
11 Both cunning folk and witches could communicate with their familiars through voice only, without a visual encounter, although specific reference to purely auditory encounters are rare (see Beaumont 1705: 175–203 for some examples).
12 Pitcairn 1833: I ii 51.
13 McPherson 1929: 130; Stuart 1841: 127.
14 Pitcairn 1833: III ii 604; Kinloch 1848: 132; Howell 1816: 854.
15 Stuart 1841: 124; Black & Thomas 1903: 103; Normand 2000: 225.
16 Martin 1716: 334.
17 Pitcairn 1833: III ii 601.
18 Davenport 1646: 12–13.
19 Rosen 1991: 69.
20 Oldridge 2000: 58 and Russell 1984: 67–9.
21 Gifford 1603: 9.
22 Glanvill 1681: 164–5.
23 The familiar names here are all taken from trial records or witchcraft pamplets. The fairy names are predominantly taken from élite writings (usually in reference to 'popular' belief) and dramatic literature. Personalized names in witchcraft confessions, which can be categorically ascribed to fairies as opposed to being tangled up with demon familiars, are few.
24 Pitcairn 1833: III ii 606.
25 Webster 1677: 301.
26 Pitcairn 1833: I ii 52.
27 Webster 1677: 301; Pitcairn 1833: I ii 52; Ibid.: I ii 163; Normand 2000: 237.
28 Gregory 1991: 36; Thomas 1991: 296.
29 Black 1903: 103; Halliwell 1845: 298.
30 Pitcairn 1833: 1 ii 52–5.
31 Webster 1677: 301.
32 Stuart 1841: 119; Pitcairn 1833: 1 ii 161–3.
33 Halliwell 1845: 298.
34 Normand 2000: 238.
35 Rosen 1991: 377.
36 Beaumont 1705: 104–5.
37 Pitcairn 1833: I ii 53.
38 Henderson 2001: 87.
39 Webster 1677: 301.
40 Rosen 1991: 69.
41 Pitcairn 1833: I ii 54.
42 Sanderson 1976: 69.
43 Dalyell 1834: 470; Latham 1930: 140.
44 Black 1903: 112. Kentish cunning woman Elizabeth Barton, who became famous for making alarming predictions about King Henry VIII in 1533, seems to have possessed a spirit familiar with possible fairy origins. Sir

Thomas More, who interviewed Elizabeth, claimed that she told him that 'of late the Devil, in likeness of a Bird, was flying and fluttering about her in a Chamber' (Kittredge 1956: 64).

45 Pitcairn 1833: I ii 55.
46 Ibid.: I ii 58.
47 Thomas 1991: 709; Sanderson 1976: 61.
48 A number of witches encountered their demon familiar soon after the death of one or more children (see Valletta 2000: 211).
49 James VI & I 1597: 35.
50 Larner 1981: 95.
51 Larner 1981: 95; Stuart 1841: 129.
52 Ewen 1933: 367; Ibid.: 299; Davenport 1646: 9; Law 1818: lxxi.
53 James VI & I 1597: 35.
54 Rosen 1991: 237.
55 Davenport 1646: 13.
56 Ewen 1833: 303; Kinloch 1848: 130.
57 Halliwell 1845: 183; Thomas 1991: 317. Alice made a good living out of the greed of gullible clients. It was also the desire for fairy treasure which prompted early seventeenth-century cunning woman Anne Taylor and her friend Susan Swapper to dig 'in a haunted place near the summer-house in Anne's garden' and 'in a field belonging to a farm at Weeks Green, just outside Rye' (Gregory 1991: 36).
58 McPherson 1929: 47.
59 See an example in Ewen 1833: 249.
60 James VI & I 1597: 35.
61 Rosen 1991: 93.
62 Normand 2000: 225.
63 Ewen 1933: 315.
64 Sharpe 2001: 116.
65 Ewen 1933: 312.
66 Pitcairn 1833: III ii 601.
67 Rosen 1991: 140.
68 Ibid.: 124.
69 Kinloch 1848: 131.
70 Davenport 1646: 5.
71 Ewen 1933: 292.
72 Pitcairn 1833: III ii 608–10.
73 Rosen 1991: 363; Ibid: 366.
74 Kinloch 1848: 123.
75 Rosen 1991: 140.
76 Ewen 1933: 372.
77 Normand 2000: 231–46.
78 Halliwell 1845: 298.
79 Pitcairn 1833: II 537.
80 Black 1903: 109.

81 Sanderson 1976: 56; Burton 1896: 1219.
82 Henderson 2001: 87.
83 Briggs 1978: 57.
84 Briggs 1976: 45–9.

CHAPTER FIVE **The Working Relationship**

1 Pitcairn 1833: I ii 52–6; Rosen 1991: 67–71; Latham 1930: 140; Pitcairn 1833: II 537–8; Ibid: I ii 163; Latham 1930: 174; Stuart 1841: 119–25.
2 Davenport 1646: 9–10; Ewen 1933: 283; Davenport 1646: 5–6; Ewen 1933: 298; Davenport 1646: 1–2; Howell 1816: 856–8.
3 Rosen 1991; Kittredge 1956; 211; Rosen 1991: 74 & 128; Ibid.: 152, 138 & 184; Ibid.: 121, 125 &139; Ibid.: 85; Ewen 1933: 83; Rosen 1991: 133.
4 Davenport 1646: 8.
5 Rosen 1991: 359.
6 Sanderson 1976: 56.
7 Murray 1921: 207–8.
8 Rosen 1991: 183; Ewen 1933: 326; Kinloch 1848: 122; Henderson 2001: 120.
9 Normand 2000: 238.
10 Howell 1816: 848–9.
11 Stuart 1841: 120.
12 Kittredge 1956: 211.
13 See Thomas 1991: 323 and Halliwell 1845: 298.
14 Bovet 1975: 104–5; Rosen 1991: 68.
15 Henderson 2001: 131.
16 Pitcairn 1833: I ii 51.
17 Rosen 1991: 68–9.
18 Normand 2000: 244–5.
19 Webster 1677: 301.
20 Gregory 1991: 36.
21 Rosen 1991: 123; Halliwell 1845: 297.
22 Henderson 2001; 87.
23 Pitcairn 1833: I ii 52.
24 Sanderson 1976: 56–7.
25 Normand 2000: 238.
26 Rosen 1991: 187–8.
27 Ewen 1933: 239 & 277.
28 Kinloch 1848: 121.
29 Ewen 1933: 152.
30 Ibid.: 449–50.
31 Pitcairn 1833: I ii 53, 54 & 57.
32 Rosen 1991: 187. Nearly sixty years later Essex witch Rebecca Jones claimed to have suffered from an equally over-zealous familiar (see Howell 1816: 855).

33   Rosen 1991: 360.
34   Ibid.: 111.
35   Normand 2000: 242.
36   See Pitcairn 1833: II 537 for a typical example.
37   Ibid.: 3 603.
38   Ibid.: I ii 56 & 53.
39   Davenport 1646: 9; Rosen 1991: 123.
40   Law 1818: xcii.
41   Pitcairn 1833: I ii 56.
42   Only a minority of accounts of journeys to the sabbath or into fairyland are richly detailed; nevertheless, these sources can be used as blueprints with which to read between the lines of the less-detailed accounts. In relation to the lengthy confessions concerning the sabbath from Forfar and Auldearn, Christina Larner wrote that they 'do not appear to represent the tip of an iceberg in the sense that many more as rich and detailed lie in the archives unpublished. The examination of numbers of unpublished confessions suggests that the most colourful confessions were published in the nineteenth century. The typical unpublished confession is scrappy. Those of Forfar and Auldearn, however, are typical in the sense that all the features which they mention in such detail are echoed in the often more fragmented confessions still in the archives' (Larner 1981: 153). For reasons which are still unclear, descriptions of both visits to fairyland and attendance at the sabbath occur far more frequently and are far more detailed in Scottish trial records than in those from England. Nevertheless, English descriptions, like the more fragmented ones from Scotland, fit very well into the blueprint provided by the more detailed Scottish accounts.
43   The fullest extrapolation of this hypothesis can be found in Carlo Ginzburg's *Ecstasies* (Ginzburg 1991), although his previous micro-study of the Italian Benandanti, *Night Battles* (Ginzburg 1983) gives a focused introduction into the subject. Follow-up studies such as Gustav Henningsen's '*The Ladies from Outside: An Archaic Pattern of the Witches' Sabbath'* (Henningsen 1990) support Ginzburg's ideas, as do the frequent references to visits to fairyland, and fairy gatherings, in folk tales and ballads throughout Europe since the early Middle Ages.
44   Stuart 1841: 119–25; Pitcairn 1833: III ii 602–14; Rosen 1991: 362–3.
45   Latham 1930: 175.
46   Bovet 1975: 105.
47   Kinloch 1848: 124.
48   Ibid.: 120.
49   Ewen 1933: 342–3.
50   Ibid.: 343.
51   Larner 1981: 155.
52   James VI & I 1597: 74.
53   Pitcairn 1833: I ii 161–3.
54   Webster 1677: 301.

55   Pitcairn 1833: III ii 602–14.
56   That Nairnshire witch Isobel Gowdie's descriptions of travelling in a fairy whirlwind, for example, were firmly rooted in popular belief of the period is corroborated from many quarters. An anecdote containing many of the elements in Isobel's story was sent to John Aubrey in the late seventeenth century by James Garden, Professor of Theology at Aberdeen (see Hunter 2001: 153–4 & Aubrey 1972: 94–5). The late sixteenth-century account of the 'Aerial Adventures of Richard Burt' is also highly relevant here, as are the references to fairy whirlwinds in John Campbell's *Superstitions of the Highlands and Islands of Scotland* (see Rosen 1991: 204–9 and Campbell 1900: 24–5 & 68–9). References can also be found in folk tales from throughout Europe, such as in the Irish tale of *Guleesh* (see Jacobs 1994: 5).
57   Pitcairn 1833: II 537
58   Bovet 1975: 104–6.
59   Larner 1981: 154; Normand 2000: 226. Flight experiences were also intimated by Somerset witch Elizabeth Style, when she claimed that at the end of the sabbath 'all were carried to their several homes in a short space' (Ewen 1833: 343).
60   In trial records from both England and Scotland we find testimony describing encounters with animals which were believed to have been transformed witches. And witches often confessed to such transformations. It was commonly thought that any form of damage to such animals would directly affect the body of the witch. A typical account can be found in Glanvil's *Saducismus Triumphatus*, where the theologian Dr Henry More cites a report about 'an old witch, who being in the shape of a huge cat, had her back broken, and the same night was found dead in her bed injured in like manner' (Ewen 1933: 454).
61   Law 1818: lxxi.
62   Pitcairn 1833: III ii 604 & 611
63   Sharpe 2001: 118.
64   Rosen 1991: 121–5.
65   Ewen 1933: 289. Huntingdonshire witch Francis Moore (1646) claimed that her two familiars, in the form of a black dog, called Pretty, and a white cat, called Tissy, 'crept under her cloathes, and tortured her so that she could not speake' (Davenport 1646: 6).
66   Law 1818: lxxi . Angus witch Helen Guthrie (1661) claimed that cannibalistic acts safeguarded her against breaking such taboos: herself and four companions went 'up to the church wall about the southeist doore, and raisit a young bairn unbaptised, and took his feet, the hands, a pairt of the head and butock, and maid a py thereof, that they might eat of it, and by that meins might never mack a confessione' (Kinloch 1848: 114).
67   Thomas 1991: 733.
68   Halliwell 1845: 183.
69   Henderson 2001: 172.
70   Pitcairn 1833: I ii 163.
71   Ibid.: I ii 56.

CHAPTER SIX   **Renunciation and Pact**

1 Briggs 1959: 202. This is an excerpt from Tom Tit Tot, a traditional English version of Rumpelstiltskin.

2 The Sea-Maiden, Jacobs 1994: I 144.

3 Normand 2000: 67–8.

4 The records from the trials of Scottish witches Thomas Paton and Bessie Graham state that ' the custome of the Justice court is to find charmes relevant, onlie when they proceid from express pactioun with the divell, or from tacite pactioun and whither this be so or not the Lords will judge by the circumstances' (Levack 1992: 358).

5 Aubrey 1972: 203.

6 Pitcairn 1833: I ii 52.

7 Ibid.: I 163.

8 Webster 1677: 301.

9 Black & Thomas 1903: 113.

10 Briggs 1959: 116.

11 Rosen 1991: 377.

12 Campbell 1900: 40–1.

13 In a popular edition of classic fairy tales by Iona and Peter Opie, at least ten of the 22 traditional tales feature supernatural beings offering help to humans, and in at least five of these help is not given freely, but involves some kind of 'deal' or 'contract' (Opie 1992).

14 Pitcairn 1833: I ii 52.

15 Howell 1816: 839; Ewen 1933: 296.

16 Kinloch 1848: 132.

17 Briggs 1959: 5.

18 Thomas 1991: 317; Halliwell 1845: 300; Cowan 2001: 86–7. Similarly, John Webster claimed that the fairy-like spirit described in an anecdote could not have been an 'evil spirit' because 'it was such a sportful and mannerly Creature, that it would leave them, and not disturb them at their devotions; as also . . . because it denied that it was a Devil, and professed that it hoped to be saved by Christ' (Latham 1930: 47).

19 Stuart 1841: 119–64.

20 Pitcairn 1833: I ii 52.

21 Martin 1716: 392.

22 Ewen 1833: 297.

23 Sanderson 1976: 56.

24 McPherson 1929: 70.

25 Law 1818: 27.

26 Ibid.: lxxi.

27 Shades of similar rituals can be found in other seventeenth-century Scottish sources. James Garden, in a letter to John Aubrey, describes how some Highlanders claimed that: '[the seer] does communicate the same [second-sight] to another: & that in the mean time of the apparition, if on sett his foot upon his who hath it, he will see what he sees, but once given cannot be

recalled or taken away again which scares many from their curiosity' (Hunter 2001:147). For other examples see Hunter 2001: 60 & 191.

28 Sanderson 1976: 64.
29 Rosen 1991: 73–4.
30 Pitcairn 1833: I 163.
31 Ibid.: I ii 52.
32 Ibid.: I ii 53.
33 Rosen 1991: 358.
34 Davenport 1646: 12.
35 Rosen 1991:377.
36 Pitcairn 1833: III ii 608.
37 James VI & I 1597: 39.
38 McPherson 1929: 130.
39 Pitcairn 1833: III ii 602–12; Law 1818: 27.
40 Bovet 1975: 104–6; Murray 1921: 245.
41 Briggs 1976: 394; Pitcairn 1833: I 163.
42 Such beliefs were still extant in relatively modern times. One folklorist maintained that in the early twentieth century the Scots believed that the fairies would abduct you if you broke their taboos. He records a woman claiming, 'Oh it wasna safe to be talking o' the gude folk: maybe they wad be spriting her awa' next' (Mc Pherson 1929: 106).
43 Purkiss 2001: 117.
44 Pitcairn 1833: I ii 53.
45 Pitcairn 1833: I ii 53 & 56.
46 Davenport 1646: 12–13.
47 Ewen 1933: 284.
48 Kinloch 1848: 132. In the following year Isobel Gowdie claimed of the Devil that 'The nixt tyme that I met with him wes in *the New Wardis of Inshoch*, and haid carnall cowpulation and dealling with me. He wes a meickle, blak, roch man, verie cold; and I found his nature als cold within me as spring-wall-water' (Pitcairn 1833: III ii 603).
49 Hole 1977: 45. Ellen's confession reflects the popular belief that fairies invited or coerced humans to mate with them in order to replenish fairy stock. Ellen probably believed that her real children had been taken to fairyland while inferior fairy replicas, that is – changelings – had been left in their place.
50 Howell 1816: 842.
51 Malleus Maleficarum 1971: 243–54.
52 Stuart 1841: 119.
53 Black & Thomas 1903: 112–13.
54 Kittredge 1956: 64.
55 Briggs 1978: 93–117.
56 Halliwell 1845: 58–63.
57 Ibid.: 123.
58 Sanderson 1976: 62.
59 Kittredge 1956: 119.

60 Murray 1921: 88.
61 Ewen 1933: 287.
62 Davenport 1646: 9–10.
63 Ewen 1933: 290.
64 Evans-Wentz 1981: 127–8.
65 Campbell 1900: 20.
66 Rosen 1991: 128.
67 Sanderson 1976: 97.
68 Ibid.: 59–60.
69 Ibid.: 59.
70 Robertson 1910: 262.
71 Rosen 1991: 74 & 122–3 & 125.
72 Howell 1816: 848.
73 In the early twentieth century folklorist Evans-Wentz recorded an old Manx belief which links fairy dogs with trooping fairies. An 86-year-old gentleman claimed that 'This used to happen about one hundred years ago, as my mother has told me: Where my grandfather John watterson was reared, just over near Kerroo Kiel (Narrow Quarter), all the family were sometimes sitting in the house of a cold winter night, and my great grand-mother and her daughters at their wheels spinning, when a little white dog would suddenly appear in the room. Then every one there would have to drop their work and prepare for *the company* to come in: they would put down a fire and leave fresh water for *them*, and hurry off upstairs to bed. They could hear *them* come, but could never see them, only the dog. The dog was a fairy dog, and a sure sign of their coming' (Evans-Wentz 1911: 122).
74 Aubrey 1972: 203; Burton 1977: 193; Scot 1972: 48.
75 Scot 1972: 48.

CHAPTER SEVEN   **Demon and Fairy: The Interface**

1 Pitcairn 1833: I 58.
2 Briggs 1976: 47.
3 Chambers 1870: 324.
4 Rosen 1991: 377.
5 Pitcairn 1833: II 537.
6 Davenport 1646: 12; Rosen 1991: 76 & 358; Black & Thomas 1903: 112.
7 Normand 2000: 207.
8 Ibid.: 245.
9 Black & Thomas 1903: 108–9.
10 Rosen 1991: 107–8.
11 Ibid.: 108.
12 Pitcairn 1833: I ii 55.
13 Éva Pócs observes the same transformatory process occurring in early modern Hungarian witch trials, claiming that: 'In the context of witch trials, the guardian and helping spirits of the witch, or their doubles performing in these

roles, were basically bad, demonic creatures with only a few exceptions. However, this was exactly the point in the witch trials, where witch-hunting demonology and the élite culture in general is rightly presumed to have had a strong influence. During our investigations, it turned out that something else was behind this stratum of demonologized, satanic bewitching spirits: the figures of the "good" dead and "good" guardians.' She then goes on to conclude that 'the partner of the healing witches and their "good" helping spirits show a great similarity to the fairy magicians and their guardian spirits. The reason for this lies in the presumed relationship, a collateral relationship, so to speak, between Central and Eastern European fairies and witches of the early Modern Age' (Pócs 1999: 110–11).

14 Rosen 1991: 382.

15 Ewen 1933: 273.

16 Ordinary people in the medieval period attributed a similar ambivalence to the saints (see Wilson 2000: 62–5).

17 Kinloch 1848: 132.

18 In *Magic in the Middle Ages*, Richard Kieckhefer explores the possibility that 'necromancers held an amoral conception of God, as a being who could be influenced (if not coerced) by prayer to bestow his aid in all sorts of dubious enterprises' (Kieckhefer 1990: 168). The moral ambivalence of learned magicians in the period, and their ambiguous view of both God and familiar spirits, is discussed in more detail in chapters TWELVE and THIRTEEN.

19 Assize records state that in 1566 Essex witch Elizabeth Francis was not given the death sentence despite – if a pamphlet recording the trial is to be believed – having confessed to performing maleficium with the aid of a demon familiar (Cockburn 1978: 48; Rosen 1991: 73–6). Around the middle of the following century, Webster's northcountry cunning man was acquitted, despite his confessed dealings with spirits easily recognizable as fairies (Webster 1677: 301–2).

20 Ewen 1933: 459.

21 Pitcairn 1833: I ii 57.

22 Howell 1816: 847–9; Ewen 1933: 325.

23 Ewen 1933: 212.

24 Law 1818: 23.

25 Some openly confessed to being uncertain of the moral status of the spirits they worked with. Perthshire cunning woman Isobel Haldane (1623) indicated that she was uncertain which spiritual agency had been responsible for carrying her to fairyland several years before (claiming that she had been 'taikin furth, quhidder be God or the Deuill, scho knawis nocht'). This uncertainty, however, did not prevent her from employing the services of the 'man with ane gray beird' whom she met there as a familiar spirit (Pitcairn 1833: II 537). Several decades later, clergyman George Hickes claimed that when he asked young Scottish seer Janet Douglas 'if she thought it [her second-sight] proceeded from a good or evill cause' she cleverly 'turned the question upon me, and asked me what I thought of it' (Hunter 2001: 172).

26 Ewen 1933: 297.
27 Ibid.: 296.
28 Burton 1896: II 8.
29 Normand 2000: 139.
30 Pitcairn 1833: I ii 52.

Introduction to Part II

1 See Gibson 1999.
2 In recent years a number of scholars have examined Nordic literary and oral traditions in an attempt to gain insight into the shamanistic beliefs and practices of pre-Christian Northern Europeans. While these studies have uncovered some fascinating material, specific information relating to beliefs and practices surrounding familiar spirits is still difficult to find (see Blaine 2002).
3 See Thomas 1991 and Macfarlane 1971.
4 See Ginzburg 1983.
5 See Ginzburg 1991.
6 Prominent among these are Klaniczay 1990; Pócs 1989 and 1999; Behringer 1998; Henningsen 1990 and Dömötör 1980.
7 Klaniczay 1990: 144.
8 Harvey 2003: 1. For recent general works on shamanism see Harvey 2003; Hutton 2001; Kalweit 1988; Lyon 1998; Narby 2001; Vitebsky 2001 and Walsh 1990.

CHAPTER EIGHT   **The Shaman's Calling**

1 Gillin 1956: 133; Campbell 1984: 161; Kalweit 1988: 133 & 132 & 120 respectively.
2 Lyon 1998: 351.
3 Olson 1967: 143.
4 Kalweit 1988: 40. In the narratives of both cunning folk, witches and contemporary shamans you can find the attire of the familiar spirit described as 'old-fashioned' (see Pitcairn 1833: I ii 51). 'Old-fashionedness' is also more generally cited as a feature of fairy attire (see Briggs 1976: 110–11).
5 Halifax 1980: 121. This is very similar to the description of a familiar given by Dorsetshire cunning man John Walsh in 1566. Walsh claimed that the familiar 'would sometime come unto him like a gray-blackish culver, and sometime like a brended dog, and sometime like a man in all proportions, saving that he had cloven feet' (Rosen 1991: 69).
6 Drury 1996: 44.
7 Kalweit 1988: 9.
8 Olson 1967: 143; Rasmussen 1927: 127.
9 Drury 1996: 42.
10 Kalweit 1988: 138.

11 Eliade 1989: 39.
12 Rasmussen 1908: 146.
13 Narby 2001: 56.
14 Kalweit 1988: 120. For a full account of this remarkable shaman's experiences see Gillin 1956: 131–6.
15 Rasmussen 1908: 306. Bereavement was also the trigger for a Californian Wintu shaman who described how 'When I sorrowed for my son, through that I received command of a spirit power'. Similarly a North American Quinault shaman met his whale helping spirit after 'His brother had died and as the surviving brother he went every day to a rocky island to mourn' (Lyon 1998: 261 & Olson 1967: 154 respectively).
16 Olson 1967: 152. The North American Twana shaman, 'Sore-Eye Bill', on the other hand, sought out his helping spirits when suffering less dramatic, but nevertheless keenly-felt, misfortunes. An account reads that one day the shaman watched his father gamble away all his possessions: 'And when his father had lost everything he turned to Bill, took the blanket off his back, bet it, and lost that too. This was such a shame to . . . [Sore-Eye Bill] that he went up to . . . Tekiu Point, a point about nine miles north of Dewatto, intending either to get power or commit suicide' (Elmendorf 1993: 166).
17 Eliade 1989: 53.
18 Lewis 1975: 61.
19 Kalweit 1988: 138.
20 Lyon 1998: 230.
21 Kalweit 1988: 128.
22 Lewis 1971: 50.
23 Lyon 1989: 208.
24 Fortune 1969: 38.
25 Olson 1967: 144.
26 Kalweit 1988: 88.
27 Lyon 1998: 210.
28 Campbell 1984: 161.
29 Rosen 1991: 122–3.
30 Park 1938: 23.
31 Kalweit 1988: 120.
32 Eliade 1989: 305.
33 Halifax 1980: 52.
34 Densmore 1922: 129.
35 Hutton 2001: 54–5.
36 Lyon 1998: 176.
37 Ibid.: 148.
38 Bourgeois 1994: 48–9. The abilities which helping spirits can confer in this quarter can be extremely powerful. One Canadian Iglulik shaman claimed that his spirits enabled him to see 'far ahead of him, through mountains, exactly as if the earth were one great plain, and his eyes could reach to the end of the earth. Nothing is hidden from him any longer; not only can he see things far, far away, but he can also discover souls' (Rasmussen 1929: 113).
39 Dixon 1905: 265; Bourgeois 1994: 60.
40 Dixon 1905: 282.
41 Since the work of Margaret Murray has been discredited historians have shied

away from considering the possibility that individuals may have grouped together to perform magical ritual in the period. The perspectives drawn in this book, however, suggest that we cannot rule out the possibility that 'ecstatic cult', that is, groups of individuals who came together for the purposes of communal trance experience, may have existed in some parts of Britain in this period. The subject awaits further investigation.

42 Hutton 2001: 91.
43 For a summing up of North American beliefs surrounding the vision quest see Lyon 1998: 361–3. Knud Rasmussen, R. F. Fortune and Roland Dixon mention similar invocatory procedures (see Rasmussen 1927: 82–4; Fortune 1969: 53–7; Dixon 1904: 24–6).
44 Hutton 2001: 91.
45 Rasmussen 1908: 154.
46 Densmore 1922: 128.
47 Rasmussen 1927: 31.
48 Ibid.: 122. For an early modern example see Hunter 2001: 149.
49 Kalweit 1988: 122.
50 Ibid.: 187.
51 Eliade 1989: 306.
52 Halifax 1980: 88.
53 Du Bois 1935: 97.
54 Rasmussen 1908: 148.
55 Kalweit 1988: 187.
56 Hutton 2001: 66 and 67.
57 Kalweit 1988: 138.
58 Elwin 1955: 149.
59 Some shamans describe being stripped down to the bones and then given new or cleansed flesh, organs or blood: others witness their flesh and other body parts being torn apart or cut into pieces and then consumed (sometimes after being cooked or dried) while others allow worms to drain their blood until they fall into unconsciousness.
60 Eliade 1989: 108.
61 Kalweit 1988: 106.
62 Rasmussen 1908: 307.
63 Rasmussen 1927: 149. In an elaboration of this belief, the Siberian Yakut believe that the part of the body which the spirits devoured during initiation will determine the compass of the shaman's healing abilities. If, for example, the spirits devour the leg of a shaman he will then be skilled at curing diseases of the leg and so on (Kalweit 1988: 107–8).
64 Ibid.: 307
65 Rasmussen 1908: 357.
66 Eliade 1989: 43.
67 If this belief is considered in the light of the fact that some traditional Arctic communities, to the present day, eat raw flesh as a matter of course, it does not seem so outlandish.

68 Olson 1967: 144.
69 Eliade 1989: 307.
70 Ibid.: 308.
71 Specific beliefs surrounding the sucking of blood by animal familiars (as opposed to the more widespread beliefs concerning the giving of 'drops' of blood to the Devil), are almost exclusively found in the South East of Britain, and as such are likely to have been a regional British version of this ancient belief. References to bloodsucking are not so common on the Continent in this period, but instead we find scattered but consistent references to the removal of bones, being torn to pieces, dismembered and devoured, all of which are directly suggestive of shamanic beliefs. Since the work of Ginzburg et al. it is now customary for scholars to refer to these beliefs as related to 'shamanistic initiation' (Pócs 1999: 84).

CHAPTER NINE **Spirit Worlds and High Gods**

1 Rasmussen 1976: 119.
2 Kalweit 1988: 141; Eliade 1989: 147; Lyon 1998: 22; Eliade 1989: 91; Lyon 1998: 78.
3 One shamaness who entered the lower world 'through a narrow opening in the ground' found herself 'in a country with a thick dark-blue sky over her. It was not light there, as it is up here; the sun was smaller and paler than the sun on earth, and it seemed to derive its light from above' (Kalweit 1988: 69). This account is redolent of a seventeenth-century cunning man's description of fairyland: 'being asked by the Judge whether the place within the Hill, which he called a hall, were light or dark, he said indifferent, as it is with us in the twilight' (Webster 1677: 301). The folk tale *Elidor and The Golden Ball*, recorded by Girald Cambrensis in 1188, describes fairyland as beautiful but 'nevertheless obscure, and not brightened with the open light of the sun' (Hazlitt 1875: 353).
4 Rasmussen 1908: 134.
5 Kalweit 1988: 69.
6 Ibid.: 39.
7 Eliade 1989: 105. Like some cunning folk and witches, some shamans seem very keen to accept the invitations of their helping spirit. For a 'trance-dancer' from the Malaysian Temiar, the eagerness to enter the spirit world is intimately tied up with sexual longing: 'There is a male spirit of the fruits that desires to sleep with me [she claims]. Even when I dream, he's there. After a while one doesn't feel right, one's heart is shaky, one thinks only of him, one wants to go off into the jungle' (Harvey 2003: 190).
8 Kalweit 1988: 89. Similarly Bessie Dunlop claimed to have 'lay seik until Thom came agane bak fra thame' after refusing just such an invitation (Pitcairn 1833: II ii 53).
9 Eliade 1989: 216.
10 This is a simplification. Beliefs in 'multiple souls' are commonly found in

primitive cultures, including those of Siberia and the Americas (see Eliade 1989: 215–16). It is possible that such beliefs lay behind early modern Scottish notions surrounding 'co-walkers'. Robert Kirk describes co-walkers as ethereal replicas of a man, replicas who are in 'every way like the man, as a Twin-brother and Companion, haunting him as his shadow and is oft seen and known among men (resembling the Originall) both befor and after the Originall is dead' (see Sanderson 1976: 52 & Briggs 1976: 80).

11 Kalweit 1988: 22.
12 Ibid.: 21.
13 Ibid.: 22–3.
14 Ibid.: 136.
15 Campbell 1984: 160.
16 Ibid.: 161.
17 Rasmussen 1927: 126.
18 Halifax 1980: 105.
19 Kalweit 1988: 141.
20 Elwin 1955: 139.
21 Elmendorf 1993: 213.
22 In the Scottish folk tale *The Smith and the Fairies*, the smith's fourteen year-old son suddenly changes, and 'lay in his bed, silent, yellow and pining' and the local 'knowledgeable' man told him that 'the People of Peace [the fairies] had changed the boy, and left a "sibreagh" [changeling] in his place' (Briggs 1959: 215). In the later Irish tale of *Ethna the Bride*, on the other hand, the newly-married Ethna was bodily carried into fairyland by the fairy king. Under threat of destruction from Ethna's enraged human spouse, the fairy king sent Ethna's motionless bodily form back to the human world but kept her soul with him in fairyland (Briggs 1976: 125–7).
23 Pitcairn 1833: I ii 51.
24 Rasmussen 1927: 28–9.
25 Elmendorf 1993: 213.
26 In *The Smith and the Fairies,* quoted above, the smith retrieves his son by boldly travelling into a fairy hill, armed with his Bible, and retrieving him from his captivity. A short while after the boy was cured 'and the smith and his son prospered' (Briggs 1959: 216). Similarly, the mortal husband of Ethna the Bride finally managed, with magical aid, to retrieve her soul from fairyland and reunite it with her body, after which the couple lived out their mortal lives 'in great happiness' (Briggs 1976: 125–7). In the Irish tale, *Soul Cages*, a young man travels to the bottom of the sea to free the 'poor imprisoned souls' who had been caught by a sea spirit and locked into wicker baskets (Briggs 1959: 228–30).
27 Pitcairn 1833: I ii 55–6 & 58.
28 Eliade 1989: 212.
29 Law 1818: 27; Pitcairn 1833: III ii 602–12.
30 Kalweit 1988: 141.
31 Barbeau 1958: 76–7.

32 Eliade 1989: 203.
33 Kalweit 1989: 142. There are many ancillary correspondences between shamanic journeying and fairyland and sabbath experiences. Like cunning folk and witches, shamans sometimes claim that their journey into the spirit world to become a shaman involves the acquisition of a new identity and a new name, and/or that they are forbidden by the spirit who guides them to either speak to the dead or eat their food. Some of these correspondences have been explored by Ginzburg and others, however there remains much work to be done in this area.
34 Lyon 1998: 405 & 338 respectively.
35 Eliade 1989: 226; Lyon 1998: 19–20. For accounts of John Fian and Isobel Gowdie's experiences (see Normand 2000: 225–6; Pitcairn 1833: III ii 604 and 611.
36 Eliade 1989: 93.
37 Rasmussen 1927: 79.
38 Rasmussen 1908: 313.
39 Park 1938: 10.
40 Lyon 1998: 239.
41 Ibid.: 114.
42 Du Bois 1935: 97.
43 Eliade 1989: 106.
44 Balikci 1967: 200. Some shamans could even perform harmful magic from beyond the grave (see Donner 1954: 75).
45 Hutton 2001: 56.
46 Ibid.: 66.
47 Lyon 1998: 98.
48 Eliade 1989: 113–14.
49 Ibid.: 113–14.
50 Rasmussen 1908: 308.
51 Rasmussen 1927: 39.
52 Kalweit 1988: 187.
53 Halifax 1980: 201.
54 Lyon 1998: 124.
55 Rasmussen 1927: 385–6.

CHAPTER TEN **Phantastics and Phantasms**

1 Thomas 1991: 274.
2 Despite making such comments, Valetta is one of the few British historians to consider questions of ontology in any detail. See Valletta 2000: 6.
3 Davies 2003: 183.
4 Gibson 1999: 1.
5 Harner 1982: 20.
6 James V1 and 1 1591: 41.
7 Bovet 1684: 106.

8   Ewen 1933: 342–3.
9   See Murray 1921.
10 See Cohn 1993.
11 See Ginzburg 1989 & 1992.
12 See Henningsen 1990; Klaniczay 1998 & 1990; Pócs 1999; Behringer 1998; Edsman 1967.
13 Klaniczay 1990: 144; Behringer 1998: 152; Pócs 1999: 14.
14 Gaskill 1994: 134; Maxwell-Stuart 2001: 78–9.
15 Sharpe 2002: 222.
16 Purkiss 2000: 88.
17 McPherson 1929: 130; Sanderson 1976: 54.
18 Glanvil 1681: 157.
19 Halliwell 1845: 183.
20 Ewen 1933: 168.
21 Ibid.: 134.
22 Examples of trance states caused by possession, bewitchment and haunting can be found in Cecil Ewen's encyclopaedic *Witchcraft and Demonianism*. See the accounts of the bewitchment of William Avery, the Fairfax daughters and the Muschamp children (Ewen 1933: 209–11 & 241–4 & 317–19 respectively).
23 See Hunter 2001.
24 Kalweit 1988: 130.
25 Ibid.: 123.
26 Pitcairn 1833: III ii 603.
27 Stuart 1841: 121–2.
28 Davies 2003: 182.
29 Pitcairn 1833: I ii 52.
30 Ewen 1933: 289; Rosen 1991: 377.
31 Davenport 1646: 12.
32 Ewen 1933: 366.
33 Rosen 1991: 88; Ibid.: 79–80. In a variation on this theme, Essex witch Joan Cunny (1589) was believed to possess two spirits which were like black dogs but 'faced like a toad' (Ewen 1933: 168).
34 Ewen 1933: 168 & 241& 284–5.
35 Valletta 2000: 167; Ewen 1933: 221.
36 Ibid.: 307.
37 Ewen 1933: 273; Rosen 1991: 123–4. Familiar-encounters were associated with other, equally strange, physical experiences. Alice Samuel, from Warboys, Huntingdonshire, claimed in 1593 that she had six familiars in the form of 'dun chickens' and that on one occasion she knew they had ceased performing maleficium because they 'are now come into her, and are now in the bottom of her belly, and make her so full, that she is like to burst' (Ewen 1933: 170).
38 Rosen 1991: 93.
39 Ibid.: 187; Hole 1977: 45.

40 Pitcairn 1833: I ii 56.
41 Rosen 1991: 185.
42 Ibid.: 184.
43 Ewen 1933: 304; Rosen 1991: 377; Ewen 1933: 229.
44 Rosen 1991: 74.
45 Murray 1921: 63. Jane is also cited as 'Joan' in contemporary sources.
46 Ibid.: 63.
47 Ornstein 1973: 218–19.
48 Christina Larner emphasizes the fact that the common people in early modern Scotland frequently got together for festive and ritual purposes and that after the Reformation these gatherings often had a 'clandestine' status. However post-Murray historians have been reluctant to consider the possibility that such events were ritualistic, in the sense that they were used a vehicles to facilitate individual or communal trance-experiences, as modelled by some ecstatic cults in continental Europe during this period (see Larner 1981).
49 Hunter 2001: 196.
50 Pitcairn 1833: III ii 608. The stiffness and seeming lifelessness of the body undergoing catatonic trance experiences probably lies behind the notion of 'fairy stocks', that is, the belief that when the individual is either taken, or goes voluntarily into fairyland 'in body', the fairies leave a stiff, lifeless replica of the individual in their place.
51 James VI and I 1597: 74.
52 Sanderson 1976: 98.
53 Reichel-Dolmatoff 1988: 44. This ritual position is found in shamanic cultures throughout the world.
54 Walsh 1990: 119 & 176.
55 Harvey 2003: 367.
56 Walsh 1990: 119.
57 Sanderson 1976: 73–4.
58 Briggs 1959: 104.
59 Agrippa 1651: 450.
60 Hunter 2001: 149.
61 Davidson 1989: 13.
62 Sanderson 1976: 75 & 77.
63 Hunter 2001: 177.
64 Campbell 1984: 156.
65 Hutton 2001: 149.

CHAPTER ELEVEN   Psychosis or Spirituality?

1 Pitcairn 1833: I ii 50.
2 Kittredge 1956: 6; MacCulloch 1921: 243.
3 Henderson 2001: 4; Rosen 1991: 182 & 32.
4 Larner 1981: 152.
5 Nicholson 1987: 54.

6 Narby 2001: 120.
7 Walsh 1990: 74–5.
8 Ibid.: 226.
9 Addison 1921: 19. In his polemic *Of Ghostes and Spirites Walking by Nyght* sixteenth-century Calvinist Ludwig Lavater spends a considerable amount of time illustrating how spirit-sightings could be attributed to melancholia, fear, poor sight or hearing, inebriation, sickness and deception before devoting the rest of the book to marshalling arguments in support of the reality of spirits and the veracity of spirit-sightings (see Lavater 1572).
10 Sanderson 1976: 64.
11 Ibid.: 98.
12 Ibid.: 98.
13 Martin 1716: 335.
14 Normand 2000: 207.
15 Hunter 2001: 150.
16 Howell 1816: 4 847.
17 Ewen 1933: 69 & Valletta 2000: 129.
18 The visionary experiences described by children and adults were truly fantastic. Some good examples can be found in Ewen 1933. See also the pamphlets describing the experiences of Richard Galis and Margaret Cooper.
19 Ewen 1933: 372.
20 See Purkiss 1996 & 2001 and Roper 1994.
21 Purkiss 2001: 90–6.
22 Gaskill 1994: 137.
23 It has been suggested that the word 'shaman' itself is derived from the Tungus verb meaning 'to know' (see Walsh 1990: 8).
24 Walsh 1990: 226; Narby 2001: 98; Harvey 2003: 311.
25 Rasmussen 1927: 386.
26 Lyon 1998: 240.
27 Ibid.: 333.
28 See Frazer 1993.
29 Smart 1977: 75.
30 Collins English Dictionary: Third Edition.
31 Kalweit 1988: 241. Also see Noel 1997: 26–41 for a recent in depth critique of Eliade's work.
32 Walsh 1990: 235.
33 Ibid.: 235.
34 The six personal levels are, in order of ascendance: Sensoriphysical; Phantasmic-emotional; Rep-mind; Rule/role mind; Formal-reflexive and Vision-logic (Wilber 1986: 69–72).
35 Wilber 1986: 72.
36 Walsh 1990: 236.
37 Wilber 1986: 73.
38 Ibid.: 73–4.
39 Walsh 1990: 237.

40 Some shamans describe experiences and insights which suggest that their subtle-level experiences open up into causal or even absolute states, however such suggestions are difficult to prove, and as such are a subject of controversy among scholars. Wilber put forward the 'evolutionist' view that the predominantly subtle-level visionary encounters of the shaman represent a less-evolved level of mystical experience and that the predominantly non-visionary mystical states recorded by classical or 'higher' mystical traditions represent a more advanced and profound level of human consciousness. Rasmussen and Eliade, however, make it quite clear that they believe some shamans capable of attaining highest level mystical realizations, Eliade claiming that the shaman's experiences 'often have the same precision and nobility as the experiences of the great mystics of East and West' (see Campbell 1984: 171 and Eliade 1989: xix & 507).

41 Jung 1986: 326–7.

42 Walsh 1990: 222.

43 Lyon 1998: 298.

44 Drury 1996: 77.

45 Rasmussen 1927: 385.

46 Rasmussen 1976: 118–19.

47 Campbell 1984: 179.

48 Drury 1996: 12.

49 Eliade 1989: 299. As is the case with Catholic saints (and mystics from all the world's developed religions), parts of the shaman's body can be venerated and used as fetish objects.

50 For an insight into the psychological dynamics behind this metamorphosing process see Walsh 1990: 121–37.

51 Rasmussen 1976: 113.

52 Lewis 1975: 37.

53 Rosen 1991: 186–9.

CHAPTER TWELVE **The Unrecognized Mystics**

1 Peters 1978: xi.

2 Thomas 1991: 320–1.

3 Behringer 1998: 142.

4 Thomas 1991: 314; Ibid.: 314 & 246–51.

5 Davies 2003: 31.

6 Thomas 1991: 317. Thomas's view that cunning folk generally worked within a 'materialistic' sphere may have been influenced by comments such as the following, made by the Reverend Thomas Pickering in 1618: 'As the ministers of God do give resolution to the conscience in matters doubtful and difficult' so the 'ministers of satan, under the name of wise men and wise women, are at hand by his appointment to resolve, direct and help ignorant and unsettled persons in cases of distraction, loss or other outward calamities' (Thomas 1991: 314).

7   Larner 1981: 157.
8   McIntosh 1990: 298.
9   See Wilson 2000.
10 Davies 2003: XIII.
11 Purkiss 2001: 85 & 147.
12 CAR 1985: 108.
13 Ewen 1933: 125.
14 Kalweit 1989: 244. Some shamans do not talk about their experiences for other reasons. North American Sioux shaman Lame Deer claimed that 'there are certain things one should not talk about, things that must remain hidden. If all was told, supposing there lived a person who could tell all, there would be no mysteries left, and that would be very bad. Man cannot live without mystery. He has a great need of it' (Kalweit 1989: 244).
15 Ibid.: 241.
16 Ibid.: 241.
17 Coomaraswamy 1977: 296–7.
18 Campbell 1964: 171. Coomaraswamy's condemnation was originally intended as a comment on modern man's inability to appreciate primitive folklore in general, claiming that 'The content of folklore is metaphysical. Our failure to recognise this is primarily due to our own abysmal ignorance of metaphysics and of its technical terms' (Coomaraswamy 1977: 287).
19 Davidson 1989: 2.
20 Rosen 1991: 377; Davenport 1646: 4.
21 Davies 2003: 196.
22 Eliade 1989: 30.
23 Campbell 1984: 168.
24 Walsh 1990: 102–3.
25 Ibid.: 105.
26 Rasmussen 1927: 122.
27 Campbell 1984: 169.
28 Ibid.: 171.
29 Rasmussen 1927: 382.
30 Campbell 1984: 169.
31 Halliwell 1845: 189. If Alice was ever challenged she would 'cunningly, when they were most suspitious of her, put them off with some evasion or other, shadowing all her craft with a kind of simplicitie' (Halliwell 1845: 187).
32 Ibid.: 187.
33 Ibid.: 187.
34 Thomas 1991: 299; law 1818: 23; Murray 1921: 50; Law 1818: 26.
35 See Kieckhefer 1997: 115 & Kieckhefer 1990: 168–71.
36 Thomas 1991: 320.
37 Law 1818: 23.
38 Ibid.: 22–3.
39 Underhill 254–5.
40 Watts 1978: 43.

41 Johnston 1985: 58.
42 Gifford 1603: 116.
43 Thomas 1991: 314; Ibid.: 764; Ewen 1933: 69.
44 Thomas 1991: 316.
45 Ibid.: 299–300.
46 Scot 1972: 7.
47 Perkins 1618: 638 and 652.
48 Thomas 1991: 314 and 317.
49 Ibid.: 316–17.

CHAPTER THIRTEEN **Greedigut and the Angel Gabriel**

1 An easily accessible and first-hand introduction into Jung's thought is found in his autobiography *Memories, Dreams and Reflections*. The book is also a unique insight into the workings of the contemporary visionary mind (see Jung 1986). For a clear and concise exposition of Jung's life and thought see *On Jung* (Stevens 1990).

2 See Hillman 1972 & 1983, Moore 1992, 1994 & 1996 and Watkins 1984.

3 I have taken these examples from Kalweit 1988: 124–6.

4 See the case of Leicestershire cunning woman Anne Baker in Rosen 1991: 374.

5 Although the initial encounter with a familiar was likely to have been visual, it is possible that subsequent to this event, when a cunning woman 'asked' or 'conjured' her familiar in order to gain divinatory or healing advice, a purely auditory response may often have been sufficient. This communication may have occurred in conjunction with a memory of the visual appearance of the familiar (gained from previous visionary encounters) but the memory would have resembled an ordinary act of imagination (similar to holding a picture of a friend in the 'mind's eye' while thinking of them) as opposed to a visionary experience proper. In this sense, day-to-day recourse to familiars could have resembled the process of prayer, as much as the process of conjuration.

6 Kempe 1994: 169; Goodman 2002: 107. Christian traditions describe different kinds of auditory phenomena, ranging from those experienced through the 'bodily ears' to the more profound communications received through the 'ears of the soul'. Although there is no scope to go into these differences here, an examination of this subject would undoubtedly contribute to our understanding of the relationship between magical practitioners and their familiars.

7 Ward 1994: 327–8. For specific examples see Smoley 2000: 7–10 and Nicholson 1988: 184. The idea of the mystical guide was strong in neo-platonic belief, magician Cornelius Agrippa claiming that every man possesses a personal spirit, or 'genius', which is 'given by God, it being universal, and above Nature' and that this spirit 'directs the Soul, still suggesting good Thoughts, and enlightens us, tho' it be not always observ'd:

But when we are purify'd, and live in a Calm, then it's perceiv'd by us; then it speaks, as it were, with us . . . and labours continually to bring us to sacred Perfection' (Beaumont 1705: 5).

8   A good discussion on these themes, which highlights the influences of both contemporary religious and pre-Christian beliefs in the visionary experiences of Swedish cunning women, can be found in Carl-Martin Edsman's paper titled *A Swedish Female Folk Healer from the Beginning of the 18th Century* (see Edsman 1967: 120–65). See also Behringer 1998 & Klaniczay 1984 & 1990.

9   Gibson 1999: 34.

10 Goodman 2002: 105.

11 According to Denise Baker adepts were encouraged to develop 'an imaginative participation in the events of Jesus' life. The meditator is encouraged to close the gap between the present time and the past time of historical Christ by being engaged "either as an eyewitness or as an actor in the drama of the event."' In a fourteenth-century translation of *Meditationes vitae Christi* the adept is urged to cast behind him 'all other occupations and business; and he who makes himself present in his thought as if he saw completely with his bodily eye all the things that befell concerning the cross and the glorious passion of our lord Jesus, not briefly and fleetingly, but lovingly, busily, abundantly, and lastingly' (see Baker 1994: 44–5).

12 In the medieval Christian tradition, distinctions were made between Corporeal visions (in which the individual experiences 'a sensation equivalent to that which an external object would produce'); Imaginative visions (in which the vision 'is the sensible representation of an object by the action of the imagination alone'); and Intellectual visions ('in which no sensible image is perceived, but the intelligence is enlightened directly'). The visionary experiences of cunning folk and witches, like those of shamans, seem to correspond most closely to the Corporeal and Imaginative categories (which also correspond to phenomena experienced on Wilber's 'subtle level' of mystical experience) – although, as argued in previous chapters, these experiences may have opened up to higher levels of contemplation (see Julian of Norwich 1952: xvi–xix). A deeper look at the precise ways in which the visionary experiences of shamans, cunning folk and witches fit into this categorization system would be an interesting line of research.

13 Klaniczay 1990: 95–110 & 129–50.

14 Hilton 1957: 11–12.

15 Teresa of Ávila 1987: 304.

16 Halliwell 1845: 300.

17 Henderson 2001: 86–7; Thomas 1991: 317.

18 Rosen 1991: 117–25.

19 Pitcairn 1833: I ii 51; Pitcairn 1833: 2 537; Normand 2000: 225; Black & Thomas 1903: 103.

20 Normand 2000: 257; Larner 1981: 141; Davenport 1646: 12.

21 See Ewen 1933: 241; Davenport 1646: 13; Howell 1816: 834 for some examples.

22 Lavater 1929: 108.

23 Many of the spirits and deities found in non-Christian religions, seem strange to modern western eyes, though they are wholly congruent with their surroundings: the jackal and crocodile-headed deities of the ancient Egyptians; the fauns and centaurs of Ancient Greece; the bloodthirsty Kali of the Hindus, with her necklace of skulls; or conversely, Ganesh – a little pot-bellied being with an elephant's head and a penchant for good food and business – who is currently one of the most popular and revered gods in India. Sacred beings as represented by tribal societies, which tend to an even higher level of zoomorphic representation, are even more incongruous to modern western eyes.

24 Thomas 1991: 726: Latham 1930: 31.

25 Glanvil 1681: 164–5; Pitcairn 1833: I ii 57; Halliwell 1845: 297.

26 Briggs 1976: 425–6.

27 Henderson 1879: 257.

28 Thomas 1983: 94.

29 Ibid.: 95.

30 Smith 1999: 75.

31 Picard 1997: 181.

32 Ewen 1933: 285.

33 Byrne 1961: 162.

34 Thomas 1983: 98.

35 Ibid.: 98.

36 Lyon 1998: 351; Olson 1967: 143.

37 Fortune 1969: 69.

38 Rosen 1991: 184; Davenport 1646: 3–4; Howell 1848: 840.

39 Lavater 1929: 246; Kempe 1994: 42; Pitcairn 1833: III ii 603; Ewen 1933: 289.

40 Hilton 1957: 12.

41 Kieckhefer 1984: 156.

42 St Teresa of Ávila confirmed to her companions that she had seen a recently deceased mutual acquaintance 'ascend into heaven with the greatest joy' and claimed elsewhere that 'It has pleased the lord to show me the degrees of glory to which some souls have been raised, and he has shown them to me in the places assigned to them' (Theresa of Ávila 1987: 292 & 294).

43 Kempe 1994: 147 & 79. Margery Kempe herself claimed that the priest to whom she dictated her experiences 'asked her questions many different times about things that were to come – things of which the outcome was unsure and uncertain to anybody at that time – asking her to pray to God and discover when our lord would visit her with devotion, what the outcome would be' (Kempe 1994: 90).

44 Ibid.: 89–90. Margery claimed that she had 'Many more such revelations' but like a true Christian, she was always very wary of them (ibid.: 90).

45 Normand 2000: 238.
46 James 1961: 62.
47 Kieckhefer 1997: 42.
48 Thomas 1991: 321.
49 For a typical example see Ewen 1933: 69.
50 Duffy 1992: 160.
51 Julian of Norwich 1952: 67.
52 Kempe 1994: 301, 115 & 80.
53 Goodman 2002: 107.
54 Kempe 1994: 52 & 256.
55 Petroff 1986: 182.
56 Kempe 1994: 129 & 196.
57 Ibid.: 179–80.
58 Petroff 1986: 19.
59 Pitcairn 1833: III ii 601; Ibid.: I ii 52; Stuart 1841: 39; Ewen 1933: 299; Rosen 1991: 377; Davenport 1646: 9; Ewen 1933: 341; Kinloch 1848: 121.
60 Larner 1981: 95; Ewen 1933: 372.
61 Law 1818: 27; Pitcairn 1833: I ii 54.
62 Teresa of Ávila 1987: 301.
63 Pitcairn 1833: II 537.
64 Ibid.: I ii 163.
65 Kalweit 1988: 143. See Evola 1983 for a wide-ranging and in-depth analysis of the subject.
66 Petroff 1986: 196. Margery Kempe claimed that Christ came to her and said 'Therefore I must be intimate with you, and lie in your bed with you. Daughter, you greatly desire to see me, and you may boldly, when you are in bed, take me to you as your wedded husband . . . Therefore you can boldly take me in the arms of your soul and kiss my mouth, my head, and my feet as sweetly as you want' (Kempe 1994: 126–7).
67 Ibid.: 123.
68 Black & Thomas 1903: 113; Howell 1816: 842.
69 Baker 1994: 143; Kempe 1994: 250; Teresa of Ávila 1987: 301.
70 Kieckhefer 1984: 157.
71 Ibid.: 158. St Teresa of Ávila provides us with an equally evocative description: 'In a rapture, I saw a representation of her [the Virgin Mary's] ascent into heaven, of the joy and solemnity with which she was received, and of the place where she now is. It would not be possible for me to explain how this happened. My spirit was filled with great bliss at the sight of such glory, and the vision had great fruits. For I was left with a strong desire to serve that lady, because of her great merits' (Teresa of Ávila 1987: 305).
72 Purkiss 2001: 147.
73 Pitcairn 1833: I ii 163 ; Ewen 1933: 342; Normand 2000: 237; Law 1818: lxxi; Stuart 1841: 121.
74 Pitcairn 1833: III ii 611.
75 Ibid.: I ii 52.

76 See the case of Suffolk witch Thomas Everard (Ewen 1933: 287) and of course Essex witch Joan Prentice (Rosen 1991: 186–9).

77 Sweet smells and tastes are frequently recorded by contemplatives who reach high stages of meditation. The anonymous author of *The Cloud of Unknowing*, with characteristic austerity, warns that such experiences are distractions created by the Devil and should be guarded against (Underhill 1922: 237–8).

78 Valletta 2000: 168.

79 James VI & I 1597: 74.

80 Rasmussen 1976: 119.

81 Ibid.: 120.

82 Eliade 1989: 291; Rasmussen 1927: 28–9. Eliade claims that this desire for mystical joy can set the shaman apart from his community, in the sense that it lies behind his 'liking for solitude, his long dialogues with helping spirits, and his need for quiet' (Eliade 1989: 291).

83 Ewen 1933: 69; Ibid.: 152; Ibid.: 450; Purkiss 2001: 127.

84 See note 5, chapter 13.

CHAPTER FOURTEEN   **The Freedom of Magic**

1 Walsh 1990: 119.

2 Pitcairn 1833: I ii 52.

3 Rosen 1991: 43.

4 Walsh 1990: 162.

5 Rosen 1991: 43.

6 Thomas 1991: 20.

7 Valletta 2000: 121.

8 Gaskill 1994: 133.

9 Rasmussen 1927: 381.

10 Johnston 1985: 131& 136. The link between suffering and mystical insight has another facet. Johnston notes later that 'the further one enters the thicket of the joyful and ecstatic mystical life the greater becomes one's capacity for suffering – a suffering that is redemptive' (Johnston 1985: 136).

11 Olson 1985: 543–7.

12 Similarly, Dewi Rees claimed that out of 293 Welsh widows and widowers almost half admitted to experiencing a 'hallucination' of their dead spouse within ten years of the latter's death (Rees 1971). W. F. Matchett revealed that hallucinations are common among North American Hopi Indian women, the bereaved claiming to 'speak to the apparition [of their dead spouse] as if it was real' (Valletta 2000: 212).

13 Thomas 1991: 21.

14 See Matossian 1989.

15 Sanderson 1976: 54.

16 Briggs 1959: 163.

17 Latham 1930: 33.

18 Lavater 1929: 222.
19 Scot 1972: 86.
20 McPherson 1929: 296.
21 Donner 1954: 69.
22 In *An Introduction to the Mystical Qabalah*, Alan Richardson claims that for Jung 'it was vital that Western Man rediscover magic. He saw life in terms of myths and rituals and the religious quest. Over and above all the self-styled Adepts and Hierophants, *Jung was by far the greatest magician of this century* [my italics]' (Richardson 1981: 16).
23 See Davies 1999.
24 See Thomas 1991.
25 Larner 1989: 157.
26 Lewis 1975: 205.
27 Walsh 1990: 116.
28 Rasmussen 1927: 385.
29 Thomas 1991: 730–1.
30 Drury 1996: 90.
31 Fries 1996: 5.

BIBLIOGRAPHY

Addison, Joseph (1921) *Essays of Joseph Addison*, ed. John Richard Green, London: Macmillan and Co. Ltd.

Agrippa, Heinrich Cornelius (1651) *Three Books of Occult Philosophy*, trans. J. Freake, London: Gregory Moule.

Aubrey, John (1972) 'Remaines of Gentilisme and Judaisme', in J. M. Cohen (ed.), *Three Prose Works*, Sussex: Centaur Press Ltd.

Baker, Denise Nowakowski (1994) *Julian of Norwich's Showings: From Vision to Book*, Princeton, New Jersey: Princeton University Press.

Balikci, Asen (1967) 'Shamanistic Behaviour Among the Netsilik Eskimos', in J. Middleton (ed.), *Magic, Witchcraft and Curing*, New York: Natural History Press.

Barbeau, Marius (1958*) Medicine-Men on the North Pacific Coast*, National Museum of Canada, Bulletin No. 152. Anthropological Series No. 42, Canada: Department of Northern Affairs and National Resources.

Barry, J., Hester, M. and Roberts, G. (eds) (1996) *Witchcraft in Early Modern Europe: Studies in Culture and Belief* (Past and Present Publications), Cambridge: Cambridge University Press.

Beaumont, John (1705) *An Historical, Physiological and Theological Treatise of Spirits, Apparitions, Witchcrafts, and Other Magical Practices,* London.

Behringer, Wolfgang (1998) *Shaman of Oberstdorf: Chonrad Stoeckhlin and the Phantoms of the Night,* trans. H. C. Erik Midelfort, Charlottesville: University Press of Virginia.

Black, G. F. and Northcote W. Thomas (eds) (1903) *Examples of Printed Folklore Concerning the Orkney & Shetland Islands,* London: David Nutt.

Blain, Jenny (2002*) Nine Worlds of Seid-Magic: Ecstasy and Neo-Shamanism in North European Paganism,* London and New York: Routledge.

Bourgeois, Arthur, P. (ed.) (1994) *Ojibwa Narratives of Charles and Charlotte Kawbawgam and Jacques LePique, 1893–1895,* Detroit: Wayne State University Press.

Bovet, Richard (1975) *Pandaemonium, or the Devil's Cloyster,* Wakefield: E. P. Publishing.

Briggs, Katharine (1959) *The Anatomy of Puck,* London: Routledge and Kegan Paul.

—— (1976) *A Dictionary of Fairies*, London: Penguin.

—— (1978) *The Vanishing People: A Study of Traditional Fairy Beliefs*, London: Batsford Ltd.

Briggs, Robin (1996) *Witches & Neighbours: The Social and Cultural Context of European Witchcraft*, London: HarperCollins.

Burton, Robert (1896) *The Anatomy of Melancholy*, ed. Rev. A. R. Shilleto, London: George Bell & Sons.

Byrne, M. St Clare (1961) *Elizabethan Life in Town and Country*, London: Methuen.

Campbell, John Gregorson (1900) *Superstitions of the Highlands and Islands of Scotland*, Glasgow: James Maclehose and Sons.

Campbell, Joseph (1984) *The Way of the Animal Powers*, London: Times Books.

CAR (1985) *The Calendar of Assize Records: Home Circuit Indictments. Elizabeth I and James I*, ed. J. S. Cockburn, Introduction, London: H.M.S.O.

Chambers, Robert (1870) *Popular Rhymes of Scotland*, Edinburgh: W. and R. Chambers.

Cockburn, J. S. (1972) *A History of the English Assizes 1558–1714*, Cambridge University Press.

Cohn, Norman (1993) *Europe's Inner Demons: The Demonization of Christians in Medieval Christendom*, London: Pimlico.

Coomaraswamy, Ananda (1977) *Selected Papers: Traditional Art and Symbolism*, ed. Roger Lipsey, New Jersey: Princeton University Press.

CSD (1977) *Chambers Scots Dictionary*, ed. Alexander Warrack, Edinburgh: W&R Chambers Ltd.

Dalyell, John Graham (1973) *The Darker Superstitions of Scotland*, Norwood, PA: Norwood Editions.

Davenport, John (1646) The *Witches of Huntingdon*, London.

Davidson, Hilda Ellis (ed.) (1989) *The Seer in Celtic and Other Traditions*, Edinburgh: John Donald Publishers Ltd.

Davies, Owen (1999) *Witchcraft, Magic and Culture, 1736–1951*, Manchester: Manchester University Press.

—— (2003) *Cunning Folk: Popular Magic in English History*, London: Hambledon and London.

Deikman, Arthur (1973) 'Deautomatization and the Mystic Experience', in R. E. Ornstein (ed.), *The Nature of Human Consciousness*, California: W. H. Freeman and Co.

Densmore, Frances (1922) *Northern Ute Music*, Bureau of American Ethnology, Bulletin 75, Washington: Government Printing Office.

Dixon, Roland B. (1904) 'Some Shamans of Northern California' in *The Journal of American Folklore*, 17: 23–7.

—— (1905) 'The Northern Maidu' in *Bulletin of the American Museum of Natural History*, 17: 119–346.

Dömötör, Tekla (1980) 'The Cunning Folk in English and Hungarian Witch Trials' in *Folklore Studies in the Twentieth Century*, ed. Venetia Newall, Woodbridge: Brewer.

Donner, Kai (1954) *Among the Samojeds in Siberia*, New Haven.

DOST (1931–90) *Dictionary of the Older Scottish Tongue*, ed. W. A. Craigie, A. J. Aitken *et al.*, vols 1–7, Chicago: University of Chicago Press; Oxford: Oxford University Press.

Drury, Nevill (1996) *Shamanism*, Dorset: Element.

Du Bois, Cora (1935) 'Wintu Ethnography', *University of California Publications in American Archaeology and Ethnology*, vol. 36, No. 1, Berkeley, California: University of California Press.

Duffy, Eamon (1992) *The Stripping of the Altars: Traditional Religion in England 1400–1580,* New Haven and London: Yale University Press.

Edsman, Carl-Martin (ed.) (1967) 'A Swedish Female Folk Healer from the Beginning of the 18th Century' in *Studies in Shamanism*, Stockholm: Almqvist & Wiksell.

Eliade, Mircea (1989) *Shamanism: Archaic Techniques of Ecstasy*, trans. Willard R. Trask, London: Arkana.

Elmendorf, William (1993) *Twana Narratives: Native Historical Accounts of a Coast Salish Culture*, Seattle and London: University of Washington Press.

Elwin, Verrier (1955) *The Religion of an Indian Tribe*, Bombay: Oxford Univerity Press.

Evans Wentz, W.Y. (1981) *The Fairy-Faith in Celtic Countries*, Gerrards Cross, Buckinghamshire: Colin Smythe Ltd.

Evola, Julius (1983) *The Metaphysics of Sex*, London and The Hague: East-West Publications.

Ewen, C. L'Estrange (1933) *Witchcraft and Demonianism*, London: Heath Cranton Ltd.

Fortune, R. F. (1969) *Omaha Secret Societies*, New York: AMS Press.

Frazer, James George (1922) *The Golden Bough: A Study in Magic and Religion,* London: Macmillan.

Fries, Jan (1996) *Seidways: Shaking, Swaying and Serpent mysteries,* Oxford: Mandrake of Oxford.

Gaskill, Malcolm (1994) 'Witchcraft and Power in Early Modern England: the case of Margaret Moore', in Jenny Kermode and Garthine Walker (eds), *Women, Crime and the Courts in Early Modern England*, London: University College London Press, pp. 125–45.

Gibson, Marion (1999) *Reading Witchcraft: Stories of Early English Witches*, London: Routledge.

Gifford, George (1603) *A Dialogue Concerning Witches and Witchcrafts*, London.

Gillin, John (1956) 'The Making of a Witch Doctor' in *Psychiatry*, vol. 19: 131–6.

Ginzburg, Carlo (1991) *Ecstasies: Deciphering The Witches' Sabbath*, trans. R. Rosenthal, London: Penguin.

—— (1992) *The Night Battles: Witchcraft and Agrarian Cults in the Sixteenth and Seventeenth Centuries*, trans. John and Anne Tedeschi, Baltimore: The Johns Hopkins University Press.

Glanvil, Joseph (1681) *Saducismus Triumphatus*, London.

Goodcole, Henry (1621) *The Wonderfull Discoverie of Elizabeth Sawyer a Witch, late of Edmonton, her Conviction and Condemnation and Death*, London.

Goodman, Anthony (2002) *Margery Kempe and her World*, Harlow: Pearson Education Limited.

Gregory, Annabel (1991) 'Witchcraft, Politics and "Good Neighbourhood"', *Past and Present* 133: 31–66.

Guiley, Rosemary Ellen (1989) *The Encyclopedia of Witches and Witchcraft*, New York: Facts on File, Inc.

Halifax, Joan (1980) *Shamanic Voices*, Harmondsworth: Penguin.

Halliwell, James (1845) *Illustrations of the Fairy Mythology of A Midsummer Night's Dream*, London: The Shakespeare Society.

Harner (1982) *The Way of the Shaman*, New York: Bantam.

—— (1987) *The Ancient Wisdom in Shamanic Cultures*, in S. Nicholson (ed.), Shamanism 3–16, Wheaton Illinois: Quest.

Harvey, Graham (2003) *Shamanism: A Reader*, London: Routledge.

Hazlitt, William Carew (1875) *Fairy Tales, Legends, and Romances, Illustrating Shakespeare*, London: Frank and William Kerslake.

Henderson, Lizanne and Edward J. Cowan (2001*) Scottish Fairy Belief: A History from the Fifteenth to the Nineteenth Century*, East Linton: Tuckwell Press.

Henderson, William (1879*) Folk-Lore of the Northern Counties of England and the Borders*, London: W. Satchell, Peyton and Co.

Henningsen, Gustav (1990) '"The Ladies from Outside": An Archaic Pattern of the Witches' Sabbath', in B. Ankarloo and G. Henningsen (eds), *Early Modern European Witchcraft: Centres and Peripheries*, Oxford: Clarendon Press.

Heywood, Thomas (1888) *Plays*, ed. A. Wilson Verity, London: Vizetelly.

Hillman, James (1972) *The Myth of Analysis*, Evanston, Ill.: Northwestern University Press.

—— (1983) *Healing Fiction*, Dallas: Spring Publications.

—— (1994) *The Essential James Hillman: A Blue Fire*, ed. Thomas Moore, London: Routledge.

Hilton, Walter (1957) *The Ladder of Perfection*, Harmondsworth: Penguin.

Hole, Christina (1977) *Witchcraft in England*, London: B.T. Batsford Ltd.

Howell, Thomas Bayley (1816) *A Complete Collection of State Trials: and Proceedings for High Treason and other Crimes and Misdemeanors from the Earliest Period to the year 1783 with notes and other Illustrations*, 10 vols, London: Longmans.

Hunter, Michael (2001) *The Occult Laboratory: Magic, Science and Second Sight in Late Seventeenth-Century Scotland*, Woodbridge, Suffolk: Boydell Press.

Hutton, Ronald (2001) *Shamans: Siberian Spirituality and the Western Imagination*, London: Hambledon & London.

Jacobs, Joseph (ed.) (1994) *Celtic Fairy Tales*, London: Senate.

James VI and I (1597) *Daemonologie, in form of a dialogue, diuided into three bookes*, Edinburgh.

James, E. O. (1961) *Comparative Religion*, London: Methuen & Co.

Johnston, William (1985) *Silent Music: The Science of Meditation*, Glasgow: Fontana.

Julian of Norwich (1952) *Revelations of Divine Love: Shewed to a Devout Ancress by Name Julian of Norwich*, edited from the manuscript by Dom Roger Hudleston O. S. B., London, Burns Oates.

Jung, C. G. (1986) *Memories, Dreams, Reflections*, trans. Richard and Clara Winston, London: Fontana.

Kalweit, Holger (1988) *Dreamtime & Inner Space: The World of the Shaman*, trans. W. Wünsche, Boston & London: Shambhala.

Kieckhefer, Richard (1984) *Unquiet Souls: Fourteenth-Century Saints and their Religious Milieu*, Chicago; London: University of Chicago Press.

—— (1990) *Magic in the Middle Ages*, Cambridge: Cambridge University Press.

—— (1997) *The Forbidden Rites: A Necromancer's Manual of the Fifteenth Century*, Stroud: Sutton Publishing.

Kempe, Margery (1994) *The Book of Margery Kempe*, trans. B. A Windeatt, London: Penguin.

Kinloch, George (1848) *Reliquae Antiquae Scoticae*, Edinburgh.

Kirk, Robert (1976) *The Secret Commonwealth of Elves, Fauns and Fairies*, ed. Stewart Sanderson, Cambridge: The Folklore Society.

Kittredge, George Lyman (1956) *Witchcraft in Old and New England*, New York: Russell & Russell.

Klaniczay, Gábor (1990) 'Hungary: The Accusations and the Universe of Popular Magic', in B. Ankarloo and G. Henningsen (eds), *Early Modern European Witchcraft: Centres and Peripheries*, Oxford: Clarendon Press.

—— (1990) *The Uses of Supernatural Power: The Transformation of Popular Religion in Medieval and Early-Modern Europe*, trans. Susan Singerman, ed. Karen Margolis, Cambridge: Polity Press.

Larner, Christina (1981) *Enemies of God: The Witch-hunt in Scotland*, London: Chatto and Windus.

—— *(1985) Witchcraft and Religion: The Politics of Popular Belief*, ed. Alan Macfarlane, Oxford: Basil Blackwell.

Latham, Minor White (1930) *The Elizabethan Fairies*, New York: Columbia University Press.

Lavater, Ludwig (1929) *Of Ghostes And Spirites Walking By Nyght*. Reprint of 1572 version, ed. J. Dover Wilson and May Yardley, Oxford: Oxford University Press.

Law, Robert (1818) *Memorialls*, Edinburgh.

Levack, Brian P. (ed.) (1992) *Witchcraft in Scotland*, vol. 7 of *Articles on Witchcraft, Magic and Demonology*, New York and London: Garland Publishing.

Lewis, Ioan (1975) *Ecstatic Religion: An Anthropological Study of Spirit Possession and Shamanism*, Penguin: Harmondsworth.

Lyon, William S. (1998) *Encyclopedia of Native American Shamanism: Sacred Ceremonies of North America*, Santa Barbara, California: ABC-CLIO.

MacCulloch, J. A. (1921) 'The Mingling of Fairy and Witch Beliefs in Sixteenth and Seventeenth Century Scotland', in *Folk-Lore, Transactions of the Folk-Lore Society*.

Macfarlane, Alan (1991) *Witchcraft in Tudor and Stuart England*, London: Waveland Press, Inc.

McIntosh, Alastair (1990) 'Review of The Seer in Celtic and Other Traditions edited by Hilda Ellis Davidson' in *The Christian Parapsychologist* 8:8 298–300.

McPherson, J. M. (1929) *Primitive Beliefs in the North-East of Scotland*, London, New York and Toronto: Longmans, Green and Co.

Martin, Martin (1970) *A Description of the Western Isles of Scotland*, London 1716, Facsimile edn, Edinburgh: Mercat Press.

Matchett, W. F. (1972) 'Repeated hallucinatory experiences as part of the mourning process among Hopi Indian women', *Psychiatry* Vol. 35: 185–94.

Matossian, Mary Kilbourne (1989) *Poisons of the Past: Molds, Epidemics and History*, New Haven: Yale University Press.

Maxwell-Stuart, Peter G. (2000) *Satan's Conspiracy: Magic and Witchcraft in Sixteenth-Century Scotland*, East Linton: Tuckwell Press.

Miller, Joyce (2002) 'Devices and Directions: Folk Healing Aspects of Witchcraft Practice in Seventeenth-Century Scotland', in Julian Goodeare (ed.), *The Scottish Witch-Hunt in Context*, Manchester: Manchester University Press.

Moore, Thomas (1992) *Care of the Soul*, New York, HarperCollins.

—— (1994) *Soul Mates*, New York: HarperCollins.

—— (1996) *The Re-Enchantment of Everyday Life*, New York HarperCollins.

Murray, Margaret (1921) *The Witch-Cult in Western Europe*, Oxford: Clarendon Press.

Narby, Jeremy and Huxley, Francis (eds) (2001) *Shamans Through Time: 500 Years on the Path to Knowledge*, London: Thames & Hudson Ltd.

Nicholson, Shirley (ed.) (1987) *Shamanism: An Expanded View of Reality*, Wheaton, Illinois: Theosophical Publishing.

Noel, Daniel (1997) *The Soul of Shamanism: Western Fantasies, Imaginal Realities*, New York: The Continuum Publishing Company.

Normand, Lawrence and Roberts, Gareth (eds) (2000) *Witchcraft in Early Modern Scotland: James VI's Demonology and the North Berwick Witches*, Exeter: University of Exeter Press.

Oldridge, Darren (2000) *The Devil in Early Modern England*, Stroud: Sutton Publishing Ltd.

—— (ed.) (2002) *The Witchcraft Reader*, London: Routledge.

Olson, Ronald L. (1967) *The Quinault Indians*, Seattle: University of Washington Press.

Opie, Iona and Peter (1992) *The Classic Fairy Tales*, Oxford: Oxford University Press.

Owens, Lily (ed.) (1996) *The Complete Brothers Grimm Fairy Tales*, New York: Gramercy Books.

Park, Willard Z. (1938) *Shamanism in Western North America: A Study in Cultural Relationships*, Evanston and Chicago: Northwestern University Press.

Perkins, William (1618) *A Discourse on the Damned Art of Witchcraft*, Cambridge.

Peters, Edward (1978) *The Magician, the Witch and the Law*, Hassocks, Sussex: Harvester.

Petroff, Elizabeth A. (ed.) (1986) *Medieval Woman's Visionary Literature*, New York: Oxford University Press.

Picard, Liza (2000) *Restoration London*, London: Phoenix.

Pitcairn, Robert (1833) *Ancient Criminal Trials in Scotland 1488–1624*, Edinburgh, Bannatyne Club.

Pócs, Éva (1989*) Fairies and Witches at the Boundaries of South-Eastern and Central Europe*, Helsinki: F.F. Communications, no. 243.

—— *(1999) Between the Living and the Dead*, trans. Szilvia Rédey and Michael Webb, Budapest: Central European University Press.

Purkiss, Diane (1996) *The Witch in History: Early Modern and Twentieth-Century Representations*, London and New York: Routledge.

—— (2001*) Troublesome Things: A History of Fairies and Fairy Stories*, London: Penguin.

—— (2001) 'Sounds of Silence: Fairies and Incest in Scottish Witchcraft Stories' in Stuart Clark (ed.), *Languages of Witchcraft: Narrative, Ideology and Meaning in Early Modern Culture*, Basingstoke, Hampshire: Macmillan Press Ltd.

Rasmussen, Knud (1976) *Intellectual Culture of the Iglulik Eskimos*, New York: AMS Press Inc.

—— (1927) *Across Arctic America*: *Narrative of the Fifth Thule Expedition*, London: G. P. Putnam and Sons.

—— (1908) *The People of the Polar North*, London: Kegan Paul, Trench, Trübner & Co.

Rees, W. D. (1971) 'The Hallucinations of Widowhood', *British Medical Journal* 4: 37–41.

Reichel-Dolmatoff, Gerardo (1988) *Goldwork and Shamanism*, Colombia: Medellin.

Richardson, Alan (1987*) An Introduction to the Mystical Qabalah*, Wellingborough, Northamptonshire: The Aquarian Press.

Robertson, Revd C. M. (1910) 'Folk-Lore from the West of Ross-shire' in *Transactions of the Gaelic Society of Inverness*, vol. 26.

Roper, Lyndal (1994) *Oedipus and the Devil: Witchcraft, Sexuality and Religion in Early Modern Europe*, London and New York: Routledge.

Rosen, Barbara (ed.) (1991) *Witchcraft in England, 1558–1618*, Amherst: The University of Massachusetts Press.

Russell, Jeffrey B. (1972) *Witchcraft in the Middle Ages*, London: Cornell University Press Limited.

—— (1990) *Lucifer: The Devil in the Middle Ages*, New York: Cornell University Press.

Sanderson, Stewart (ed.) (1976) Robert Kirk's *The Secret Commonwealth of Elves, Fauns and Fairies*, Cambridge: D. S. Brewer for the Folklore Society.

Scot, Reginald (1972) *The Discoverie of Witchcraft*, London, 1584; reprinted and with an introduction by Montague Summers, New York: Dover Publications.

Sharpe, James (1996) *Instruments of Darkness: Witchcraft in England 1550–1750*, London: Penguin.

—— (2001) *Witchcraft in Early Modern England*, London: Pearson Education Limited.

—— (2002) 'The Witch's Familiar in Elizabethan England', in *Authority and Consent in Tudor England: essays presented to C. S. L. Davies* (eds) George W. Bernard and S. J. Gunn, Aldershot: Ashgate.

—— (ed.) (2003) *English Witchcraft 1560–1736*, London: Pickering and Chatto.

Simpson, Jacqueline (1996) 'Witches and Witchbusters', *Folklore* 107: 5–18.

Smart, Ninian (1977) *The Religious Experience of Mankind*, Glasgow: Collins.

Smith, Bruce (1999) *The Acoustic World of Early Modern England: Attending to the O-Factor*, Chicago and London: The University of Chicago Press.

Smith, J. Irvine (1972) 'Introduction' to *Selected Justiciary Cases 1624–1650*, vol. 2, 2 vols, Edinburgh: Stair Society.

Smoley, Richard 'The Source of Wisdom', in *Parabola: Myth, Tradition and Search for Meaning*, vol. 25, Number 3, August 2000.

The Life of St Teresa of Ávila By Herself (1987) trans. J. M. Cohen, London: Penguin.

Stevens, Anthony (1990) *On Jung*, London: Penguin.

Stuart, John (ed.) (1841) *The Miscellany of the Spalding Club*, Aberdeen.

Thirsk, J (ed.) (1967) *The Agrarian History of England and Wales 1500–1640*, vol. 4, Cambridge University Press.

Thomas, Keith (1991) *Religion and the Decline of Magic*, London: Penguin.

—— (1983*) Man and the Natural World: Changing Attitudes in England*, London: Allen Lane.

Trevor-Roper, H. R. (1969) *The European Witch-Craze of the 16th and 17th Centuries*, Harmondsworth: Penguin, 1969.

Underhill, Evelyn (ed.) (1922*) Cloud of Unknowing*, London: John M. Watkins.

Valletta, Frederick (2000) *Witchcraft, Magic and Superstition in England, 1640–70*, Aldershot: Ashgate.

Vitebsky, Piers (2001) *The Shaman: Voyages of the Soul, Trance, Ecstasy and Healing from Siberia to the Amazon*, London: Duncan Baird Publishers.

Walsh, Roger N. (1990) *The Spirit of Shamanism*, London: Mandala.

Ward, Keith (1994) *Religion and Revelation*, Oxford: Clarendon Press.

Watkins, Mary (1984) *Waking Dreams*, Dallas: Spring Publications.

Watts, Alan (1978) *The Meaning of Happiness: The Quest for Freedom of the Spirit in Modern Psychology and the Wisdom of the East*, London: Rider & Company Ltd.

Webster, John (1677) *The Displaying of Supposed Witchcraft*, London: J. M.

Wilber, K., Engler, J. and Brown, D. (eds) (1986) *Transformations of Consciousness: Conventional and Contemplative Perspectives on Development*, Boston: New Science Library/Shambhala.

Wilby, Emma (2000) 'The Witch's Familiar and the Fairy in Early Modern England and Scotland', in *Folklore* III: 283–305.

Wilson, Godfrey and Monica (1945) *The Analysis of Social Change,* Cambridge: Cambridge University Press.

Wilson, Stephen (2000) *The Magical Universe: Everyday Ritual and Magic in Pre-Modern Europe,* London; New York: Hambledon and London.

INDEX

Aberdeenshire, magical practitioners from, 17, 36, 56, 61, 62, 68, 70, 71, 72, 78, 79, 97, 106, 170, 240, 264n, 265n

Achomawi (California), 137, 142, 145, 148, 155. *See also under* shamans

Addison, Joseph, 187, 250

Agrippa, Henry Cornelius, 6, 180, 288n, 289n

Alaskan Inuit, 153, 158, 195, 209, 210, 211, 215. *See also* shamans

Allen, Robert, 'The God of Norfolk', 217

alliance theory, 71, 72

Americas, 7, 126. *See also* shamans

amulets, magical. *See* magical objects

analytic psychology, 4, 252

Andro Man, 17, 36, 56, 57, 61, 62, 68, 77, 78, 85, 97, 106, 264n, 266n; and visionary experience, 174, 240

angels, 4, 17, 158, 193, 214, 220, 221, 223, 231, 236, 238, 239; as familiars, 3, 17, 56, 57, 62, 97, 118, 201; guardian, 4, 289n; in Christian iconography, 225; angel lore, modern, 4

Angel Gabriel, 220, 221, 235

Angus, magical practitioners from, 60, 62, 71, 73, 74, 75, 78, 83, 86, 97, 105, 117, 118, 271n, 272n

animal metamorphosis: by fairies, 19, 63; by cunning folk & witches, 88, 89, 163; by shamans, 154, 163, 286n

animals: value of, 32, 228–9; human proximity to, 228–30; as evil spirits (general), 63, 226, 227; as envisioned spiritual guides, 226–31

animal familiars/helping spirits, 58, 63, 65, 85; animal forms; ape, 175; bear, 129, 144, 207; bee, 63, 138–9; bird, 63, 129, 150, 226, 268n, 269n; calf, 70; cat, 36, 63, 74, 78, 88, 110, 170, 175, 176, 226, 231, 272n; chicken, 283n; crow, 89; dog, 31, 36, 63, 72, 75, 78, 82, 83, 85, 97, 110, 130, 135, 144, 166, 175, 176, 188, 226, 231, 266n, 275n, 277n, 283n; dove, 63, 226; duck, 35, 129; ermine, 131; ferret, 63, 82, 176, 185, 197, 226, 235; fish, 129; fowl, 37; frog, 35, 63, 230; grasshopper, 63; hare, 89, 230; hedgehog, 49, 170; horse, 63, 129, 175; lamb, 63, 226; lion, 73, 110, 135, 226; mole, 90, 129, 226, 230, 231; mountain marmot, 151; mouse, 63, 89, 97, 131; owl, 49, 129; polecat, 70; rabbit, 107, 129, 230; rat, 70, 85, 109, 129; raven, 78, 129; reindeer, 129; rook, 89; seal, 129; snail, 63, 226, 229; snake, 129, 144, 226; spider, 35, 63; stag, 63; tiger, 130; toad, 109, 170, 171, 226, 283n; whale, 129, 130, 150; wolf, 129, 130

animism: definition of, 128; in early modern Britain, 14, 15, 17, 159, 201, 202, 204, 224, 228, 256; in tribal societies, 125, 126, 128, 158, 159, 163, 202, 204

anthropological perspectives on early modern witchcraft, 6, 124–7, 163, 164

Apache (North America), 196

apothecaries, 32, 174

Araucanians (South America), 132

archetypal psychology, 4, 218

Arctic, 131, 147, 153, 190, 191, 196, 281n. *See also* shamans

Argyllshire, magical practitioners from, 60, 85, 86, 90, 91, 102

Armstrong, Anne, 89

asceticisms, to induce trance states: deliberately cultivated, 79, 129, 130, 177; naturally occurring, 245, 247